Gifts of Deceit

GIFTS OF DECEIT

Sun Myung Moon,

Tongsun Park,

and the Korean Scandal

ROBERT BOETTCHER

with Gordon L. Freedman

Holt, Rinehart and Winston   New York

Published by Holt, Rinehart and Winston, 383 Madison Avenue, New
York, New York 10017.
Published simultaneously in Canada by Holt, Rinehart and Winston of
Canada, Limited.

Library of Congress Cataloging in Publication Data
Boettcher, Robert B.
Gifts of deceit.
Includes bibliographical references and index.
1. United States—Relations (general) with Korea.   2. Korea—Relations
(general) with the United States.   3. Corruption (in politics)—United
States.   4. Moon, Sun Myung.   5. Park, Tongsun.   I. Freedman, Gor-
don L., joint author.   II. Title.
El83.8.K7B6   301.29'73'0519   79-20192
ISBN 0-03-044576-0

FIRST EDITION

Designer: Joy Chu
Printed in the United States of America
10 9 8 7 6 5 4 3 2 1

To Aunt Grace and Uncle Lou
and in memory of Billy

Note on Korean Names

Korean custom is to put the family name first, followed by given names; for example, President Park is Park Chung Hee. This book adheres to the custom except in cases of Koreans whose names have become known in this country in the Western order, such as Sun Myung Moon, Tongsun Park, Bo Hi Pak, and Hancho Kim.

ACKNOWLEDGMENTS

Significant portions of this book were written in collaboration with Gordon Freedman. Most of the material on Tongsun Park's activities was derived from his expert investigative work, research, and preliminary drafts. Gordon and I are both indebted to former Congressman Richard Hanna for the very helpful cooperation he gave.

It was my great fortune to have known and worked with Congressman Donald M. Fraser and the staff of his subcommittee's investigation of Korean-American relations. Throughout our long association, they contributed to the creation of this book in more ways than they could be aware.

In addition to the thousands of pages published on the Korean scandal, a considerable amount of new information was needed. Those who supplied it were both willing and patient with my repeated checking and double-checking. In this regard, I am thankful to Steve Hassan, Lee Jai Hyon, Ed Baker, Gregory Henderson, Ed Gragert, and An Hong Kyoon.

John Marks, in a formal sense my agent, was more importantly the good friend who continues to be helpful after so many years. Margaret Ameer Cataldo, Kathy Panciera, and John

Buckley were willing to assist with the typing when needed. And special thanks to Cynthia Reed, who, by offering the right advice at the right time, may have saved the project.

From the time of my first meeting with Marian Wood, I knew she was the kind of person I wanted as an editor. In the ensuing months, my respect for her grew as she was demanding, patient, laudatory, and critical. Supported by her able assistant, Judy Karasik, Marian's professionalism got this novice author through his first book.

CONTENTS

Prologue 1

PART ONE

1 His Excellency 11
2 The Lord of the Second Advent 31
3 The Charmer 56
4 The Origins of the Influence Campaign 78
5 Tongsun and His Congressmen 99
6 Minions and Master 144

PART TWO

7 Washington Looks the Other Way 189
8 Three Who Stood in the Way:
  Ranard, Habib, Fraser 213
9 Koreagate 241
10 Inviting Tongsun Back 267

xi

11 Kim Dong Jo: The Still-Untold Story   290
12 Dueling with the Moonies   307
13 The Menace   325

     Notes   351
     Index   389

Gifts of Deceit

PROLOGUE

WHEN LEE JAI HYON WALKED INTO the conference room on the third floor of the Korean Embassy in Washington, everyone else was already there. He hurried to his usual place near Ambassador Kim Dong Jo's chair at the head of the long table. Looking around the room, he saw the usual cast of characters: the Counselor for Political Affairs, the Economic Attaché, the Counselor for Commercial Affairs, the Defense Attaché, the Consul General, and the Education Attaché. Seated nearest the ambassador on the left was Yang Doo Won, head of the Korean Central Intelligence Agency (KCIA) in the United States. Lee wondered for a moment if he were the only one with no idea of what the meeting was about. As the Embassy's chief spokesman, with the title of Chief Cultural and Information Attaché, he was usually told in advance so he could prepare.

With all the senior officials present, Ambassador Kim began to speak. "This meeting will be devoted to sensitive matters of the highest importance to our government. It is therefore necessary to take special precautions for security." Nothing from the meeting was to be discussed outside the room, he said. Those who attended were not allowed even to talk about it among

1

themselves. As for written records, notes taken during the meeting were to be left on the table and destroyed.

"Does everyone understand?" the ambassador asked. Heads nodded around the table.

Ambassador Kim then turned the meeting over to KCIA station chief Yang Doo Won. Like the American intelligence agency abroad, the Korean CIA had its own organization within the Embassy. And like the American CIA, the head of that unit was called the station chief. Yang Doo Won was known in Washington by an assumed name, Lee Sang Ho, as was customary for the KCIA in foreign countries. A few months later, when the State Department would quietly tell the Korean Embassy that he was no longer welcome in the United States because of his harassment of Koreans living here, he returned to Seoul under his real name and became Assistant Director of the KCIA.

"We all have a responsibility to retain the support of the United States for His Excellency's policies," he began. "The United States is our strongest friend against another attack by the northern puppet." The term "northern puppet" was standard parlance among South Koreans when referring to North Korea or its leader, Kim Il Sung. In the same way, North Koreans referred to the Seoul government as "the stooge of American imperialism." Yang was describing the world as the South Korean government saw it: locked in deadly confrontation between fervent Communists and fervent anti-Communists.

Yang Doo Won went on to praise the wisdom of President Park Chung Hee, newly referred to as "His Excellency," for promulgating the Yushin Constitution in October 1972, six months before. Yushin, which blocked all criticism of the government, was, Yang pointed out, a necessary step to ensuring national solidarity.

So far, none of this was news to his listeners. It was the standard government line, and any one of them could have made the same little speech, perhaps with varying degrees of enthusiasm.

The KCIA chief was worried, though, about trends in the United States. Americans, he lamented, never hesitated to criticize governments, their own and others. It was the time of Watergate, and Korean officials were amazed by the attacks on Richard Nixon. Although he was confident Nixon would not interfere with Yushin, he was not so sure about Congress and the public.

"Will Americans meddle in our internal affairs by preaching about American-style democracy?" he asked gravely. "What if they condemn the Yushin policy and withdraw their support?"

Yang then asserted the "absolute necessity" for the Embassy to reach out and convince Americans in all walks of life to give "His Excellency" full support. He urged more frequent contacts with Congressmen and other government officials, businessmen with vested interests in Korea, journalists, and university professors. "We must use all such persons for the vital task of enhancing the image of our government if we want to retain American support."

The meeting ended after about half an hour. No one had said anything from around the table. Lee Jai Hyon sensed the others shared his puzzlement over Yang Doo Won's curious lecture. Never before had there been a meeting where the KCIA did all the talking. The KCIA always worked apart from the rest of the Embassy; there were no day-to-day contacts with its officers in the course of business.

Lee Jai Hyon was sick of trying to make Park's dictatorship look good in the United States. He knew the only reason Park had dumped the old constitution was to stay in power. Whatever the KCIA chief was getting at, Lee intended not to be affected by it for very long. He had already decided to resign quietly from government service as soon as he and his wife, a registered pharmacist, could arrange for jobs in Seoul.

In the weeks that followed, there were more secret meetings, never announced more than a day in advance and always with the stringent security measures. During the course of six sessions over a period of about five weeks in the spring of 1973, KCIA intentions came into focus. A conspiracy was being outlined. Bit by bit the pieces of the puzzle fell into place as the KCIA chief, cautiously at first, made words like "manipulate," "coerce," "threaten," "co-opt," and "seduce" a part of the vocabulary of his talks. After a few meetings, he felt confident enough to declare, "If you know something bad about a person, you can use it to manipulate him."

The KCIA chief also spoke of "buying off" Americans. Lee had reason to think that delicate matter was being handled personally by Ambassador Kim Dong Jo. There had been the incident several months earlier when Lee walked into the ambassador's office and found him busily stuffing packets of $100 bills into unaddressed white envelopes. Feeling awkward about the strange activity he was witnessing, Lee pretended not to notice and proceeded to raise the matter he had come to discuss. But the ambassador brushed him aside. "I can't talk to you now; I'm on my way to Capitol Hill," he said hurriedly. Lee excused himself and left the room.

It seemed to Lee that the ambassador and the KCIA were trying to recruit the whole Embassy. Apparently a lot of manpower was needed. "Front men" and "undercover agents" were mentioned. Lee began to wonder about certain Koreans in the Washington area.

Tongsun Park was one. A wealthy socialite often seen with Congressmen, he obviously had some powerful connections in Seoul. Lee knew Ambassador Kim detested Tongsun but had been told by President Park not to interfere.

For an outsider, Bo Hi Pak was also very close to the KCIA. Lee Jai Hyon had learned Pak used the KCIA's secret telecommunications facilities to send messages. At first, it had not seemed important to Lee that Bo Hi Pak was a follower of Sun Myung Moon. In Korea, Lee vaguely remembered Moon as a crackpot evangelist. But Moon had become very active in the United States lately. And there was the time the KCIA had hired some new secretaries on Pak's recommendation, through the Freedom Leadership Foundation whose founder was Moon.

AT THE END OF APRIL, Han Hyohk Hoon, Lee's senior assistant, resigned and went into hiding. That was the beginning of more trouble for Lee.

The Korean Minister of Information, calling from Seoul the day after Han's defection, told Lee to persuade Han to return to Korea. Lee said there was nothing he could do because the man was already gone.

Things escalated quickly with another call the following night from a very angry minister. "I cannot believe you would hesitate to exert every possible effort to make that traitor return to Seoul. You should be making it clear to Han in no uncertain terms that he must come back at once. That is your duty without even being told," the minister said.

"I cannot force him to return, Mr. Minister. The American government is processing him for a change in visa status so he can stay here as long as he wishes," Lee explained.

"That should be no problem for you," the minister retorted. "You can issue a public statement saying Han is a Communist agent who fled because he knew we were about to catch him after discovering his espionage contacts with North Koreans. The Americans will then turn him over to you gladly."

It was all Lee could do to restrain his mounting anger. "Mr. Minister, I cannot frame an innocent man. All he did was to leave quietly. He hasn't denounced the government publicly. And what he tells his friends will do us no harm. I appeal to you: Let him go."

"I may as well tell you that some of us here are beginning to have questions about your own loyalty. You had better do something to bring Han back or you may be in deep trouble yourself."

Lee began to worry. What would happen if the government held him responsible for Han's defection? He wondered whether retirement in Seoul would be safe. He was only a month or so away from announcing his resignation and returning to Korea. But perhaps the plan was no longer workable.

For the next several days there were no calls from Seoul, nor pressure at the Embassy. Instead, the Lee family found itself under surveillance in an unusual way. Embassy colleagues began dropping by the house unexpectedly every night with their wives—not close friends, but casual acquaintances who rarely if every had visited the Lee home. Each couple would stay several hours, and at least one couple paid a "social call" each evening. Both sides—callers and hosts alike—knew exactly what was going on. But both sides, faithful to the rules of Korean etiquette, maintained a pleasant demeanor throughout. To do otherwise would have been unpardonably rude. There could be no personal umbrage, neither taken by the Lees nor intended by the callers. That the callers had been organized to serve as watchdogs over the Lees was a fact lost in the flow of pleasant conversation. So the evenings passed amid the cordial exchange of inconsequential chitchat about the weather, children, the cost of living, mutual friends, and the like, ending each time with the warmest of farewells.

On June 4, 1973, another secret session with the KCIA was held at the Embassy. Lee was still among those invited. This one lasted only about fifteen minutes. As Lee rose from his chair to leave the conference room, the KCIA station chief placed a hand on his shoulder and said, "Dr. Lee, I want to interrogate you in my office now."

The two men walked together in silence to Yang Doo Won's office, where another KCIA officer was waiting. Lee Jai Hyon sat in the chair offered him. Seated behind the desk, Yang slowly read to himself a two-page cable from KCIA headquarters before addressing Lee. The questioning then began, politely but professionally, as if straight from an interrogator's manual: Name, address, date of birth, family, education, and professional background. Lee felt as if he were in a police station. Then to the crux of the matter:

"Why don't you cooperate with us to get Han Hyohk Hoon back to Korea? Where is he? Surely you know. Talk to him. Pressure him. If that doesn't convince him, let us persuade him." And so forth, returning repeatedly to questions whose answers had not been satisfactory.

Lee recalled stories he had heard about KCIA torture techniques. The interrogation, he realized, was only the first step in breaking him down. After about three hours, the KCIA chief decided to stop for lunch and resume two hours later. Lee Jai Hyon walked out into the commotion of midday Washington traffic. He never went back to the Korean Embassy again.

TWO YEARS and six days later, on June 10, 1975, Professor Lee Jai Hyon of Western Illinois University was sitting at the witness table in the cavernous hearing room of the House International Relations Committee in Washington. He had been invited by Congressman Donald M. Fraser of Minnesota, chairman of the Subcommittee on International Organizations, to appear as a witness at one of the subcommittee's hearings on human rights in South Korea and the implications for United States policy.

The witnesses preceding Lee had given accounts of Park Chung Hee's repression: torture of political prisoners, mass arrests, prolonged detention without trial, constant surveillance by the KCIA, media censorship, rigged elections, and an emasculated National Assembly.

Concurring with the other witnesses as he took the stand, Lee announced, "I will testify on other aspects that have not yet been touched upon."

He now felt safe enough to blow the whistle on the KCIA. The time and place were right.

The KCIA's nefarious activities were not limited to Korea, he said, but also had been exported to the United States in an ambitious plan of clandestine operations based on "seduction, payoff, and intimidation," to mute criticism of Park Chung Hee's rule and to buy supporters in the United States. This was something the subcommittee had not expected to hear.

"It took me two years to come here today to tell these things," Lee declared, "and I am very grateful I can do it here."

He then revealed a detailed plan, drawn from the secret meetings he had attended at the Korean Embassy in 1973.

The KCIA, he said, was trying to "buy off American leaders," especially members of Congress. American businessmen who had invested in Korea were to be pressured into lobbying for President Park's policies in Washington. Academic conferences were to be rigged to "rationalize Park's dictatorship," and friendly professors were to be rewarded with "free VIP trips to Korea." The KCIA was to send undercover men into the Korean community in the United States to use newspapers and broadcasting for propaganda, control Korean residents' associations, and intimidate uncooperative Koreans by threatening the safety of their relatives in Korea.

Congressman Fraser was alarmed by what Lee Jai Hyon said. If the statements were true, the activities of the KCIA amounted to outright subversion by a supposedly friendly country. He therefore instructed the subcommittee staff to begin making inquiries about Lee's allegations at the Justice Department and among Korean-Americans. At the time, he had no idea where the inquiries would lead. But in fact, "Koreagate" had begun.

PART ONE

I

His Excellency

A MOUNTAIN CALLED Kumo San towers over the surrounding rice land in North Kyongsang Province. Korean folk theory has it that great men are born in areas with an impressive mountain close by. Near Kumo San, in the village of Kumi on the Nakdong River, Park Chung Hee was born in 1917.

At one time, Park's father had been a county official, which had meant some status but very little money. By the time Park Chung Hee was born, the father was again tilling the soil with his other sons. Life was hard for the many poor farming families like Park's. They lived in thatch-roofed houses with mud walls. The winters in Kumi are bitter, cold, and windy. In 1917, good fuel was hard to come by, since the Japanese forbade cutting the trees around Kumo San in order to conserve forests. Mostly, farmers burned straw and pine needles.

Park Chung Hee was two years old at the time of the 1919 independence movement. All over the country, hundreds of thousands of Koreans staged peaceful protest demonstrations against Japanese rule. It was a burst of nationalism that ended in a bloodbath. Six thousand people were killed by Japanese police,

11

sixteen thousand wounded, and another twenty thousand arrested.

The location of Korea—"the land of the morning calm"—between two powerful neighbors, China and Japan, had created problems throughout its history. Except for one century of Mongol rule, the Koreans had managed to maintain their own cultural identity as a separate nation for almost two thousand years. But while Korea had for the most part run its own affairs, it was nonetheless forced to pay tribute to China as the elder in the Confucian family of nations. Two or three times a year, a mission from the Korean king would journey to Peking to acknowledge the Chinese Emperor as the Son of Heaven. Such tribute did not guarantee peace. Although Korea had no great militarist tradition, it was at times the battlefield for the wars of others. Twice in the late sixteenth century the peninsula was ravaged by Japan, which was trying to use Korea as a route to invade China. In the seventeenth, it was overrun by the Manchus, who needed to protect their flank while conquering China. The Koreans came out of these experiences with the tough resilience for which they have always been noted.

For many centuries, they have also shown remarkable artistic and technical creativity. One of the world's first uses of movable metal type was in Korea. The Korean alphabet, *hangul,* is today still considered one of the most accurate and practical of all writing systems. In the sixteenth century, a Korean admiral invented the world's first iron-clad ships to help turn back the Japanese invasion. In the arts, Korea traditionally has excelled in ceramics, painting, woodwork, textiles, and architecture. In the present day, some of the most accomplished pianists, violinists, and singers are coming from Korea.

In politics, factionalism has been a permanent plague. Factionalism was a major cause of corruption and stagnation during the Yi Dynasty, whose collapse led to Japanese domination. The

Tonghak Rebellion of 1894 began as a peasant uprising led by intellectuals. Unable to control it, the Yi Dynasty called in Chinese troops. Japan, viewing the Chinese move as a dangerous unbalancing of power in the region, dispatched its own forces as well. In the ensuing Sino-Japanese War, Japan replaced China's longtime influence in Korea and, in 1910, formally annexed Korea. The Tonghak rebels' hopes for economic betterment and civil rights ended in exploitation of the whole country by Japan.

Over the years, the Japanese tried to stamp out everything Korean and turn the people into second-rate Japanese. The one national characteristic of the Koreans that the Japanese made use of was industriousness. Japanese landowners and businessmen took full advantage of Korean labor to provide the Japanese Empire with food, raw materials, and basic industries. At school, the language of instruction for Park Chung Hee was not Korean, but Japanese. Teachers discouraged him from using Korean even at home; if he was caught speaking it at school, he was punished.

Park's classmates remember him as a smart and upright boy who was conscientious about satisfying those above him. After finishing normal school, usually the highest level of education for the poor, he became a primary school teacher at Mungyung, not far from Kumi. There was not much for him to look forward to on his father's farm, and teaching was an opportunity to get away from the drudgery.

While teaching school, he married a girl from Kumi of one of the Kim clans. About half the people in Korea have the surname Kim, Park, or Lee and trace their family line many centuries back to ancestors with those names. For a Park to marry another Park could be considered a kind of incest, however remote. The custom has the effect of limiting the choice of spouses.

When he was twenty, Park volunteered for Japanese army officer training. It was not unusual for younger Korean sons to go off to the Japanese army. Staying home kept them subordinate to the father and older brothers in accordance with the strict hierarchy of Korean family relationships. Park went to the military academy in Manchukuo, the Japanese puppet state formerly known as Manchuria. A highly disciplined person by nature and experience, he was well suited for military life. With an outstanding record in two years of training in Manchukuo, he became one of the few Koreans chosen to attend the Imperial Military Academy in Tokyo.

In 1941, all Koreans had to reregister with Japanese names. As required, he changed his name. He was now Lieutenant Okamoto.

Park served in Manchukuo during World War II. There, he became acquainted with Chung Il Kwon, a fellow officer who many years later was to become President Park's Prime Minister and Speaker of the National Assembly. Park remained steadfastly loyal to Imperial Japan throughout his service, and as the war ended, he had become unchangeably influenced by Japanese discipline and organization.

KOREA'S LIBERATION from Japan in 1945 was a tarnished triumph. The country was divided in half between a Communist north and a non-Communist south. Korea was again a pawn of the big powers, this time the Soviet Union and the United States. The Russians, accepting the surrender of Japanese forces north of the 38th parallel, set up a Communist government there as they had done in East Germany. In the south, the American occupation authorities arrived knowing nothing about Korea; at first they relied on the Japanese for help and then later turned to Koreans who had collaborated with Japan. Korean democrats were assumed to be too far to the left.

To lead the new free South Korea, the Americans brought in Syngman Rhee, a reactionary politician who had spent the previous thirty-five years in the United States. Since Rhee had no power base of his own in Korea, Koreans formerly with the Japanese colonial administration formed the backbone of his regime. Funds to support him were given largely by those who had made money under the Japanese.

In 1946, Park Chung Hee was admitted to South Korea's new military academy. One of the cadets entering in 1948 was Kim Jong Pil, who later married Park's niece; in 1961, he would help Park take over the country. He would also establish the Korean CIA, organize Park's political party, and see that the Park regime gave its blessing to the activities of Sun Myung Moon's Unification Church.

Amid the political turmoil following liberation, Park's family turned leftward. One of his brothers, Mu Hee, was killed as a Communist during a general strike in 1946. Park Chung Hee's own sympathies were moving in the same direction.

Completing the short training course in 1946, Park stayed on at the academy as a student battalion commander. It was during that period that he became a Communist. He was induced to join a planned Communist military uprising by Lee Chung Op, a former teacher of his and member of the South Korean Labor party, which was Communist. Park in turn indoctrinated younger officers and persuaded them to take part. He was not present when the rebellion at Yosu and Sunchon was crushed by the South Korean army in 1948, but an investigation found he was one of the brains behind the action. Heading the investigation was General Kim Chang Yong, known as "Snake" Kim, a former Japanese military police sergeant, a fanatical anti-Communist, a torturer. After some very rough treatment, Park was court-martialed and sentenced to death. He managed to signal some high-ranking friends—including Chung Il Kwon—that if spared he would reveal the Communist network in the army. The chief of military intelligence agreed to the proposal.

Park joined "Snake" Kim's search group and gave away the

conspirators. His actions resulted in the purge of hundreds of army officers and the death of many former friends. His death sentence was commuted, but he was dismissed from the army. Soon afterward, he got a job as a civilian in military intelligence.

When the Korean War broke out in June 1950, the army desperately needed officers. Park's senior friends had him quietly reinstated immediately. His loyalty was not questioned after that.

No strangers to misfortune, the Korean people suffered as never before during the Korean War. Cities were devastated in both North and South Korea, more than two million people were killed, and the homes of millions of others were destroyed. The fledgling Republic of Korea (R.O.K.) army had been completely unprepared to deal with the attack; it lacked the necessary size, experience, and training. Intervention by the United States, under the United Nations flag, eventually turned back the Communist invasion. The rescue created a feeling of eternal gratitude among Koreans toward the United States.

During the war, Koreans did not hesitate to speak out against President Rhee when he moved to change the constitution so as to assure his reelection. He solved the problem by locking out the opposition members of the National Assembly and ramming the amendment through with his own supporters. It was a tactic to be used again in the future by President Park Chung Hee.

On July 27, 1953, the Korean War ended with the signing of an armistice agreement at Panmunjon. An abortive political conference was held to work out terms for the peaceful reunification of Korea, but progress beyond the armistice agreement proved impossible. Koreans lived on in fear of another war.

PARK CHUNG HEE EMERGED from the war a brigadier general. He was not a part of the power structure, though, and remained a backwoods general throughout the fifties. He remarried, having divorced his first wife several years before. A great many of Park's fellow officers were doing the same thing. The war had brought higher social status and more power to Korean military men than ever before. Wives from the farm were considered too coarse for the sophisticated company the men were now keeping. So they found more suitable women from among the more educated and cultured. Old wives were packed off back to the land and discarded. In Park's case, the first wife went to a Buddhist convent. His second wife, Yook Young Soo, was to become a popular First Lady.

Already a poverty case before the war, South Korea was now faced with the overwhelming task of reconstruction. The economy was in shambles. President Rhee made matters worse. He had little penchant for economic planning and believed the country should concentrate its efforts on reunification. Economic development could come later. Because the Japanese had concentrated industrial development in the North, the country's economy would be sound when North and South were back together again, he contended. Under American pressure, Rhee did approve some proposals for development planning, but his heart was not in it. His axiom was that improving the economy was a disincentive to American aid: the better Korea did, the less it would get. Reconstruction was also hampered by a government riddled with corruption. American officials despaired over foreign aid money going down a rat hole. There was sizable Korean opposition to what Rhee was doing, but he played factions off against each other, and those he couldn't manipulate, he bought. The Rhee regime became more and more repressive as the years went by. After he rigged his reelection in 1960, massive student demonstrations forced Rhee to resign.

Park Chung Hee took over in 1961.

The mastermind of his coup d'état was Lieutenant Colonel Kim Jong Pil, Park's nephew-in-law. Kim had been dreaming of a takeover for a long time. For years, while serving in army intelligence, he had been an avid reader of histories of coups, both successful and unsuccessful. Conditions for a decisive move seemed perfect in the spring of 1961. The Rhee regime had been succeeded by an elected democratic government less than a year before. Power was no longer concentrated in one man. The constitution had been amended to limit the authority of the President, Yun Po Sun, and give more power to the National Assembly. The government was run by a moderate Prime Minister, Chang Myon. Chang had dared to take some measures for reforming the economy, and people were grumbling about some of them, such as higher rates for electricity and trains. Free expression, after Rhee's controls, appeared to some to be an open door for chaos. In the National Assembly, the factions were trying to do each other in. Chang did not keep a close watch on the military. Quite a few young officers were objecting to slow promotions as well as to corruption and factionalism among generals.

The senior man in Kim Jong Pil's plot was Park Chung Hee. Most of the core group of about a dozen were men below the rank of general. Several were graduates of the eighth class of the military academy, including Kim Hyung Wook and Kim Jong Pil himself.

With a force of about 3,500 troops, the coup leaders moved into Seoul in darkness early in the morning of May 16. Overcoming slight resistance, they secured radio stations, power plants, police stations, and some public buildings. Kim Jong Pil made a telephone call to General Chang Do Young, the army chief of staff. At first the sleepy general thought Kim was drunk. But after checking out what Kim had said, he capitulated. At 5:00 A.M., General Chang announced the takeover in his own name, as ordered by Lieutenant Colonel Kim Jong Pil. It was as simple as that.

Convincing the Americans to go along was more difficult. The Embassy had no ties with the men who apparently had just taken over the government. Several weeks earlier, Peer de Silva, the CIA's top man in Korea, had heard rumors that a military takeover was in the making. Prime Minister Chang had ordered the stories checked, but the checking took too long. As soon as de Silva heard about the army chief of staff's announcement, he quickly put in a call to the Prime Minister's home, identified himself, and asked to speak to Mr. Chang.

The voice on the other end of the phone sounded nervous. "I am Major Park Chong Kyu and I represent the People's Revolution," it declared in good English. Park said he was a top aide to Kim Jong Pil dispatched to arrest the Prime Minister, but was unable to find him.

Park Chong Kyu? People's Revolution? De Silva did some checking to find out more about these people.

He learned that Park Chong Kyu was a protégé of Kim Jong Pil and that Kim had been kicked out of the army the previous year for taking part in the "16 Colonels Incident." Hardly an attempted coup, the incident had amounted to a group of young officers bursting into the chief of staff's office and demanding that some generals resign for corruption. Gregory Henderson, the Embassy's cultural attaché, remembered Park Chong Kyu as a pistol-packing, leather-jacketed ex–army officer who used to drop by his office occasionally to talk to Henderson and the staff. Now it was clear Park Chong Kyu had been scouting out Henderson's attitude about a possible change in government. Henderson also recalled having been invited to dinner by another man whose name presently appeared as a coup associate, Lee Tong Won. Lee's questions had been probes about whether Henderson thought the Chang Myon government could survive. The reply was not what Lee wanted. Acknowledging the young government's fragile position, Henderson had said he believed it should be given every chance. Henderson, a longtime scholar of Korea with many contacts, was one of the few Embassy people able to come up fast with information on the coup members.

No one at the Embassy was acquainted personally with the head of the coup, but an old file on Park Chung Hee detailed his Communist past. There was also reason to think Kim Jong Pil and others might be crypto-Communists. The Embassy people were deeply worried. It was an ominous situation. At best, the government had been toppled by a bunch of military men the Americans didn't even know; at worst, South Korea could be falling into the hands of Communists.

Statements disapproving the coup were issued immediately by Chargé d'Affaires Marshall Green from the Embassy, and General Carter Magruder as Commander in Chief of the United Nations Command in Korea. Green urged that the elected government be restored to power. Magruder called on all South Korean military personnel to remain under authorized command, of which he was the head.

In a meeting with Magruder, Kim Jong Pil angrily turned down the general's request that the coup group return the R.O.K. military to American control under the United Nations Command. Park, however, felt it unwise to hold out. He was not prepared to put South Korea in the position of having to defend itself alone against an attack from the north. Restoring the U.N. Command could also be the first step toward full American recognition of his takeover, which he also had to have. A day or two after the coup, he decided to talk to the Americans himself.

The headquarters for the military junta was an old Japanese department store building. General Magruder was ushered down corridors lined with men in fatigue uniforms holding submachine guns. Park Chung Hee's cluttered makeshift office was in a corner on the top floor. Kim Jong Pil was included in the meeting, but Park did most of the talking. Park was very accommodating, much to Kim's surprise. He began by apologizing for any trouble the coup might have caused. Then he agreed to return R.O.K. forces to the U.N.–U.S. command. Magruder thanked him and left.

Park was not so amiable with his next American visitor that day. Marshall Green was the acting head of the Embassy during the interim period of a regular change in ambassadors. Park preferred not to be bothered by the Embassy. To him, it was a nest of Chang Myon supporters. His collaborators in the coup had told him that such sympathies were held by Green, Henderson, and Donald Ranard, the political counselor. Park was more comfortable dealing with military men. A deal had just been struck with an American general. That seemed enough for the time being.

Marshall Green spoke in diplomatese, a language even more foreign to Park than English. But despite the phrasing, the message was clear. In effect, Green was telling Park to go back to wherever he came from.

Taking one long drag after another on his cigarette, Park was typically stone-faced as he listened to the translation. Having heard as much as he wanted to hear, he turned to the interpreter and asked, "Is the American finished talking yet?"

Before sending Green away, Park stated firmly that the coup had been necessary to keep South Korea strong against the threat from the North. It was the same scare tactic he was to use from then on whenever he needed justification for anything he wanted to do. The North Korean threat was the reason the Americans were in Korea to begin with. And it was the biggest fear of the South Korean people. Park would play on it repeatedly as an argument-stopper through the years.

Park's rationale was not backed up by what the American government knew about North Korean intentions. The CIA's Peer de Silva and other North Korea watchers saw nothing in the way of a buildup in the spring of 1961. The threat seemed about the same as it had always been. The CIA certainly had not prompted Park to seize control. The junta's propaganda was claiming the Chang Myon government had been hopeless, that chaos had reigned supreme, weakening the nation's defenses. De Silva saw it in a different light. When Henderson asked him about the junta's charges, he replied, "The government definitely was not hopeless. On the contrary, it was bright with hope."

Whether Park liked the American Embassy or not, he knew he had to deal with it. The Embassy was in a similar situation vis-à-vis Park. A few days after giving Green the brush-off, Park invited him for drinks at an out-of-the-way café.

Park apologized to Green, but said little else of substance. The two men engaged in stiff small talk over a good many drinks. Before getting up to leave, Park shook Green's hand and announced, "We're friends now." It was not the fullest mending of relations, but for Park it was a good start.

The Americans did not like the looks of Park's crowd, but the takeover was obviously real. Park clearly entertained no thought of handing the reins of power back to Chang Myon. Military force could have been used to put down the coup, but only a month earlier President John F. Kennedy had gotten a black eye from the Bay of Pigs intervention in Cuba. Perhaps most pointed, the fear that Park and the others might be Communists was gradually proving unfounded.

It was decided to give Park full diplomatic recognition. The Kennedy administration, however, stepped up its determination to work toward restoring democracy in South Korea. For more than ten years, the U.S. government had been saying aid to Korea was intended to help develop democracy. The only encouraging sign on that score had been the nine months between Rhee and Park. Washington wanted the military government to be temporary. At every opportunity, American officials were to press the junta to hold elections and restore civilian control as soon as possible.

A few weeks after the coup, the new ambassador, Samuel Berger, arrived and presented his credentials to Park Chung Hee. In that first meeting, Berger conveyed Washington's message in crystal-clear terms.

THE JUNTA STARTED OFF with a big anticorruption show. Park's governing body, the Supreme Council for National Reconstruction, proclaimed one of its main objectives to be the elimination of corruption. Immediately, more than two thousand politicians were arrested for corruption, including Chang Myon. Within four months, seventeen thousand civil servants and two thousand military officers had been arrested. An estimated 41,000 officials were fired. Park's distinction between corrupt officials and political opponents was never very clear, however.

In order to wage the anticorruption crusade and make the nation safe from the North, the junta said, it was necessary to dissolve the National Assembly, outlaw political activity, disband most social organizations, and control the press.

Responsibility for wiping out corruption was given to a new arm of the government organized by Kim Jong Pil—the Korean Central Intelligence Agency. The KCIA was set up "to supervise and coordinate both international activities and criminal investigations by all government intelligence agencies, including the military."

With such a sweeping mandate, the KCIA could and did intrude into all aspects of life in South Korea. In American terms, the KCIA was empowered to do what police do on the local level, what the FBI does on the national level, what the CIA does on the international level, and more. Prior to the coup, the American CIA had favored some pulling together of foreign intelligence activities by the R.O.K. government. The KCIA, however, was not what American intelligence men had had in mind. When Kim Jong Pil began organizing, the USCIA urged him not to combine domestic and foreign intelligence functions. As for what the new agency should be called, the CIA was against the Koreans using its own name. Kim ignored their advice, and the impression was left that the USCIA had created a South Korean counterpart in its own image. Through the years, the CIA would have regular liaison with the KCIA and exert some influence, to a lessening degree as time went by.

The KCIA had a modest predecessor under the Chang Myon government, the Combined Intelligence Research Center. Without the secret police powers of the KCIA, it had been encouraged by the USCIA. Its head, Major General Lee Hu Rak, had worked especially closely with the Americans. Viewed as too much of a U.S. man by the Park junta, he was arrested on charges of corruption in office. To please the Americans, Lee was released. In a very short time, he endeared himself to Park Chung Hee and became Park's chief of staff. During the early seventies, he was to be a particularly notorious director of the KCIA.

The anticorruption arrests and purges enabled Kim Jong Pil to place political corruption firmly under his own control for a while. Rival politicians, whether corrupt or not, were simply eliminated. Big businessmen were threatened, jailed, or shut down. That left the field clear for Kim to make a killing by using the authority of the KCIA. In 1962, construction of the Walker Hill casino and resort near Seoul brought several million dollars in rake-offs for the KCIA. For turning on the Japanese financial spigot between October 1961 and February 1962, Kim used Israeli businessman Shoul Eisenberg as a go-between with big businessmen in Japan. Large kickbacks for importing Japanese cars followed. Covert manipulation of the Korean stock market turned a profit of about $40 million for Kim and the KCIA in the spring of 1962.

The Americans were pushing for elections, and Park Chung Hee intended to be the one elected if elections had to be. Preparing for that event, Kim Jong Pil organized the Democratic Republican party in February 1963. The idea was to overcome factionalism and pull in lots of campaign money. A unified party was a threat to the entrenched factions, so they let it be known that Kim Jong Pil had arranged for a $20 million payment to the party from the Japanese government. At that time, before Korea and Japan had signed a post–World War II treaty, dealing with the Japanese government was guaranteed to bring instant unpopularity to Korean politicians. The stock market juggling had also become a public scandal. In February, Park forced Kim to resign and sent him into exile for a few months. Kim had become a liability to Park because too many people knew about the corruption. More important, though, Park saw Kim as a growing threat to his own power.

Park had promised elections would be held in 1963. In March of that year, he announced a change of mind. Military rule, he stated, would go on for another four years. The Kennedy administration was determined not to let him get away with that. Two years of the junta was already too long as far as Washington was concerned. Economic aid to Korea was turned off, and Park relented.

The election was held in the fall. Park won with the help of the KCIA, and large forced contributions from Japanese and American businessmen. He was now officially President of the Republic of Korea.

Corruption continued unabated. It was more diffuse now that Kim Jong Pil was not running the KCIA. Others had more of a chance. Competition broke out among the major money-grabbing politicians. In 1964, two of Kim's competitors were able to get President Park to exile Kim for another short period. With more foreign business coming in as the Korean economy expanded, the foreigners had to pay under the table for the privilege of doing business in Korea. Extortion of Korean businessmen was already a routine well established.

Four politicians, in particular, were the main points for pulling in money for the government and themselves during the mid to late sixties. S. K. Kim, the finance chairman of Park's party, usually collected funds to be paid by check. Kim Hyung Wook, director of the KCIA, collected cash and converted S. K. Kim's checks into cash through the KCIA's access to foreign exchange outlets. The KCIA director kept at least $750,000 from S. K. Kim for himself. Lee Hu Rak, Park's chief of staff, managed large bank accounts in Switzerland for President Park. These three men—S. K. Kim, Kim Hyung Wook, and Lee Hu Rak—worked together to counterbalance the fourth, Kim Jong Pil. His large power base made him a more formidable fund raiser than the others. Park Chung Hee had the job of keeping them all under control in service to him. Of the four, Kim Jong Pil was the most difficult to handle. His goal had always been to run the country one day.

President Park kept a large pile of cash, usually supplied by Lee Hu Rak, in a cabinet behind his desk in the Blue House, the presidential mansion. The President used the money to pay off Korean politicians when they visited. His supporters were well taken care of, but many opposition members of the National Assembly also were bought. As an army man, he worried about loyalty from military commanders, so they got especially large payments. Single payments of $50,000 are known to have been made by Park from his office cache.

He won a second four-year term in May 1967, in an election considered to have been fairly clean as far as the voting went. With 51.4 percent of the vote, he defeated Yun Po Sun, who had been President during the ill-fated Chang Myon government. Park's campaign was financed through extortion of large funds from foreign businesses. Gulf Oil later was to admit having made a lump payment of $1 million. The National Assembly elections a month later, however, were marred by widespread ballot box stuffing, vote buying, and intimidation of voters. A Korean news agency, Hapdong, called the Assembly elections that year the "most fraudulent and corrupt in the history of the Republic of Korea."

With Park officially installed for another four-year term, Koreans living overseas got a grim reminder of the KCIA's long reach. In June, thirty-four students and professors were kidnapped from Europe by the KCIA in the so-called East Berlin spy case. They were brought back to Korea, jailed, tortured, tried, and convicted for espionage. Three were sentenced to death and hanged.

At the end of the 1960s, South Korea was no longer the basket case it had been only a decade before. Its rapid economic development began to be one of the great success stories of the decade. The economy had grown by more than 9 percent a year, one of the highest rates in the world. The Gross National Product rose from $2.2 billion in 1960 to $5.6 billion in 1970, and was to reach $25 billion in 1976. Phenomenal strides were made in industrializing the country. Exports of manufactured goods increased by more than 1,000 percent during the 1960s. Korea became an important producer of textiles, electrical machinery, and plywood, with the United States and Japan as its biggest customers.

The government had formulated five-year development plans, to be enforced rigidly. Under authoritarian labor conditions, the people responded and the goals were met. Other poor countries also had carefully worked-out plans with plenty of American money and advice, but in Korea it was the people that made the difference. Barren of much in the way of useful raw materials, Korea compensated with human resources: educated, industrious, disciplined people.

Economic development was as good for Park Chung Hee as it was for the people. His long-term economic strategy was designed to keep him in office and reduce dependence on the United States. Critics were hard put to deny that the economy was on the upswing. Having no particular philosophy of economics himself, Park was guided by instinct and experience. He instinctively respected organization and was a genius at running organizations. His model for economic development had been Manchuria, already set firmly in his mind twenty years before he came to power. In the 1930s, the growth there under Japanese administration had been the most impressive in the world. The Japanese had done it through a tight organization run by a right-wing business-military clique. Democracy had been absent.

Park had the same kind of clique but also a large cadre of smart young economists, many of whom had been trained in the United States. He was able to build on his Manchurian impressions with modern economics. During the mid-sixties he often was tutored by Dr. Joel Bernstein, the head of the American Agency for International Development (AID) in Korea.

KUMI, PARK'S HOMETOWN, became a model of modernization. The roads were paved, the area was electrified, and a large industrial complex was built. The primary school Park attended had been rebuilt and given the best of facilities and teachers. Along with progress came pollution and plowing up of ancestral graves. Kumi was far from typical of small-town Korea, but Park hoped eventually to do as much all over the country. The other side of Kumo San, the mountain, was a good illustration of what still needed to be done. In appearance, it was something out of the old era: still poor and underdeveloped, without electricity or paved roads. Park and his organization men could not do everything at once. Industry came first. Unless a rural area was scheduled for a factory, it had to wait longer for progress. Agriculture was neglected during the sixties. Farm prices were kept low for the millions of people flocking to the cities. Industry had created new jobs, and incomes were on the rise for the majority of South Koreans.

It was a far cry from the subsistence living of so many people just a few years before. Koreans had never had it so good. And it had all happened under Park Chung Hee.

Corruption, militarism, and dictatorship also happened under Park. Korea had been repeatedly blighted by all three for a long time, leading many Americans to believe that that was just the way Koreans were. The Park regime encouraged that belief by both word and deed. Korean officials lectured Americans on the difference in values between East and West. They contended a free system of government was not the right kind for the Korean people. Since elections under Park were bought, manipulated, or denied, that point was never tested.

Park played along with the forms of democracy because the Americans insisted on it. Unless he held elections and allowed some criticism in the newspapers, the money and political support he wanted from Washington could be jeopardized. His strong preference for full dictatorship was held back during most of the sixties. Later, when the country was stronger and less dependent on the United States, his natural tendency would assert itself full force.

Corruption followed logically from Park's distrust of democratic government. He was in power and intended to stay there. It was also understandable that an organization with such a concentration of power as the KCIA should also be the center of corruption. When money scandals erupted in public, Park went through the motions of cracking down on the KCIA director or other officials. The exercises made him appear to be a wise, righteous monarch who was above it all. His success in buying Korean politicians was to encourage him and his KCIA associates to attempt the same thing with Americans later—sometimes successfully.

Beginning as a poor farmer, Park developed through successive stages: collaborator with the Japanese, Communist, anti-Communist, militarist revolutionary, and corrupt elected President. In 1972, he was to become an absolute dictator.

2

The Lord of the Second Advent

SUN MYUNG MOON leaves no room for doubt about where he and Korea stand in the eyes of God: he is the new Messiah and Korea is God's chosen nation. This is the culmination of God's six-thousand-year quest to restore man from the fall of Adam. It was revealed to him by God when he was a young man, Moon tells his cult followers. God said, "You are the son I have been seeking, the one who can begin my eternal history."

Moon felt no humility. After all, it was God's will to choose him after an exhaustive search through thousands of years and billions of lives. The title "Son of God" could go to only the rarest of individuals, he says, one capable of winning victory over all human history. He was proud to inherit God's Kingdom.

Moon's theology, the Divine Principle, teaches that man can be restored to original goodness by restoring Adam, Eve, and three archangels. Adam's fall resulted from Eve's being seduced by the archangel Lucifer, who was jealous because God gave Eve to Adam instead of to him. Human history has been a constant replay of the same interaction among Adams, Eves, and archangels. God's eternal plan for man's perfection has been thwarted as potential Adams are undone by Eves and archangels. The po-

31

sitions of Adam, Eve, and the archangels are occupied by persons, nations, and movements identified as such by Moon. Ultimately, Adam must dominate after successfully going through three stages: formation, growth, and perfection. But if an Eve or an archangel is at a higher stage than Adam, they must help restore Adam to perfection so he can assume his rightful role in the unified system of things.

Moon is Perfect Adam, so he must be obeyed without question. Jesus, the most important Adam between the original one and Moon, attained spiritual perfection but was a flawed Messiah. His mission was foredoomed by John the Baptist, who spent his time baptizing people instead of becoming Jesus' obedient disciple for influencing the politics of the Herod regime. Making things worse, Jesus was a child of adultery, not immaculate conception, according to Moon. Mary was impregnated by Zachariah. Jesus had an unhappy home life because Joseph was jealous of Zachariah and resented Jesus.

The Divine Principle therefore teaches family unity as dictated by Moon. When Jesus grew up he failed as a leader because he was unable to love his disciples enough to motivate them to kill for him or die in his place. Moonies are taught that because Moon's love is not of the weak Jesus kind, their love for Moon must be strong enough to do what Jesus' disciples were unprepared to do. Since Jesus was incapable of perfect love, owing to his unwholesome upbringing, he was also unable to marry as intended by God.

"The reason why Jesus died was because he couldn't have a bride. Because there was no preparation of Bride to receive Jesus, that was the cause of his death," Moon preaches.

Political action is central to Moon's mission, although the cult denies that it engages in politics at all. Moon views Jesus' failure as a political failure for not gaining control of the government of Israel. Jesus was able to establish a spiritual kingdom, but that was only half of what God wanted. Moon is taking up where Jesus left off by uniting the spiritual kingdom with a physical kingdom on earth. The trouble with Christians, he says, is that they have accepted the myth that the Messiah will return as a spirit "on the clouds." To Moon it is obvious that if this were true, God would have made it happen long ago. The long delay was necessary because God intended for the Lord of the Second Advent to appear as a person who will complete Jesus' mission on earth among the living. He sees Christian churches as furthering Satan's cause by rejecting him.

Israel was God's chosen nation, but the Jews, falling prey to Satan's power, rejected Jesus. God punished them with centuries of suffering, and finally cleansed them by killing six million in World War II. But the Jews had missed their chance. God had to find a new Messiah and a new Adam nation because, Moon explains, it is God's principle not to use the same people and the same territory twice. Korea was ideally suited for several reasons. It is a peninsula, physically resembling the male. Like the Italian peninsula, cultures of islands and continents can mingle there to form a unified civilization corresponding to the Roman Empire. Korea had maintained its own cultural identity through invasions by China and Japan over the centuries. And at Panmunjon, the military demarcation line represents the division between not only the Communist and non-Communist worlds but God and Satan as well.

Japan is in the position of Eve. Being only an island country, it cannot be Adam. It yearns for male-like peninsular Korea on the mainland. Moon sees the Japanese generally as effeminate people who want to be dominated by stronger, manly powers. But as Eve prevailed over Adam in the Fall, Japan prevailed over Korea in the colonial period. And like Eve in the Fall, Japan became a Satanic power.

America is an archangel country. Its mother is England, another island country in the position of Eve. The archangel America helped the Adam country Korea by sending Christian missionaries, rescuing it from Japanese rule, and stopping the advance of Satan's Adam—Communist North Korea. America is too arrogant and individualistic, however. It cannot remain the world's leader, because God has destined America to serve Korea.

Korea's mission, therefore, is to restore the Eve country Japan and the archangel America, and become the center of the new unified world civilization. This is to be accomplished through Moon and his Unification Church.

In Moon's unification thought, politics cannot be separated from religion. His political views have been conditioned narrowly by South Korea's two prevailing political phenomena during his lifetime—nationalism and anti-Communism. What he sees as politically imperative for Korea, he has applied to all of God's universe. World history is now centered on Korea, he preaches, and what happens to Korea centers on him. He claims the Korean War could have been avoided had he been accepted as the Lord of the Second Advent. The archangel America had created the right conditions by making Korea independent from the Eve country Japan. But the Koreans, failing to rally around Moon, were divided between Communist and free-world forces. Though tragic, the division carried forward God's plan that Korea be the flag bearer for the world. The battlefield for the showdown between God and Satan would be Korea. God's chosen people would triumph through suffering. America, Japan, and all other nations could be restored by helping Korea's anti-Communist cause. Only in Korea could the civilizations of East and West be unified. In the end, Moon declares, even North Korea's Kim Il Sung could be restored if he answered the call to follow the Divine Principle.

Details about Moon's early life are not clear because of his efforts to tell the story himself only in terms of being the Son of God. He was born in 1920 in north Korea. He was raised as a Presbyterian in a middle-class family, was a good student, and studied engineering at a university in Japan during World War II. He was married in 1944 and divorced in 1950. He was arrested twice by the Communist government in North Korea for activities as an evangelist and was sentenced to five years in prison in the fall of 1947. During the Korean War, when United Nations forces reached Hungnam prison, he was released halfway through his sentence. He resumed his evangelical activities in Pusan on the southeastern coast. With a small handful of followers in Seoul, he founded the Holy Spirit Association for the Unification of World Christianity, which became known as the Unification Church, in 1954.

Rumors reached the American Embassy that Moon was a ritual womanizer. Reportedly, young girls underwent sexual initiation into his cult; he would thus purge them of the Satanic spirits that inhabited Eve and lead them to the Divine Principle. He was jailed for three months in 1955 by South Korean authorities on charges reported by newspapers and government agencies as draft evasion, forgery, "pseudo-religion," and false imprisonment of a university coed compelled to adopt his religion. The charges were dropped, and Moon's followers hotly deny that Master was a fornicator.

Moon's own account of his life is heavy on allegory supporting the Divine Principle. The episodes he relates to his cult are like parables, always with a direct tie-in to his teachings. He presents his life story as the unfolding revelation of the Divine Principle, with himself as the example to follow for what he preaches.

There was a minister named Kim who was Moon's John the Baptist. According to Moon, after Kim received a revelation from God, he placed his hand on Moon's head and blessed him as the heir to King Solomon and the glory of the whole world.

Unfortunately for Kim, the women in Kim's following—also responding to divine revelations—became attracted to Moon. The rivalry resulted in Moon's leaving after a short time. But Moon could not hold himself responsible for what happened. When Kim gave Moon his blessing, God rightfully transferred all that Kim had to Moon.

God revealed Moon's divine mission to his fellow prisoners in North Korea, Moon tells. They were in awe of him because he could do twice as much work as they on half the rice quota. He thought of half a bowl as his full quota and the other half as an extra gift from God, which he gave to the other prisoners. He disciplined himself to the most distasteful work: carrying 1,300 bags of fertilizer to the scale every day. For the Son of God no amount of labor was too much. Others needed rice for survival, but Moon was living on the spirit of God. While working he imagined he was the star of a movie being shown to his ancestors and descendants. He resolved to teach his followers to ignore the limitations of their physical bodies and be sustained by spiritual strength.

There was a woman named Ho Ho Bin in prison with Moon the first time he was arrested. Whenever she had divine revelations, her stomach muscles wobbled. This was God's way of reminding her that the new Messiah would come as a real person from a mother's womb. Several times Moon tried to contact her, but she refused to have anything to do with him. He wanted to tell her that if she put her faith in him and lied about her revelations, the Communists would release her. Finally he slipped her a note:

"The writer of this note is a man of heavenly mission, and you should pray to find what he is. If you deny everything you have received, you will be released."

Mrs. Ho would have none of it. She wanted to destroy the note immediately, but the guard, tipped off by another prisoner, grabbed it. Moon was interrogated, accused of being an Ameri-

can spy, and tortured. But he denied her revelations and was released after less than three months in jail. He says Mrs. Ho and
all her followers were killed by the Communists when the Korean War started in 1950.

Mrs. Ho's fate dramatizes the peril of not accepting Moon as
the Messiah. Disobeying him led to her death. She refused to follow the Lord of the Second Advent. By disregarding Moon's
counsel, she violated his Doctrine of Heavenly Deception.

Moon teaches that lying is necessary when one is doing
God's work, whether selling flowers in the street or testifying under oath. The truth is what the Son of God says it is. At the Garden of Eden, evil triumphed by deceiving goodness. To restore
original perfection, goodness must now deceive evil. Even God
lies very often, he says. God's lies bring far greater gifts than man
thinks are possible. If Mrs. Ho had believed in Moon and lied she
would have been released. If released, she might have become
Perfect Eve with Moon.

Moon claims to have found Perfect Eve in the seventeen-
year-old girl he married in 1960, Han Hak Ja. He told the cult
that her preparation for Bride to receive Moon began at the age
of four; in 1947 she was blessed by Mrs. Ho. Being so young at
the time, she did not remember the experience. But Moon was
aware of it from the moment he met her. Once the vows of matri-
mony were exchanged, Moon as Perfect Adam could not let himself fall into the same trap as the first Adam. He "snatched her
out of the Satanic world" and taught her to obey. Since Adam
fell by being dominated by Eve, he had to reverse the precedent
by achieving complete domination over his wife. Obedience training went from formation to growth and perfection, to the point
where, after three years, he says, she would sacrifice her life if he
so ordered.

Since Adam and Eve fell from grace and Jesus never married, it remained for the Third Adam to restore the Perfect Fam-

ily. Moon and his wife became True Parents, known as Father and Mother.

Only True Parents can consecrate the heavenly marriage needed to create a heavenly home. Before Moon grants permission for Unification Church members to marry, they must serve him for at least three years, corresponding to Jesus' ministry of three years. Mates are chosen by Moon, often at random in a large group, and couples are not supposed to consummate the marriage until they have Moon's approval.

In order to rule the world, Moon had to start with Korea. It was essential that he have loyal cultists inside the government. They had to be well placed so they could sway powerful persons and become influential themselves. They must be skillful in portraying the Unification Church as a useful political tool for the government without revealing Moon's power goals. By Moon's serving the government, the government would be serving him. Avenues to more power could be opened. Recognition at higher and higher levels could come. His service could become indispensable. The government could come to need him so much that he would be able to take control of it.

Four of his early followers were young army officers close to Kim Jong Pil, the chief planner for the Park regime and founding director of the KCIA: Kim Sang In (Steve Kim), his interpreter, later to become KCIA station chief in Mexico City; Han Sang Keuk (Bud Han), who became ambassador to Norway; Han Sang Kil, who became Moon's personal secretary after serving at the Korean Embassy in Washington; and Bo Hi Pak, Moon's advance man in Washington during and after Pak's service as assistant military attaché at the Korean Embassy.

Kim Jong Pil made a two-week official visit to the United States as KCIA director in the fall of 1962. Included in his entourage was Steve Kim as interpreter. The Korean Embassy mobilized for the occasion, and the Kennedy administration rolled out the red carpet. Lieutenant Colonel Bo Hi Pak was the Embassy's officer in charge for Kim's meetings with CIA Director John McCone, Secretary of Defense Robert McNamara, and Defense Intelligence Agency head Lieutenant General J. E. Carroll.

En route home, Kim Jong Pil met secretly in his room at the St. Francis Hotel in San Francisco with a small group of Moon's early activists, who had been sent to proselytize on the West Coast, and some American converts. Kim Young Oon, beginning in Eugene, Oregon, in 1959, had moved to Berkeley, California. Choi Sang Ik, having established the church in Japan, had moved to San Francisco. Kim told them he sympathized with Moon's goals and promised to help the Unification Church with political support from inside the government. He said he could not afford to do so openly, however, which fit Moon's plans perfectly.

Kim Jong Pil had learned from Moon's followers in the KCIA that Moon was a zealous anti-Communist. That could be useful to the government. He was also aware of Moon's ambition to build influence in Korea and beyond. That could create problems for the government if the influence were not properly channeled. Moon was anxious to increase church membership in cities and villages throughout the country. Fine, thought Kim, just as long as they don't get out of bounds. The KCIA must be the one calling the shots. He decided the Unification Church should be organized satisfactorily to be utilized as a political tool whenever he and the KCIA needed it. Organizing and utilizing the Unification Church would be a simple matter anyhow. After the military coup overthrew the elected government in 1961, all organizations in Korea were required to apply for reregistration with the government. Undesirable elements were identified through a process of reevaluation and dealt with accordingly. Kim could maintain effective ties with Moon's organization through the four army officers, but the Moonies had best not be told of Kim's plans to manipulate them. It was a situation favorable both to Moon's plans for expanding via the good graces of the government and to Kim Jong Pil's plans for building a personal power base.

Bo Hi Pak's work for Moon in America was of crucial importance. Pak is a model Moonie. For him, Master always comes first. From the time he joined Moon in 1957, he endeavored to make everything he did contribute in some way to Moon's divine mission. Assignment to the Embassy in Washington in 1961 was a precious opportunity to do missionary work in the United States. As a diplomat, he could foster Moon's interests within the R.O.K. government and keep Moon apprised of important intelligence. It was God's providence that he go to America, he believed, and he must make the most of it.

Pak "witnessed" tirelessly for Moon. Every new acquaintance was a potential convert. His home on North Utah Street in Arlington, Virginia, was a recruiting center. Every social gathering there was a potential study group. He was assisted in his ministry by his wife and another Moonie living with them, Jhoon Rhee, who later became well known as the owner of a chain of Korean karate schools. In 1963, Pak established the Unification Church in Virginia. The incorporation papers declared the church to be totally independent from any other organization and affiliated with the original movement in Korea only on a doctrinal basis.

Airline pilot Robert Roland and his wife were cultivated patiently by Pak over a period of several months without a hint about the connection with Moon. The Rolands and the Paks became close friends.

On one occasion, Roland asked what the duties of an assistant military attaché were. Pak was candid about his intelligence role at the Embassy. He explained that in addition to routine diplomatic work he was responsible for liaison between South Korean and American intelligence agencies, which often required his visiting the supersecret National Security Agency (NSA) located at Fort Meade, Maryland. Roland asked about the work the NSA did.

Pak volunteered that it dealt mainly with secret codes and monitoring of radio transmissions. Roland, a bit startled by the information, was finding his new friend to be an intriguing person.

One evening, the Rolands found that they were the only guests invited. Previously, others had always been present. As small talk wore on at the dinner table, Roland sensed his hosts were leading up to something carefully planned. When the meal was finished and they were settled comfortably in the living room, Pak revealed step by step how the destiny of mankind was in the hands of a Korean named Moon. Pak's life was devoted to helping Moon fulfill his divine mission.

"You've noticed that I sometimes seem tired and overworked," he said to Roland. "That is because I am so busy working for Master that I have time for only three or four hours of sleep. My boss at the Embassy criticizes me for neglecting my duties there, but I know the Korean Government favors our movement. If necessary, I would work twenty-four hours a day for Master."

"What are you trying to accomplish in Washington?" Roland asked.

"I must lay a firm foundation for Master by making influential political and social contacts."

Roland was curious to know if Moon had remained celibate until he married at the age of forty.

Pak's expression became serene and he nodded with sincerity. "Yes, most pure virgin."

It all sounded like fascinating hogwash to Roland, but his wife was taken in. Her devotion to Moon led to divorce years later and estrangement between Roland and their daughter after

she, too, became a Moonie. But it was not until many months
after that first talk that Roland became outwardly hostile to the
movement. In the meantime Pak attempted to convert him, and
Roland learned interesting details he was later to use during a
thirteen-year effort to expose the Moon organization.

AFTER ATTENDING A CONCERT by the Vienna Boys Choir, Pak
conceived the idea of organizing a troupe of young girls to perform traditional Korean songs and dances. The propaganda value could be enormous with the right kind of management. Moon
could double what the Austrians had done with the Vienna Boys
Choir: little girls as ambassadors of good will for Moon and Korea, dancing their way into the hearts of millions, including presidents, prime ministers, and kings. Moon liked the idea and
founded the Little Angels in 1962.

The Little Angels were one of the first of hundreds of
"front" groups designed to further Moon's universal objectives.
The groups follow a consistent pattern. Moon may be listed as
the founder, but ties with the Unification Church are denied.
Moon stays in the background while Moonies such as Bo Hi Pak
promote the group for Moon's ultimate benefit. The technique at-
tracts large numbers of people who are uninterested in Moon's
religion. To the extent that they know Moon is affiliated, they see
him as a man with varied worthwhile interests apart from religion. The fact that his religious interests encompass everything
he does is artfully hidden from the public. But even while the Little Angels project was still in the planning stage, Pak stated the
purpose clearly in the application for tax-exempt status for his
Virginia branch of the Unification Church. He wrote in his statement to the Internal Revenue Service: "It is hoped that the future
will allow sponsoring a Korean dancing group in various cities as
a means of bringing the Divine Principles to more people and to
thus further the unification of World Christianity." As evidence
that his organization was a bona fide church, he submitted a let-

ter signed by Korean Ambassador Chung Il Kwon, which Pak had drafted, certifying that the Unification Church "has been the recognized Christian religion in Korea since 1954." At the time of the letter, 1963, most Koreans had not yet even heard of Moon's church.

In Korea, the Little Angels were getting organized. Instructors were hired, girls were recruited, and the government provided a building free of charge for the training center. But a great deal of money would be needed to elevate the scheme to the level intended by Pak and Moon. Pak hit upon the idea of an American-based foundation to sponsor not only the Little Angels but other Moon projects as well. The foundation should have broad-based appeal, so it could not be identified openly with the Unification Church. Promoting people-to-people relations with Korea and opposing Communism seemed lucrative themes. Americans would contribute money to those causes, especially if recommended by distinguished leaders. Unknowingly, they would be serving Moon, but in the long run they would be rewarded by Moon's establishing the Kingdom of Heaven on earth.

Thus was born the Korean Cultural and Freedom Foundation (KCFF) in 1964. Unlike some other front groups, the KCFF acknowledged no affiliation with Moon. Bo Hi Pak would pretend his practice of Moon's religion and his work for KCFF were unrelated. Moon's founding of the Little Angels would be downplayed so that Pak and the KCFF could get the maximum advantage of appearing independently successful. However, KCFF money would be used to help make the Unification Church strong in America.

The foundation would require more of Pak's time than was allowed by moonlighting; he could no longer afford to waste his work days at the Embassy. His position there had opened the right doors in Washington, but had outlived its usefulness. The moment had arrived to start working full time for Master. With the church's government connections in Seoul, he arranged for early retirement from the army. Although now a private citizen, he was able to return to the United States on a diplomatic visa, backed by a letter from the Ministry of National Defense saying he was performing an unspecified special diplomatic mission.

The key to successful fund raising and propaganda was endorsement by influential people. It was essential, therefore, to have the right names in the top positions, although Pak would see to it that he alone ran the foundation. He found a useful figurehead in the person of Yang You Chan, R.O.K. Ambassador to the United States during the Korean War. Retired and settled in Washington, Yang was known and respected by American government leaders from the fifties and still carried the title of Ambassador-at-Large. He was especially noted for his staunch anti-Communism. Yang agreed to be executive vice-president and persuaded retired Admiral Arleigh Burke to accept the presidency. Bo Hi Pak was vice-president. Burke and Yang gathered an impressive list of names for the KCFF letterhead: former Presidents Truman and Eisenhower as honorary presidents; Kim Jong Pil as honorary chairman; the directors and advisers included Richard Nixon, George Meany, Perle Mesta, Senator Hugh Scott, Senator Homer Capehart, General Matthew Ridgway, and Congressman Clement Zablocki.

The foundation's first annual dinner was a formidable event held in the Washington Hilton's International Ballroom. It featured speeches by Admiral Burke, Korean Ambassador Kim Hyun Chul, and Assistant Secretary of State William Bundy. Bo Hi Pak was master of ceremonies for the evening's entertainment: the "Gala National Premiere" of the Little Angels, presented by noted Washington impresario Patrick Hayes.

Moon, like Tongsun Park, is skillful at transforming the illusion of power into real power. Both seized every opportunity to be seen with influential persons and especially to be photographed with them. This technique helped increase their power in Korea by convincing government leaders that they were close to the most important people in America. Likewise, in the United States they exaggerated their actual importance in Korea, which opened more doors to American influence.

During Moon's first visit to the United States in 1965, Bo Hi Pak arranged through Ambassador Yang for him to meet Dwight Eisenhower at Gettysburg. There was the customary picture-taking. A contingent of Little Angels was brought along to charm the Eisenhowers with a private performance. By receiving Moon, the former President was doing what was expected of him. Moon commented that Eisenhower "paid his bill in full" by opening doors to further recognition by national and international leaders. The pictures from Gettysburg also were put to effective use for recruiting church members.

Admiral Burke resigned in 1965 after about a year as KCFF president. He had originally accepted the position with the understanding that it would be temporary, but in the meantime he had developed misgivings about the organization. Robert Roland had sent him material on the Unification Church describing Pak's ties with Moon and the hidden purposes of the Little Angels. Also, Bo Hi Pak's explanations about where the money was going had seemed unconvincing to Burke. Apparently, Burke was never sufficiently alarmed to warn the other prominent persons whose names were being used. Despite the resignation, Pak persisted in using Burke's name, both on the letterhead and in lobbying for the foundation. Burke, too, had "paid his bill" by acquiring high-level respectability for KCFF.

It was intended that the Little Angels gain prestige for Korea and Moon, and in this they succeeded admirably. Acclaimed by critics for their artistry and charm, they were a hit in the world's leading concert halls during the sixties and early seventies. They performed before audiences of dignitaries, including an appearance before Queen Elizabeth, and a rare performance at the United Nations, where Secretary General Kurt Waldheim and Governor Nelson Rockefeller were listed as patrons. It was during the United Nations appearance that, for the first time, Moon was publicly acknowledged as the founder. Characteristically, deception was employed for hard-sell effect. In Las Vegas, the Moonie managers conned Liberace, with whom the troupe was performing, into announcing falsely that an invitation had just come from President and Mrs. Ford for a White House performance.

The Korean government took full advantage of the propaganda opportunities afforded by the Little Angels. They were billed as "unofficial ambassadors of good will," and Korean embassies all over the world eagerly promoted visits by the troupe. KCIA Director Kim Hyung Wook expedited the issuing of passports (which are hard for Koreans to get and must be re-issued for each trip) for the girls whenever Pak requested them. The government financed overseas tours and donated choice land outside Seoul for a multimillion-dollar school and performing center.

Pak peddled the widely believed story that the girls were orphans, when actually most came from upper-middle-class families who competed to get their daughters in. He discovered the Little Angels could be convenient vehicles for bringing cash for the KCFF into the United States from Japan, where the Moon organization had abundant sources of money. Large amounts could be divided among members of the company before passing through Customs. They could then be divested of the money at Pak's home, which he maintained as a logistics center whenever the Angels were in the United States. In 1972, a Little Angels traveling group delivered 18 million yen ($58,000).

Moon always regarded the Little Angels as an instrument for exerting influence over social and political institutions. After a successful appearance by them in Japan, he told his followers that "we have laid the foundation to win the embassy personnel stationed in Japan to our side—and through them we can influence their respective nations." In Korea, where rumors about ties

to Moon were becoming a problem because of his growing notoriety, Pak ran a newspaper ad denying that the Little Angels had
anything to do with the Unification Church. The troupe's booking agent, fearful that links with Moon would harm their otherwise excellent reputation, asked for official reassurance. The
KCFF board chairman informed him that Moon was merely a
friend and supporter of the Little Angels, not unlike millions of
others. American Moonies were ordered not to promote them
too openly or else "Satan will attack by saying that Reverend
Moon is exploiting these children for his own glory."

For more than ten years the truth about Moon's scheme was
kept from non-Moonies on the KCFF board and from the many
thousands of Americans who gave money to the foundation.

THE NEXT PROJECT for KCFF was Radio of Free Asia (ROFA),
launched in 1966. The idea, modeled on Radio Free Europe, was
to broadcast anti-Communist programs from South Korea to
North Korea, China, and North Vietnam. Moon and Pak gave it
a special twist, however. They would conduct mass mailings to
Americans asking for money to pay for broadcast facilities in Korea but arrange for free use of transmitters and studios through
the KCIA. The money could be pumped into the Unification
Church or other Moon activities, as needed. KCFF's list of
American luminaries could be used for promoting ROFA, since
the radio was a KCFF project. It was another multipurpose
Moonie venture with benefits above and below the surface: promoting anti-Communism, becoming more valuable to the Korean
government, gaining greater prominence in the United States,
and making money for Moon. Bo Hi Pak was thrilled by it. It
was described to prospective contributors as "one of the most
daring undertakings against the Communists on the mainland of
Asia in the last thirty years."

Larry Mays was someone Pak thought could be useful without getting in the way. Mays was a mortgage broker in Baltimore

when Pak met him in 1965. He was uninterested in Unification Church theology but was drawn to Pak through a shared devotion to anti-Communism. They became good friends. During lunch at the Washington Hilton in June 1966, Mays was surprised to hear Pak suggest to Ambassador Yang that Mays become the first international chairman of Radio of Free Asia. Flattered, Mays accepted immediately. A few weeks later, Pak had him elected to the KCFF Board of Directors.

Bo Hi Pak found Mays a genial, malleable sort. He was enthusiastic and didn't ask questions about where the money came from or went. He was a good anti-Communist. Though he had no power himself, he had a few moderately influential connections. He could provide a joint Korean-American veneer to the ROFA leadership. Pak could run things easily with Larry Mays around.

The target date for ROFA's first broadcast was only two months off. The immediate business at hand was for Pak, Yang, and Mays to go to Korea to negotiate with the government for approval to begin operating. Pak expected to use a 500,000-kilowatt transmitter belonging to the government-owned KBS network, and Mays thought ROFA money would be used to pay for it. Pak told Mays that as international chairman, Mays's presence in Korea would be important at meetings with President Park, the Prime Minister, and other notables. But before leaving, Pak said, there was one matter that had to be taken care of. He needed approval from the Korean Ambassador to the United States, Kim Hyun Chul, to go to Korea to complete the ROFA negotiations. Mays asked why. Pak explained that Ambassador Kim had complained that since the Little Angels had come to the United States the previous year without adequate financing, he didn't believe KCFF had enough money to take on a new project.

Actually, Pak had put KCFF in the red by more than $20,000 with the Little Angels' visit. Ambassador Kim was worried about the Korean image in Washington if KCFF got into serious financial trouble. He thought the Little Angels project was basically good for Korea, but he was leery about the way Bo Hi Pak handled money. Since Pak had connections at the top of the government in Seoul, Kim's ability to control him was limited. He did not want to be caught in the middle getting the blame if Pak got into hot water in Washington.

Mays thought ROFA had plenty of money. "Didn't you tell me we already have more than forty thousand dollars in contributions?" he asked Pak. Mays had never asked to see the financial records. He just assumed everything was in order after reading the brochure.

"Yes, that's true," Pak assured him. Mays recalls Pak then saying it would be more convincing to Ambassador Kim if Mays were to tell him ROFA was Mays's idea and that Mays was paying for the trip with a check made out to Pak, which Pak would show to the Ambassador. Mays agreed to write a $10,000 check for Pak to take to their meeting at the Embassy the next day.

As planned, Mays told the Ambassador it was he who had conceived the idea for ROFA and proposed it to former Ambassador Yang, who in turn informed Pak and obtained approval from the KCFF directors. Ambassador Kim was convinced. The trip to Korea was on.

In Seoul, Pak orchestrated a program to keep Mays busy with trivia while Pak and Yang handled the real work. Mays was assigned a protocol secretary and a chauffeur. He presented an engraved trophy (furnished by Pak) to Prime Minister Chung Il Kwon. In a call on KCIA Director Kim Hyung Wook, Mays received a plaque inscribed: "To Lawrence L. Mays—Behind the scenes toward the goal." He had arrived in Korea with only superficial knowledge of the ROFA project, but even that was of little use at meetings because most of the conversation was in Korean. He did pick up an important piece of information in English though: Pak told the government broadcasting director that $70,000 had been received in contributions from Americans.

Back at the Bando Hotel, Mays mentioned the difference between this figure and the $40,000 Pak had told him about in Washington.

"Yes, we received about seventy thousand dollars altogether," Pak said matter-of-factly.

Mays spoke sternly for the first time. "You will have to account for the difference, then."

"No need to worry. I had to use the additional money for other expenses."

"For what?" Mays pressed.

Pak explained that the money had gone to the Unification Church, Mays recalls. The church had been helped by Jhoon Rhee, he said, who had turned over all the profits from the karate schools for Pak to use for upkeep of the church headquarters on S Street in Washington. But more money was needed to feed and house church members.

Mays wondered where Pak drew the line between KCFF and the Unification Church—indeed, whether there was a line at all.

The target date for ROFA's first broadcast was August 15, the anniversary of Korea's liberation from Japan. The date had been set by Pak many months in advance, and he placed symbolic importance on meeting the deadline. That seemed impossible. August 15 arrived after three days of negotiations with the government and there was no approval yet. Mays went to the President's Independence Day reception assuming it would take considerably more time to get ROFA going. Much to his surprise, he was greeted by the Minister of Public Information with a big handshake and "Congratulations! President Park has just given word that Radio of Free Asia will go on the air tonight at eleven o'clock."

Bo Hi Pak really delivers, Mays said to himself. He felt very satisfied that night when he heard the first broadcast, although he had no idea what the announcer was saying. Nor did he know that Pak had delivered via the friendly intervention of Kim Hyung Wook, the director of the KCIA.

It was not until the morning of August 16 that Mays deviated from Pak's carefully planned schedule. He called at the American Embassy to talk to Ambassador Winthrop Brown and his staff. They had many questions about ROFA: its affiliation with KCFF, the amount of advance preparation, and how it was that approval was obtained so quickly from the R.O.K. government. Mays, of course, was unable to provide details, but he assured the Embassy the project was well funded with contributions from Americans and that he, as international chairman, would control the content of all programs. Ambassador Brown then came to the point. He had information that the man KCFF had hired to be ROFA's operations director in Seoul, Kim Kyong Eup, was working for the KCIA. Mays was astonished and promised to look for a replacement. It was clear Ambassador Brown distrusted Bo Hi Pak and felt the prominent Americans on KCFF's letterhead were being drawn into something they knew nothing about.

It was important to Mays that the U.S. government look favorably on ROFA. He was hoping that the Voice of America and ROFA could work together in support of anti-Communist goals. He never dreamed the operations director was a KCIA man, but he did remember Ambassador Yang's saying that the R.O.K. Minister of Public Information had sent him a message in Washington asking KCFF to hire Kim Kyong Eup.

Bo Hi Pak was at the hotel when Mays returned from the Embassy. Ambassador Yang came immediately at Mays's request. Mays told them Ambassador Brown was not satisfied with Kim Kyong Eup and wanted him replaced, not mentioning the KCIA connection. Pak and Yang spent most of the day on the telephone and finally found that Kim Dong Sung, a former Minister of Public Information, was available for the job. The Embassy told Mays there was no objection. The KCIA connection was still there, however. Kim Dong Sung previously had been an aide to former KCIA Director Kim Jong Pil.

The following morning Mays and Pak drove to the outskirts of Seoul to visit the Little Angels school. They were treated to a performance of new dances being prepared for the next American tour. They then went back downtown for lunch with Moon and Kim Jong Pil, at that time the chairman of President Park's Democratic Republican party. Lunch was a cheerful affair, with most of the talk in Korean. Moon was happy that ROFA was now on the air, and he presented Mays with a pair of silver chopsticks. Kim Jong Pil, the silent "Godfather" of Moon's special relationship with the R.O.K. government, said very little.

Mays returned to Washington alone. Pak and ROFA were not what he had thought. He viewed himself as an American patriot who wanted to do something about Communism; ROFA was to have been a noble undertaking for this cause. But Pak's overriding loyalty to Moon was diverting ROFA's money into the Unification Church. The KCIA was involved, too, apparently working with Pak and Moon behind his back and getting ROFA into trouble with the U.S. government. Then there was the $10,000 check. He didn't mind going along with the little game to get the Korean Ambassador off Pak's back, but the check was supposed to have been destroyed or returned to him. When he asked about it as they were departing for Seoul, Pak said he would return it when they arrived back in Washington. But Pak's secretary had telephoned them in Seoul to report that the check had bounced after it was deposited. Pak apologized casually, explaining that his secretary must have deposited the check by mistake. Mays didn't like being duped.

He was through with Pak, but he still wanted to salvage ROFA. This might be done by incorporating ROFA as an entity separate from KCFF, as should have been done in the first place and as Ambassador Brown had suggested. He gave the whole story to General John Coulter, the president of KCFF. They both resigned from KCFF. On the same day they incorporated ROFA as a separate entity in Baltimore.

The second ROFA was a futile paper exercise. Bo Hi Pak had the organization, the facilities in Korea, and by far the greater determination. He kept ROFA going for nine years. Americans continued to mail in contributions, thinking their money was paying for a privately owned and operated project. Pak was spending at least some of the money on the Unification Church, according to what he had told Mays. And he was using Korean government transmitters free of charge, and leaving the broadcasts under the control of the KCIA.

The Korean Cultural and Freedom Foundation reaped large benefits for Moon. By the end of the sixties his designs on America had shaped up nicely. Bo Hi Pak had been remarkably effective cultivating the American elite. Nixon, Eisenhower, Truman, and others were working for Moon without even knowing it. He could have his picture taken with almost anyone. The Little Angels—secretly his "Divine Principles children"—were winning the hearts of millions. Radio of Free Asia had paid off with money to nourish the young Unification Church in the United States and free air time for anti-Communist broadcasts. Kim Jong Pil's early support of the Unification Church had been justified for the Korean government many times over in the successes of the Little Angels, the attention to Korea from KCFF's influential supporters, and the church's anti-Communism and loyalty to the Park regime. There was a mutually advantageous relationship wherein the Moon organization and the Korean government served each other. There was little mutual trust though; each side was suspicious of the other's designs on it. But both made maximum use of the indulgence of Americans. Moon and the Korean government had done well indeed by Bo Hi Pak's diligent labor.

UNTIL HE AND KOREA take over the world, Moon says, it is God's will that America have custody of all the world's land that is not Communist. As an archangel, it had been vested with stewardship over all of God's property. But America had failed. The first failure was at the end of World War II when the Communists were allowed to join the United Nations. The decline continued: not enough was done to fight Communism, especially in Korea, so America was punished with the death of President Kennedy. Drug problems, free sex, crime in the streets, and family disunity were all grim evidence of Satan's undermining power. Among American leaders, Moon saw not a single true patriot, but only small men obsessed with authority. Moon resolved that he alone would train future leaders. Into the moral void the Lord of the Second Advent would go so that "someday they will realize that I am truly the most noble and precious VIP that ever came to America."

In 1969, Moon decided it was time to get his rank and file in America busy combating Communism. He had been waging extensive anti-Communist campaigns in Korea and Japan under the aegis of his International Federation for the Extermination of Communism, with political and financial support from Ryoichi Sasakawa and Yoshio Kodama and other powerful Japanese right-wing figures. He organized the Freedom Leadership Foundation (FLF), the American branch of his international federation. Its president, Allen Tate Wood, mobilized Moonie groups throughout the country to lobby for the hawk position in Vietnam and try to diffuse the peace movement.

Wood and eight other American Moonie leaders attended the annual conference of the World Anti-Communist League in Kyoto, Japan, in September 1970. The conference was the biggest ever held by the world league, largely because the sponsoring organization that year was a Moon group, Shokyo Rengo, the Japanese branch of his international anti-Communist federation. Master ordered the Japanese Moonies to prepare for the event with a massive fund raising drive, which reportedly yielded $1.4 million brought in by selling flowers in the streets. Through

KCFF, the Moon organization was able to engage Senator Strom Thurmond as guest speaker.

Allen Tate Wood then proceeded to Korea to meet Master. The fall of 1970 was an opportune time for briefing the head of the Moonies' American political organ. The Korean government was just then making plans for an influence campaign in the United States. Wood had several private audiences with Moon. It was clear that Master was preparing for a major expansion into the political field in the United States with a new sense of urgency. According to Tate, Moon said:

> "FLF will probably win first the academic community. Once we can control two or three universities, then we will be on the way to controlling the reins of the certification for the major professions in the United States. That is what we want to do because universities are the crucible in which young Americans are formed. So if we can get hold of those, then we can move out into politics, into economics, and so on."

But above all, Master stressed, "We must guarantee unlimited military assistance to South Korea and prevent further withdrawal of American forces." Those were exactly the two objectives of the Korean government's campaign to influence United States policy. It had been approved in secret by President Park only a few weeks before, and the Moon organization had been assigned a key role.

The Charmer

TONGSUN PARK had his father's affection but not his respect. The spread of about eight years between Tongsun and his two older brothers was one reason. In Korean family tradition, they were expected to take on responsibilities in the family's coal and oil distributing business. While Tongsun was still a schoolboy, they reached maturity, and the father was strict and demanding toward them. Tongsun was not the kind of child who responded to demands even if his father had been inclined to impose any. He was adorable and loving, eliciting the warmth his father held back from the older brothers.

Tongsun's mother, not legally married, was also the object of deeper affection from the father than the mother of the half-brother and half-sister. With Tongsun's mother, the father found the love that had been absent in the relationship with his legal wife. The separation of feelings within the family was widened when the father moved to Seoul for business reasons, with his two older sons and their mother after Korea was liberated from Japan in 1945. For the time being, ten-year-old Tongsun stayed with his mother and half-sister in Sinchang in North Korea, where Tongsun had been born in 1935. As travel between the two

Koreas became difficult, Tongsun's father eventually brought the rest of the family to Seoul.

The Park family was wealthy but not active politically. Tongsun's mother was civic-minded, however, and her devotion to good works won respect in Seoul. She established a school to teach textiles and light technical skills to girls and heavier industrial skills to boys. It was important to her that her son have full standing in the family and in society. She was concerned that although he was charming and agreeable, no one took him seriously. She was protective toward Tongsun against the brothers' jealousy of all the affection he got. They considered him flighty and spoiled and thought he would always be a child. But his mother remained confident in her high hopes for Tongsun. Only she had faith in him, and he adored her. The loyalty and love between mother and son was to be a permanent feature of Tongsun's life.

In Tongsun's quest for recognition, he was to make full use of his greatest personal asset: charm. His carefree nature could bring positive reactions because he put it across as congeniality. He could make up for not bothering to study the details of heavy problems by making friends of people who did. Popularity could compensate for his lack of diligence. His brothers made it by being respected, but he could make it by being liked. Money could enable him to meet the right people; charm could do the rest. It was politics, pure and simple. Others had done it without pretending to be profound, so why couldn't he?

A very ambitious Tongsun Park arrived in the United States in 1955 after finishing high school in Seoul. He spent a few months at King College in Tennessee before moving to Washington to enroll in Georgetown University's School of Foreign Service. His mother had thought him well suited to become a diplomat, a profession his father also approved of. Living in Washington and majoring in international relations was just what he wanted. Washington was an ocean of politics, and he jumped in at the campus level. His goal was to become president of the student body. He entertained at his fine apartment in Georgetown, wore the latest clothes, and drove friends around in a shiny new Buick Riviera. Campus politics and socializing kept him too busy to spend much time studying, so he invited good students to dinner for briefings from their course notes before exams.

Korean students got at least as much of Tonsun's eager attention as his American classmates: a large number of them—bright and well connected—attended Washington-area universities. Tongsun's Sunday dinner parties at the Yenching Palace Restaurant gathered Korean students for leisurely table talk over several courses of Chinese food and built a political base for Tongsun. At the end of his freshman year, he was elected president of the Washington-area Korean students association. By his junior year, he had became vice-president of the Georgetown student body and national president of the Korean students association. He was less successful as a scholar, however; his poor grades got him suspended for a year. But he made the best of it. The University of Puget Sound accepted him as a transfer student and voted him 1959 "Campus king" in a popularity contest after some good campaigning. Forced to abdicate as Georgetown student body vice-president, he retained the presidency of the Korean students and toured the country speaking to Korean-Americans about student life in the United States. After a year, it was time to go back to Georgetown and the Washington mainstream, but Puget Sound had been a nice diversion with some West Coast experience to balance his East Coast interest.

He graduated from Georgetown in 1962 without ever becoming president of the Georgetown student body, but he made a number of very helpful friends: future Indiana Congressman John Brademas, with whom he shared a house; Joseph Montoya,

Jr., son of the New Mexico Senator; Louise Gore, wealthy owner of Washington's Jockey Club and future Republican National Committeewoman; former Korean Ambassador to the United States Yang You Chan; Park Chung Soo, future aide to the Prime Minister; and Lee Bum Jun (Park Chung Soo's wife), who later became a member of the Korean National Assembly. Of particular long-range importance was his friendly acquaintance with the then-current Korean ambassador, Chung Il Kwon—the same Chung who had served as a Japanese army officer with the young Park Chung Hee in Manchuria. Chung, every bit as gregarious as Tongsun, took a special liking to the enterprising young student politician.

Now an up-and-coming citizen of the world, Tongsun was begrudgingly let into the family businesses in Seoul. His brothers gave him the presidency of Miryung Sangsa, an oil tanker firm.

After getting established in the Seoul business world, he began traveling to Washington more frequently because, as he later said, "a citizen of the free world should participate in the political process in Washington." Since South Korea needed help from the United States to handle its security, he believed Koreans had a responsibility to advise "political friends" in America about the situation in Korea. Among his "political friends" was Washington lawyer Tom Corcoran, confidant of Democratic Presidents, who literally could walk in on Lyndon Johnson almost any time. He did just that with Tongsun at the Blair House in 1965. Johnson and Park Chung Hee were chatting through an interpreter during a state visit by the Korean President. Corcoran and Tongsun came in unannounced. Tongsun met the two Presidents, shook hands, had his picture taken with them, and left with Corcoran.

He felt safe masquerading to American friends as a cousin of President Park Chung Hee, thinking word would never get back to distant Seoul. Ambassador Kim Hyun Chul picked it up in

Washington in 1966, however, and reported by letter to KCIA Director Kim Hyung Wook. Tongsun found himself in a jam on his next arrival in Korea. He was arrested by the KCIA at the airport, interrogated all night, and released the following day with a stiff warning to stop the impersonation. Two or three days later, KCIA Director Kim got a phone call from Chung Il Kwon, the former ambassador to the United States who was now Prime Minister and who was becoming Tongsun's mentor. Chung said Tongsun was a fellow who could be very useful because of his many important friends in Washington. He urged Kim to have a talk with Tongsun to hear "all about the United States."

Two days later Tongsun was a guest in the KCIA director's office. Again, Kim raised the matter of his pretending to be President Park's cousin.

Tongsun explained that Americans must have misunderstood his meaning when he said he and the President were both from the Park clan. Every Korean, including the Korean ambassador, knew that didn't imply a family relationship. He said he was sure the ambassador had complained simply because of jealousy over Tongsun's friendship with so many members of Congress and other prominent people in Washington society.

Kim counseled him to be more discreet so as not to create any unfounded misunderstandings in the future.

When KCIA Director Kim arrived for a dinner at Prime Minister Chung's invitation a week later, Tongsun was there too. He assured Kim he could do many useful things for the Korean government through his influential friends in Washington. Kim invited Tongsun to stop by his office again. He was interested in this young man.

Before returning to the United States, Tongsun called on Kim. Since he could be so helpful to the government, he hoped Kim could help him too. He asked for nothing specific. Kim suggested Tongsun contact the KCIA station chief at the Embassy in Washington if he needed anything.

BACK IN WASHINGTON, there were problems with his new business venture, the George Town Club. The fundamental problem was that Tongsun was running it. Not only did he lack managerial skill; he was also broke. Rich as he was in Korea, he had little money available in the United States in 1966, and Korea's strict currency controls kept him from converting large amounts into dollars. He had spent too much money outfitting the club, borrowing heavily and charming his friendly creditors into waiting for payment. The club was impressive-looking—a nineteenth-century brick townhouse with original paneling and dark hardwood floors and beams. It was decorated with Oriental rugs, knight's armor, Arabian rifles, oil paintings, and antique Oriental vases. Tongsun had formed Suter's Tavern Corporation in the early sixties with stockholders including Charles Bressler, Paul Enton, Louise Gore, Robert D'Ambry, and himself. By the time the corporation opened the George Town Club in March 1966, Tongsun had bought out the other stockholders with promissory notes payable in ten years. (The notes were finally settled between 1972 and 1974 at 50 cents on the dollar.)

Tongsun was anxious to meet a certain Congressman who had made a favorable impression on Prime Minister Chung while visiting Korea—Representative Richard Hanna of California. A mutual friend, Dr. Shin Dong Shik, called Hanna for an appointment to introduce a young Korean who needed help. When Tongsun arrived, Hanna saw a well-dressed man who, in small talk, emerged as exceptionally polished. Smoothly and with a sense of humor, Tongsun told Hanna about the George Town Club and its failing finances. The Congressman accepted the invitation to come down to the club for a firsthand look at the enterprise. A lunch date was set.

Hanna was interested but skeptical about playing any role. He imagined a place far below the class of Washington's F Street Club, the University Club, or the Cosmos Club. He was surprised to find it beautifully appointed and with excellent food and service. He was shown the list of prominent members and noticed a former Eisenhower aide and several leading Washington attorneys dining. Tongsun Park seemed to be a natural host, but it was obvious he was no manager. Hanna learned from the cook and maître d' that the staff sometimes went for several weeks before getting paid. Still, he thought, the club had great potential and Tongsun Park was a fascinating fellow. Hanna told Tongsun he could best help by attracting more big names for the membership list. Tongsun suggested the Congressman invite some prominent Washingtonians to a George Town Club party. Better than that, Hanna said, have a dinner party for Speaker of the House John McCormack.

Hanna approached the Speaker, telling him, "John, you are entitled to the recognition you don't always receive from your colleagues. They want to invite you to dinner in your honor."

Invitations were sent out, including one to the President. Though no reply came from the White House, several hours before the party secret service agents came unannounced to inspect the building. In the middle of the party, Lyndon Johnson arrived and paid his respects to John McCormack and the crowd of guests assembled. The next day, the newspapers gave a lot of coverage to Tongsun Park, the gracious host at the George Town Club on Wisconsin Avenue.

In Hanna, Tongsun had discovered an unusually generous man willing and able to help him rise in Washington's social and political circles and gain prominence with the Korean government. Hanna, for his part, was learning that his new friend's charm often seemed counterbalanced by the problems he was able to attract. Hanna was subsidizing Tongsun's rise with loans to help meet the payroll at the George Town Club. When he first visited Tongsun's home, the cook complained about immigration problems. Hanna helped out. At the time, there was nothing in it for Hanna other than friendship. But Tongsun wanted more. Although the club was giving him publicity, which showed the Seoul government he was accepted by important Americans, that was not enough. He wanted to amass a fortune in the United States and he wanted more recognition from the Korean government as someone advancing its cause in Washington.

"Dick, I'm never going to be anything but in a desperate situation as a club owner. I have to get something going to make money," complained Tongsun in late 1967. By now Hanna was used to Tongsun's whining so he paid little attention at first. But Tongsun went on. He began describing a rice shortage in Korea, the worst the country had experienced in years.

It was unusual for Tongsun to have mastered so many details. He spoke of the American rice surplus and the possibility of arranging a big sale of rice to Korea from the United States. Hanna doubted whether they could be instrumental in anything as grandiose as the rice deal outlined by his friend. He was planning to visit Korea in connection with his work on the international finance subcommittee during the Christmas holidays though, so he made a mental note of Tongsun's urging him to check the rice situation.

Prime Minister Chung Il Kwon rolled out the carpet for Hanna in Seoul. Most of Hanna's free time was spent with the Prime Minister, dining at good restaurants, playing Ping-Pong at Chung's home, and partying. Eventually, Chung got down to serious business: rice production, consumption, pricing, and politics. Political careers in Korea, Chung stressed, could be made or broken by these issues. He was concerned about stabilizing prices for the continued well-being of the ruling Democratic Republican party. Domestic production was down, but rice was available on the international market and they would have to buy large quantities. The amount was greater than Hanna had suspected or Tongsun had quoted.

One of the purposes of Hanna's trip was to examine ways to help bring Korea's debt ceiling to a reasonable level. A foreign rice purchase on the scale Chung had described would cut deeply into the country's foreign exchange holdings. But if Korea bought California rice financed under the Food for Peace Program, the payment would be spread over a long period at low interest rates. Hanna talked to the American ambassador, William Porter, before leaving. Porter was well aware of the situation and agreed it was important that Korea buy from the United States. He noted one thing in favor of the United States: the other contender, Japan, insisted that Korea buy a large amount of other unrelated commodities in return for getting Japanese rice at a competitive price.

Upon returning to Washington, Hanna's first words to his Korean friend were, "Tongsun, you were right!" Tongsun smiled humbly, as was his way when being praised. He then revealed why he was so interested in the rice problem. He wanted to be the middleman for all sales of American rice to Korea. Hanna's role as conceived by Tongsun would be to convince the Korean government to use Tongsun as the exclusive sales agent.

The usual arrangement was for the sellers to find an agent who would offer and arrange the sale to the foreign government. The system Tongsun envisioned was based on the leverage the Korean government could exert because a "buyer's market" existed. Hanna listened as Tongsun asked him to intercede with the Korean government by suggesting that an exclusive agent chosen by the buyer, not the seller, could be of great political advantage to it. It would be fairly easy, he said, to convince the government that an American agent would not try to get the best deal for Korea and would be less likely to share commissions generously with Korean officials. It didn't follow, however, that the government would see that Tongsun was the right Korean for the job. That was where Hanna came in: the government would take Tongsun seriously if he were backed up by an important American Congressman.

Hanna was a bit annoyed. Here was Tongsun, again asking a large favor. He was hard to turn down under normal circumstances, but this time he was asking a lot. It meant Hanna would have to work hard in Korea to convince the government and then go through a similar routine with the California rice growers. Tongsun needed Hanna's cooperation though, and was willing to offer a part of the commissions on the sales.

"What the hell? I thought this was over!" Hanna snapped at Tongsun. He had already checked out the situation in Korea for Tongsun, had become sympathetic to the Koreans' need for rice with easy financing, and was prepared to work as a Congressman to sell them California rice under the Food for Peace program. But with Tongsun it never seemed to be over; there was always the next stage.

"I have to get the confidence of the Korean government," Tongsun replied earnestly, "and only you can help me do that."

Reflecting for a few moments, Hanna saw the proposal as a private business deal acceptable for a Congressman outside official duties. In effect, what he would be getting from Tongsun was a finder's fee. If Tongsun also shared proceeds with Korean officials, that was his business and had nothing to do with Hanna. He decided to help Tongsun get the rice agency.

In Seoul, to sell the plan to the Korean government in August 1968, Tongsun was at Hanna's side constantly. Prime Minister Chung Il Kwon threw a party for Hanna at the Daeha Restaurant the first night. It was obvious that Tongsun was very close to the Prime Minister, but Hanna had no inkling that Chung and Tongsun were using him in a scheme to gain more power among the factions in the government. General Kim Hyung Wook, the KCIA director, was introduced to Hanna at the party. Hanna was also unaware that like himself, General Kim, too, was playing a role in both of Tongsun's current U.S.-related projects—the George Town Club and the rice deal. The previous year, after Hanna had attracted President Johnson and Speaker McCormack to the club, Tongsun had asked General Kim to help him borrow money for the club, promising to use it as a Korean lobbying center. Kim had then arranged a transfer of $3 million in Korean government money to Tongsun's bank to facilitate loans for the club.

Hanna listened as Chung extolled Tongsun's virtues to General Kim. Kim then turned to Hanna and said he had heard of all the fine things the Congressman had done for Korea, starting with helping an orphanage during Hanna's first visit to Korea in 1965. He was looking forward to seeing the Congressman in his office the next morning. Hanna was pleased. Chung and Tongsun had told him earlier that without the KCIA director's cooperation, Tongsun could not get the rice agency.

Before going to KCIA headquarters, Tongsun and Hanna discussed an added dimension of the rice deal, one certain to appeal to General Kim. The rice sale was important to the interests of the United States, and Tongsun intended to spread the word around Congress in order to help Korea's cause. Hanna himself, quite apart from Tongsun's urgings, thought Korea should have an effective organized lobby much as Israel, Greece, and Taiwan had. He had advised Korean officials on a couple of occasions that their lobbying in Washington was misdirected. Rather than relying on friends in the White House, State Department, and the military, he thought, they should turn their attention to Congress. Hanna went along, therefore, when Tongsun said part of the profits from the rice sales should be used to contribute to congressional election campaigns.

Seeing General Kim on his own turf at KCIA headquarters,

Hanna perceived a man seriously concerned that his image reflect his position. Kim Hyung Wook lacked Chung Il Kwon's wit and was rough-hewn in comparison; in Korean political circles, he was known as "the bear." The KCIA director began the conversation by emphasizing the threat to South Korea's security. He spoke of some 290 incidents of North Korean infiltration during the previous year and a half alone. Hanna said something about supporting the American commitment to defend South Korea and then launched into his pitch to sell California rice.

He clicked off the major points: Korea needed rice, the United States had a surplus, Japan was also a contender, Korea could get a better deal from the United States. Kim acknowledged the points, and Hanna moved on to the next phase of his prearranged presentation. Buying American rice would enhance Korea's standing with American politicians. He then described Tongsun's suitability for the job of sales agent, saying Tongsun was popular among Congressmen and was prepared to contribute some of the commission money to election campaigns. The wording was not as strong as what Tongsun had pestered him to say— he did not say Tongsun's qualifications were unique in the entire world—but Kim got the message.

At this point, Tongsun chimed in eagerly with a statement in Korean. The KCIA director's expression changed and he nodded with approval. Unknown to Hanna, Tongsun had said the Congressman would play a key role in distributing proceeds from the sales commissions around Congress.

It was an easy matter for Kim to call the director of the R.O.K. Office of Supply and tell him Tongsun was to be the agent in the United States for the upcoming big rice purchases. A simple request from the KCIA director was enough to throw the bureaucracy into action.

General Kim instructed Tongsun and Hanna to talk things over with the Office of Supply. The meeting there on the same day was short and perfunctory. Director Kim Won Hee okayed

Tongsun. With deep hidden joy, Tongsun phoned KCIA head-quarters to inform General Kim that "everything was taken care of."

Tongsun was jubilant. He was on his way to a multimillion-dollar income in the United States. The Korean side of the deal was set.

On the American side, the problem was the California Rice Growers Association. Again, Tongsun could not clear the hurdle without Hanna's help. The Congressman was to set up appointments with the right people so that he and Tongsun could persuade them to fire whatever agent they had and hire Tongsun. Right after returning from Korea, he began badgering Hanna about getting in touch with the California rice growers.

"All I can do, Tongsun, is introduce you to Mayor Alioto. Then it's up to you," Hanna said. Joseph Alioto, the mayor of San Francisco, had been the attorney representing the Rice Growers Association. Meeting Alioto might be enough, Tongsun felt, for the time being.

Shortly after Alioto returned from giving the nominating speech for Hubert Humphrey at the 1968 Democratic Convention in Chicago, he received a call from Hanna asking for a meeting. When Tongsun and Hanna arrived in Alioto's office, the mayor seemed not at all sure what the meeting was to be about. He had assumed Hanna wanted to talk about Democratic politics. But there was Tongsun explaining to a somewhat impatient mayor about his interest in selling California rice to the Korean government. Alioto responded quickly that he was devoting very little time to the Rice Growers Association; business could be best conducted with Robert Freeland, the association's chief executive officer.

Meeting with Tongsun and Hanna toward the end of September, Freeland said he was not interested in changing agents. Later, he and Alioto discussed the matter further and decided to ignore Tongsun despite a cable Alioto received from the R.O.K.

Office of Supply stating that Tongsun Park would be instrumental in diverting the sale from Japan to the United States. They believed the rice growers' business could be handled better by Woodward and Dickerson of Philadelphia, the current agent, which the year before had arranged with a Korean consortium the largest commercial rice sale in history. However, that transaction was to pale in comparison to Tongsun's U.S. government-financed sales in subsequent years.

Freeland arrived in Korea in mid-October to propose the next sale through William Wurster, Woodward and Dickerson's representative in Seoul. Wurster told him it appeared they would have to deal directly with the Korean government instead of businessmen, now that U.S. government financing was available for large rice purchases. Freeland attempted to set up a meeting with the R.O.K. Office of Supply. Director Kim Won Hee refused even to see Freeland if his agent, Wurster, accompanied him. Freeland went without Wurster and was told that Wurster's company had fallen into disfavor with the Korean government. This was hard to understand, said Freeland, since Woodward and Dickerson had handled the huge rice sale the year before, with Wurster working day and night. Kim Won Hee brushed aside the objection and suggested the California Rice Growers engage Tongsun Park. Kim did not rule out Wurster altogether; he could work under Tongsun.

Wurster wanted nothing to do with Tongsun Park. A year or so earlier, Tongsun had sold him a membership in the "George Town Club of Seoul," which was to have been a high-class retreat for American businessmen and the upper crust of Korean society. Wurster parted with $3,000 for his membership. He never saw the money again, or the promised club.

Freeland thought perhaps the American Embassy could save him from being saddled with Tongsun. He and Wurster made an appointment to see Ambassador Porter. The ambassador listened somberly as they described the overall predicament.

A sympathetic smile crept onto his face as Tongsun's name was mentioned over and over. All Porter could do was to shake his head and say, "Frankly, gentlemen, I would like to help you, but there is nothing I can do."

The Embassy had been the last hope for Freeland and the California Rice Growers. He could read from Porter's demeanor that this was probably not the first time Tongsun had interposed himself between the two governments. Tongsun, with no technical knowledge to help the rice growers, was being foisted on them by the Korean government. Freeland could not take chances. The sale was too large for that—400,000 tons, the entire amount of California's rice surplus. It was Tongsun or no sale. He said goodbye to Wurster and took Tongsun.

By chance, Wurster saw Tongsun Park once more. Several months after Wurster had lost his rice agency, Tongsun happened to be sitting across the aisle on a flight between Seoul and Tokyo. Tongsun leaned over and said, "I think you should cooperate in this rice business in Korea."

Wurster shot back angrily, "Are you threatening me?"

The charm vanished from Tongsun's eyes as he said coldly, "I don't need to threaten you. I am too strong."

Being the sole selling agent for U.S.-Korean rice trade was to bring Tongsun more than $9 million in commissions, some $850,000 of which he spent on members of Congress. Hanna's services were rewarded with about $200,000 over the years. Ironically, Hanna was sometimes in the position of having to lend money to his wealthy friend. Tongsun's spending habits were as flamboyant as his personality, so he seldom had much on hand; his lavish plans were always one step ahead of his bankbook. His first payment to Hanna was $3,000 in February 1969, almost three years after the Congressman started advancing funds to him.

The advice he got from Hanna was far more valuable than the relatively small amount of money he had borrowed from the

Congressman. Tongsun developed his congressional lobbying strategy through long talks with Hanna, who argued that the Koreans had to turn their attention from the White House to Congress so as to influence important votes. The plan was simple. The Korean government should know the economic interests of the districts of key Congressmen. When Korea was making large purchases in the United States, the economic link between Korea and the particular district should be made known to its Congressman. Korean lobbyists would then contribute to the Congressman's campaign.

The rice deals were calculated on this theory. The Californians in Congress would reap political benefits by Korea's purchases of vast rice reserves. Later, political careers in Louisiana would be helped by similar rice purchases. Korea was buying rice from the Congressman's district and contributing to his campaign. He would feel indebted to Korea. On the next important vote it would take only a casual call to remind the legislator of his favorable stance on Korean issues.

From the beginning, Hanna knew Tongsun intended to put money from rice sales commissions into congressional campaigns—although he was not told how much or to whom. He even encouraged it. Rationalizing his own role to himself, he could view Tongsun narrowly as a private businessman instead of an R.O.K. agent. That way, neither the percentage he was getting nor the campaign contributions should be illegal. On the other hand, Hanna did not go around talking about it. That Tongsun was doing some valuable lobbying for the Korean government was clear to Hanna. And he knew his friend had to cut some deals with high officials in Seoul in order to keep the business going. But that was Tongsun's affair, not his.

The money Tongsun Park made from rice commissions enabled him to expand with other business operations in the United States, also worth millions, such as Pacific Development, Inc., Five Star Navigation, Three Star Navigation, and restaurants in

Washington. Specializing as a middleman, he was to receive several million dollars for consulting services. For his settlement of one contract dispute in 1975 between Burma Oil of Britain and Japan Lines, he was paid a fee of $3 million. Not surprisingly, he sometimes failed in business ventures. His boasting about influence with Korean and American officials did not convince the E-Systems Corporation to make him its agent for a large contract to provide backpack radios to the Korean Ministry of National Defense in 1975. One of the reasons he lost out was that E-Systems had heard he was working for the KCIA. He backed out of an agreement to purchase 22,000 tons of rice from the American Rice Company of Houston for export to Korea; the company eventually decided not to press a lawsuit for breach of contract. Tongsun had his greatest successes when the power of his government connections—both Korean and American—left businessmen with the choice forced on the California Rice Growers: Tongsun or nothing.

"WOULD YOU PLEASE amplify to your friends in Congress about our problems with North Korea?" KCIA Director Kim Hyung Wook had asked Congressman Hanna during their meeting with Tongsun about the rice agency in August 1968. Hanna did better than that. He organized the largest congressional delegation ever to visit South Korea. In March 1969, twenty-three Congressmen were shown in person that only 30 miles north of Seoul there was a hostile and unpredictable Communist army.

The idea for the visit, as well as most of the work, came from Hanna. He got Speaker McCormack to approve the trip as a way of showing that Congress remained committed to defending South Korea at a time of lagging support for the war in Vietnam. He persuaded Majority Leader Carl Albert to lead the delegation. He had the Korean National Assembly issue a formal invitation to the House of Representatives. And he advised

KCIA Director Kim on how best to impress congressmen with the need for military aid.

Hanna believed South Korea's cause was just. He also gained satisfaction from being treated by the Koreans as an important person. In the United States, there were 434 other Congressmen. But in Korea he was *the* Congressman.

Tongsun needed to get some credit for the big congressional delegation; it would show General Kim he was delivering on the promises he had made about winning influence for Korea in Congress. Hanna did not fail him. When Hanna informed Kim by letter that the delegation was coming to Korea, he added, "Our mutual friend, Tongsun, will be working as a liaison."

The twenty-three Congressmen got quite a welcome at Seoul's Kimpo Airport: a regiment of government dignitaries headed by Prime Minister Chung Il Kwon and the Speaker of the National Assembly, a chauffeured car to take each Congressman to the hotel escorted by an English-speaking member of the National Assembly, and orphan girls (from the orphanage Hanna had helped during his first visit to Korea) to hand every Congressman a bouquet of flowers. Strung across the observation deck of the terminal building was a huge banner reading WELCOME CONGRESSMAN HANNA. It was the choice item on the Korean government's menu of exuberant overkill. Hanna was the brunt of little jokes from his colleagues, who said it looked like he was the King of Korea.

Apparently General Kim was favorably impressed by the way things went. After the Americans left, he informed President Park that the visit seemed certain to create better relations with Congress and ultimately would generate wider pro-Korean sentiment in the United States.

TONGSUN'S NEXT OPPORTUNITY to appear influential with Congress and the Korean government came in late 1969 when the

Republic of Korea asked that Congress earmark an extra $50 million in military aid for Korea. The request coincided conveniently with Tongsun's second big rice sale.

Although technically he was agent for the seller, the California Rice Growers Association, he was at least equally a Korean government agent. Most of all he represented himself and endeavored to use both sides for his own benefit. With the rice growers, it was easy; they had to take him. With the Korean government he had to give—money and something else. His unwritten contract with Prime Minister Chung and KCIA Director Kim stipulated some Korean victories in Congress.

The pawns in Tongsun's game plan were the Congressmen. Hanna was always a big help, but getting the $50 million approved by a Congress souring on foreign aid was something Hanna could not do alone. Tongsun chose three avenues beyond the help Hanna could extend. The first was to work with Congressmen from the recent delegation to Korea. The second was to use the rice sale as leverage with members whose districts produced rice. (As he put it himself years later, "If my friends want me to help sell their surplus rice, which has always been a political headache for them, then they ought to show their support for military aid to Korea.") And the third was to make inroads in the powerful committees.

Democratic Congressmen John McFall of California and Otto Passman of Louisiana were both members of the powerful House Appropriations Committee. Both were from rice districts. McFall was an obvious target, being from California. As for Passman, Tongsun correctly assumed he was aware of Korea's potential as a market for Louisiana's rice surplus.

Tongsun had not met McFall or Passman prior to the $50 million aid proposal. But no matter. He could use both without meeting them, by shaking up the California Rice Growers Association. Tongsun told the association's sales promoter, Curt Rocca, that Korea was getting pressure to buy the next load of rice—another colossal 400,000 tons—from Japan, but if Congress approved the $50 million in military aid, there would be no need for the California rice growers to worry.

Rocca alerted McFall. McFall took his concern to Passman. The two men met to discuss how to save the rice sale. They agreed on two proposals by Passman: get the Department of Agriculture to come up right away with attractive financing for the Koreans to buy American rice; and attach an amendment to the military aid appropriations bill for the $50 million the Koreans wanted.

Within a week, the Agriculture Department had approved financing for the rice sale on terms much easier than Japan's.

McFall and Passman then went into action in the Appropriations Committee. The money was approved in Passman's subcommittee, but deleted by the full Appropriations Committee. Congressman William Broomfield of Michigan, a staunch Korea supporter on the Foreign Affairs Committee, reintroduced the provision when the aid bill was taken up on the House floor. Hanna led the debate and produced a supporting letter from Defense Secretary Melvin Laird. Passman declared he had received "intelligence information underscoring the urgent need for the appropriation." The Broomfield amendment passed the House.

The Senate was an obstacle, however; it was known to be down on more military aid. Senator Fulbright, for one, had argued against special earmarking of funds, complaining about foreign government agents who were able to "finagle" such funds. But McFall and Passman won out in the House-Senate conference committee on the appropriations bill, through Passman's dogged determination and adroit compromises on other provisions.

McFall was only too willing to see Tongsun when he called to ask for an appointment. After Tongsun gave his life story highlighting long friendships with Congressmen, McFall moved anxiously to the point. "We now have the money in the foreign aid bill, so we will be able to sell the rice," he assured the powerful Korean lobbyist.

As staged by Tongsun, the United States was giving Korea $50 million in extra military aid so Korea would buy 400,000 tons of rice from California through easy financing under the Food for Peace program. He had paid lobbying calls on thirty-five Congressmen. At his request, McFall wrote three letters thanking him for helping with the military aid and the rice sale. Then, after the $50 million was approved, Hanna wrote to Prime Minister Chung Il Kwon to say that "the members of our delegation to Korea who are on the Appropriations Committee did staunchly support funds for Korea." In addition, he gave credit to himself, Broomfield, and Tongsun.

Tongsun was doing all right. He got his rice commission, played power broker for legislation that originally had nothing to do with him, and created more influence for himself with both the American and the Korean governments.

KCIA DIRECTOR KIM HYUNG WOOK was pleased with Tongsun Park. In a short time, the freewheeling young businessman had become a KCIA agent of influence. Kim's method of giving orders to Tongsun bypassed the Korean Embassy in Washington. When he couldn't personally tell Tongsun what he wanted, he would do so through the KCIA station chief at the United Nations, Yang Doo Won. Tongsun was supposed to keep Yang informed of his activities so Yang could report back to Kim. This was done when Tongsun and Hanna set up the junket to Korea for the twenty-three Congressmen. Tongsun was not the KCIA's most obedient servant, however. Kim had told him to make payments to congressmen and lobby to ensure that Congress kept up the special allowance to Korea for Korean troops fighting in Vietnam. Tongsun did not have enough American money to contribute to Congressmen before the rice commissions started.

When he began getting commissions in 1969, he kept most of the money and planned to give some to Congressmen later, although Prime Minister Chung and KCIA Director Kim received a share as his mentors in Seoul. He did little if any lobbying for the special allowance for the Vietnam War, but more than made up for it by appearing to engineer singlehandedly the $50 million in extra military aid.

Although KCIA Director Kim was to say years later, "He was my agent," Tongsun never saw it that way. In his own mind he was nobody's agent but his own. From his standpoint, everybody was working for Tongsun's dual goals of money and recognition: Kim, the Congressmen, the California Rice Growers.

Through the years no one was used by Tongsun more than Hanna. They were the closest of friends. Tongsun frequently reminded Hanna of his affection by saying Hanna was "like a brother" to him. Ken Park, Tongsun's older brother, told Hanna he could not understand why a Congressman would want to have anything to do with someone as shallow as Tongsun. Hanna stood to make a lot of money via Tongsun, to be sure. But it had started partly because of his own good nature, partly out of fascination and affection for Tongsun, and partly because of a certain amount of recognition that came with the association.

Tongsun told friends he wanted to be the Korean ambassador to the United States someday. That title would be a supreme acknowledgment that his way of gaining recognition worked. He was at his best, though, as a behind-the-scenes manipulator and probably lacked the courage or confidence to be out front. At the end of 1969, his way was working beautifully and the future looked promising. With a combination of shrewdness and charm, Tongsun Park's star was on the rise.

4

The Origins of the Influence Campaign

AMBASSADOR WILLIAM PORTER was out walking his dog the evening of January 21, 1968, when he heard gunshots from the direction of the Blue House. He immediately asked an aide to find out what had happened. Over the next few hours information came in fragments outlining a grave situation. A group of armed men wearing R.O.K. army uniforms had had a shootout with the police. A policeman was killed. Four of the attackers were killed. Several got away. One had been captured. They were North Korean. They had been trying to reach the Blue House.

Around midnight, Ambassador Porter was called to the Blue House to meet with President Park Chung Hee. By then both men had learned that the shootout with South Korean police had stopped the advance of a North Korean assassination squad on its way to the Blue House to kill President Park. Some thirty commandos had crossed the demilitarized zone and made their way to Seoul, armed with automatic rifles, pistols, and hand grenades.

President Park was enraged. He was intent on striking back, he told Porter, and vowed to have South Korean forces in the

North Korean capital of Pyongyang in two days' time. Porter said if the President tried that he would have to do it alone. Park warned that Porter too had been in danger because the American ambassador was the North Koreans' "number two target." But the United States was not prepared to go to war over a foiled commando raid.

Park Chung Hee was very dissatisfied over the Americans' failure to retaliate. The raid on the Blue House was a scary reminder of the South Korean capital's vulnerability to infiltration from the North. It was the most serious penetration of Seoul since the Korean War. He could not attack the North without American approval, so there was nothing he could do except again gird the people for vigilance against the Communist menace.

Two days later there was another shock from North Korea. The intelligence ship USS *Pueblo* was captured 15 miles offshore near the North Korean port of Wonsan. Eighty-two crew members had been taken prisoner, though they had managed to destroy most of the ship's intelligence-gathering equipment. One sailor had been killed. In North Korea, after the crew underwent torture, Captain Lloyd Bucher was forced to sign a confession that the *Pueblo* had been caught inside North Korea's 12-mile territorial sea.

American forces in northeast Asia went on the alert. President Johnson ordered 350 more warplanes to South Korea. The carrier USS *Enterprise* was positioned off the North Korean coast. At the United Nations, Ambassador Arthur Goldberg angrily brought up the *Pueblo* seizure in the Security Council. The American response was a great show of strength, but no shots were fired. North Korea refused to return the *Pueblo* crew, and the United States was not willing to go to war over it. Vietnam was more than enough to deal with; no one wanted another Asian war.

The *Pueblo* incident compounded Park Chung Hee's dissatisfaction with his American allies. In his view, the Americans had not done nearly enough about a major provocation, the Blue House raid; now they were doing much more about something he considered not as serious. If he had had his way, North Korea would have met armed retaliation for both incidents. Since that was not possible, it rankled him all the more that the *Pueblo* was getting more attention in the United States than the Blue House raid. Defense Minister Kim Sung Eun made Park's attitude clear when he complained to Lieutenant General Robert Friedman that the United States showed little concern when commandos came within 800 meters of taking President Park's life, yet one "pig boat" could move heaven and earth. Park saw the *Pueblo* seizure as a side issue not deserving the commotion it was causing in Washington.

On January 31, Park's government staged rallies where 100,000 students demanded assistance from the United States and the United Nations to prevent further North Korean commando raids. The *Pueblo* seizure was not mentioned. The next day, Foreign Minister Choi Kyu Ha told reporters the Park government was "categorically opposed to any tendency in Washington" that gave the *Pueblo* a higher priority than the infiltration problem. On the same day, however, Washington and Seoul both raised the priority for Vietnam as the Communists launched the great Tet Offensive.

There was no doubt in Lyndon Johnson's mind that the Tet Offensive and the North Korean provocations were related. He was convinced the North Koreans had been trying to divert American military resources from the Indochina area and induce South Korea to recall its two combat divisions from Vietnam. It was equally firm in Park Chung Hee's mind that the United States was not tough enough with Communists in either Korea or Vietnam. Moreover, he felt, with South Koreans helping the United States in Vietnam he was entitled to more help from his American friends when North Korea caused trouble at home.

South Korea's participation in Vietnam was indeed important to the United States. It was the most visible evidence of non-American support for the war against the Vietnamese Communists. Other nations had made supportive statements; some had sent relief aid, military advisers, or small combat contingents; but no ally came near South Korea's level of support—sixty thousand fighting men.

Park Chung Hee was deeply committed to resisting Communism both at home and abroad. The South Koreans saw their first experience with combat outside their own country as a sign of growing national maturity and prestige—a formerly beleaguered nation taking on big responsibilities to help another country against Communist aggression. At least as important as this symbolism, however, was a more tangible benefit. Korea was making an enormous amount of money. The Vietnam War was proving to be a boost to Korea's economy comparable to the effect the Korean War had had on the Japanese economy. Park Chung Hee had exacted a good price from Lyndon Johnson—$1 billion in special allowances for South Korea. Benefits included greatly increased military aid, lucrative Korean contracts in Vietnam, and foreign exchange advantages. The United States provided funds to pay Korean troops at about the same level as American forces, but the R.O.K. government paid them at a much lower rate and kept the difference.

The Tet Offensive did not divert Park Chung Hee's attention from the threat of infiltration at home. Like Lyndon Johnson, he too saw a link between Korea and Vietnam. At Ambassador Porter's suggestion Johnson decided to send a special presidential envoy to calm Park's nerves. He asked Cyrus Vance, a private attorney at the time, to go to Seoul and talk to the South Korean President. Vance returned to Washington with Park's promise not to attack the North on his own. In return, Vance had assured Park that the President of the United States stood firmly with South Korea and would support a bill in Congress for $100 million in supplemental military aid. Johnson and Vance were satisfied that Park Chung Hee had been placated.

There was much in the talks with Vance that displeased Park. He had not gotten the assurance he wanted for "automatic response" to North Korean aggression. Still, the Vance mission showed that the President of the United States was giving South Korea his attention even while the Tet crisis raged in Vietnam. Though Johnson had not reacted to North Korea with the force Park desired, at least the South Korean president had been accorded the dignity of a special envoy bringing reassurance direct from Johnson. Confidence depended on the belief that there was a special relationship with the United States. The R.O.K. army, one of the world's best-trained, was larger than North Korea's. South Korea had a more advanced economy and a larger population. Even so, from President Park on down, South Koreans believed that only the awesome power of the United States could prevent another wholesale onslaught from North Korea. One of Park Chung Hee's greatest pillars of political strength was his claim that he, better than anyone else, could keep American support from wavering, through a special relationship he had built with Washington. Particularly in times of crisis it was crucial for him to show that the Americans were with him. The Vance mission was seen in Korea as a sign that the special relationship was real.

Real though it might be, the special relationship carried disadvantages. Park knew he and Lyndon Johnson had different notions about what the life-or-death issues were. North Korean commandos had come within 800 meters of taking Park's life, not Johnson's. American Presidents viewed the threat from North Korea against the backdrop of America's global responsibilities. There would always be differences in the way he and his American allies perceived the world. South Korea must therefore become prepared to fend for itself. Park and his advisers were troubled by conflicting feelings about the American big brother: their need to depend on him, their determination not be dominated by him, and their fear of losing him.

Uncertainty about America deepened the following month. Park Chung Hee was dismayed when Johnson halted the bombing of North Vietnam and declared he would not seek reelection. The bombing halt showed further flagging of resolve to resist Communism. The decision not to run again meant Park would have to build another special relationship with a new leader in Washington. At a scheduled meeting between the two Presidents in Honolulu three weeks later, Park turned down Johnson's request for more R.O.K. troops in Vietnam. The limited war Johnson was fighting in Vietnam appeared unpromising, and Park wanted the troops at home to deal with the infiltration problem.

During the same month as the Honolulu meeting, April 1968, the Korean government let Washington know it was interested in starting its own arms industry. In particular, the Koreans wanted to produce the American M-16 rifle under license from the U.S. government. State Department officials were sympathetic to the idea, since the goal of foreign aid was for countries to be able eventually to take care of their own needs. If Korea could make its own rifles, the United States could reduce military assistance. The U.S. government considered the idea throughout 1968 without approving it. A large part of the problem was that the Koreans wanted to manufacture everything for the rifles themselves, from springs to barrels and magazines. To meet that request, Colt Industries, the M-16 patent holder, would have to make arrangements for the Koreans with the subcontractors who made parts of the rifle for Colt. In 1969, Colt yielded to pressure from Deputy Defense Secretary David Packard to help the Koreans build the rifle plant. Thereafter, the United States went along with Korean production of a wide variety of American-patented military equipment.

PARK CHUNG HEE PREFERRED Hubert Humphrey over Richard Nixon in the 1968 election. For all of Park's growing concerns about American dependability, overall he had been very pleased with the Johnson administration. Humphrey was a part of that administration and a man Park liked and trusted. With Humphrey as President, Park could expect continuation of a good though imperfect relationship.

The prospect of a Nixon presidency worried Park. Although Nixon had a proven anti-Communist record, he had become somewhat of an unknown quantity in Seoul by 1968. He was seen as an opportunist who put winning the presidency before principles and might try to end the war in Vietnam as quickly as possible to appease antiwar sentiment in the United States. Nixon seemed also to be hinting at less support for South Korea. Park's advisers had gotten a glimpse of Nixon's thinking from an article he had written in the fall of 1967 for the prestigious journal *Foreign Affairs*, and they were disturbed over what it might mean for Korea. In the article, "Asia After Vietnam," Nixon wrote:

> One of the legacies of Vietnam almost certainly will be a deep reluctance on the part of the United States to become involved once again in a similar intervention on a similar basis. . . .
>
> The role of the United States as world policeman is likely to be limited in the future. To ensure that a U.S. response will be forthcoming if needed, machinery must be created that is capable of meeting two conditions: (a) a collective effort by the nations of the region to contain the threat by themselves; and if that effort fails, (b) a collective request to the United States for assistance.

The article concluded that "the central pattern of the future in U.S.-Asian relations must be American support for Asian initiatives."

To the Koreans, this kind of thinking portended a pullback from the American commitment to defend them. Although Nixon had also stressed that the United States should not abandon treaty obligations, he seemed to be saying that the United States would fight in a war against North Korea only after South Korea and some allied Asian nations had failed to win.

The same month Nixon won the election, North Koreans landed a force of about a hundred guerrillas on the coast of South Korea. The infiltrators eventually were killed or captured in a joint R.O.K.-U.S. hunt. Three months after Nixon entered office, there was a North Korean provocation similar to the *Pueblo* incident. A large U.S. navy reconnaissance plane was shot down outside North Korea's territorial sea limit. All thirty-one crew members were killed. President Nixon and his national security adviser, Henry Kissinger, considered retaliating with a strike against a target in North Korea, but decided instead to continue the reconnaissance flights with armed escort planes added. They believed a retaliatory strike carried too great a risk of trouble from the Soviet Union and China. Defending the decision not to hit North Korea, Secretary of State William P. Rogers said, "The weak can be rash; the powerful must be restrained."

President Park's dilemma was the same as it had been the year before. He warned there were likely to be more incidents, called for tough countermeasures by the United States, and asked for more military aid. His dissatisfaction deepened.

ONE POINT in Nixon's *Foreign Affairs* article had been encouraging to Park Chung Hee. Nixon had said parliamentary democracy might not be the best kind of government for some Asian countries. Americans should be tolerant of nondemocratic regimes, he had suggested.

The South Korean constitution set a limit of two terms for a president. Campaigning for his second term in 1967, Park promised that if elected he would step aside four years later as re-

quired by the constitution. But he was determined to amend the
constitution so he could run for a third term. With Nixon in the
White House, the Americans would not interfere as they had
when Kennedy made Park end the military junta in 1963. The
problem this time was opposition from within his own Democratic Republican party (DRP). Kim Jong Pil wanted to succeed
Park. After eight years of waiting and working to keep himself
powerful, the founder of the KCIA felt it was his turn to be president. Kim Jong Pil's most important ally was S. K. Kim, one of
Korea's biggest financiers and treasurer of the DRP. Together
their influence reached deep into the National Assembly, where
President Park would need a two-thirds majority for his third-
term amendment.

Park could not simply buy off Kim Jong Pil. Kim had already amassed a fortune as KCIA director through stock market
manipulation and deals with Japanese businessmen. It was influence in the Korean government that Kim wanted, and he was being blocked by some of his worst enemies close to President Park.
Kim would agree to support the third-term amendment only if
the President got rid of KCIA Director Kim Hyung Wook and
the chief of the Blue House secretariat, Lee Hu Rak, who was
Park's H. R. Haldeman. Park's acceptance of these conditions
solidified the DRP.

THE ONLY MEETING between Richard Nixon as President and
Park Chung Hee took place in San Francisco in August 1969.
Park saw the meeting as a reaffirmation of the special relationship. It could benefit his drive for the third-term amendment and
show that Korea was exempt from Nixon's new policy for Asia.

That policy, known variously as the "Nixon Doctrine" or
"Guam Doctrine," had been unveiled in general terms on Guam
in July. Nixon had stopped on the island during the first leg of a
round-the-world trip. At an informal press briefing he had unex-

pectedly told reporters that the United States would expect its Asian allies to assume the primary burden for their own defense. When requested, economic and military assistance would be furnished if it seemed appropriate. The United States would keep treaty promises to help allies and would provide a shield if nuclear powers threatened certain non-Communist nations. In non-nuclear situations, American troops would not automatically appear on the scene to fight; allies would be expected to rely on their own manpower. The clear message was that the United States would avoid getting bogged down in future Asian wars like the one in Vietnam.

Park Chung Hee saw no reason why he could not live with such a policy as long as it applied mainly to other countries and meant no cutback in Korea. His advisers' fear about Nixon's article in *Foreign Affairs* had seemed unfounded in the time since Nixon became President. So far, relations with Nixon had been about the same as with Johnson. In light of the Vietnam experience, it was understandable if the United States did not take on new obligations to fight in Asia. Nixon had made clear, though, that he would stick to the treaties America already had in Asia, and Korea had such a treaty.

Still, Park was uneasy about the danger that Nixon might be sending the wrong signal to the Communists. He would have preferred a general proclamation about holding the line firm against Communism everywhere. The Nixon Doctrine might alter the psychological status quo in Asia, Park feared.

Ambassador Porter accompanied President Park to San Francisco. President Nixon asked the ambassador to join him for a private talk in his hotel room prior to a closed meeting of the two presidents. There, Nixon stated flatly to Porter than he was "dead serious" about withdrawing a large number of American troops from Korea. His reasoning included a need to put the Nixon Doctrine into practice and public sentiment against the Vietnam War, but the main reason was pressure from Congress. There was a strong drive in Congress to "bring the boys home" from foreign countries where they had been stationed in such large numbers for what was felt to be too long a time. In particular, the President was getting pressure from Congressman Wilbur Mills, powerful chairman of the House Ways and Means Committee. Mills wanted to cut spending overseas, and with so much money going to Vietnam, wished to economize by cutting down the military presence in Korea. Besides, Mills was angered by the damage that cheap Korean textile imports were inflicting on southern textile manufacturers in the United States.

"If I can't get moving on the matter of removing troops from Korea, the Administration will have real problems with Mills," Nixon said. He asked if Porter thought troop reduction would be manageable with the Koreans.

Porter replied that it would probably be manageable if the pace were not too fast.

Nixon proceeded to the meeting with Park Chung Hee accompanied by Henry Kissinger. When Park raised the matter of American military presence in Korea, Nixon told him the United States had no intention of reducing troop levels in the foreseeable future.

For the Koreans, the Nixon-Park meeting could not have been more important. Years later, however, when Kissinger was asked about the meeting he could not recall what had been discussed.

Park's party returned to Seoul reassured that the special relationship was intact and that they could count on Richard Nixon.

The San Francisco meeting was put to use also for the third-term amendment. Despite Nixon's pointed refusal to offer support, his public comment about South Korea's "remarkable progress" under Park's leadership was played up by the Korean government and press to denote American approval for the proposed change in the constitution.

In the National Assembly the opposition parties were vehemently against the third-term scheme. The DRP Assemblymen therefore pulled it off alone. They held a secret session at 2:30 A.M. on September 14 and approved the amendment "unanimously." The final step would be the national referendum on October 17. Park threatened to resign in midterm if he did not succeed in the referendum. The amendment carried with a vote of 65 percent. It failed to carry the Seoul area, however, and there were allegations of fraud and cash payments to rural voters. Reportedly, the DRP spent $15 million on the referendum.

IN FEBRUARY 1970 the National Security Council completed the study on U.S. troops in Korea begun secretly on Nixon's orders a year before.

The President was given a decision memorandum containing three options: remove both U.S. army divisions, remove one division, or leave just a few brigades. The President was supposed to check the option he chose. When the memorandum was returned to John Court, the staff officer handling the project, Nixon had checked all three options. Bewildered, Court took the memorandum to General Alexander Haig.

"You won't believe this unless you see it yourself. He checked all three options. What do we do? Send it back to him?" Court handed the papers to Haig.

Haig seemed less than astonished. "No," he shrugged. "We'll just act on the option we recommended. Remove one division."

Thus was decided the biggest change in American policy toward Korea in more than fifteen years.

The State Department instructed Ambassador Porter to arrange a meeting with President Park as soon as possible. Porter

broke the bad news to Park at the Blue House on March 26, 1970.
Calmly and carefully, he explained that the United States had decided to withdraw one division, numbering about 20,000 men, as
part of an overall policy of reducing overseas troop deployments.
Some 42,000 American military personnel would stay. The United States was proposing that the Korean government take the initiative of making a formal request for the withdrawal of some
troops on the grounds that the Korean armed forces had become
strong enough to do without them.

Porter then proceeded to describe the sweeteners Washington was offering. The timing of troop reduction could be negotiated. There would be no further reductions before Korean forces
returned from their Vietnam assignment. A great deal more military aid was offered to enable South Korea to modernize its military forces: $1.5 billion spread over five years. Economic aid was
to include a continuation of Food for Peace shipments of not less
than $50 million per year.

Park was more than displeased. He was intransigent. The
South Korean President told Porter he would not allow the
American troops to leave Korea. The United States government
had no right to take them out, he insisted, so he simply would not
permit it to happen.

Porter had expected displeasure, but he was hardly prepared
for an outright refusal Park had no authority to make. He told
Park that although their countries were close friends, the United
States had no intention of surrendering control of its military
forces to the Korean government or any other government for
that matter. The President of the United States was Commander
in Chief of the armed forces and would remain so. The meeting
ended with Park still adamant that the troops could not be withdrawn. Porter returned to the Embassy shaken but undeterred.
Give him time, he thought. Let him absorb the initial shock.

A few days later Porter was called to a meeting with Prime

Minister Chung Il Kwon. Chung asked that troop withdrawal be postponed until after the 1971 Korean presidential election, a delay of about one year. But Nixon's mind was made up. Waiting a year was out of the question. The troops had to come home sooner so he could make good on what he had said at Guam. He saw Korea as the best place for it, since the South Korean military was strong enough to do just as well with fewer Americans. And he had to do something fast to ease the pressure from Congress.

Prime Minister Chung began making threats. He told Porter if an attempt were made to fly the Seventh Division out of Korea, he personally would lie down on the runway to keep the planes from taking off. Porter replied in jest, saying, "Do that, my good friend, but let me take a picture before the planes begin to roll." Furthermore, Chung vowed, Korean forces would refuse to occupy the areas where the departed American forces had been positioned, leaving them open to attack. If North Korea invaded the South, it would be the fault of the United States. Porter knew Chung was posturing for dramatic effect, but he realized he was headed for some tough negotiations.

Park Chung Hee and his advisers were furious over what was being done to them, but ultimately helpless to do anything about it. They were not being asked how they would react to a proposal to reduce American troops. They were being told the decision had already been made. Richard Nixon had disregarded the special relationship they believed was so secure. He had broken what they thought was a promise not to withdraw troops. They had believed the Nixon Doctrine would not be applied to them. Why, they wondered, was Nixon weakening their defenses against North Korea? Nixon should know as well as anyone that Kim Il Sung was determined to overrun the South. Hundreds of thousands of Communist soldiers had guns pointed southward only 30 miles from Seoul. Hadn't South Korea been the most faithful of all United States allies? It was one of the few countries where everyone really *liked* America. They not only liked the American people, but also—rarity of rarities—they liked the American government as well. The cry "Yankee Go Home" was never heard in South Korea. Koreans were dying in Vietnam in common cause with the United States, partly out of gratitude for the sacrifices Americans made during the Korean War. The people of the two countries were blood brothers in a very real sense.

The question was not whether keeping 62,000 American soldiers in Korea could be justified for purely military reasons. It was the psychological reason for keeping them that was important to South Koreans. If Kim Il Sung thought American support for South Korea was wavering, he might seize the opportunity for an attack. South Korean and American forces could turn the North Koreans back, but the cost would again be bloodshed and destruction in the South. Park Chung Hee maintained that withdrawal of twenty thousand American troops would be the wrong signal to send to Kim Il Sung.

The 1971 presidential election was at least as much on Park's mind. He had had little to worry about until troop reduction came along. The constitution had been changed so he could run for a third term. The economy was booming. Money for a big campaign would be no problem because he would have American companies foot the bill as he had done in the past. It was the American government that had always insisted on his having elections, so his party, the DRP, simply extorted money from American companies. Some American businessmen called it the "J Factor," meaning "juice." Without the juice, they were told, they could not do business in Korea. For the 1971 election, at least $8.5 million of Park Chung Hee's campaign money was to come from U.S. corporate sources. Two oil companies provided the bulk: $3 million directly from Gulf Oil; and $4 million (of which $1 million was termed "loans") paid by Caltex Petroleum going through its Korean partner, Honam Oil.

Troop reduction could cloud Park's bright prospects for a third term. He had intended to make a major campaign theme of the special relationship he was credited with having built with the United States. He wanted to claim that the good life South Koreans were living was due to the secure conditions he and big brother had created together. Withdrawal of twenty thousand American troops would give his election opponent the opportunity to charge that Park had little influence with the United States and that the touted special relationship was a fraud.

American negotiators faced stiff Korean resistance throughout the summer of 1970. The two sides found themselves talking about two entirely different things. The Koreans were negotiating over whether any troops would be withdrawn. As they saw it, there could be no withdrawal without an agreement for withdrawal, and they were not agreeing. The United States, having already decided to withdraw troops, was negotiating over the timing of withdrawal and the terms of the aid package for military modernization. Park Chung Hee insisted the U.S. troop level remain unchanged for at least five years. He regarded the proposed military modernization package as woefully inadequate grounds for him to give "permission" for the troops to leave. Porter reminded Park that his permission was neither sought nor required.

Threats continued. After the U.S. government made the first public announcement on troop withdrawal in July, Prime Minister Chung told Ambassador Porter he would resign along with the entire cabinet if the troops were actually pulled out. Kim Dong Jo, the Korean Ambassador in Washington, told a reporter the United States might think twice about taking the troops out if Korean forces in Vietnam suddenly were to return home. American officials paid little heed, however, since they were convinced the Koreans were getting far too good a financial deal in Vietnam to make it worthwhile to carry out that threat.

At a conference in Honolulu in July, the Korean Defense Minister, Jung Nae Hiuk, told Deputy Secretary of Defense David Packard that his orders were to prevent troop withdrawal. As the negotiations proceeded to get nowhere, Jung Nae Hiuk tearfully related a story from Korean history about an envoy who had to commit suicide because he failed in his mission. The American negotiators left Honolulu believing negotiations were now over and the withdrawal of troops could begin immediately. Not so. The R.O.K. government told the press the issue had not been settled in Honolulu and that negotiations would continue.

Policymakers in Washington were exasperated. The problem would have to be handled at a higher level if there was to be any progress. In part, this was because the Koreans said they had been treated discourteously by Packard and his delegation in Honolulu. Nixon decided to dispatch Vice-President Spiro Agnew to Seoul for a meeting with President Park. As an acknowledged "hawk," Agnew believed he was the right man to convince Park that Nixon was not abandoning Korea and that American support would be just as firm with twenty thousand fewer troops.

If the Koreans had seemed difficult in Honolulu, it was only a warm-up for the Park-Agnew meeting. For that event, they pulled out all stops. Agnew was on their turf, so they had complete control over his visit.

The Koreans' schedule for the Vice-President started with a morning visit to the National Assembly, where the Prime Minister paraded out several opposition Assemblymen for an especially hard sell against troop withdrawal. They seemed to Agnew to have been thoroughly programmed. Movies were then shown depicting the magnitude of the threat from the North. Agnew thought they were overdoing it, and he was getting a little annoyed.

Next he was driven to the Blue House for a meeting at ten o'clock with President Park, listed on the schedule to last about an hour. What followed was a grueling six-hour marathon with no breaks for coffee, lunch, or the rest room. Agnew's aide, General John Dunn, remembered the session as "brutal and absolutely offensive," with Park Chung Hee in "a performance by a head of state unlike any I had ever seen."

It was apparent, though, that Park Chung Hee had already realized the twenty thousand troops would go. Therefore, his objectives with Agnew were to delay withdrawal and guarantee the military aid. He was as tough as possible so as to leave no doubt to anyone—Agnew, Nixon, or the Korean officials in the room—that Park Chung Hee was not to be taken lightly.

Agnew lectured Park on the division of powers in the American government: while the President makes foreign policy, Congress decides funding; the President's foreign policy depends on the granting of funds by Congress. President Nixon would give his all-out support for the $1.5 billion for military modernization but because Congress was independent of the President, he could not make the flat guarantee Park was demanding. It seemed to Agnew that Park misunderstood the role of Congress, no matter how Agnew tried to explain. Park kept demanding that Nixon make certain the money be approved. The two men stated the same points over and over, hour after hour.

Mercifully, the meeting at last ended. Agnew left the Blue House with greatly reduced respect for Park Chung Hee. He was glad to leave Korea the following day. Before departing, though, he made the mistake of saying offhandedly to reporters that it was necessary to get on with removing the troops, since all American ground forces would be out of Korea within five years anyway. No such decision had been made in Washington, but despite strenuous efforts by the State Department, Park and his men no longer would accept words of reassurance. They were panic-stricken.

Three days after Agnew left, the Koreans discovered that, unknown to them, some ten thousand American troops had already been withdrawn right out from under their noses.

AGNEW HAD GONE to great lengths emphasizing the importance of Congress in getting the military aid. Ambassador Porter had always conditioned his aid offers with the caveat "subject to the approval of Congress." And it was Congress that seemed to have pressured Nixon into the troop cut. The stakes were too high to rest on the assurances of Nixon and the diplomats. Park now saw that Congress had to be won over.

They would have to get at Congress in every possible way. Direct approaches by the Korean Embassy in Washington would be used, but these alone would not suffice. The Embassy had neither the manpower nor the extensive contacts needed. Embassy officers had the added disadvantage of being known civil servants whose job was to promote the government's position. A variety of American opinionmakers would have to be cultivated, including businessmen, scholars, journalists, and religious leaders. A more effective way of making approaches to such people seemed to be to use persons not known to be government agents. The influence operation needed well-established Koreans in Washington who already had good contacts. Tongsun Park and Bo Hi Pak certainly qualified as agents of influence.

The concerted Korean influence campaign was born at a meeting in the Blue House chaired by President Park only a few days after Agnew's visit ended on August 26, 1970. The most powerful men in the government attended. Everyone agreed it was urgent that Congress approve the maximum amount of military aid and that there be no further American troop reductions in the near future. They recognized the need for a major campaign to influence U.S. government policy and public opinion. Support for the goals and for an influence campaign was unanimous, but there were arguments over who should be in charge.

It was not surprising that Prime Minister Chung's proposal drew opposition. He wanted Tongsun Park to run everything. Under the proposal, Tongsun, as chief Korean government lobbyist in the United States, was to have control over the KCIA at the Embassy, Bo Hi Pak of Moon's inner cirlce, and General Kang Young Hoon, who headed the Research Institute on Korean Affairs, an R.O.K. government front operation in the Washington area. Dealings with Congress were to be centralized. The operation would use Congressmen, Korean National Assemblymen, and scholars and businessmen from both countries.

Chung Il Kwon should have known better. Tongsun's name was not one that brought instant harmony to discussions among Korean politicians. A fight among factions erupted and the meeting ended without agreement.

Tongsun's chief opponent was Blue House aide Park Chong Kyu, who had risen from brash army major during the 1961 coup to chief of the Presidential Protective Force. He disliked Tongsun intensely and denounced him for keeping the rice commissions for himself instead of turning over the customary 50 percent to President Park's party. He also suspected Chung Il Kwon was getting a kickback from Tongsun. Chung defended his protégé by insisting Tongsun needed the money to make payments to Congressmen. Tongsun's wheeling and dealing were beyond Park Chong Kyu's control, but as the President's right-hand man at that time, he blocked the access to Park that Tongsun sought. He had an ally in Ambassador Kim Dong Jo, who had earlier complained to President Park that Tongsun's solo lobbying was interfering with the Embassy's efforts to make useful contacts in Washington.

Through Bo Hi Pak and the Korean Cultural and Freedom Foundation, Park Chong Kyu also could see a chance of acquiring an asset in Washington comparable to what Prime Minister Chung had with Tongsun, since he had been dealing with Pak for years. But he failed to realize that Pak's ultimate loyalty was to Moon.

More meetings were held in the Blue House to plan the influence campaign. Park Chong Kyu proposed making more use of Bo Hi Pak. Prime Minister Chung had to come up with something to push back the anti-Tongsun forces. He produced a list, obtained from Tongsun, of fifty-one visits Tongsun had made to Capitol Hill, detailing the subject of each visit and the ongoing results. Congressmen who had visited Korea in 1969, for example, were shown to have responded later to Tongsun's requests for help on military aid or the third-term amendment.

By September 23, Tongsun had hurriedly incorporated the Conference for the Development of Free Institutions in Washington for the effect it might have at the Blue House meetings. The organization's stated purpose was to promote understanding between Congress and the Korean National Assembly. For more than a year he had been talking up the idea with Congressmen without launching it formally. Organizations were not his forte. Its list of endorsers was impressive—thirty-six Senators and Congressmen plus several lawyers and scholars.

The planners of the influence campaign could not ignore Tongsun's record of accomplishments, but putting him in charge of everything was out of the question. The rival factions could not agree on anyone in the United States to head the campaign. President Park saw that if the competition among factions were kept within bounds, no one person would grow too powerful and their motivation for receiving recognition from him might lead to getting more accomplished. Things had to be centralized in some way, however. After a few weeks, it was decided to continue the separate lobbying activities in Washington and establish a special Blue House review committee to coordinate things. This meant Tongsun, Ambassador Kim, the KCIA at the Embassy, Bo Hi Pak, and General Kang each would deal directly with Seoul. In the Blue House committee, Park Chong Kyu would have a chance to take control if he could. But centralized control was to prove impossible. Everyone went his own way for power and profit.

Tongsun and His Congressmen

TONGSUN PARK was hardly a visionary. His natural impulse was to win friends and influence people, and he had many friends in Washington. He did not have to be a great student of history to realize the Korean government would always welcome good connections in Washington. Unlike Sun Myung Moon, who told people he controlled the fate of the universe, Tongsun was more concerned about controlling the fate of his rice agency by taking advantage of political opportunities in Washington and Seoul. Moon might say God moved Nixon to cut the troops so the Korean government would come to him begging for help, but Tongsun made no such claim. It was heady enough stuff for Tongsun when President Park and his top men debated for weeks over how to use Tongsun's talents. Nixon's troop decision had catapulted him to the center of attention. He was in great demand for doing what he enjoyed most—cultivating Congressmen. He loved it.

By incorporating the Conference for the Development of Free Institutions (CDFI) in September 1970 while the Blue House meetings were going on, Tongsun was able to make the skeptics in Seoul think he was doing things in an orderly and perhaps dependable way. CDFI was supposed to be a broadly based organization for involving politicians, businessmen, scientists, and scholars in pro-Korean government activities. It could serve as a respectable cover for the KCIA to pay for trips to Korea by influential Americans. The skeptics were pleased that CDFI seemed institutional rather than personal; that is, it did not have Tongsun's imprimatur of self-gain stamped all over it.

CDFI got Tongsun's foot in the door with some Senators and Congressmen he had not met before. House Speaker John McCormack's endorsement had been a big help. As a result of Tongsun's maneuvering, the Speaker had circulated a "Dear Colleague" letter to all members of the House. "Let us be generous . . . and join our Korean friends in their epic struggle for freedom and human dignity," he had written. Within a month after CDFI was incorporated, Tongsun had contributed to the election campaigns of about half the Senators and Congressmen on the list of endorsers.

He had little use for CDFI, however. It lacked style. Organizations were more in Bo Hi Pak's line: the Korean Cultural and Freedom Foundation, Radio of Free Asia, and a myriad other Moon groups. Putting CDFI together had been largely the work of Kim Kwang, Tongsun's cousin and employee. Kim even boasted that CDFI was his own operation, and the idea for the organization actually may have originated with him.

Kim Kwang had been studying in New York for several years when Tongsun invited him to move to Washington in 1970. Tongsun thought his cousin could be a useful addition to his operations. As an intern on Congressman Hanna's staff with his salary paid by Tongsun, Kim had direct access to the inner workings of Congress. By the time CDFI was incorporated, Kim had been moved to Congressman Cornelius Gallagher's office. Kim Kwang was ambitious in his own right and privately was discontented with the junior cousin role. To Tongsun, he was a pawn. Kim made efforts to impress the KCIA at the Embassy as an independent operator, but it was only when Tongsun transferred him to Gallagher's office that the KCIA station chief became interested. Gallagher was a senior member of the House Foreign Affairs Committee.

Tongsun let CDFI wither. He had no use for it after its formal incorporation had helped convince President Park and his planners to give Tongsun a piece of the influence campaign. He would rather do things his way. He felt more confident relying on his proven one-on-one charm.

WITH 9,000 MILES between Washington and Seoul and no one he had to answer to in Washington, it was easy for Tongsun to fudge a little. He was supposed to have been spreading money around Congress since the first rice commissions began in 1969, but that simply had not been possible. He needed that money to maintain his life style. He was always overcommitted, and even his friendly creditors would not wait forever. It took a lot of money to keep up the George Town Club and his luxurious home near the Korean Embassy with its $35,000 stereo system. His parties were lavish, but they had to be if he was to live up to the title he had given himself—"the male Perle Mesta." Yet the Blue House influence planners apparently were having doubts about his veracity. He had to show them positive proof he was making payments to Congressmen. In a rare departure from his usual practice of giving out cash to people, he sent checks to twenty-five Senators and Congressmen for the 1970 elections just as the last Blue House meeting was being held. The contributions were not very large—from $500 to $1,000 each—but the canceled checks would dispel the doubts in Seoul.

With the canceled checks to prove he was doing what he was supposed to do, Tongsun expected the exaggerated reports he was sending to Seoul in October 1970 to be taken seriously.

He boasted of having converted 150 members of Congress to Korea's cause. This achievement had cost only $1 million, he claimed, all generated from his own rice commissions. In comparison to the $15 million to $20 million he said other countries were spending, that was cheap. He gave the impression that, compared to the cash he had spent on lobbying, his contributions by check were small. The October contributions, made for their effect on the Blue House influence planners, were given his own expert rationale as to timing: "The effect of monetary contributions during election campaigns is worth 100 times more than at other times."

Showing impressive results, he urged that the government subsidize him so he could do more. He suggested he be given more government-granted business concessions like the rice agency and that the KCIA provide funds directly to him. Several members of Congress particularly helpful to Korea had been, he claimed, "secretly" requesting contributions: Senators Joseph Montoya, Stuart Symington, George Murphy, and Harry Byrd, Jr., and Congressmen William Broomfield, Cornelius Gallagher, Richard Hanna, and William Minshall.

The list was more a projection of his own need than a statement of reality. What Tongsun needed was a small group of strategically placed Congressmen in his pocket. They had to be willing to work with him and in a position to give important help. He believed the best chance for achieving full support from Congress as a whole for himself and Korea was by maneuvering an inner core of Tongsun loyalists. He needed more men like Hanna. A charmed circle was not likely to come cheaply, so he was willing to pay. If he could develop such a group, the powers in Seoul would respect him as a mature and formidable agent of influence.

He had already picked the members for the charmed circle. Besides Hanna, he had in mind Congressmen William Minshall, Cornelius Gallagher, and Otto Passman.

KOREA HAD no special economic interest in William Minshall's district in Ohio. Cleveland was not a rice-producing area where Tongsun could make a commission. Minshall interested Tongsun as the senior Republican on the Defense Appropriations Subcommittee and a good friend of Defense Secretary Melvin Laird. The cultivation of Minshall had begun as soon as Laird left Congress to head the Pentagon early in 1969. At Tongsun's request, Minshall made a *Congressional Record* statement supporting President Park's third-term amendment. He was sympathetic to Tongsun's lobbying against Nixon's troop reduction in the summer of 1970. When it became apparent that the troop decision was firm, Tongsun urged Minshall to go to Korea to meet top officials. The chairman of the Appropriations Committee authorized the use of committee funds in August for the trip. Minshall accepted Tongsun's offer of $5,000 for travel expenses, which was more than the cost of the trip. Since his committee was already paying these costs, he regarded Tongsun's cash as a campaign contribution.

The timing of Minshall's trip in September 1970 could not have been better for Tongsun. While Park Chong Kyu was trying to downgrade Tongsun's value as a lobbyist at the Blue House meetings, Tongsun produced a powerful Congressman in Seoul who was a personal friend of the Secretary of Defense. Minshall met with the R.O.K. defense minister and the director of the KCIA.

The Minshall visit did a lot to dampen Park Chong Kyu's charges against Tongsun, and Tongsun made even more of it in his reports to Seoul after Minshall returned home. He said Minshall had gone to Korea after hearing the USCIA soft-pedal the North Korean threat, but his meetings with Korean officials, especially KCIA Director Kim Kye Won, had "changed his view." Tongsun said he was certain Minshall's improved attitude would have "great impact" on Melvin Laird and the U.S. defense budget. According to Tongsun, Minshall had brought back an urgent request from General John Michaelis, the American commander in Korea, to get President Nixon and Secretary Laird to expedite the funding for modernizing the South Korean military.

Through Minshall, Tongsun later was able to get to Laird personally and pull off two coups that made him look better than ever to the Seoul hierarchy. Early in 1971, Tongsun succeeded in getting an appointment for former Prime Minister Chung Il Kwon to see Laird, over the objections of the State Department. The following year, Tongsun and Minshall persuaded Laird to attend the annual R.O.K.-U.S. Defense Ministers Conference. Previously the meeting had almost always been handled by the Deputy Secretary of Defense. To maximize the impact of this power play, Tongsun saw to it that Colonel Lim Kyuil, a KCIA officer at the Korean Embassy, was present when Minshall and Tongsun talked to Laird.

Through the years, Tongsun continually pumped Minshall for information on defense matters, and his personal ledgers show payments to Minshall amounting to $31,000.

Tongsun's cash probably did not induce Minshall to do much that he would not have been willing to do without it. The Ohio Congressman already believed in the toughest stance against North Korea and the fullest support for the South. He saw South Korea as one of the few true friends the United States had in a world full of ungrateful allies and anti-American neutrals. He would have preferred that Nixon leave all the troops in Korea, but as a good Republican he went along with the withdrawal decision. Since the State Department did not say very much to Congress about Nixon's offer of $1.5 billion in military aid, talking with Tongsun did make Minshall more aware of the Koreans' strong desire for it. He resolved to work in Congress to get the full amount funded so Korea could modernize its military forces to compensate for the departure of twenty thousand American troops.

IT WAS NOT IDEOLOGY that qualified Congressman "Neil" Gallagher for the charmed circle, nor access to high officials of the Nixon administration. Gallagher was a liberal Democrat. Korea was not a potential market for products from his hometown of Bayonne, New Jersey. Close ties with a Korean lobbyist could not bring direct benefits to Gallagher in the voting booth. However, Tongsun said his first meeting with Gallagher was a kind of "love at first sight." Gallagher had a basic view of reality that Tongsun liked: he could be bought.

Their acquaintance began in February 1969, when Tongsun invited Gallagher to join the twenty-three-man junket to Korea. Membership on the House Foreign Affairs Committee made Gallagher a logical target for influencing. He was unable to make the trip to Korea but did comply with Tongsun's request in October 1969 to urge other Congressmen to support President Park's plans for a third term. And Gallagher provided a job in his office for Tongsun's cousin Kim Kwang in July 1970 in the midst of the heavy lobbying against troop reduction. Tongsun paid Kim's salary and $13,000 to Gallagher for starters.

After a visit to Korea in August featuring an appointment with President Park, Gallagher had some advice for Korean lobbying. He told Tongsun that the standard South Korean line about the threat of an attack by North Korea was wearing thin with Washington; for years they had used it so heavily that the Nixon administration wasn't paying much attention any more. It would be smarter, the Congressman suggested, for the Korean government to say to the Americans, "If you reduce your troop level, it will cause political chaos in South Korea," since the United States had justified troop reduction on the grounds that South Korea was not only militarily strong but also politically stable.

Gallagher's suggestion made a lot of sense to Tongsun. The threat of political chaos might make the Americans decide against future troop cuts. And more important, it could make them appreciate Park Chung Hee for maintaining order. Tongsun was sure the leaders in Seoul would be pleased with the advice he had drawn from Gallagher. It would fit into President Park's election campaign plans to insist that only he could prevent chaos in the wake of the troop cut. According to another of Tongsun's Capitol Hill friends, Henry Kissinger recently had told congressional leaders that the United States had better proceed with caution so troop reduction would not upset Park Chung Hee's stable government. Tongsun's report to Seoul boasted, "This cannot be but the result of Mr. Gallagher's input."

The investment in Gallagher paid further dividends when he became chairman of the Subcommittee on Asian and Pacific Affairs in 1971. With Kim Kwang working on Gallagher's staff, Tongsun and the KCIA had a listening post inside the subcommittee responsible for policy on Korea in the House of Representatives. Korea was the subject of Gallagher's first set of hearings. Claiming credit for the hearings, Tongsun assured Seoul they would be helpful by bringing out the latest American intentions on modernizing the South Korean armed forces. Kim Kwang did more, though. Dealing directly with the KCIA at the Embassy, he made sure the witnesses for the hearings were acceptable to the government, passed classified information to the Embassy from the closed sessions, and paid Gallagher for it with KCIA money. He took credit for the hearings himself.

THE CHARMED CIRCLE could never be complete without Otto Passman. His combined assets of power and rice proved irresistible to Tongsun. From a major rice-producing state, Louisiana, Passman was the powerful chairman of the Foreign Operations Subcommittee, which controlled appropriations for both military and economic aid to foreign countries. Since he neither smoked nor drank, he said, his great pleasure was "kicking the hell out of the United States foreign aid program."

Passman was convinced the money was going down a rathole in the receiving countries. Agencies such as the Peace Corps, the United States Agency for International Development (AID), and United Nations organizations were mainly for "tens of thousands of fat cats, drawing big salaries, flying all over the world." He was a great traveler himself, with an average of more than two trips per year to both Geneva and Hong Kong to pursue his fascination with watches. His large collection of timepieces was impressive. Jewelers and watchmakers in those cities knew him well for his regular bartering visits. Sometimes he brought along Louisiana friends as special "consultants"—a Cadillac dealer, an insurance man, a rice grower—all traveling first class at government expense.

The State Department and AID lived in terror of Passman. Weeks were spent getting ready for his foreign aid hearings. Written statements and briefing books were put together painstakingly to anticipate his inevitable objections. Armed with pounds of paper, high State Department officials would take their seats at the witness table in Passman's hearing room. After listening to the chairman's summary of the pitfalls he saw in that year's request for foreign aid, they would bravely begin reading the prepared statement. No more than a few sentences or paragraphs into State's testimony, it was often Passman's wont to break in with a remote detail. That usually meant the prepared testimony was over and that the briefing books might just as well have been left at the State Department. They would then be treated to the famous "Passman dance"—the chairman's fidgeting and gesturing through a rambling diatribe on foreign aid waste.

Passman could not be bothered with the rationale behind foreign aid, but he was a master of the far-flung details. Once, when an AID official came to discuss a program to help poor countries control population growth, Passman cut him off with a complaint that the United States was losing out to West Germany in the world market for prophylactics. AID had been buying some quantities of condoms from foreign countries.

"I'm trying to make a pitch to bring this volume of business back home," Passman stressed.

"The demand exceeds the U.S. productive capacity," answered the AID official.

By 1969, Passman had reached an agreement with the White House to go easy on military aid if he could work his own way on humanitarian aid. The pact was a result of the friendship Passman had made in 1947 with a fellow freshman Congressman from the other party, Richard Nixon. Military aid was crucial to Nixon because of the war in Indochina. Passman was happy to oblige. His affection for Nixon was to continue through Watergate. Insisting he would never have voted for impeachment, he called Nixon "the greatest President in the history of the United States."

The cantankerous Passman made no secret of his disdain for Tongsun. He had seen Tongsun inject himself into Congress's business with the $50 million in military aid for Korea in 1969. Ambassador Kim Dong Jo had told him Tongsun was an opportunist who was always butting into the Embassy's business. Tongsun was undeterred. Passman's listening to Ambassador Kim made it doubly important to bring him into the charmed circle. The ambassador was both a detractor and a competing lobbyist. The best way to quash the competition would be to take away its assets. Passman was one. For the same reason Tongsun had his sights on Congressman William Broomfield, a member of the Foreign Affairs Committee, whose ear the ambassador had also. Passman, though, would be a more valuable prize. He was an intriguing challenge worth a lot of effort. Tongsun was even willing to work patiently, something he was not used to doing.

The leaders in Seoul would not believe Tongsun if he claimed Passman was already working for him in the fall of 1970. They knew Passman was on Ambassador Kim's side in the matter of Tongsun. The most he could get away with saying about Passman in his October reports was that if Korea was to buy Louisiana rice, Passman "would aggressively support Korean issues . . . in return."

Tongsun had been slow to see the benefits of pushing sales of Louisiana rice to Korea. Looking back, he realized it had been a big mistake. Foolishly, his initial interest in Passman had been for his power, not his rice. Tongsun should have gone after both. He had been making plenty of money from California rice and mistakenly thought Louisiana did not grow the kind Koreans liked to eat. He had passed up a golden opportunity in 1969 when his friend Congressman David Pryor of Arkansas had introduced him to Louisiana Congressman Edwin Edwards. Edwards's approach had been antagonistic, chiding Tongsun for the "sweet deal" he had with the California rice growers.

In defense, Tongsun retorted, "Korean housewives are familiar with California brand names."

"That's true only because California rice is all you get for them." Edwards pointed out that Louisiana produced a large amount of the same kind of rice grown in California.

This had been news to Tongsun. But he was not interested in Louisiana rice at that time. He liked his "sweet deal" with California.

Promoting a big sale of rice to Korea was not merely a passing fancy for Edwards. He had had his eyes on the governorship for four years and saw the selling of Louisiana rice as the key. He had been chairman of the 1969 Washington Mardi Gras, a Louisiana promotional dinner and ball where the theme was rice. The big event of the evening was the crowning of a "Rice Queen." Her cut-glass tiara and scepter would later have an honored place

on display in the Governor's Mansion in Baton Rouge, symboliz-
ing the importance of rice to Edwards's victory. In attendance at
the ball were ambassadors from the major rice-consuming nations. Ambassador Kim was there, eager in his most diplomatic
fashion to buy Louisiana rice.

Passman was an active backer of his junior colleague's drive
for the governorship. Together, he and Edwards had managed to
sell a small amount of rice to Korea in 1969. But Tongsun had
the market cornered, so the bulk of Korea's business was with
California. Hoping to be elected governor in 1972, Edwards was
determined to engineer a big sale in 1971. He and Passman had
begun meeting with Ambassador Kim around August of 1970.
Kim had sounded encouraging. The three men issued a joint
press release announcing that Korea and Louisiana Congressmen
were "discussing sales of southern rice."

That had been the danger signal for Tongsun. It was then
that he realized the folly of having brushed off Edwards the previous year. It had boomeranged. Working with Edwards was the
man Tongsun wanted working for him, Otto Passman. And the
two of them were now in league with his arch enemy, Ambassador Kim, who would like nothing better than to cut Tongsun out
of the rice business altogether. A renewed interest in Edwards
was definitely in order. It was time to start courting him.

Edwards was glad to see Tongsun coming around. If Tongsun and Ambassador Kim both were interested in Louisiana rice,
so much the better. He and his wife Elaine found Tongsun personally a congenial fellow, and their children loved the gifts he
always brought. But Edwards had no intention of leaving the
crucial rice deal in the hands of Korean middlemen. He wanted
to go to Korea and talk to the leaders of the government himself.
He persuaded Passman to go with him. With Passman's clout
they might be able to get an appointment with President Park.
As soon as Tongsun got word of the trip, he begged Edwards to

let him join the party. It seemed not a bad idea to Edwards. Passman would have to be convinced, however. Since Edwards knew Passman had no love for Tongsun, he pointed out that taking the Korean selling agent along made sense in a strategy of covering all bets. For the sake of Edwards and the big rice sale, Passman was willing to swallow his distaste for Tongsun for the moment.

Not so Ambassador Kim. At the mere suggestion of bringing Tongsun in, he was unequivocal. He told Passman if Tongsun went they could forget about meeting President Park. Personally, Passman was relieved to know he would not have to put up with Tongsun on the trip. He told Edwards the ambassador was opposed to Tongsun's going, without giving Edwards the details of the Tongsun-Kim feud. Edwards did not want to offend Tongsun, so he softened things by telling him simply that since the trip was for official business it was limited to government officials.

There still remained a problem about having Edwards's travel expenses paid by Congress. Passman, as chairman of the Foreign Operations Subcommittee, could get approval for his own overseas travel anytime. But it was not very plausible to say that Edwards, a member of the Judiciary Committee, would be conducting committee business on a trip to Korea to sell rice for his gubernatorial campaign. Passman had influence with the old-timers in the House though. Judiciary Committee chairman Emanuel Celler made an exception for Edwards's trip.

A gun salute and senior Korean officials greeted the Louisianans upon their arrival at the Seoul airport in December 1970. Edwards turned to look as he heard a familiar-sounding voice from behind. It was Tongsun. Edwards and Passman had been in Korea less than five minutes. At the first sight of him, Passman moved in the other direction, missing for the moment the important news Tongsun had brought. Edwards took Tongsun's copy of that morning's *Korea Herald* and read a disturbing story on the front page. President Park had announced a decision to buy 400,000 tons of rice from Japan. Former Japanese Prime Minister Kishi had been in Seoul the day before to propose the sale to Park.

It looked as if the Louisianians had been preempted. But Tongsun was ready with advice.

"I can tell you how to bust the deal with Japan," he said to Edwards in the airport VIP reception room. "Tell President Park the southern congressional bloc won't vote for military aid to Korea if Korea doesn't buy the American rice. And tell the President just like that, because he will understand only if you are blunt."

As the motorcade departed the airport, Passman became riled when he saw Tongsun riding in one of the official cars. He ordered the cars to a halt and demanded Tongsun be separated from the motorcade. With Tongsun removed, the motorcade proceeded.

Attending the official reception for Passman and Edwards that night were all the top American and Korean officials. Everyone felt a little uncomfortable when Tongsun arrived unexpectedly. The story about Passman's pique in the motorcade had spread through town quickly that day. No one wanted to be rude as Tongsun circulated through the room, joining in the cocktail conversation. Passman had no qualms, though. He took Tongsun aside and told him to "get lost."

Tongsun was not that easy to get rid of. He had come to the reception to ask Edwards something important. He finally managed to buttonhole the younger Congressman. Could he go with Passman and Edwards to the meeting with President Park the next day?

Edwards was as pleasant to Tongsun as Passman was unpleasant. He wanted to keep the peace. He assumed Tongsun would be the agent for the rice deal, if there was going to be a rice deal. He fell back on his earlier escape clause: since the meeting with the President was official congressional business, it would not be possible for Tongsun to come along.

"Well, at least tell President Park I have lots of friends in America," Tongsun pleaded.

Edwards said he would.

PASSMAN DID NOT WANT to be in the same room or the same motorcade with Tongsun, but he was not above taking Tongsun's advice through an intermediary. The rice deal had to be wrested from the Japanese somehow. Edwards told Passman what Tongsun had suggested at the airport. The hard-nosed approach sounded good to Passman. If anyone knew how to be blunt, it was he.

Park Chung Hee's office in the Blue House was a large, rather stark room. Discussions took place around a coffee table surrounded by large overstuffed chairs with white embroidered coverlets across the top. Park had only an interpreter with him for the meeting with the two Congressmen. After an exchange of amenities, the talk shifted to the subject of rice.

"I am sorry the United States did not get to sell rice to the Republic of Korea," Passman began.

Nodding, his face expressionless, Park said the final decision had not been made.

Passman was ready. He relayed warm greetings from President Nixon. Park nodded again, saying he was always pleased to hear from the American President.

Then Passman launched his hard sell. "It will be touch-and-go back in Congress," he said. "We will need the majority support of the seventy-eight members of Congress from rice-producing states in order to legislate what Mr. Laird proposed in updating the Korean military establishment." Since President Park had not yet made a firm commitment to buy Japanese rice, Passman urged him to take another look at the American offer. He added that the United States had always done a lot more for Korea than Japan.

Park was not about to jeopardize military aid with Japanese rice. He said he would buy American rice if the United States could match Japan's financial terms. Passman assured him that would be no problem.

Now that they were over the hurdle, Edwards tried to say something about Tongsun. Park's expression became stern. The interpreter looked up without putting Edwards's sentence into Korean. Passman turned and snapped, "Goddamnit, don't mention that name!"

Edwards moved on to a different subject, a stipulation that at least half of the rice would come from the American southern states. The President told Edwards it did not matter where the rice came from as long as the quality was the same.

The meeting ended with Park giving his permission for Passman and Edwards to issue a press release stating that Korea had agreed to buy 400,000 tons of American rice.

Passman and Edwards surmised the Korean government had timed the story about a rice deal with Japan in order to scare them into bettering Japan's terms. The Koreans had ended up having to take American rice on terms only as good as Japan's because Passman had threatened the all-important military aid. The idea for bludgeoning the Korean President had come from Tongsun, something Passman probably would not acknowledge even to himself.

The financing of the rice deal featured a curious turnabout in Washington. Korea was not eligible for more financing under the Food for Peace Program, so Passman had to find another way.

Dr. John Hannah, the head of AID, found it hard to believe that the perennial foe of economic aid was promoting a development loan to Korea. It was unprecedented, as was the proposed use of the loan: to finance the sale of American rice. But Hannah, like President Park, had no choice in the matter. He was in no position to buck the combined wills of Otto Passman and the White House.

With the sale agreed to, Tongsun moved briskly to associate himself with its success and to downplay Ambassador Kim's role. The day after Passman and Edwards left Seoul, he showed up at the American Embassy to announce proudly that he had it from the Congressmen that the financing was all set with the White House. The Embassy ignored Tongsun's puffing. Ambassador Porter knew the Passman-Edwards visit had been arranged by Ambassador Kim. Porter was wise to Tongsun anyhow.

BACK IN WASHINGTON, Tongsun sent Seoul another one of his overstated reports. Relations with Passman were quite close, he intimated, and Passman had "promised that he would not reduce, even by one dollar, the administration's proposed military aid bill." He recommended paying Passman $30,000 as "expenses" for his trip to Korea.

He was slipping badly, more than he realized. Ambassador Kim had been complaining about Tongsun to both the Korean and the American governments. To the Americans, he said Tongsun did not represent the Korean government. To the Koreans, he said Tongsun could not be trusted with the responsibility of lobbying Congress. Everyone in Seoul knew the powerful Passman held Tongsun in open contempt. Word had even gotten to President Park. Chung Il Kwon, removed after five years as Prime Minister, no longer could protect his protégé.

By April, Tongsun knew it was time to begin the paperwork for the rice sale, but there had been no word from Grover Connell, the rice exporter. California and Louisiana had been pooling rice under Connell after a 1969 Supreme Court decision that had barred agricultural cooperatives from negotiating sales as single entities. The ruling did not affect selling agents, so Tongsun had continued as middleman, much to Connell's regret. He decided to get things going by contacting Connell himself. He was broke again.

Connell's response was a shocker: "You are no longer acceptable as our agent." He had a new Korean agent, he explained, a company chosen by the Korean government. Tongsun was out.

The coveted rice agency, his ticket to both money and recognition, had been taken away from him. It had happened without the Korean government's even telling him. He had been done in by Ambassador Kim Dong Jo with help from his own crass behavior. The ambassador had kept him out of the Louisiana rice deal from the start. Tongsun's attempts to horn in and take some credit had served only to reveal him as a phony. Kim had convinced the powers in Seoul they could do quite well without Tongsun.

Tongsun would no more accept the loss of his rice agency than he would leave a reception just because Otto Passman told him to get lost. His American empire had been built on the rice agency, and he was determined to get it back.

In dire straits, he turned to the man he trusted most, Congressman Hanna. First he needed money. Could Hanna loan him $25,000?

Hanna had always been easy to take advantage of. It therefore surprised Tongsun that his old friend's response was rather businesslike.

"This isn't just acting as a friend or just using my influence as a way of setting up an opportunity," Hanna stressed. "I expect you to be a little more sure in seeing that I get some participation out of whatever you are going to make." Tongsun had never paid him anything near the long-promised 25 percent of rice commissions.

As always, Tongsun was reassuring. "You can be certain. You are not only my brother, you are my business partner as well. When I get a net return, you will get a return along with me."

Hanna went along, but with formality. Tongsun had to execute a written note and pay finance charges and interest. The Congressman provided the money over strong objections from Mrs. Hanna. She tried to tell her husband he was being taken by Tongsun, but he refused to listen.

Next it was some good words with Seoul that Tongsun needed. Again Hanna was accommodating. He wrote a long letter to KCIA Director Lee Hu Rak defending Tongsun and blaming Ambassador Kim for the disrepute Tongsun had lately fallen into. The "pique and contention" coming out of the Tongsun-Kim feud served no useful purpose, he argued. He suggested the Korean government step in to settle "the personality conflicts between the Embassy operation here in Washington and Mr. Tongsun Park."

Hanna's letter to Lee Hu Rak was not enough for Tongsun. He was afraid the KCIA director might be powerless or not sufficiently interested to aid him in his plight. If President Park himself were showered with tributes to Tongsun, it could make a real difference. He decided to cash in on some of the investments in good will he had made the previous fall. Seoul had copies of the canceled checks from his contributions to Congressmen for the 1970 elections. He simply called on the Congressmen and asked them to write President Park on his behalf. To save time and make sure they got it right, he provided a sample—a letter to Park that Hanna had already written. Fourteen Congressmen obliged during the spring of 1971. With some variances in style and length, they all followed the same form. Each began by congratulating President Park on his reelection in April. Next came an account of the things the Congressman had done for Korea.

Last but not least, the Congressman said his pro-Korean activities had resulted from his association with Mr. Tongsun Park.

Solvent for the moment, thanks to Hanna's loan, Tongsun was able to take a trip to Seoul in July. He wanted to size up his predicament and try to do something about it. Things did not look very encouraging. Clearly, he had fallen from grace. Kim Hyung Wook, the former KCIA director, listened sympathetically to Tongsun's tale of woe and accepted a cash gift of $10,000, but was unable to help. With morale at a low point, a very candid letter arrived from Hanna. It had the qualities of genuine concern but said some things Tongsun did not want to hear.

"Your problem, Tongsun, is in not having one dominant view of yourself," Hanna wrote. "You can't be many things to many people. You must decide what you want to be and be that on your own. . . ." Hanna suggested he settle down in Korea, marry into a respectable family, and concentrate on his family's businesses. "And keep your friendships within the limitations of your commitments."

Holding the letter in his hand, Tongsun reread several lines: ". . . a substantial gap between the quality of your service in Washington and the judgement of your performance as seen by Korean leaders. . . ." And the next line was worse: "There are those here in Washington who are impressed more by the style of your performance than by its substance."

The letter hurt. It sounded like what his brothers used to say. He thought his successes in Washington had laid their criticism to rest. Now his best friend was saying the same thing. It had to be the loan that had caused Hanna to write such a letter. Hanna must be bitter over having to help him with money when he was down and out. If money was all their friendship meant, Hanna could get it soon enough, he vowed, once the rice agency was regained.

A few hours after arriving back in Washington on July 29, he had lunch with Neil Gallagher at the AV Restaurant on New

York Avenue. Gallagher was scheduled to depart for Korea six days later. He had helped put together the biggest congressional visit to Korea since the Hanna-Tongsun delegation in 1969. The group was to be led again by Carl Albert, who was now Speaker of the House. Tongsun was not involved. Ambassador Kim had seen to that. Kim Kwang, Tongsun's cousin on Gallagher's staff, had worked closely with the Korean Embassy on the arrangements for the trip. Gallagher explained that he had tried to have Kim included as a staff member of the delegation. Unfortunately, Carl Albert had not resisted when the State Department objected to Kim, so Kim would not be able to go. Tongsun wished Gallagher a bon voyage with $30,000. He had been able to replenish his American bank account with funds from a black-market transaction in Korea. A few days later he paid the $25,000 he owed Hanna.

Kim Hyung Wook's visit in November 1971 offered a glimmer of hope. The former KCIA director, now a member of the National Assembly, was on a world tour with a group of Assemblymen to inspect Korean Embassy operations. If Kim saw things in Washington Tongsun's way, it could be helpful when the group made its report in Seoul. The $10,000 Tongsun had paid him in July might return some political dividends after all.

The former KCIA director got an earful of the Tongsun-Kim feud during his stay in Washington. Yang Doo Won, head of the KCIA in the United States and an old friend of Kim Hyung Wook, said Ambassador Kim was arrogant and not well liked by Embassy officers. Tongsun contended the ambassador really had no business dealing with Congress and should stick to regular contacts with the executive branch. The ambassador was jealous, Tongsun charged, and was trying to destroy Tongsun's good relations with Congress so he could be the undisputed "main character" himself. Tongsun's arguments were echoed by Hanna.

Kim Hyung Wook finally took the problem up with Ambassador Kim personally. "Why do you have this conflict with Tongsun Park?" he asked.

Ambassador Kim replied candidly: Tongsun's activities were damaging the ambassador's reputation and would reflect badly on President Park.

Kim Hyung Wook returned to Seoul feeling Tongsun and the ambassador were in a continual struggle trying to undercut each other. But his sympathies were with Tongsun. The feud reminded him of his first encounter with Tongsun five years before. Then, he had had Tongsun arrested because the previous ambassador had been complaining about him. It seemed the present situation was just another case of a jealous ambassador trying to hold back this enterprising young fellow. Korea's best interests were not served that way, he felt, because Tongsun was willing and able to do some good lobbying.

He made a personal appointment with President Park and reported what he had heard in Washington. He told the President the feud was damaging the influence campaign. In his judgment the best course of action would be for the President to remove Kim Dong Jo as ambassador.

Kim Dong Jo was not removed, but the important thing to Tongsun was that his message was getting through to President Park. As long as he did not look bad to the President, it would be easier for him to work his way with Lee Hu Rak, the KCIA director. Decisions about the rice agency were made by the KCIA director after getting a feel for the President's overall likes and dislikes. Tongsun felt he was making progress. It was again time to put the charmed circle to work on the Korean government directly. He turned to its most useful members, Hanna and Gallagher.

He and Hanna went to Korea in November. Hanna was willing to work hard. With all the money and effort he had already put in, he had a personal business interest in Tongsun's getting the rice agency back. On this trip, he was traveling as a representative of both California and Louisiana rice interests. He had brought letters for Lee Hu Rak from Congressman Edwards, Senator Allen J. Ellender of Louisiana, and Congressman Chet Holifield of California. Both states were eager for more big rice sales to Korea and were not content to rest on Ambassador Kim's assurances. The rice Congressmen did not understand Korean factional politics and were confused by the rift between Tongsun and the ambassador. If Hanna had a direct line to the KCIA director, they wanted to use it.

In Seoul, Tongsun coached Hanna without end. The Congressman listened tolerantly, but he knew how to talk to officials and had no use for Tongsun's overkill approach. He had already decided how he would present their case to Lee Hu Rak. Tongsun need not have worried; Hanna was fully committed to getting the rice agency back.

Hanna gave Lee Hu Rak the letters, noting that Senator Ellender was chairman of the Senate committee that controlled foreign aid appropriations. There was no letter from Passman, but Edwards's and Ellender's letters both mentioned Passman's power over foreign aid and their close ties to him. Hanna's pitch had two main points: that congressional interest in Tongsun Park had not changed regardless of what was being heard in Seoul, and that it was important to restore the rice agency because it would put Tongsun in a position to bring Senator Ellender and Congressman Passman onto the actively pro-Korean team. Lee Hu Rak said he appreciated Hanna's and the other Congressmen's offer to sell more rice to Korea. He promised to take the matter of the rice agency under consideration.

Gallagher's assignment in November was to write two letters to President Park extolling Tongsun. He had met Park Chung Hee with the other Congressmen in Carl Albert's August delegation. His letters described Congress as preoccupied with a number of overriding domestic and foreign issues. Such a situation required a "renewed effort" to keep Senators and Congressmen apprised of Korea's needs. Gallagher said the way to do that was for the Korean government to support Tongsun Park fully. A grateful Tongsun took the occasion of Thanksgiving dinner at Gallagher's home in New Jersey to thank the Congressman with another $25,000 in cash.

Tongsun could see the tide turning in his favor. Things were falling into place. His assets were performing well. Kim Hyung Wook had interceded with the President on his side of the feud with Ambassador Kim. The charmed circle was saying the right things to the President and the KCIA director. And his goodwill commodities—the Congressmen indebted to him for campaign contributions—had supplied helpful letters to the President. The only asset not yet pumped was his family. It was next.

Ken Park, Tongsun's older brother, was a man widely respected in Seoul. He and KCIA Director Lee Hu Rak were good friends. Now that Lee had heard the political arguments, Tongsun thought a personal plea might clinch the rice agency. His brother agreed to try.

Ken Park asked Lee Hu Rak to give Tongsun a break. The KCIA director was amenable. He gave the go-ahead for Tongsun's reinstatement in early December. Tongsun's joy was boundless, and Hanna wrote Lee Hu Rak a grateful letter.

The reinstatement was conditional, however. The KCIA would be watching Tongsun. His performance was to be judged on the basis of KCIA reports to Seoul, not his own embroidered accounts. If he wanted them to recognize him as their best agent of influence in Washington, he could not lie about it. He would be required to turn over a large chunk of his commissions to the President's party, the DRP, through the KCIA. The DRP was short of funds after Park Chung Hee's expensive reelection in April, notwithstanding the millions extorted from American

companies. They were looking for something in the neighborhood of $1.5 million to $2 million from Tongsun over the next
year or two.

Considering the mess he had been in for months, Tongsun
was now in remarkably good shape with the powers in Seoul. As
always, though, he wanted more. The director of the KCIA had
been won over and President Park was not objecting to him. But
he wanted President Park's personal blessing and a free rein in
Washington. He did not want to be accountable to the KCIA at
the Embassy. Still unable to get an appointment for himself because Park Chong Kyu barred his way to the President's office,
he decided to send Gallagher. He slipped Gallagher $5,000 more
and they were off to Korea in January 1972.

Gallagher briefed President Park on the latest U.S. defense
policy information from Melvin Laird, obtained by Tongsun
through Congressman Minshall. Then to the heart of the matter,
the real reason he had been paid to come to Korea: Gallagher
recommended that President Park make Tongsun the head of the
influence campaign in the United States, in addition to being the
agent for all rice sales to Korea.

Park was not a man to be wildly enthusiastic about anybody,
least of all Tongsun. Predictably, he was noncommittal. He was
surprised at the way this Congressman was pushing himself into
internal Korean government affairs.

Four days later, Tongsun was on his way to Hong Kong for
some very important business. Sitting in his first-class seat on the
plane, he reviewed the Passman situation from beginning to end.

Getting the rice agency was one thing. Keeping it was quite
another, as Tongsun had learned in the tribulations of 1971.
With the KCIA looking over his shoulder and Ambassador Kim
still anxious to trip him up if he could, he would need a solid base
of support in Congress. Now more than ever, Otto Passman had
to be brought in. Passman had had a lot to do with his losing the

rice agency in the first place. He had sided with Ambassador Kim, been openly hostile to Tongsun, and negotiated the Louisiana rice deal with President Park himself. He was capable of doing more damage to Tongsun in the future. As a member of the charmed circle, he could be its greatest asset; otherwise, he would probably be Tongsun's greatest liability.

Passman had seemed immune to Tongsun's blandishments, so unlike the others. Hanna was generous, Minshall was politically sympathetic, and Gallagher seemed to be up for sale. But Passman was independent, very much his own man.

The nearest he had been able to get to Passman was Congressman Edwards. Edwards's value to Tongsun had always been his closeness to Passman. Tongsun had visited him two months before in New Orleans at the "Edwards for Governor" headquarters in the Monteleone Hotel. He had had in mind giving Edwards a little positive encouragement to solicit Passman's cooperation. Edwards had been full of talk about how well the campaign was going and the importance of rice to his political good fortune.

Selling Louisiana rice was good for him, too, Tongsun had said—as he held out an envelope with an offer to help with the campaign. Edwards had politely turned him down, thanking him warmly all the same.

He had gone downstairs for an appointment with Elaine Edwards in the coffee shop. She and Tongsun were rather close. After hearing her describe the rigors of campaign life, he had said, extending the envelope, "Edwin says he doesn't need any help, so here is something for you and the kids." She had thanked him and dropped it in her purse without opening it.

Tongsun really didn't mind parting with $10,000 for Elaine and her children. He liked the Edwardses. But it was not likely to gain any headway for him with Passman, which is what the money had been intended for.

Tongsun's one source of influence over Passman was the rice agency. Korea would buy only the rice Tongsun Park negotiated for. A feeling of power ran through Tongsun as the plane landed in Hong Kong. Otto Passman was there for one of his visits to watchmakers and jewelers.

The seduction of Otto Passman had been planned well by Tongsun. Passman's membership in the charmed circle should be enjoyed by them both. He felt no vengeance toward the elderly Congressman for past unpleasantries. The power he now held would be unspoken. Satisfaction of security for Tongsun came from just knowing he had Passman where he wanted him. Not by coincidence, Tongsun recently had begun collecting watches.

Gallagher had preceded Tongsun to Hong Kong. He was on hand as a kind of closet adviser. For the first couple of nights they had dinner together to discuss Tongsun's approach to Passman.

Gordon Dore was a prominent Louisiana rice miller who was traveling with Passman. Edwards, soon to be governor of Louisiana, had asked Dore to meet Tongsun before leaving on the trip to the Orient. Since Tongsun was to be the agent for the upcoming big rice sales, Edwards wanted Dore to try to keep the peace between Passman and Tongsun. Over dinner at the George Town Club, Tongsun and Dore had agreed it would be best to wait until everyone was in Hong Kong before telling Passman that Tongsun was there. Passman might cancel the trip otherwise.

It was no secret that Tongsun had regained the rice agency. Passman already knew that, and he did not like it. He insisted a foreigner had no business pulling in commissions from an American sale. And he took pride in his role in having gotten Tongsun dumped a year before. In Hong Kong, he busied himself with watches and jewelry as usual, spending time with his old friend Kevin Hsu, who owned a chain of jewelry shops. He was staying at the Ambassador Hotel on the Kowloon side. For eighteen years he had stayed at no other hotel since the time the manager of the Ambassador had given him a room when there were no vacancies in the city. When Dore brought the news that Tongsun was in town and wanted to have dinner with them, his reaction was predictable: "I don't want that son of a bitch around!"

"If we want to sell the rice, Otto, we've got to deal with him. He's the agent," Dore reminded him.

Passman grudgingly consented. Dore asked him to try to make the best of it.

When Tongsun got a phone call from Dore confirming the dinner date, he took out his pocket diary and jotted down "Otto, Dore, Charles Pang—Miramar Theater Supper Club," for January 17, 1972. Directly below his notation was the diary's printed quotation, from General Douglas MacArthur. It read: "There is no security on this earth; there is only opportunity."

Otto had been around long enough to know the value of flexibility. In politics, necessity was a great changer of attitudes. Tongsun proved to be a charming dinner host. He picked up the tab at the Miramar Theater Supper Club, which had featured a traditional Chinese show, and at the Korea Gardens the following night. Otto was delighted to discover he and Tongsun shared an interest in watches. Tongsun seemed to know a great deal about his favorite subject.

When their conversation turned to business, Otto told Tongsun that besides rice, Louisiana had a surplus of dehydrated yams in his district. Tongsun was interested. He promised to buy a thousand cases himself and see what he could do about selling the yams to Korea too.

With all the entertainment expenses, Tongsun's cash on hand was running low. Between Gallagher and the Passman entourage, he had spent about $1,500. He asked if Dore could advance him some money until they returned to Washington. Dore loaned him $5,000. Tongsun gave it to Passman in exchange for some watches. Years later he would testify under oath that, while in Hong Kong, he had promised Passman $50,000 per year in campaign contributions for three years.

Within a week, Otto was saying, "I feel that I now know you and understand you better and I look forward to working with you in the future."

A luncheon in Seoul seemed an ideal way to let the world know the Tongsun-Otto alliance had come into being. On January 21, the day after Passman arrived in Seoul from Hong Kong, he played host for a gala affair at the Chosun Hotel. The Korean chefs outdid themselves with Passman's Louisiana recipes. Rice and sweet potatoes were featured prominently on the menu. The guests included high officials of the R.O.K. government, businessmen, and American Embassy officers. The only thing attracting more attention than the Louisiana cuisine was the presence of Tongsun Park as one of Passman's invited guests.

The highlight of the event was Passman's phone call to candidate Edwards, then in the final days of his runoff election campaign. The conversation was hooked to loudspeakers in the Chosun Hotel banquet room. On the Louisiana end, Edwards had it taped for radio broadcast. The message was Passman's news about Korea's great interest in Louisiana farm products.

Underscoring the importance of the alliance, Tongsun's new friend in Congress had paid a courtesy call on President Park right after the luncheon.

Urgent business kept Tongsun in Korea when Passman returned to the United States on January 22. For the time being, he and Otto had to put off their plans for a visit to Louisiana together. The all-important rice agency took priority. Although the KCIA director had approved Tongsun, and Otto had joined the charmed circle, Tongsun wanted two more favors from the Korean government. American rice sellers did not like dealing with Tongsun. This was especially true of Grover Connell, who handled about 90 percent of the business. Tongsun believed the only way to get Connell and the others to accept him as the exclusive sales agent was to have the Korean government tell them they had to. The R.O.K. Office of Supply was reluctant to use that kind of open coercion.

Tongsun also felt some compensation was due him for the income lost in 1971 after Ambassador Kim had him dumped. He wanted the Korean government to pay damages. KCIA Director Lee Hu Rak was willing to try to work something out, but it would take time.

Never one to rely on himself to solve problems, Tongsun had the charmed circle put pressure on the Korean government. If the powers in Seoul could be shown everyone in Washington was pining for Tongsun's return, they might give him what he wanted. It was a fact that Passman wanted him back for some media stunts in Louisiana. Tongsun made the most of that by getting Passman and friends to send him telegrams. One message said he was needed to go to St. Francisville, Louisiana, in Passman's district, with Governor Edwards, Dore, and Passman. They were to visit the Joan of Arc Company, which processed dehydrated yams, "where a motion picture will be made showing the four of us with the president of Joan of Arc loading the 1,000 cases of sweet potatoes destined for Korea." If Tongsun did not return by mid-February the picture could not be made, the telegram said.

The tougher the message, the better for Tongsun. Passman's telegrams complained that Tongsun had not lived up to his agreement to come back. At one point, Otto cabled a threat: "We will refer the matter to the Korean Ambassador in Washington and get him to take it up directly with President Park and . . . get the Korean government to assume your contract."

Gallagher did his bit, too, in a letter early in March. Reminding the KCIA director of the promise to make Tongsun the rice agent, Gallagher said "the delay is causing unnecessary unrest" in Congress.

The current KCIA director, Lee Hu Rak, still had not paid the damages for lost income that Tongsun was demanding. So Tongsun again enlisted the help of ex-KCIA Director Kim Hyung Wook. He called on Kim at home and showed him a list of Congressmen Tongsun claimed had been asking for contributions. If he could not make the payments, the Congressmen would wonder why. Tongsun said he did not want them to think the Korean government was keeping him from meeting his obligations. It could reflect badly on President Park in Congress. Kim Hyung Wook carried that message to Lee Hu Rak, Park Chong Kyu, and other high officials.

March 21, 1972, was a red-letter day for Tongsun. He recorded its importance with seven words in his diary: "Saw Director. Riviera resolved. Saw OSROK letter." The KCIA director had told him he would get $190,000 right away from a Swiss bank account. OSROK, the Office of Supply of the Republic of Korea, had written a letter to Connell Rice and Sugar and Continental Grain Company stipulating that his service "would be required for all our rice trade with the United States." "Riviera," the rice trade in Tongsun's personal code, had been fully resolved.

His diary's printed quotation for the day, from Victor Hugo, was: "The supreme happiness of life is the conviction that we are loved."

Tongsun wasted no time. Three days later he was entertaining Otto at Washington's expensive Rive Gauche Restaurant. His employee, Jai Shin Ryu, was on his way to Zurich to get the damage money from the KCIA transferred to Tongsun's account at Equitable Trust in Baltimore.

By March 28, Tongsun was back in business with $190,000

in the bank. In his diary, the code for the money was the letter *L*. Below "L. received," he wrote, "Passman (10 copies)," meaning $10,000. Another $10,000 payment was indicated on March 29, as "Passman (10 L. copies)."

He was now ready to keep his date with Otto in Louisiana. Passman put out a press release for home consumption saying he was returning to the district for "something more important than merely a visit." He announced he was bringing "Korean Ambassador Tongsun Park." The coming of this distinguished visitor was heralded as a success in Congressman Passman's "newly accepted self-designated assignment of promoting the sale of American agricultural commodities to foreign nations."

Home consumption was equally important to Tongsun. When he went to Louisiana in April, he took along his KCIA watchdog, Steve Kim.

It turned out to be quite an event for St. Francisville. Governor Edwards's helicopter swooped down into the little town to deliver the party of dignitaries—the Congressman, the "Ambassador," Gordon Dore, and Steve Kim. Passman told the assembled crowd the presence of the "Ambassador" marked the beginning of Korea's expanded interest in the products of Louisiana. With ceremonial flair, Tongsun presented the president of the Joan of Arc Company with a check for a thousand cases of yams. Cameras clicked throughout the proceeding.

Tongsun had not the foggiest notion of what he could do with a thousand cases of dried American sweet potatoes. Koreans certainly would not eat the stuff. He would either have to dump it somewhere or serve it at the George Town Club. Without a doubt, though, it was a sound investment. It wasn't yams he was buying; it was Otto's support. Passman's interests were well served by the act. It was an election year, and the St. Francisville yam-producing area had recently been added to his district.

When the news of Tongsun's latest impersonation reached the Korean Embassy, Ambassador Kim Dong Jo flew into a rage. The usurper had returned full force, hurling the ultimate insult. There seemed no way to rid himself of this scourge. The powers in Seoul would not listen to him; the ambassador's hatred of Tongsun was too well known. There was nothing he could do in Washington; Tongsun had his Congressmen. Still, there was one possible avenue. The Embassy's chief information officer, Dr. Lee Jai Hyon, had said he had been troubled by calls from Louisiana reporters asking for more information on Ambassador Tongsun Park. Kim Dong Jo hit upon the idea of setting up Dr. Lee to complain to Seoul. Lee had a different channel, the Ministry of Public Information, rather than Kim's Ministry of Foreign Affairs. A report from Lee might be taken more seriously than one from himself.

It didn't work. Seoul's answer to Lee's complaint was a personal letter from President Park to Ambassador Kim. The message was clear: Leave Tongsun alone.

IN THE SPRING of 1972, Tongsun called upon the charmed circle again. The letter he drafted for Hanna to send to President Park said, "We are very impressed with Tongsun doing a magnificent job in an important area."

Passman wrote President Park that because of "the Honorable Tongsun Park, a great thing has happened": Korea's purchase of 340,000 tons of Louisiana rice. He also noted Tongsun's efforts with Senator Ellender and others on military issues were "moving with significant success, and doing so without jeopardizing the relationship between your Ambassador and the Departments here in Washington."

Minshall, always useful for making it appear that Defense Secretary Laird was a Tongsun man, sent a letter in June to the KCIA director. "The Secretary," he wrote, "was greatly encour-

aged and impressed by the substantial legislative support Tongsun was able to have committed." Later in the summer, Tongsun
sent Minshall to Korea to deliver similar tributes in person.

Tongsun's six-month report card went to the KCIA the end
of September. Headquarters in Seoul had assigned two top officers to do an independent critique of his work. The idea was to
get the straight story on what he was doing and make him behave. If he was found not to be doing his job, he would lose the
rice agency and be cut out of the influence campaign. The KCIA
had picked Yang Doo Won (alias Lee Sang Ho in the United
States) and Steve Kim because they were senior officers known to
be able to get along with Tongsun. They found getting along with
Tongsun had its benefits. Yang Doo Won had acquired his job as
head of the KCIA in the United States through Tongsun's mentor, Kim Hyung Wook. Steve Kim enjoyed traveling in Tongsun's rarefied social circles. Both Yang Doo Won and Steve Kim
were delighted at not having to wait for cash gifts from Tongsun;
he was willing whenever they asked.

Tongsun was not worried about their report to the KCIA.
He helped write it.

The "T. S. Report" (T. S. referring to "Tongsun") was dated
September 30, 1972. It credited Tongsun with having 120 members of Congress under his influence. He was said to have delivered a major aid vote through "mobilization" of Senators
Ellender, Montoya, and Gordon Allott. In another category, he
had mounted a "drive to restore the reduced amount of U.S. aid"
by meeting six times with Secretary of Defense Laird and having
Passman talk to President Nixon.

Figures claimed for payments to the charmed circle were
well over what Tongsun's personal ledger showed. Other claims
were totally fictional as to name and amount. He claimed to have
given $25,000 to Wilbur Mills, $10,000 to Morris Udall, $80,000
to Governor Edwards.

The report also claimed a donation of $100,000 directly to the White House. Tongsun did put money into Nixon's 1972 campaign, but nowhere near that figure. Minshall was Tongsun's Republican bag man for this. Most of Tongsun's dealings were with Democrats, since they controlled Congress. But the charmed circle had to be bipartisan because the White House was Republican. A few days before the November election, Tongsun gave Minshall an envelope to deliver to Clark MacGregor at CREEP, the Committee to Re-elect the President. The envelope was filled with crisp hundred-dollar bills amounting to about $25,000. Minshall told MacGregor it was a contribution from the officers of the George Town Club. It was not a large sum compared to what was available to CREEP, so MacGregor put it in an office safe, unreported.

Certain "outfits" of Tongsun, the "T. S. Report" went on, added to his suitability for the lobbying job: "high-class mansion," "chauffeur-driven Cadillac," and the image of an "amicable and patriotic young businessman" who was "popular in the upper classes" of Washington. He was praised for his ability to "manipulate target persons with . . . tenaciousness." His driving force was seen as a definite plus for the influence campaign. He was "determined to prove himself really capable" and, more important, was "motivated by the fact that he is in competition with D. J."—Ambassador Kim Dong Jo.

Yang Doo Won and Steve Kim recommended that the KCIA keep Tongsun on the job. He had been performing without "serious mistakes." In the future, he could be expected to do just as well as long as he remained "under supervision" by them.

The glowing "T. S. Report" had not gone so far as to claim Tongsun had nothing to worry about. There was one line of concern which read: "A portion of the lower echelon in the State Department has been watching him closely." Just as he could exaggerate his accomplishments, he was equally able to understate his problems. The "lower echelon" he referred to included the ambassador to Korea, Philip Habib. Everyone in the American Embassy had been ordered by Habib to stay away from Tongsun. The word about Habib's boycott was slipped to Tongsun by his friend John ("Jocko") Richardson, the head of the USCIA in Korea. According to Tongsun, his cultivation of Richardson had been low-keyed. Instead of cash, he gave the CIA man small gifts such as liquor.

Habib's ostracism had Tongsun in a quandary. He felt it was uncalled for and showed Habib wasn't a very good ambassador. The problem, as he saw it, was that Habib just didn't understand Korea. He was certain Richardson and others at the Embassy did not agree with the ambassador. Habib was an obstacle he could not get around in the usual way. Tongsun was used to attacks by competitors like Ambassador Kim. That was part of the game. It motivated him to accomplish more. The same was true of Congressmen like Passman who resisted him at first. Habib presented a different kind of problem. Tongsun felt hurt, angered, and frustrated.

He went to Capitol Hill in the spring of 1973 to seek consolation from the man he regarded as "uncle," Senator Hubert Humphrey. Tongsun had wormed his way into a social acquaintance with Humphrey and his sister, Frances Howard, by courting Mrs. Howard's daughter Anne. She had been his date off and on since 1967, both at the George Town Club and for parties at his home. In 1970, Anne Howard had visited him in Korea. When Humphrey was running for the Democratic presidential nomination in 1972, Tongsun had contributed $5,000 to the campaign, hoping it would win him some political influence. Apparently, the Senator never knew about the contribution.

With a long sad face, Tongsun explained his plight over Habib to "Uncle" Hubert. The veteran "Happy Warrior" was philosophical at times like this. Smiling, he looked up and said, "Oh,

Tongsun, you know you can't always have everybody love you."
His advice was to do "the right thing" and not pay attention to
the detractors.

Humphrey's counsel calmed Tongsun's nerves somewhat.
However, Habib was coming at him from more than one direction. He had gone to the extent of having the American military
commander in Korea, General Donald Bennet, warn Passman
about Tongsun.

Otto's importance to Tongsun went up the scale with Neil
Gallagher's exit. The government had nabbed Gallagher for income tax evasion, and he went to prison in the spring of 1973
after pleading guilty. Illegal dealings with Tongsun and Kim
Kwang were also known by the Justice Department, and Gallagher had long been suspected of ties with organized crime. According to the press, federal investigators believed a corpse had
been removed from his basement in connection with a 1962 un-
derworld slaying. Gallagher had been very useful for putting the
Tongsun point of view across to President Park. Tongsun would
miss the New Jersey politician's quick trips and handy letters to
Korea whenever cash was offered.

Passman was different. Of the four members of the charmed
circle, Tongsun felt the least secure with him. His strong streak
of independence was worrisome. He was dealing with Tongsun
more out of necessity than desire. Tongsun trusted him only in
the area where Otto's need for Tongsun was greatest: rice. Now,
with Gallagher gone, more was needed from Otto than ever before—he was a better rice sales promoter than Hanna, and he
had more political influence than Hanna and Minshall combined.

Keeping Otto happy occupied a good deal of Tongsun's attention between April and June of 1973. On April 3, his diary
noted he had to pay $50,000 to Passman by April 11. Since he
did not have that kind of money on hand, he decided to try tapping rice dealer Grover Connell for some sales commissions. His

diary for April 5 reads, "Met Grover at New York," also indicating agreement for having $230,000 deposited in Tongsun's bank accounts: $80,000 to American Security and Trust in Washington and $150,000 to a Bermuda bank. (Getting paid in Bermuda had proven useful for tax dodging.) On April 9 he shuttled to Bermuda to pick up $130,000 in cash. Money in hand, he returned to Washington. According to the diary, he met the April 11 deadline: a notation indicates $50,000 for Otto, plus $75,000 for Gordon Dore.

A few days later, Tongsun and Otto set out for Korea to talk up more rice business. In June, according to Tongsun's financial records, $48,000 more was delivered to Passman's congressional office.

TONGSUN'S DIGNITY was ruffled at the airport in Anchorage, Alaska, in December 1973.

Halfway home to Washington, he deplaned Northwest Orient Flight 6 for customs inspection and a flight change. Passengers were processed through rows set up like supermarket checkout lines. To move the passengers quickly, customs officials usually made a thorough inspection of only those who seemed to be carrying a large amount of valuables. When Inspector Dennis Hazelton saw the impeccably dressed Korean with a large shopping bag from a camera shop, he decided to make a full search.

Tongsun opened a suitcase full of cameras and other expensive gifts. He insisted the items were his, for personal use. Hazelton asked for verification. Tongsun shuffled through some papers and handed the inspector a guarantee form for a hair dryer.

Hazelton began looking through manila folders in Tongsun's briefcase. When he pulled out the third folder, Tongsun clamped a firm grip on his forearm with both hands. Hazelton reminded him that customs inspectors had the right to examine luggage and suggested he let go. Tongsun released his grip. It was the first time Hazelton had ever encountered forcible resistance to a search. As he opened the file folder labeled "Congressional List," Tongsun grabbed for it, tearing off the top two pages. Having had enough, Hazelton stopped to call the chief inspector. Within seconds, Tongsun had ripped up the pages and stuffed the shreds in his pocket.

The inspectors made Tongsun hand over the shreds and his other documents. They found a long list of Congressmen and Senators, two letters from a Congressman to President Park Chung Hee, and some notes in Korean. A Korean-speaking inspector caught the word "contribution" in the Korean notes.

Customs officials had never heard of Tongsun Park or a Korean influence campaign. They just had an unruly passenger on their hands. A highly indignant Tongsun was now telling them how important he was. The very next night, he said, he was to have dinner with the Vice-President of the United States and the following night several Congressmen were to be his guests. He insisted his government connections were such that he ought to be traveling on a diplomatic passport. He jotted down Hazelton's name and badge number and promised trouble for him in Washington.

The inspectors could find no violation of customs law. They concluded there were no other reasons to detain him any longer. As Tongsun boarded the flight for Washington, Hazelton typed out a report of the strange incident with this hotheaded braggart. He included as many of the congressional names as he could remember. That was the end of it, except for occasional laughs among the Anchorage inspectors, until four years later when Hazelton was called to be a key witness in the Koreagate investigations.

BY THE END of 1973, Ambassador Kim Dong Jo had returned to Korea to become Minister of Foreign Affairs. He had ceased to

be a major problem for Tongsun more than two years earlier.
Still, Tongsun was glad his longtime foe had left Washington.
Kim's successor, Hahm Pyong Choon, posed no threat. He was a
scholar of international law, a Harvard graduate. Hahm was appointed ambassador partly because President Park had been impressed when Henry Kissinger had mentioned him favorably as
a former student during a reception. He projected a good
image for Korea, and that was what the government needed for
countering the bad press Park's dictatorship was getting in the
United States. He was an intellectual, not a politician. Tongsun
had flattened Kim Dong Jo, who was a political pro. Long before
Hahm arrived, Tongsun was well entrenched in Washington and
had the right backing in Seoul. There was no cause for him to
worry about the newcomer. The new year seemed auspicious.

Tongsun picked a new target for cultivation on Capitol Hill,
no less than House Majority Leader Thomas P. ("Tip") O'Neill.
He had no illusions of bringing O'Neill into the charmed circle,
but he wanted to see how far he could get. At the very least, the
powers in Seoul should be convinced he had an in with O'Neill.

O'Neill was the heir apparent to become Speaker of the
House whenever Carl Albert decided to retire. In the Watergate
crisis, he took on added prominence. Far more than Albert,
O'Neill guided the impeachment process in the House. Tongsun
called him the "Commander-in-Chief of the impeach-Nixon
movement." If Nixon was forced out of office, Congress would
become "almighty" and O'Neill "the most influential person in
the U.S. political scene."

The Korean government could not be left to think Tongsun
was sitting quietly on the sidelines during Watergate. He claimed
important participation. Attorney General William B. Saxbe, he
said, asked him to arrange a clandestine get-together with
O'Neill. Accordingly, Tongsun told the KCIA the two men came
to one of his parties and met "in the bedroom of TSP."

The congressional visit to Korea in April 1974 was another chance for exploitation. O'Neill was to lead the delegation. Tongsun was ready with advice to President Park for talks with O'Neill. The best way to convince O'Neill the dictatorship was a good thing would be for the President to tell him that strong leadership would bring political stability through which "economic development may be achieved and democratic institutions realized." It seemed to Tongsun that kind of argument might be persuasive. In 1969, O'Neill had put a statement in the *Congressional Record* supporting Park's third-term amendment because of the threat from North Korea.

Tongsun had yet another proposal. If past experience was any guide, there were means other than conversation to win important friends for Korea. Money should be used to help O'Neill become Speaker of the House. The way to do it, wrote Tongsun, would be for the government to make payments to the Congressmen traveling with O'Neill to Korea. They would feel indebted to O'Neill for taking them on such a profitable trip. They might also see it as a reward from O'Neill for helping him become Majority Leader. The Congressmen's wives should also be given "necessary expenses." Tongsun even claimed O'Neill had *asked* that the payments be made. (Apparently, the Korean government did take part of Tongsun's advice. A year later, some wives were offered money, but at least two of them turned it down.)

The April visit to Korea did not make O'Neill a fan of the Park government. He came back deeply disturbed by the repression he saw there.

Congressman Donald Fraser's hearings in July and August on human rights in South Korea posed a serious and perplexing problem. Like Ambassador Habib, Fraser was out of Tongsun's range. He had never been to Korea nor attended a Tongsun social affair. His hearings were to feature several very critical witnesses. Joining Fraser's Subcommittee on International Organizations for the hearings was the Subcommittee on Asian and Pacific Affairs whose chairman used to be Gallagher. Again, Tongsun lamented the jailing of his friend. If Gallagher were still around, Tongsun could have persuaded him to hold competing hearings. Witnesses would be selected to give the Park regime's point of view. To Tongsun's mind, what Fraser planned was terribly biased.

Perhaps "Uncle" Hubert could help. Fraser had been a Minnesota protégé of Humphrey's. Tongsun asked the senator to intercede with Fraser. Humphrey responded by saying, "Well, Don Fraser is a very independent-minded fellow." The hearings were held without Humphrey's ever contacting Fraser.

The Korean Embassy had made sure some of its witnesses testified at Fraser's hearings. It remained for Tongsun to show something for himself. He could not let such an important event go by without getting into the act.

"Dick, I think we should get hold of some of our friends who understand Korea," Tongsun said to Hanna, "and let them give their side of the story." Hanna agreed. They picked six Congressmen: Democrats Walter Flowers of Alabama, Mel Price of Illinois, Sonny Montgomery of Mississippi, Edward Patten of New Jersey, and Republicans Albert Johnson of Pennsylvania and William Minshall of Ohio. Tongsun and Hanna wrote the statements and gave them to the Congressmen for sending on to Fraser.

As usual, there were follow-up letters to President Park and the KCIA director. Hanna boasted that his and Tongsun's efforts had "minimized the thrust of the critics" and "neutralized the effectiveness of the hearings." Actually, the Congressmen's statements were not written until after the hearings were over. Along with other written statements and appendixes, they did not even appear in print until Fraser's hearings were published six months later.

The threat of Fraser had Tongsun worried. If it were to turn the tide in Congress against aid to Korea, he would be in trouble. His vaunted influence might be viewed in Seoul as a sham. Tongsun had no new talents, so he fell back on an old one, party-giving. In September he spent $2,950 on a campaign fund-raising party for Congressman John Brademas, his college roommate at Georgetown. On December 16, he threw his second birthday party for Tip O'Neill. Hanna and Minshall had fronted as hosts at the George Town Club for the first one in 1973. Tongsun's plans for the 1974 affair were grander. The party, twice as large and expensive as the previous one, was held at the Madison Hotel. Billing himself as the host this time, he got Minshall to persuade O'Neill to come. The birthday present was a set of golf clubs. O'Neill was told his colleagues in Congress had paid for the gift.

Tip O'Neill was a bad investment. The same week Tongsun was treating him to a birthday party, he supported the first cut Congress had ever made in military aid to Korea. A few weeks before that, he had joined Fraser and six other Congressmen in signing a letter to President Ford warning about "the destruction of democracy in Korea." The letter urged Ford to tell Park Chung Hee the United States would begin to disengage from Korea unless human rights were restored.

Testifying under oath during Koreagate, Tongsun was to admit both that O'Neill had never asked for contributions and that he had never received any money from Tongsun.

The year 1974 had begun better for Tongsun than it ended. Although he made more money than ever (his rice commissions soared to $3.7 million, five times the 1973 take), behind his back Otto was working against him. Passman tried to put through a rice sale without him, but Tongsun had squeezed in at the last minute. Commiserating in private with Grover Connell in July, Passman called Tongsun "one of the most brazen individuals that ever lived. All you can do is cooperate with him because you

are in business to make money." Three days later, Otto was prac-
ticing what he preached. He assured Tongsun he would tell the
Deputy Prime Minister of Korea how grateful he was for Tongsun's "tremendous cooperation" (1974 was an election year, and
Tongsun had promised a generous contribution).

Otto was a chameleon, and Tongsun knew it. The old Louisiana pol was proving disloyal even on the rice business, where
Tongsun had thought he could trust him. Tongsun was incensed
over Passman's promoting of a rival shipping company. St.
John's Maritime had been formed by Gordon Dore, Grover Connell, and Harry Smith, an established shipper. Passman was using his influence to have American foreign aid commodities
carried by St. John's to all receiving countries, including Korea.
This ran counter to Tongsun's plans for using his own ships.
Connell and Dore had turned an investment of about $500 into a
profit of $800,000 apiece.

Tongsun had expected great things from the April congressional delegation to Korea. Previous group junkets had always
opened new ground on Capitol Hill for him to cultivate. This
time, however, the delegation leader, O'Neill, had come back denouncing the Korean government. And two of the visiting Congressmen, Lloyd Meeds and Morris Udall, had testified jointly at
Fraser's hearings as anti-Park witnesses.

The year ended with a $93-million cut in military aid be-
cause of human rights violations. The South Korean government
was in bad shape with Congress, and Tongsun had ample reason
to worry.

A shock hit Tongsun in April 1975, involving two friends,
Jimmy and Nancy Howe. The money he had been giving them
had seemed a good investment for more recognition, since Nancy
was a personal aide to Betty Ford in the White House. But a few
days after the newspapers discovered Tongsun had funded their
expensive vacation in the Caribbean, Jimmy Howe committed

suicide. Although the death may have been brought on by the marital and financial problems the Howes had been having, it created unwanted notoriety in Washington for Tongsun.

Calamities had never deterred Tongsun. To him they were simply temporary setbacks. The rice trade with Korea was to decline after the 1974 peak, but he had diversified his businesses. He was now making millions with oil in the Middle East and shipping transactions in Japan. Congressmen were voting against aid to Korea, but they still came to his parties. They liked him. Liking led to greater recognition. Money and recognition always served each other well in Tongsun's game.

Minions and Master

AN ARMY OF obedient servants would have to be recruited and trained to restore the Kingdom of Heaven to earth under Sun Myung Moon. They would have to work as people had never before worked because there had never been such a great mission. They would have to go wherever Moon sent them to raise the $300 million he needed for making his project worldwide and the billions more he needed to control the wealth of the planet. But Moon did not have shiploads of chained tribal people at his disposal when he arrived in America in 1971. Involuntary servitude was against the law. Could he make people think they were actually willing to be slaves?

He got the answer he wanted from idealistic American youth. He and they were ready for each other. They were people in the age group eighteen to twenty-four, in transition from adolescence to adulthood, student to professional, getting in or getting out of school, family life to life alone. For one in search of a coherent view of the world, college had the effect of making things more confusing by presenting so many different approaches to life without identifying one as altogether right. In the "real" world, problems abounded, from family disunity to the threat of nuclear destruction. At best, things were in disarray; at worst, life was chaotic, depressing. Such minds were fertile soil. Their idealism was the key. Describe how happy people would be if discord could be turned into harmony. Show how this can be done through unified love for God. Then play on the distance between what a person thinks he is and what he wants to be. Hold up ideals and make him ashamed of not living up to his own standards. Instill ideas of self-worthlessness. Make him feel guilty about putting concern for himself above group unity. The burden of guilt could be lightened by working as a family with others who believe the ideals can be attained here on earth. The family has a father who will lead the way. The harder one works for Father, the closer one gets to achieving the goal. Follow Father. God has shown him alone the path to perfection because he is the Messiah.

Moon taught a clear strategy for attracting prospective converts. Until the prospect is converted, he must not know that a strategy is being used. Later he will appreciate being deceived because the motive was his own salvation. First, all church members must make as many new acquaintances as possible. Befriend them by taking a personal interest; do not disagree with their views, whether right or wrong. Do favors. Find the right style to use on each kind of person. Classify his personality. Introduce him to a church member with a similar personality, but don't reveal that he is a church member. Meet together like that two or three times. Get into conversations on current issues, ethics, or morality. Then say, "I know where there are many serious young people talking about things like this," or "I have heard of some lectures about a new philosophy, very sincere, very interesting, talking about the problems of life. I would appreciate it if you would go with me so I can get your opinion on it." The prospect will pay attention to the lecture because he has been asked for criticism. When he says it was wonderful, say, "Oh, I don't know. Not necessarily so." But suggest going again in order to learn more about it.

Chris Elkins was president of his fraternity at the University of Arizona when John Shea, a recent acquaintance, invited him to attend a lecture about something called the One World Crusade. What he heard was philosophical, nonreligious, and interesting. So he went again each week for a month or more. The One World Crusade was explained as a movement encompassing all aspects of life. He was impressed by the magnetism of the lecturer, Dr. Joseph Sheftick. He and his fifteen or twenty followers had an aura of confidence, friendliness, and sincerity. They related well to his own interests and seemed warmly concerned about him. As the lectures progressed, a Korean named Sun Myung Moon was mentioned as a great teacher, but the main stress was on the coming of a Messiah to build heaven on earth. It dawned on Elkins that Sun Myung Moon must be the Messiah in question, although no one had said he was. During dinner with the group one night, he stated that observation. Dr. Sheftick raised his head, sat up straight, and announced, "We have a new brother: Chris Elkins."

Elkins did not affirm Sheftick's declaration, nor did he deny it. He simply went along for the time being. In fact, he was seriously considering joining. The goals were so noble: peace and brotherhood at all levels. Fund raising didn't appeal to him, but he could swallow it because he felt he and the movement really belonged together. And the people gave him so much love and attention that he couldn't just say no. His best friend tried to dissuade him. When his family protested, Dr. Sheftick warned that Satanic forces work best through those most loved.

Euphoria prevailed during his honeymoon period with the Moon cult. Then the atmosphere became more serious. Elkins didn't like fasting and staying up all night praying aloud with the others. After a couple of weeks, it all seemed too heavy. Driving back to Illinois to visit his mother in the hospital, he was in a daze. He tried to think things out. What had he got into? Was this the life for him, separated from the rest of the world? The love . . . the concern . . . heaven on earth. . . . What if Moon was really what they said he was? Could he risk losing what they offered? From Illinois, he called the group. It felt good to hear their voices. He would return.

He resigned as president of the fraternity. The Moonies sent him to Phoenix to fund-raise by selling peanuts on the street. He was still restless because Satanic spirits were at work inside him, so he was grateful that another member was by his side at all times. His parents wanted the car back, but a leader chided him: "Who needs it more? Your parents or the movement?"

He was learning. The great crusade required everything he had. The attachment to Father must be total, as Father said:

> Your whole body, every cell of your body, every movement, every facial motion, even every piece of hair, every ounce of energy must be directed to this one point.

Just as other members were always with him physically, Father was always with him too:

> You must live with me spiritually all the time—while you are eating, while you are sleeping, while you are in the bathroom, while you are taking a bath, taking a rest, even in dreams you can be sitting with me and discussing with me. That's the only way. This is the secret of our movement. Whoever has that basic, fundamental attitude and that spiritual power will perform miracles.

Spiritual regeneration required mental somersaults. What once seemed true was now false. What once seemed unreal was now real. The world Elkins had known since birth was the product of original sin. The fall of Adam opened the floodgates to Satanic spirits, which had inundated the lives of Elkins's ancestors. If he gave himself to Moon completely, he could rid himself of that awful heritage and be restored:

> You will rearrange the mechanism within yourself in good order so that you will feel in the right way, think in that way, say things in that way, and act out in that way.
> So you are your body, but your mind is my mind.

Chris Elkins had sung in choirs before, so he was told that joining the New Hope Singers was something he might like to do. Rehearsals were held at the Belvedere training center in Tarrytown, New York, purchased after a nationwide candle-selling blitz had yielded about $800,000.

The schedule at Belvedere was rigorous: get up out of the bunkbed at 6:00; exercise at 6:05; clean up and get dressed at 6:15; pray at 6:35; eat oatmeal and water at 7:00; do chores at 8:00; attend training sessions at 8:45; eat bread, butter, and jelly sandwiches at 1:00; tend the grounds at 1:45; shower at 3:30; attend training sessions at 4:00; eat casserole with flecks of meat at 7:00; attend training sessions at 8:00; go to team meetings at 11:00; do individual study at midnight; go to bed at 1:30. There was no free time, and everything was done in groups supervised by a leader.

The three functions in the life of a Moonie—to be indoctrinated, to fund-raise, to recruit new members—required so much time that only a few hours were left for sleep. Working with limited rest was a purifying act of self-sacrifice that proved one's allegiance to Moon. The timetable for achieving his goals was short. In three years' time he had to have thousands of servants "marching the main streets of the capital of each nation." And by 1981, Communism was to be defeated. To keep down individual dissatisfaction about sleep, he whipped up group thinking in his training speeches:

MOON: Would you prefer to sleep seven hours instead of six hours?
CULT: NO!
MOON: Would you prefer to sleep for seven hours or five hours?
CULT: FIVE!
MOON: Would you prefer to sleep five hours or four hours?
CULT: FOUR!
MOON: Would you prefer to go to work without sleeping or sleeping?
CULT: WITHOUT SLEEPING!
MOON: I don't want you to die, so I will let you sleep barely enough to sustain your life. What I'm thinking is that although you get thin like ghosts, with big eyeballs, skinny all over and stooped down like this in walking, stuttering—but if by your doing that, by your being like that, we are successful in God's providence, I would prefer to have you do that.

Commitment was total. Cult members should commit suicide rather than fail in their duty to Master. They were even made to practice wrist-slashing techniques.

And there have been suicides.

April 3, 1975: Bill Daly went down to the railroad tracks near Moon's seminary, took off all his clothes, placed his neck over a track, and was decapitated by an oncoming train. Friends, ex-Moonies, say the cult's constant hammering about guilt had gotten to him.

June 6, 1976: Allen Staggs fell twenty stories down an elevator shaft to his death in the old New Yorker Hotel, which, under Moon's ownership, was renamed the "World Mission Center."

The Moonies said it was an accident. A policeman who investigated the incident was surprised that Staggs's fellow church members acted as if they didn't know him and appeared "annoyed that their schedule was being interrupted by the whole thing"; "they didn't seem to care." The police closed the case without ruling whether the death was an accident or suicide.

August 23, 1976: Kiyomi Ogata, a Japanese Moonie, plunged from the twenty-second floor of the New Yorker.

August 23, 1979: Junette Bayne, again the New Yorker Hotel, from the twenty-first floor. Her estranged husband, not a Moonie, said, "If she wasn't pushed physically, she was pushed psychologically out that window."

Health problems were a nuisance Moon could not be bothered with. If the spirit was strong, the body would follow. If the body was weak, there must be spiritual problems. A girl with a broken ankle was told to pray and drink ginseng tea. She fundraised for three days before getting treatment at a free clinic on her own. Another girl was left with permanently impaired eyesight after an emergency operation for a detached retina. The doctors said she would have been all right had they been able to treat her months earlier when she skipped the appointments her father had made. Listening to lectures on the Divine Principle was more important, cult leaders had said. She almost went blind. A Moonie from Kansas suffered a nervous breakdown. When Chris Edwards finally went to a hospital and was told his infected hand might have to be amputated, he felt ready to welcome the loss as justifiable "indemnity" for his sins.

Across the road from the training center, Moon and his family lived at a $600,000 estate—East Garden. Master had fresh sheets put on his bed every day and his clothes were washed three times before wearing. He told the cult his estate and fine car were necessary in order to show the world something other than the miserable side of life.

With the New Hope Singers, Chris Elkins accompanied Moon on the twenty-one city "Day of Hope" speaking tour during the fall of 1973. The tour began with three nights of lectures at Carnegie Hall in New York City. An advance team of one hundred to two hundred spent two weeks in each city at fund raising, putting up posters announcing Moon's appearance, luring dignitaries to a banquet for Moon, and saturating the local media with press releases. Among Moon's tour trophies were appointments with governors and mayors (always with a Moonie cameraman in tow), keys to cities, and many "Day of Hope" proclamations and telegrams from unsuspecting officials— including New York Mayor John Lindsay, Los Angeles Mayor Tom Bradley, Washington Mayor Walter Washington, Ohio Governor John Gilligan, and Governor Jimmy Carter of Georgia.

CHRIS ELKINS had become an accomplished fund raiser. He had learned to vary his sales pitch. Depending on the kind of person being solicited, he asked for money for drug rehabilitation, a youth center, or a new choir called the New Hope Singers. Connection with Moon or the Unification Church was not revealed. All the money was turned over to church leaders.

Elkins made a good impression on Neil Salonen, the president of the Unification Church in the United States. Salonen also headed the Freedom Leadership Foundation, one of the political arms of the Moon organization, and he thought Elkins was suitable for use in the movement's expanding political activities in Washington. Elkins welcomed the transfer. It would relieve him of what he liked least—fund raising—and involve him in Father's exciting new campaign to save Richard Nixon: Project Watergate. When Nixon's image was rehabilitated with Moon's help, Elkins was told, Nixon would be forever indebted to Moon.

Moon was standing on a mountainside in Korea one day in

November 1973 when he and God agreed it was up to him to rescue Nixon from Watergate. No one else could do it. Moon, in the position of Adam, must help Nixon the archangel. On the lower level of America rather than the universe, Nixon was an Adam, to be supported by his wife in the position of Eve and by the American people in the position of servant archangels. Since the people did not perceive this divine relationship, it was Moon's responsibility to show them. In the 1972 election, God chose Nixon to be President for four years. Since God had not given the people a different message in the meantime, they had no right to impeach him. God's command to America, through Moon, was "Forgive! Love! Unite!"

The day after returning from Korea, Moon began publishing full-page Watergate statements, featuring his picture, in fifty-one major newspapers. It was his first personal political act in the United States. Until that time, Americans had known him only as a vigorous evangelist with an unorthodox theology. Now, he initiated a forty-day prayer and fast period under his newly formed National Prayer and Fast Committee headed by Dan Fefferman (whom he had also designated to be Prime Minister of Israel when the time came). Moonies handed out leaflets, marched to state capital buildings dressed as Americana figures, prayed in public places, and collected 75,000 signatures for Moon's Watergate declaration. The drive was geared for maximum news coverage. Praying on camera was stressed, with "medium prayer" recommended as most effective (although one girl got high marks for being filmed crying as she prayed because she pulled it off with an appearance of sincerity).

Wherever Nixon traveled, a contingent of Moonies was sent to rally for him. Elkins was a point man, making sure the Moonies were up front with pro-Nixon signs so bystanders and spectators would appear to be a crowd of enthusiastic Nixon backers. Father had said they must act to make ten seem like ten thousand. Sometimes it was too much even for Nixon's White House. When Elkins went to Nashville for the President's visit to the Grand Ole Opry, the secret service asked the Moonies to tone it down since it was Pat Nixon's birthday.

They planned a big splash for the 1973 National Christmas Tree Lighting Ceremony. The D.C. Armory was rented for a closed rehearsal to turn the tree lighting into a Nixon support rally. Salonen divided 1,200 people into twelve "tribes" and choreographed them to lunge forward with a "spontaneous" cheer for the President. In a side room at the Armory, six hefty Moonies, dubbed the "Horse Team," were organized for an additional plan, kept secret from the others. On Salonen's cue, the six were to converge on Nixon and hoist him up on their shoulders. The stunt was rehearsed several times with Salonen playing Nixon's part.

A White House aide called the Christmas Tree Lighting "a fiasco." Traditionally, it was a quiet, quasi-religious event. Nixon had no desire to inject Watergate into it, pro or con. It was to be one of those cherished occasions when he could just be President. A choir sang, a minister offered a prayer, and the President read a little statement about Christmas. Just as Nixon—along with a Boy Scout—moved to press the button to light the trees, a large crowd of people tore down the fence and came rushing forward to the edge of the platform cheering and waving banners that read GOD LOVES NIXON! and SUPPORT THE PRESIDENT! News cameras flashed. Nixon hurriedly exited by the rear of the platform. The Horse Team was unable to get to Nixon because he did not leave in the direction Salonen had expected. The Moonies recongregated in Lafayette Square across from the White House, still cheering and waving banners in the bitter cold. Salonen told his flock he had faith the President would appear.

Inside the White House, Nixon was furious over the Moonies' conduct at the tree lighting. On the other hand, he thought, they were a well-organized group supporting him all the way. He would need them in the coming months. He decided to go outside and shake a few hands. When Nixon crossed Pennsylvania Avenue, they rushed him again. The Horse Team—still obsessed with hoisting Nixon—tried to get close enough to grab him, but he was surrounded tightly by secret service men. The "horses" were disappointed that the secret service stood in God's way.

When the President was ready to leave, the Moonies joined hands in two lines across Pennsylvania Avenue to block traffic. One Moonie said, "We stopped the world for him and he passed between us."

Paradoxically, Moon's effort to save the President of the United States was run by Koreans and Japanese. The same was true of all activities of the Moon organization. Salonen was a figurehead and legworker, rarely brought into important policy discussions. The Japanese handled the money and the Koreans made the big strategy decisions. Moon's word was final on any matter, and he involved himself to a surprising degree in details. Above the Americans was a power clique consisting of Bo Hi Pak, David S. C. Kim, Choi Sang Ik, Takeru Kamiyama, and Osami Kuboki. It was in accordance with the Divine Principle. America was only an archangel while Korea was Adam and Japan was Eve.

As nationality dictated one's function in the cult, so did race. Orientals were to make "spiritual" contributions. Whites should put their "analytical" abilities to work. "The talented area of black people is in (the) physical aspect," said Moon, mentioning basketball as an example.

The man behind the scenes in Moon's pro-Nixon drive was Dr. Joseph Kennedy. Kennedy had been hired by the Moon organization as a consultant to help with the "Day of Hope" program in Atlanta. He also had good connections in the White House. Whatever the exchange between Moon and God on that mountain in Korea, it was Kennedy who planted the basic ideas in Bo Hi Pak's head. In Atlanta in early November 1973, he had expressed concern to Pak over Nixon's Watergate problems, mentioning an essay by Lincoln about praying and fasting in times of national crisis.

Splendid, thought Pak. Moon thought so, too. This was what they had been waiting for. Moon could make his American political debut with the hottest issue in the country by giving it a religious slant. Unity of religion and politics was what the Divine Principle was all about. When Lincoln wrote that essay, God had tucked it away so He could bring it out for Moon a hundred years later. Moon and Pak picked up the ball and ran with it.

Dr. Kennedy, pleased with the activity for Nixon, had complied with Pak's request to have the cult admitted at the Christmas tree ceremony. He had also obtained a seat for Moon at the President's National Prayer Breakfast at the Washington Hilton to be held in January 1974. Moon's planned presence drew criticism from Congress and the clergy, so the White House stressed that he would not be sitting at the head table. Moon had to be content merely with attending alone, although he had wanted to bring along an entourage and have hundreds of his followers flood the hotel switchboard during the breakfast with calls to Forgive, Love, and Unite.

Dr. Kennedy was able to set up a meeting between Nixon and Moon the day after the prayer breakfast. The White House handled the matter quietly. The appointment did not appear on the President's published schedule for the day. Moon was ushered into the Oval Office. He shook hands with Nixon, prayed aloud in Korean, then urged the President "not to knuckle under to the pressure." Nixon thanked him for the support and gave him a pair of cuff links and a tie pin. Moon told his followers the meeting was absolute proof that Nixon would survive Watergate.

Why?

"This is the equivalent to the Roman Emperor having invited Jesus and welcomed Jesus in the past."

It was no accident of history. It was a dramatic event of the highest importance, an act of God. And Nixon realized it, said Father. When they bowed their heads and prayed together, Moon was sure Nixon knew there was only one person on earth who could save him: Sun Myung Moon. Nixon and Moon achieved spiritual unification.

From that moment forward "the Unification Church and the White House where Nixon resides can be very close places."

AT THE Freedom Leadership Foundation, life for Chris Elkins was less arduous than before. His days were not as regimented as they had been when he was on the streets or in training. At first he felt uneasy about not having someone keeping a close watch over him. But now he was able to read newspapers and sometimes even watch television. Religious indoctrination continued. Salonen made sure he spent a couple of hours each day studying the Divine Principle in a group. At work he stayed busy with Watergate and foreign affairs on Capitol Hill. The Moonies were doing a lot of lobbying to drum up support for South Vietnam, the Lon Nol government in Cambodia, and, most important, South Korea. Using phony letterheads of ad hoc committees fabricated for the occasion, Elkins worked all night sending letters to Congressmen.

Inside Congress, they were helped by unsuspecting people in the cause of anti-Communism. David Martin of the Senate Internal Security Committee staff furnished names of Senators and Congressmen to be lobbied, obtained the Senate Caucus Room for a Moonie political meeting with the press, and expedited Moon's permanent resident visa. (It was issued by virtue of his wife's permanent visa. Hers had been obtained by Bo Hi Pak's listing her as an employee of the Korean Cultural and Freedom

Foundation.) Congressman Richard Ichord obtained the House Caucus Room for a Moon meeting, and Senator Strom Thurmond continued to help the Moonies on the Hill. When Moon was having trouble getting into the country in 1971, Thurmond had intervened and Moon was admitted.

Congress was a keen concern to both Moon and the Korean government. This was particularly true in 1974 because of Watergate and the $93 million cut in military aid to South Korea resulting from Congressman Fraser's hearings. Moon and the Korean government lobbied intensively, separately but coordinately. As early as 1971, Moon had organized teams called "PR sisters" under Mitsuko Matsuda. She was Japanese, as it should be, since the archangel Americans could return to their original position only though Eve. The duties of the "PR sisters" were to cultivate friendships with members of Congress and staffs, explain the Unification Church and dispel negative attitudes, and urge full support for South Korea. Moon would thus be able to impress the R.O.K. government with his influence in the United States. Later, he issued a call for "many good-looking girls," planning to assign three to each Senator: "One is for the election, one is for the diplomat, and one is for the party. If our girls are superior to the Senators in many ways, then the Senators will just be taken in." (In fact, several Congressmen were entertained in a Washington Hilton hotel suite rented by the cult.) Everything they learned about Senators and Congressmen was to be entered in the cult's confidential file, including details of personal lives.

One such girl was Susan Bergman, a regular morning visitor to Speaker Carl Albert for two years. She prepared ginseng tea for the Speaker and his secretaries when they arrived for work. The Speaker wasn't interested in her talk about religion, but he did find her pleasant and attractive. She liked to impress others with her close relationship with him. Showing a fellow Moonie around the Capitol one day, she picked up a telephone, dialed a number, and said, "Hello, Carl, how are you? I wanted to know if you got my flowers." On another occasion, she got a long-distance call from Albert while she was at Moon's training center in Barrytown.

PRESIDENT PARK CHUNG HEE did not have to ask Moon to take up Nixon's cause, although he favored it. Moon didn't need the encouragement. Like Tongsun Park, he was self-propelling for his own purposes as well as for those of the government. Park Chung Hee viewed him as an asset for Korean influence in the United States. The Moon organization remained a key element in the influence campaign (as intended ever since the original plans were developed at the meetings in the Blue House in 1970).

While the Blue House meetings were still going on, Bo Hi Pak had rushed to Seoul with an appealing project: a letter to be signed by President Park for 60,000 Americans who had contributed to Radio of Free Asia. The mailing served the purposes of both the influence campaign and the Moon organization. In it, the R.O.K. government personally reminded Americans that the Communists were "increasing the hostilities" against South Korea; ROFA was endorsed and the contributors thanked; and Bo Hi Pak was credited by name with having informed the President about the contributors' service to anti-Communism. Without asking for money, the letters generated more contributions.

A few months later, Pak was ready with another project. A public relations man for ROFA, Donald Miller, was writing a biography of President Park. Visiting Seoul with Bo Hi Pak, manuscript in hand, Miller received the President's approval during a personal appointment. The book was never published, but no matter; the Moon organization was making the right impressions on the Blue House.

Like Tongsun Park, Moon had developed extensive contacts on Capitol Hill and was using them to support the Korean government position. Like Tongsun Park, Moon had successful businesses in Korea and the United States, with operations in a number of other countries. Both Moon and Tongsun cleverly cultivated powerful and wealthy Americans. Both were strong supporters of Park Chung Hee, cooperating closely with his senior officials, including the KCIA director. Bo Hi Pak had been the willing conduit for Prime Minister Chung Il Kwon to transfer money into his personal bank account in the United States, and other government officials had been so favored as well.

While Tongsun Park's service was both profitable for Korean officials and helpful with important members of Congress, Moon beamed his activities to a mass audience. The Little Angels were a propaganda bonanza for the government. Moon's anti-Communist campaigns, such as the 1970 conference of the World Anticommunist League and Radio of Free Asia, helped keep the world mindful of the North Korean menace at a time when the United States was more interested in negotiation than confrontation with the Communists. The attraction of American youth to Moon was seen as a welcome offset to the disturbing leftist student activities of the late sixties.

In Korea, Moon was providing anti-Communist indoctrination to government personnel at his training center at Sootaek-ri outside Seoul. Each year the government sent thousands of officials to Moon's school from local, provincial, and national agencies. Moon was permitted to stage large demonstrations in Seoul—pro-government, anti-Communist, and pro-Nixon—in the tightly controlled climate of the Park dictatorship. Industrial components of the Moon organization were awarded lucrative government contracts, including the manufacture of military weapons. KCIA Director Kim Jong Pil's decision in 1962 to utilize Moon's fledgling church had stood the test of time.

For Moon, that was fine as far as it went. But he was bigger than the KCIA and Park Chung Hee, as he often told his cult.

As he saw it, he was organizing and utilizing the R.O.K. government, not the other way around. The government officials indoctrinated at his school would be led to the Divine Principle by way of anti-Communism. Building military hardware under government contract would make the government dependent on him while providing funds for him to expand worldwide. The government was indebted to him for the cultural propaganda he had generated through his Little Angels. If he could save Nixon, his power would overshadow Park Chung Hee, and ruling the Adam country would be only a step away. He could assume his rightful position. He reminded the cult that what he was doing in Project Watergate was far more significant for its impact in Korea than in the United States.

On Capitol Hill, Project Watergate brought some early results. In January 1974, a two-day lobbying blitz for signatures on Moon's Watergate declaration yielded about a hundred Congressmen and some ten Senators. The lobbyists concealed their affiliation with the Unification Church from legislators.

Several months later, anti-impeachment leader Rabbi Korff and Nixon aide Bruce Herschenson appealed for another Moonie display of mass support for Nixon. They valued Moon's help because he could mobilize large numbers of people anywhere on short notice and with good results. Moon was cool to the request. He said no. Korff and Herschenson asked again and again, but Moon kept turning them down. The Lord of the Second Advent wanted homage from the President. Nixon should repent to Moon for his failure of leadership; then Moon would rally the troops. Salonen was caught awkwardly in the middle. He had no decision-making power. All he could do was transmit messages back and forth between the White House and Moon's Korean-Japanese, Adam-Eve hierarchy. Korff and Herschenson offered no possibility of Nixon's kneeling before Moon. Ultimately, Moon decided to hold a three-day fast on the Capitol steps—independent of White House appeals, he insisted.

It was July of 1974. Things were grim for Nixon. It was time for a miracle. If anyone could deliver, Moon said, it was he.

Chris Elkins helped staff the fast on the Capitol steps. Placards and posters were designed; literature was prepared and distributed; a press corps was set up. They hoped to get Nixon to address the fasters in person. Six hundred Moonies were shipped to Washington to do the fasting and praying. That number was chosen so as to have each Moonie pray for one Senator, Congressman, and cabinet member, with Salonen and his wife taking President and Mrs. Nixon. They prayed for releasing God's power to turn the heart of America toward forgiveness for Nixon. Nixon did not appear: he sent a telegram instead. At the end of the third day, Moon came, accompanied by Rabbi Korff. He addressed the fasters, telling them they had completed their mission successfully. It was the only time Chris Elkins ever heard Father bestowing full approval on his followers.

On the day Nixon resigned, a small group of Moonies went to the White House. Bruce Herschenson talked to them at the gate briefly. After the resignation, the members of the Horse Team from the Christmas Tree Lighting felt a heavy burden of guilt. Failure to lift Nixon up on their shoulders, Father had said, had doomed him to decline and fall.

NEIL SALONEN HAD an unusual assignment for Chris Elkins. Around breakfast time on the morning of September 14, 1974, he was told that he and four other Moonies were to throw eggs at the Japanese Embassy. A car would take them there at noon. If possible they were to hit the car carrying the Japanese ambassador to lunch. If the ambassador did not appear within thirty minutes or so, they would pelt the Embassy building and run to a car waiting to take them back to Unification Church headquarters. It was important, Salonen explained, that the timing of the incident coincide with a street demonstration by the Freedom Leadership Foundation (FLF), which was to divert police attention from the area around the Japanese Embassy on Massachusetts Avenue. A large group of Moonies, representing FLF, were to march with placards from Dupont Circle to the White House protesting the Japanese government's position on the assassination of President Park's wife in Seoul the previous month. The assassin was a Korean resident of Japan with pro–North Korean sympathies. A major crisis in Korean-Japanese relations had resulted because the Japanese government refused to take responsibility for the killing as demanded by Korea. President Ford was scheduled to visit Tokyo in November with no plans to go to Seoul. The South Korean government and the Moonies saw Ford's itinerary as an indication that the United States was siding with Japan in the dispute with Korea. The Moonies' anti-Japanese demonstration and egg-throwing were designed to show the support of the American people for Korea's position and convince Ford to visit Seoul.

The eggs were bought. Elkins and his colleagues were ready to go. He had never been told to do anything like this before. But many of the things he did for Father were new. Father worked in new and different ways and there had never been anyone like him before.

About 11:00 A.M. Salonen went into his office to call Moon for the final approval before dispatching the egg team. Fifteen minutes later he reappeared downstairs where they were waiting. Father had learned that President Ford had decided to make a stop in Seoul between Tokyo and Vladivostok, he said. That would show more than enough American support for South Korea, so the egg attack would not be necessary.

What Elkins did not know was that the KCIA had initiated the whole thing. According to U.S. intelligence reports, the KCIA had paid Moon thousands of dollars and used him to stage demonstrations at the United Nations and elsewhere to show American support for the aims of the Korean government. Moon was willing when others were not. In September 1974, KCIA headquarters in Seoul ordered anti-Japanese demonstrations in Washington, New York, Los Angeles, and San Francisco on the occasion of a visit that month by Japanese Prime Minister Kakuei Tanaka. Kim Sang Keun, a KCIA officer in the Korean Embassy, had been unable to find local Korean residents who were willing to demonstrate, so his chief, Kim Yung Hwan, arranged for Moon to stage demonstrations at the White House and the Japanese Embassy. At the last minute, the U.S. government learned of the plans through intelligence sources and objected. Kim Yung Hwan told the Moonies to cancel the operation.

WITH AN EYE ON protecting its tax-exempt status, the Unification Church insisted it never engaged in politics, especially election campaigning and lobbying for legislation. After Chris Elkins spent almost a year lobbying Congress, he was sent to Westchester County, New York, to campaign for Charlie Stephens, who was running for Congress against Richard Ottinger in the fall of 1974. The entire staff of the Freedom Leadership Foundation was mobilized. In order to keep the Washington office running, pairs of persons were rotated in and out of the campaign. Stephens was a close ally of the Moonies, having organized American Youth for a Just Peace with Allen Tate Wood in 1970. While Elkins was busy electioneering for Stephens, the New Hampshire Moonies were fully engaged in Louis Wyman's Senate campaign. Success in these two states was important because with one more state, Moon would be on his way to taking over:

> If we can turn three states of the United States around, or if we can turn seven states of the United States to our side, then the whole United States of America will turn. Let's say there are five hundred sons and daughters like you in each

state. Then we could control the government. You could determine who became Senators and who the Congressmen would be.

He was disappointed that there were only fifty states. With seventy, it would be easier to divide and conquer.

Chris Elkins liked politics, and he was looking forward to a job in Wyman's Senate office. Wyman had promised to give a church member a job if he won the election. Salonen and Dan Fefferman picked Elkins because he had more political experience than the Moonies in Wyman's campaign. The prospect of a congressional staff job was exciting. He would be serving Father and fully enjoying it for a change. Events were holding promise for Father's prophecy that:

> Some day, in the near future, when I walk into the Congressman's or the Senator's offices without notice or appointment, the aides will jump out of their seats, and go to get the Senator. They will get their Senator or Congressman, saying he must see Reverend Moon.

When Wyman lost the election, Elkins was transferred to the Columbia University campus to work in Moon's college front organization, the Collegiate Association for the Research of Principles. Father had said the Communists were stirring up trouble at Columbia.

IT WAS UNFORTUNATE for Joe Tully that Takeru Kamiyama didn't happen to like him. Being on the wrong side of Kamiyama meant trouble for a Moonie. Kamiyama was part of the Korean-Japanese power clique close to Moon. Although Tully held the position of state director of the Unification Church in New York, no one questioned Kamiyama's seniority. Tully was only an archangel.

Kamiyama set up a meeting with Moon to dispose of the problem. It was a kangaroo court. All of the New York leaders were there except Tully. Kamiyama accused him of not being able to unite with church members. Tully was arrogant and individualistic, he explained. The New York leaders gave automatic agreement. No one but Father could dispute Kamiyama. If Tully couldn't unite with members, that meant he couldn't unite with Father.

Moon asked Kamiyama what he proposed to do about it.

"Joe Tully is a good lecturer, so you could send him to Barrytown," suggested Kamiyama.

Moon laughed. "Great! That's what we'll do. We'll give him to Ken Sudo in Barrytown." Everyone joined in Father's hearty laugh over pawning off the state director.

Tully, trying not to show disappointment, was shipped off to the training center. His final humiliation was Moon's choice of a wife for him: a Japanese girl who even Kamiyama thought was "a crazy fanatic." (Moon often warned cult members he might marry them off to someone ugly or unlikely.) Moon needed to marry his foreign cult members to Americans to avoid deportation. The Immigration and Naturalization Service was bearing down on them. Tully's punishment was his "indemnity" for arrogance and individuality: he would pay a price in work and suffering.

Obedient leaders were essential to Moon's totalist system. If leaders had a slave mentality themselves, they would be better slaves to Moon. All the brainwashing notwithstanding, Moon had serious doubts that more than a few hundred of his cultists would really be willing to die for him. He saw America as the land of greatest opportunity for scaling the heights of the power he craved. If he could do it here he could do it anywhere. It would be difficult, though, because Americans had a disturbing tendency to go their own way.

When Moon moved to the United States in 1971 he was appalled by the individuality he saw. During the first months he said he was sorry he had come to America because he found no one prepared to do his work. He thought of relocating in Germany, where people "were trained in totalism," so it would be easier for his mission. He launched a crash program to tighten organization, instill discipline, recruit more members, and raise money. It was successful. Some former members recall that Nazi films on organizing Hitler Youth were shown as examples to Moonie leaders. Nothing was more important than developing a cadre of strong leaders totally subservient to his will.

Steve Hassan was such a leader. He was not only prepared to die for Moon; he felt capable of killing his own father for Moon. Bright, energetic, young, and, most important, idealistic, Hassan was perfect Moonie material. He was drawn into the cult at nineteen while a student at Queens College, having concluded that all college had to offer was memorization by rote. The Unification Church offered an ideology for bettering the world with a clear-cut path straight to eternity. After successfully completing forty days of isolation and indoctrination, Hassan was put to work. He started the Queens College chapter of the Collegiate Association for the Research of Principles, served as assistant director of the Unification Church in Flushing, lectured on the Divine Principle, managed transportation to the Moonie demonstrations in support of South Korea at the United Nations, prayed and fasted for Nixon on the steps of the Capitol, and fund-raised. He had worked loyally and hard, and he became one of Kamiyama's favorites. Kamiyama adored him so much that when Moon moved the national headquarters of the church to Manhattan from Washington, Hassan was placed in a newly formed church unit inside the national headquarters for the purpose of setting an example for Salonen and the others to follow. Kamiyama wanted them to demonstrate "the Japanese standard of sacrifice and devotion."

Hassan experienced feelings of great achievement. His life had a new worthwhile purpose. In less than a year he had come so far, yet he was still so young. And it was recognized by those he had come to respect most.

Hence, he never expected to hear what Kamiyama said to him at a meeting with all the regional commanders assembled: "You are having spiritual problems now. It's better you go out fund raising."

Spiritual problems? What had he done wrong? He lived by the Divine Principle. It was his guide for every thought, word, and deed. All questions left his mind after not more than a split second. As he bowed his head in reverent obedience, his only remaining thought was, "Dear God, not as I will, but as You will."

"It's all right," Kamiyama said. "You don't have to fund raise." He then turned to the regional commanders and stated, "This is your model for sacrifice and devotion."

It was a test like God's test of Abraham's faith when He had ordered him to sacrifice his only son Isaac. Hassan had passed— and he felt joy, not relief. Kamiyama was right. Hassan was a model. The cult had fully conquered his mind.

When Hassan did go out fund raising again several months later, it was a promotion, not indemnity for spiritual problems. He worked in Manhattan, Pennsylvania, and Baltimore as head of a model fund raising team whose proceeds went to special projects picked by Moon exclusively. As always, a special Japanese "team mother" was sent to live with the group, to cook, sew, clean house, and encourage cohesion. Her real purpose was to spy for Kamiyama by writing him detailed reports regularly. Hassan's fund raisers were out hawking flowers or candy from dawn until midnight, or later if quotas were not met. They worked the streets, supermarkets, parking lots, offices, airports, gay bars, straight bars, discotheques, factories, and house-to-house. They identified themselves as whatever seemed likely to elicit cash from a person's pocket. Sometimes a more direct approach was used by crawling along the floor in a bar or restaurant, popping up at a table to pin a flower on a woman's dress, and saying to her escort, "That will be two dollars, please." A surprising number of people paid. If the man became angry and called a waiter, Hassan made a quick dash across the floor to a far corner so he could keep working if not caught and ejected. If thrown out, he tried to slip in again and take up where he left off.

Change was sometimes hard to get once money was in a Moonie's hand. If a Moonie was handed a $10 bill, it could be a $10 contribution even if unintended. Ancestors, acting through the contributor, were paying indemnity.

At the airport, one Moonie got a dollar for pinning a flower on a nun. Discovering the solicitor was a Moonie, the nun's niece returned the flower and demanded the dollar back. There was no refund. The niece had another twenty minutes before her plane departed so she followed the Moonie around the airport, telling people: "Don't buy anything from this girl; she just stole a dollar from a nun!"

Hassan's team took in about $1,000 a day. Twice each week he took the cash to a bank and wired it directly to a Unification Church account at Chemical Bank in New York. He was never told what the money was used for, or how much was raised nationwide. He has since estimated conservatively that on the basis of a thousand Moonies collecting $75 a day per person, the annual gross would be about $28 million. A thousand fund raisers and $75 per day are low base figures, however; $100 was the minimum expected per fund raiser per day, and one-third of the Moonie membership is supposed to be out fund raising all the time.

Money is important to Moon but only as a necessary means for achieving what he wants most: power. The cult's businesses in Korea had made him a millionaire before he began his American mission. Moon enterprises were worth at least $15 million in the early seventies from manufacturing and selling ginseng tea products (Il Hwa Pharmaceutical Company), stone vases (Il Shin Stoneworks), titanium dioxide (Hankook Titanium and Dong Hwa Titanium), lathes, boilers, air rifles, and parts for military weapons (Tong Il Industries). Members of his cult were directed to set up "missions" to sell ginseng tea and stone vases in 120 countries by April 1975. One of his first American companies, Tong Il Enterprises, began marketing his tea and vases in 1973, and later became involved in his tuna fishing businesses. When the first shipments of tea arrived in America, he told his followers he planned "to explore a worldwide market for this heavenly product, along with the worldwide spread of unification principles for mankind."

Il Hwa ginseng tea, made and marketed by Moon, is on sale at most health food stores in the United States.

By 1979, Moon's world business empire included weapons, newspapers, banking, tea, chemicals, candles, vases, folk ballet, candy, fishing, movies, shipbuilding, sound recording, food processing, travel agencies, furs, jewelry, restaurants, and large real estate holdings.

In order to ensure "that the currency will be freely coming back and forth," Moon informed the cult he would establish "an international bank" by pooling the money made from his businesses. An opportunity came within a few months when the Diplomat National Bank was being organized by Charles Kim, a Korean-American businessman in Washington who was not a Moonie. Kim approached a number of Asian-Americans, including Bo Hi Pak, about buying shares in the new bank. It was another godsend. Pak arranged for Kim to meet Moon, who invested $80,000 from a $555,000 time deposit (transferred to a personal checking account at Chase Manhattan). Kamiyama put in $75,000, coming mostly from Moon's time deposit, stated as loans to Kamiyama from the Unification Church. Neil Salonen's $30,000 investment also came from persons in the church. Jhoon

Rhee, the wealthy karate master who turned over all his earnings to the cult in the early sixties, invested $100,000. Bo Hi Pak bought $75,000 of stock for himself, $18,000 for his housekeeper, and $738,000 in the names of thirteen Moonies. He arranged loans for investments of $5,000 each for two of his employees at the Korean Cultural and Freedom Foundation, Judith Lejeune and Gisela Rodriguez, instructing them to make their monthly loan payments by taking money from cash donations to the foundation. Pak even furnished the funds for bank chairman Kim's own investment of $100,000, again from cult money. Moonie money thus bought 53 percent of the bank's total stock, an investment of $1.28 million. The Diplomat National Bank had been organized under a requirement by the U.S. Controller of the Currency that no individual stockholder have an interest in more than 5 percent of the bank's total stock. Also, banking laws prohibit any organization from owning more than 25 percent of the stock in an American bank.

The day after opening for business, the bank approved two loans totaling $250,000 for Bo Hi Pak without a meeting of the loan committee, a violation of the bank's own rules. Two months later, the Controller of the Currency told the bank the loans were "in contravention of the intent of the law." Pak's two loans then had to be considered as one, with the amount reduced so as not to exceed the bank's lending ceiling.

The Moon organization was one of the bank's largest depositors, with over $7 million going into the account of the Unification Church International between December 1975 and March 1977.

Getting into the media business was important to Moon in order "to guide the academic world, including professors, the communications world and then the economic world." He told the cult it was time to start a newspaper with mass appeal. The *News World*, published in New York, began operating in December 1976. Running a deficit of over $200,000 per month, it was supported by $2,700,000 from the Unification Church International account at the Diplomat National Bank. A conscious effort was made to make it appear to be an objective, legitimate newspaper like the *Christian Science Monitor*. Some non-Moonies were included on the staff and actually paid salaries, and the paper printed material from the major wire services. The editorial board, however, consisted almost entirely of cult members and prominent coverage was given to issues of importance to Moon, such as accusing Congressman Fraser of being a Soviet agent and suggesting that the Internal Revenue Service was harassing the Unification Church. The New York newspaper strike in 1978 was seen by the Moonies as an act of God: it shut down the competition in order to bring the Divine Principle into the homes of New Yorkers, many of whom—thanks to Heavenly Deception—did not know at first that the paper was an organ of the Moon cult.

Besides newspapers, Moon's media business included movies. He told the cult in 1974 he was forming a movie company in Japan. He was looking for the right script for a film on the life of Jesus, but was open to other subjects also. He could produce films to serve his unified three-pronged purpose: religious propaganda, political propaganda, and business profit. Mitsuharu Ishii, a Japanese Moonie, became president of One Way Productions with offices in Tokyo and Los Angeles. One Way's main project was to make an anti-Communist war spectacle on General MacArthur's landing at Inchon in the Korean War. Money and actors were to come from Korea, Japan, and the United States.

At Times Square in July 1979, New Yorkers were treated to neon lights advertising the *News World* and a movie being filmed in Korea, *Inchon!*, starring Laurence Olivier, Jacqueline Bisset, Ben Gazzara, David Jansen, and Toshiro Mifune.

Moon's drive to dominate the American fishing industry

was perhaps his most ambitious business undertaking. International Oceanic Enterprises was incorporated in Virginia in November 1976, along with a subsidiary, International Seafood Corporation, located in Norfolk. Bo Hi Pak was president. The company engaged in operating fishing boats and processing and selling seafood products. With the Unification Church International pumping millions into the business, International Seafood was able within a few weeks of its incorporation to disburse monies to other components of the Moon organization, including $200,000 to Tong Il Enterprises, and $400,000 to U.S. Marine Corporation for buying 700 acres of waterfront property in Bayou LeBatre, Alabama. U.S. Marine Corporation was yet another Moonie concern. Its shipbuilding affiliate was appropriately named A-Master Marine. In Richmond, Virginia, housewives could buy fresh seafood at a store named Father's Fish. Moon's fishing and seafood tentacles spread to San Francisco; Gloucester, Massachusetts; and Kodiak, Alaska. He had a built-in competitive advantage—abundant capital flow from church sources and negligible labor costs using cult manpower. He envisioned a food crisis in the future when the world would come begging to him.

Making and selling M-16 rifles made sense both economically and politically. In public, Moon and the cult denied being involved with the M-16, the basic infantry weapon of the South Korean army. Moon conceded to *Newsweek* magazine that Tong Il Industries produced armaments for the Korean government but would not say which weapons, claiming the information was classified by his government. However, information from the U.S. State Department and American and Korean businessmen in the arms field shows that Tong Il Industries makes parts for the Vulcan antiaircraft gun, the M-79 grenade launcher, the M-60 machine gun, and the M-16 rifle. One American businessman was shown the machinery used to make the weapons during a tour of Tong Il's plant near Pusan.

H. P. Stone, vice-president of Colt Industries of Hartford, Connecticut, learned how close the operational ties are between Moon and the Park regime. His experience left the impression that with respect to the M-16 rifle, the Moon organization and the Korean government were one and the same. Colt holds the patent for the M-16 and has a co-production agreement with the R.O.K. government approved by the American government. The agreement allows the R.O.K. Ministry of National Defense to make the rifle in Korea for the R.O.K. army. Stone got a letter from Tong Il Industries in September 1977 asking for approval for Tong Il to produce the M-16 for export. Stone answered in the negative, saying his company did not have authority to approve and he was certain the U.S. government would be against the Koreans' exporting the rifles.

In October, Stone cabled the Ministry of National Defense on another matter. Since the U.S. State Department had approved Korea's request to make another 300,000 M-16s, Stone offered the Ministry a new extended contract. For several weeks there was no reply. Then, to his surprise, an answer came not from the Korean government but from Tong Il Industries. Tong Il said it would send representatives to Hartford in December to discuss the extension of the M-16 production contract. The discussions took place as scheduled, with the president of Tong Il, Moon Sung Kyun (Master's cousin), negotiating for a contract between the R.O.K. government and Colt Industries. When Stone asked if Tong Il was formally representing the Korean government, Moon Sung Kyun smiled and said, "If you ask the Ministry of National Defense, they will say no."

Father has also promised to buy Pan American World Airways and the Ford Motor Company. When the time comes, he intends to buy the Empire State Building to commemorate the restoration of Manhattan Island under him.

The manpower in Moon's business, political, and religious

enterprises has been interchangeable and unified, perfectly reflecting the totalism of his ideology. Just as money flowed freely among the various parts of his empire, so did people, whether leaders or laborers. A sample of the interlocking leadership:

Sun Myung Moon: chairman, International Cultural Foundation; director, International Oceanic Enterprises; chairman, Tong Il Enterprises; investor, Diplomat National Bank; director, One Up Enterprises; founder and chairman, Unification Church International; founder and director, *News World.*

Mrs. Sun Myung Moon: director, Tong Il Enterprises; director, Unification Church International.

Bo Hi Pak: president, Korean Cultural and Freedom Foundation; president, Little Angels; president, International Oceanic Enterprises; president, Unification Church International; director, International Cultural Foundation; investor, Diplomat National Bank; director, One Up Enterprises; president, U.S. Foods Corporation.

Neil Salonen: president, Unification Church of the U.S.A.; secretary general, Freedom Leadership Foundation; director, International Oceanic Enterprises; director, Tong Il Enterprises; investor, Diplomat National Bank; director, International Cultural Foundation; director, One Up Enterprises.

Michael Young Warder: director, Tong Il Enterprises; secretary general, International Conference for the Unity of the Sciences; director, International Oceanic Enterprises; director, Unification Church; director, One Up Enterprises; president and publisher, *News World.*

Takeru Kamiyama: director, New York Unification Church; investor, Diplomat National Bank; director, Tong Il Enterprises; director, International Oceanic Enterprises; director, One Up Enterprises.

Osami Kuboki: president, Japan Unification Church; director, International Cultural Foundation.

Judith Lejeune: secretary, International Oceanic Enterprises; director, Korean Cultural and Freedom Foundation; incorporator, Unification Church International; secretary to Bo Hi Pak; investor, Diplomat National Bank.

Mitsuharu Ishii: president, Toitsu Industries (Japan); president, One Way Productions; officer, International Cultural Foundation; president, *Sekai Nippo (World Daily News)* of Japan; financier for investments in Diplomat National Bank.

R. Michael Runyon: president, One Up Enterprises; president, U.S. Marine Corporation; vice president, International Oceanic Enterprises.

Kim Won Pil: president, Korea Unification Church; director, Unification Church International; director, International Cultural Foundation; president, Il Hwa Pharmaceutical Company (Korea).

Moon himself acknowledges his system as totalist. Oneness pervades, even in nomenclature: Unification Church, One World Crusade, Unified Family, One Up Enterprises, Tong Il ("unification") Enterprises, One Way Productions. To members of the cult, this is perfectly natural. They are reminded every day that there is only one way and that is Father's way. Father had all the answers straight from God and they covered everything.

He has promised to accomplish what the saints and sages have failed to do for six thousand years. In his lifetime, he will bring total heaven to earth at last. Adam had failed. Jesus had failed. Even God had failed.

And when Moon succeeds, God will say: " 'Reverend Moon is far better than me, the Heavenly Father.' "

In dealings with the outside world, however, the cult has denied the unity of Moon's family. The non-Moon world was in the position of Cain. The Family was in the position of Abel. Abel the good must deceive Cain the evil to reverse the sin of original deception and restore perfect goodness. The "petty" laws of the United States were the laws of Cain, so they must not interfere with Father's mission. Heavenly Deception was the way to get around them.

Accordingly, the Unification Church was granted exemption from taxes because the Moonies swore it did not engage in political or business activities. Cain's government could not be permitted to take more than a bare minimum in tax money from the Family. Hundreds of foreign Moonies were imported to work in the Family businesses, entering the United States on short-term visas as "students" or "religious trainees" and then staying for years. Millions of dollars were transferred from tax-exempt church accounts to Family business accounts and vice versa. Money moved freely from country to country. Moonie investigators gained access to the legitimate press corps by posing as journalists. Moonie money from foreign countries bought a controlling interest in an American bank without regard for banking laws and securities regulations. The Moonies lobbied for the South Korean influence campaign in Congress and staged political demonstrations, ordered and reportedly paid for by the KCIA, without registering as agents of the Korean government.

The Family not only denied any wrongdoing, it insisted defiantly that to question any of the cult's activities was an infringement of First Amendment rights to freedom of religion. From that point of view, it made perfect sense. In Moon's totalist system, *everything* can be religion: owning a bank, working for the KCIA, selling weapons of war, brainwashing, destroying families, buying the Empire State Building, taking over the world.

The press, the Fraser Subcommittee, and federal, state, and local investigators began exposing illegal and deceptive activities of the Moon cult in 1976. Salonen and Bo Hi Pak, as the chief spokesmen, were models of Heavenly Deception. Fund raisers in the street would have done well to emulate them: Moon "never received KCIA money, not one red cent"; Moon had nothing to do with running the Unification Church in the United States; the components of the Moon organization were completely independent of one another; the Korean Cultural and Freedom Foundation and the Unification Church had nothing to do with each other; the Little Angels and the Unification Church had the same founder but nothing else in common; the money for the Diplomat National Bank stock came from a long-established "Unification Church Pension Fund International" for family assistance to elderly church members; there was never any plan to throw eggs at the Japanese ambassador; Bo Hi Pak was a private citizen who had nothing to do with the Korean government; listing Moon as "chairman" or "founder" of corporations and having him sign corporate checks were merely symbolic gestures. (Concerning this claim, a New York judge wrote, "Such contentions strain the credulity of this Court.")

In the North Korean prison thirty years earlier, Mrs. Ho had ignored Moon when he told her she would be set free if she denied her revelations from God. She was killed instead. Salonen and Pak would not make the same mistake.

Moon was not cowed by the bad publicity. He welcomed it. It was part of his strategy to shake the world. He needed opponents besieging him from all directions so he could be "a lightning rod." That would be "the quickest strategy to take over the rest of the world." His opponents—the established churches, the Frasers—were striking out at him because they feared him, he said. He saw the negative press as a definite plus. Without it, he would get only an inch or two of coverage now and then; with it, the world knew who the Reverend Moon was.

WITH ALL THE controversy over Moon in the United States, President Park Chung Hee felt it best to give the outward appearance of putting himself at a distance from the New Messiah. Park's own image was at an all-time low in America and was still sinking. Ambassador Hahm issued a statement in Washington saying the R.O.K. government and Moon had nothing to do with each other. It was similar to statements made about relations with Tongsun Park, except for the inclusion of some emphasis on freedom for all religions in Korea.

Moon understood. Both he and the government had to conceal their close working ties in the influence campaign. It came easy to him. Whatever Park Chung Hee and Ambassador Hahm had to do for the sake of appearance, Moon and the government continued to work hand in hand. And he told the cult the Korean government was strongly on his side, "begging for our opinion and actions." The banquet held in his honor in Seoul in 1975 was a good sign, he said. It was attended by a host of dignitaries including Chung Il Kwon, Speaker of the National Assembly and former Prime Minister. Other things, not told to cult members, revealed even closer ties, such as Bo Hi Pak's reported access to the secret telecommunications facilities at the South Korean Embassy.

THOMAS SCHARFF wanted to know what had happened to his son's life. It had been a year since Gary dropped out of Princeton and moved in with the Moonies in Louisville. Increasingly, Gary had become a stranger to his father and mother, especially after three months of indoctrination at Belvedere. He was living in Philadelphia as the Pennsylvania state director of the Unification Church, apparently not at all interested in going back to college. W. Farley Jones, then president of the Unification Church, had assured the elder Scharff that Gary would return to Princeton in the fall. If his son could just get back in school away from the cult's controlled environment, Scharff thought, maybe he would begin to lead his own life again. Scharff wrote to Moon demanding to know what had been done to his son.

Moon couldn't be bothered with parents. Who were they to question the Lord of the Second Advent? He ignored the letter and had it returned unopened. When another letter came, it got the same treatment. Scharff then angrily threatened to "expose

Moon to the world." David S. C. Kim of Moon's inner circle moved to head off a possible problem by talking to Gary.

"What would it take to appease your parents?" Kim asked.

"Oh, they'd be satisfied if I went back to school, even though I've made it clear that's not what I want." Gary had important work to do for Father.

"Well, you had better go, then. They could cause trouble if you don't. But they will burn in Hell for insulting the Messiah."

Gary graduated from Princeton the following spring after writing his senior thesis on the Divine Principle. Every spare moment during the school year was spent with the cult, working at the Philadelphia center, demonstrating for Nixon at the Christmas Tree Lighting, lecturing, and setting up a speaking engagement for Moon at Princeton.

Parents had no right to resist Moon's control over their children. They were only "physical" parents anyhow. Moon and his wife were True Parents, to be revered and obeyed absolutely as Father and Mother. The members of the cult were their children, all brothers and sisters in the Unified Family. There was no question of choice between the Unified Family and the physical family. Moonies had a divine duty to deny parents, brothers, and sisters. Hold fast to Father. Cling to him. If parents try to drag you back to the outside world of Cain, stand against them firmly and say: " 'I'm the son of God before being your son.' "

If they insist you are a member of their family, tell them: " 'I want to be a member of the Unified Family, rather than of this small family.' "

Ties with enemies must be severed and, said Moon, "Your utmost enemy is in your family."

STEVE HASSAN lay helpless on the sofa at his sister's house with his leg in a heavy cast. His father had taken away his crutches. People kept coming in saying terrible things about the Family, and there was no way for him to escape to the nearest Moonie haven. He would still be fund raising in Baltimore if he hadn't fallen asleep at the wheel of a church van and run into a truck after three days with no sleep. Now he was captive to his father's conspiracy to turn him away from Master. He wanted to strangle his father, but decided it wasn't necessary since he was determined to get away somehow soon. He told his parents they were wasting their time with him. He was Kamiyama's model of sacrifice and devotion. This was another test of his faith and he was sure he would pass just as he always had. Father had taught him to withstand the temptations of the Satanic world. The deprogrammers' arguments seemed feeble. They tried to prove faults in the Divine Principle, but he knew Father's teachings better than they. After eight hours of talk the first day, he went to sleep contentedly. This was going to be easy, he thought.

After breakfast the next morning, he was moved to an unfamiliar apartment in Queens because the deprogrammers had learned the Moonies were on their way to rescue him from his sister's house. Disabled with a broken leg, and his family having eluded his brethren, he agreed to stay for a week, no more.

As the harangues continued he was told he had been suckered, manipulated, and used by the cult. Impossible. How could he believe he was exploited by someone he had committed everything to? At first he refused to let himself think about it. Each night he went to bed repeating to himself, "I cannot leave! . . . I cannot leave! . . . I cannot leave! . . ." He remembered a showing of *The Exorcist*, held on Moon's orders, and Moon's stern admonition that the movie was a prophecy of what would happen to those who did not stand firmly with him. But after three or four days Hassan was saying, "I cannot leave! . . . I cannot leave. . . . Why can't I leave?" He was forced to consider the possibility that Moon might not be the Messiah. As he listened to each negative point raised about the cult, worse points entered his mind that he could not counter.

By the fifth day, he had found himself again. He realized the cult had robbed him of all reference points. Having been manipulated to believe Moon's goals were desirable, he had had to believe they were true also. If they were true, then all the degradation and deceit had to be desirable. He felt he had been riding on a slave train that never stopped.

Free from the cult, Steve Hassan began to think for himself again. In the absence of mind control, he was unsure of himself at first and had to rely heavily on his family and friends for help. It took about a year for him to fully regain his former confidence.

Chris Elkins left the cult, too, in a rare instance of voluntary departure after two years as Moon's slave. Gary Scharff also got out, having been rescued by his parents.

THERE WERE OTHERS not so fortunate. Moon's devastation of Wendy Helander and her family still continues after more than five years. She was taken by the cult suddenly during her first semester at the Univerity of New Hampshire, a month after her eighteenth birthday. Spending the 1974 Christmas holidays reluctantly with the family in Guilford, Connecticut, she said she was happy being a member of the Unification Church. But she cried every day. Her parents wanted to know more about the movement that had caused her to drop out of school and move in with other members only a few days after she had been invited on a weekend "camping trip" with them. It was so unlike Wendy. She had always excelled in class and a variety of activities. In high school she had been a cheerleader, played flute in the band, and loved arts and crafts. A fluent speaker of French, she had visited France twice. Her only answer to her parents' questions about the Unification Church was to invite them to a three-day training workshop at Barrytown.

Elton and Carolyn Helander found a strange world at Barrytown. When they arrived, Wendy and about forty others were in a pandemonium of frenzied prayer, shouting over and over out of unison: "Dear Heavenly Father, forgive my sins! You have suffered so much for me; now I will sacrifice everything for you!" In another ritual, a group faced toward Korea with hands in the air and cheered for Master and the Fatherland: "Mansei! Mansei!" When the Helanders felt the urge to get up and leave a training session, the lecturer's eyes locked on theirs and they stayed in their seats. One young man left his seat and attempted to walk out. They were shocked to see him dragged back, yelling and kicking, by five leaders. Later they were to learn that another trainee, Bill Giannastasio, was able to escape from a weekend workshop only by jumping out of a second-floor window.

The lecturer for the weekend was one of the cult's best, Gary Scharff. Skillfully weaving Moon's convoluted logic, he emphasized points by gliding his open hands outward, repeating, "This is true. . . . This is true. . . . This is true . . . ," softening each repetition until the last was a whisper. He was like a hypnotist.

The Helanders were the only parents among the seventy-two trainees that weekend. On the one occasion when they were allowed to have a meal with Wendy, Gary Scharff was there to chaperon. She was happy, she said, and would stay.

Elton and Carolyn Helander were horrified by everything about the cult. The inexorable "love" bombardment was overbearing and phony. There was no such thing as free will at Barrytown.

The cult had taken control of Wendy's mind. The Helanders were determined to give her the chance to make choices for herself again. An opportunity came when they heard about deprogrammer Ted Patrick a few days later. The following Sunday, Wendy was allowed to spend the day with her parents. She remained with them and was then "deprogrammed." She seemed happy to be free after two months of enslavement. Her sense of humor began to return, and she busied herself redecorating her room. But the cult would not leave the family alone. Wendy's sister Holly was frightened by a Moonie who entered her college apartment, set his suitcase inside the door, and threatened to spend the night unless she put him in contact with Wendy. Vans were seen cruising slowly past the Helanders' house. Moonies wrote letters and came to the door. They appeared in town fund raising on the chance of meeting Wendy to intimidate her with the warning that she would die within a year unless she returned to the cult. Wendy was worried about her own vulnerability, so she made a sworn statement. It requested "immediate action by the authorities to come and physically remove me from the cult" if she were retaken because "regardless of what I may say or do, I will not be acting of my own free will."

Wendy went out to do some shopping one afternoon, saying she would be back in a few minutes. That evening her brother found the family car abandoned on the Connecticut Turnpike. The cult had enticed her back after only a month.

The FBI reported she was in Washington. With the authority granted by Wendy's affidavit, the Helanders expected no serious problem in freeing her. They were wrong. She did not appear in court when ordered by a writ of habeas corpus. Instead, Moonie lawyers played a tape of Wendy's voice: speaking in a monotone, she said she was acting on her own free will and wanted to stay in the Unification Church. The judge dismissed the case on September 23, 1975, for lack of evidence. The cult touted the decision as legal proof that there was no brainwashing. For Wendy and her family, the nightmare continued.

The family heard nothing from Wendy for weeks. Then in November she invited them for a visit to Barrytown. Her parents managed to walk alone with her to the edge of Moon's vast estate. There they were met by their two sons with a car in which to rescue her.

For the next three months the entire family lived away from the house in Guilford. The harassment had been so heavy before that they feared for their own safety this time. Elton Helander and son Joel moved in with a relative. Forrest, Wendy's younger brother in high school, lived with a neighbor. Carolyn Helander and Wendy moved around through seven states trying to elude the cult's searchers. In the meantime, the neighborhood in Guilford was again harassed. Vans cruised regularly and neighbors got phone calls asking probing questions about the Helanders. When some Moonies were apprehended by police in Warwick, Rhode Island, for prowling around the house of another ex-member, they were found to be carrying photographs of Wendy and her parents, a Japanese wooden sword, a can of Mace, and a Bible containing a devil mask used to frighten defectors into returning. The same van had been seen in the Helanders' neighborhood a few hours earlier.

After three months the Helanders received a summons to appear in court. Wendy was the plaintiff in a suit charging them with false imprisonment. She knew nothing about it but recalled having signed something at one time or another; she now realized it had probably been power of attorney for the cult.

Numerous ex-Moonies had been helping to rehabilitate Wendy. It was therefore not unusual when Richard Conrad visited the home where she was staying in Ohio in February 1976. He seemed such a nice young man, so Mrs. Helander did not object to his suggestion that he could help best by talking to Wendy alone. He reported good progress and after three days took Wendy out for a walk. They never returned.

Six days later Michael Runyon, an official of the Moon organization, proudly announced to the press that "a young man from the Unification Church pretended to undergo the deprogramming, and after gaining the confidence of the deprogrammers, brought about the escape." Now that the cult had her back, the false imprisonment suit against her parents was dropped.

For ten months the Helanders tried in vain to contact Wendy. In September they journeyed to Washington, hoping to see her at the big "God Bless America" rally Moon was mounting.

They plied through the mass of Moonies with no sign of their daughter. Then they caught sight of Richard Conrad among uniformed cult members in white jumpsuits emblazoned with Moon's emblem.

"What happened on the short walk?" asked Carolyn Helander, controlling her anxiety.

"It was extended," Conrad replied casually.

"How could you do such a thing?" cried Wendy's mother.

Conrad pointed skyward and smiled. "Only one person knows." He turned to walk away.

"Don't back off!" exclaimed Mr. Helander. "Where's Wendy? How is she?"

"I don't know." Conrad shrugged and walked away to tend to Master's work.

Former Moonies had reported that Wendy was in poor condition emotionally and physically. Because of her parents' previous efforts to get her out of the cult, she was being kept from sight, held like a prisoner. The Helanders were contacted by a stranger who told them Wendy wanted to escape but was afraid to try. They went to New York to meet her at a hotel where she was to have been brought by someone in the cult supposedly concerned about her. She did not appear.

In May 1977, Wendy Helander filed a $9 million lawsuit against her parents and the deprogrammers for kidnapping and forcibly violating her right to freedom of religion. Her parents countersued the cult for abducting their daughter. The suits were dropped in September 1978 by mutual agreement. Wendy agreed to restore close relations with her family; her parents agreed not to interfere with their daughter's "religion."

The Helanders have had no personal contact with Wendy since February 1976 when she was enticed back to the cult by Richard Conrad. She and her parents have seen each other in courtrooms, where she appeared sad and frightened, her chin quivering, seated between the cult's lawyers, Richard Ben-Veniste and Jeremiah Gutman. She seemed a robot in her movements and statements. The Helanders well remember, in the courtroom, the lawyers coaching Wendy constantly and even insisting successfully that a United States marshal be positioned, as Gutman said, "so the parents will not kidnap her again."

The Moon cult has controlled Wendy from the age of eighteen well into her twenty-fourth year. She has become a national cause célèbre in the cult's drive to use freedom of religion to serve Moon's megalomania. The Moonies have paraded her out as a "show" witness at hearings in state legislatures, flanked on either side by her leaders, where she mouths the cult's position in a lifeless tone that seems alien to the person she used to be. Having performed her public function, she is then returned to isolation from non-Moonies. Neil Salonen, Unification Church president, explained the purpose for using her: "The Wendy Helander lawsuit is designed to set a legal precedent against deprogramming."

Normal life has become an illusion for the Helanders. Carefree relaxation at home is a thing of the distant past. In terms of money alone they have been hit with more than $60,000 in legal bills. With the cooperation of their church, a group of friends started "The Wendy Fund" to help pay. Far worse than the financial drain are the feelings of anguish and frustration. If money could save their daughter, Elton and Carolyn Helander say, they would be willing to give up their house. Although they know money can never restore the free will of Wendy's former self, they do not know what can.

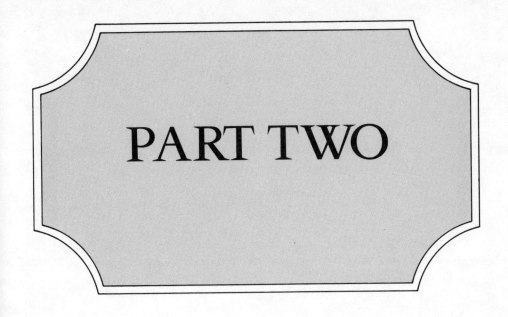

PART TWO

7

Washington Looks the Other Way

FROM SEOUL in the fall of 1970 it was clear to Ambassador William Porter that the Koreans, having failed to get Nixon to change his mind about withdrawing troops, were taking their case to Congress. They were bringing friendly Congressmen to town and organizing press conferences to show American support for Park Chung Hee. With the Korean presidential election coming up, Park had to convince the people he still had a special relationship with the United States despite the troop reduction. When the Congressmen returned to Washington, they were urged by the Koreans to put statements in the *Congressional Record* praising President Park, supporting more military aid for Korea, and opposing further troop withdrawals.

No one worked harder at it than Tongsun Park. Porter saw him lavishing favors on Congressmen, showing up whenever a delegation from Capitol Hill came to town. Tongsun was often seen with high Korean government officials. Since free movement with dignitaries was not possible without very special connections, Porter felt sure Tongsun had an assignment from the KCIA to concentrate on the American Congress. Wherever there were Congressmen, there was Tongsun, getting into the act and upstaging the American Embassy. Porter decided to say something to Prime Minister Chung Il Kwon. He would take a cautious approach without mentioning Tongsun or the KCIA by name. This was important because Tongsun was close to the Prime Minister. Chung, having been an ambassador himself, understood diplomatic language and would get the message.

Porter made an appointment for October 16. He told Chung there was a lot of "amateur" lobbying going on in Washington outside the regular contacts made by Korean Embassy officials. Such lobbying was not helpful, and the Korean government would be better off relying on the "residual good will" of Americans toward Korea instead.

Chung Il Kwon said he felt great appreciation for the good will of Americans toward his country.

To strengthen his message, Porter told Chung he had learned that the State Department's legal office was preparing a diplomatic note for foreign embassies in Washington urging that their lobbying activities stay within acceptable bounds.

Chung was disturbed to hear that the State Department was taking it so seriously. He burst through the diplomatic silkscreen and asked, "Is it Tongsun Park's activities you are concerned about?"

Porter remained the polished ambassador. "Basically, the people involved in such activity outside of the people in the Korean Embassy are amateurs and are harming the Republic of Korea's cause. Tongsun Park might be one of the offenders," he suggested, "among others."

No noticeable change followed this meeting. Three weeks later, Porter went to see Chung Il Kwon again. This time he was more specific about troublesome lobbying. He urged Chung to "try to restrain the lobbying of those Koreans who, rightly or wrongly, claimed to represent the Korean government"—particularly at that time, when Congress was considering $150 million in additional military aid for Korea. Porter wanted to make it clear that Tongsun Park wasn't the only problem. He told Chung that the U.S. government was also concerned about "irregularities" within Radio of Free Asia and its parent organization, the Korean Cultural and Freedom Foundation—in particular, their fund-raising activities. If the newspapers found out about it, they would probably play it up, which would embarrass President Park, since he had sent letters to sixty thousand Americans on behalf of ROFA just a month before.

Chung was reassuring. "The President does not wish to be involved in anything irregular. Please make it clear to anyone interested that President Park's motives for supporting the project are well-intentioned." Chung said he was certain President Park would not allow his name to be used for letters soliciting funds for ROFA in the future.

Things got worse when a group of Congressmen visited Seoul with Tongsun during the first week of January. Congressman William Broomfield informed Porter that he had turned down an offer of $1,000 from Tongsun Park. Broomfield said other Congressmen also got offers of money, but none of them said anything to Porter about it. Porter now viewed Tongsun Park as a menace, not just an annoying buffoon. The cash gifts could cause a scandal that would jeopardize all the efforts to get congressional approval for the big increase in military aid Nixon had promised the Koreans. He cabled the State Department. He and Ambassador Brown at the Department agreed Tongsun must somehow be withdrawn from the United States. Since they were sure Tongsun was under Korean government control, it was decided Porter should seek a remedy through the Prime Minister. It would be undiplomatic to tell Chung about the bribe offers. Instead, he would say the problem of Tongsun Park had reached serious dimensions and try to determine the best way to have Tongsun "recalled."

Chung Il Kwon did not disagree in principle. Certainly, he said, the government didn't want anyone at large who would put Korea in a bad light. But it was hard for him to believe that Tongsun was the culprit. "American Congressmen tell me when they visit here that Tongsun Park is very effective." He promised to take up the matter personally with President Park, however.

What Porter did not know was that Chung Il Kwon was getting kickbacks from Tongsun's rice commissions himself.

Tongsun was not "recalled" to Korea. He continued to shuttle back and forth between Washington and Seoul.

As the ambassador in Seoul, Porter never thought he should be the one responsible for curtailing lobbying in Washington. It was all happening in Washington, so that seemed the place to do something about it. Complaining to Chung Il Kwon was no substitute for calling in Ambassador Kim Dong Jo to the State Department for a stiff reproach by the Undersecretary of State. Yet it was left largely to Porter.

The Koreans, hearing nothing from the top echelon of the State Department, paid no attention to the American ambassador. From his own vantage point, Porter sensed an attitude of permissiveness toward the Korean influence campaign: Washington knew what was going on but apparently was letting it pass. The State Department thought about warning all embassies about improper lobbying, but never did it. Porter assumed the permissiveness was due to a lack of desire to make things difficult for an ally who was doing so much to help in Vietnam. There was nothing more he could do about it in Seoul, and he would be completing his tour as ambassador to Korea soon.

JULY 16, 1971: The courier from the FBI handed the sealed envelope to Laura Simcus in the office of the President's Assistant for National Security in the White House. It was from J. Edgar Hoover and marked "Top Secret Eyes Only" for her boss, Henry Kissinger. She placed it on his desk with other envelopes similarly marked. Kissinger opened it when he returned later that day. The secret memo was about Congressman Cornelius Gallagher. U.S. intelligence had learned that Gallagher had been paid by Kim Kwang, a KCIA operative on his staff, for conducting hearings favorable to Korea in Gallagher's Subcommittee on Asian and Pacific Affairs, and that Kim Kwang had passed classified information from the subcommittee to the Korean Embassy.

Kissinger would later assert that he never paid much attention to Hoover's Top Secret Eyes Only letters. It seemed the FBI director was always sending them over to show he was doing his job. Hoover should handle it himself if he thought it was so important. Kissinger had no time to worry about Gallagher, the KCIA, or Korea. He concentrated on the big issues: the Vietnam War, the Soviet Union, and China. He had just returned from the historic secret mission to China that resulted in Mao Tse Tung's invitation to President Nixon to visit Peking. He and Nixon looked at the big picture, not the little snapshots. Other matters were relegated to the State Department, and he assumed his staff would maintain the necessary contacts with State.

The National Security Council (NSC) staff could have served to ensure that Nixon and Kissinger paid attention to a wider range of subjects, but that was not the way Kissinger operated. It became his private staff, confined to the same few issues he was occupied with. Even that would not have been a problem if the State Department were functioning normally; however, Kissinger had enfeebled State to its weakest point since World War II. Kissinger and Nixon made the decisions that guided foreign relations. Secretary of State William Rogers was reduced to running an international messenger and reference service. Among Kissinger's most successful power devices were the National Security Study Memoranda, called NSSMs, whereby he would keep State busy coordinating studies on various world

questions. When a study was completed after several months, he
would object to certain points and send it back to State for weeks
or months of revising. NSC staff members followed both his priorities and style. They stayed busy keeping him well informed on
his big issues and assumed the State Department would take care
of the rest. The result was reduced attention to such matters as
the developing countries, relations with Japan and Western Europe, Africa, and the United Nations.

To the extent that Kissinger thought about Korea at all, it
had to do with Korean forces in the Vietnam War and the withdrawal of twenty thousand American troops from Korea under
the Nixon Doctrine. He considered it important to hold the line
against North Korean aggression, but that was a matter being
well taken care of without his attention. In Kissinger's world of
big-power politics, South Korea's chief importance was as an
anti-Communist buffer for the security of Japan. His only previous awareness of Korean lobbying had been from a conversation
with Secretary of Defense Laird. Laird had told him the Koreans
were getting to be a problem in Washington because they were
pressuring Congress to reverse the President's decision to reduce
troops. Laird intended to complain to the State Department
about it and Kissinger said to go ahead. Kissinger thought the
Koreans' approach was clumsy but he had sympathy for their
concern that China and North Korea could view troop reduction
as a retreat by the United States from Korea and Asia.

Kissinger returned Hoover's memo to him and moved on to
the big issues in his in box. As other "eyes only" letters from
Hoover were delivered, he was too busy to read them. On September 30, Hoover reported that two congressional staff aides
were connected with the KCIA: Suzi Park Thomson in Speaker
Carl Albert's office and Kim Kwang of Gallagher's staff. On November 24, a letter said Tongsun Park had made payments to
Congressman Hanna with money from rice deals; that Tongsun

Park was controlled by the KCIA; that the R.O.K. government had spent large amounts of money to control American and Korean journalists in the United States; and that the Blue House had been involved in contributing several hundred thousand dollars to the Democratic party (which later Koreagate investigations were unable to verify). On February 3, 1972, Hoover reported that Congressman Gallagher had asked President Park to contribute to his election campaign and recommended that Tongsun Park be appointed both as head of the influence campaign and as chief agent for American rice sales to Korea. Each of Hoover's letters referred to the information in the previous letters.

Intelligence agencies had been sending Kissinger's office detailed reports ever since Park Chung Hee approved the plans for a concerted influence campaign in the fall of 1970. Kissinger claimed none were brought to his attention. They were ignored by his staff as well. If an intelligence report were really important, he felt, the director of the CIA should deliver it to him personally.

Normally the FBI did not make special efforts to monitor the activities of intelligence agents from friendly countries like Korea. The KCIA did not pose a threat on the order of the KGB, the Soviet intelligence service. But the Gallagher case was different in that it appeared a Congressman was being paid for espionage by the KCIA. FBI officers William Sullivan and W. B. Soyars considered tapping Gallagher's phone. They reviewed the criteria for authorizing a national security intercept. The Attorney General was vested with power from the President to authorize an intercept "to protect the nation against attack, to obtain foreign intelligence information, to protect national security information, to protect against the overthrow of the Government, and any other clear danger to the structure of the Government." The Gallagher case seemed to qualify under two of those conditions: to protect national security information and to obtain foreign intelligence information. The day before Hoover's July 16 letter to Kissinger, Sullivan and Soyars sent Hoover a note asking how to proceed with the phone tapping if Attorney General John Mitchell or Assistant Attorney General Robert Mardian authorized it. Hoover agreed with the proposal for an intercept and wrote at the bottom of the note: "Yes, but I will do so only on request of Attorney General, not Mardian."

All of Hoover's Top Secret Eyes Only letters were sent to Mitchell as well as Kissinger. Mitchell made no moves against Gallagher's Korean activities because he knew Gallagher was already being investigated for income tax evasion. Since an indictment appeared likely, he decided not to merge the two issues.

For some unknown reason, Mitchell apparently never saw Hoover's November and February letters. He regretted it years later when he heard about them: he and Nixon would have loved to have known about the alleged Blue House contribution of several hundred thousand dollars to Hubert Humphrey's 1968 campaign for President.

Mitchell did read Hoover's letter of September 30 and decided to warn Speaker Albert about Suzi Park Thomson. On October 14, he paid a brief visit to Albert at the Capitol. Suzi Park Thomson had been identified as working with the KCIA, he reported.

Albert was surprised. He described Suzi as a nice girl, an American citizen with a good education. Did Mitchell think she should be fired?

If she were handling sensitive material it might be best to let her go, Mitchell replied.

"Well, there's nothing sensitive about Suzi's job," Albert assured him. "She just does routine clerical and administrative work. I'll check to make sure she doesn't handle anything that could be compromising." Mitchell departed and Suzi remained in the Speaker's office for five more years. Albert ran a standard FBI background check on her and nothing negative turned up.

FOR ALMOST five years, the State Department had been concerned about Radio of Free Asia, run by Bo Hi Pak and Moon. Undersecretary of State U. Alexis Johnson outlined the problem to Mitchell during a break at a National Security Council meeting at the White House in the spring of 1971. Johnson said ROFA was soliciting hundreds of thousands of dollars in the United States by mailing letterheads featuring the names of prominent Americans, many of whom did not even know their names were being used. The money was supposed to pay for anti-Communist broadcasts to North Korea and China, but ROFA was using R.O.K. government broadcast facilities free of charge with KCIA control over program content. The U.S. government was unable to determine what the money was actually being used for. Johnson was worried about a scandal bringing disrepute to prominent Americans. President Park apparently also was involved. Mitchell asked Johnson to give him the details in writing so he could evaluate the problem and make recommendations.

Johnson responded with memos and letters requesting an investigation. Mitchell assigned the responsibility to Assistant Attorney General Mardian. Justice received information from State describing ROFA as a creature of the Korean government and suggesting criminal activity under several laws. Mardian thought State was overreacting to "a thorn in the flesh and a potential source of embarassment." He confined the investigation to a possible violation of the Foreign Agents Registration Act, which was little more than a recordkeeping requirement low on the priority ladder at the Justice Department. All Justice and the FBI did was to interview Bo Hi Pak and close the case by concluding there was not enough evidence to establish that ROFA was an agent of the Korean government.

Bo Hi Pak assured the FBI agents that everything about ROFA was strictly legal and proper. He persuaded them not to interview Ambassador Yang because he was very old and not well. Before being interviewed by the FBI, Pak had become nervous over signs that the State Department was trying to discourage Congressmen from connections with ROFA. He decided to hire a lawyer to come up with legal grounds to prevent State from getting in his way. Robert Amory, a Washington attorney formerly with the CIA, was retained. Amory learned from a CIA friend that there was circumstancial evidence of a close relationship between ROFA and the Korean government. Amory then called on Ambassador Brown at the State Department. Brown, an old friend, advised him to have nothing to do with ROFA or the KCFF, its parent organization, because they were being investigated for illegal ties with a foreign government.

Deputy Attorney General Richard Kleindienst had been Amory's student at Harvard. In April 1972 he asked Kleindienst to expedite the investigation and suggested it was unfair not to inform ROFA why it was being investigated. Though Kleindienst had closed the case the previous month, three or four months passed before he notified Amory. Amory wrote Bo Hi Pak in August that he had been "confidentially informed at the highest level" that no further action would be taken. Pak and Moon were greatly relieved. Their operation was safe.

Pak would later proclaim that he and ROFA, having "survived the worst test" under this "most comprehensive investigation," had been "proven innocent."

IN MARCH OF 1972, Tongsun's trophy after more than a year of persistent politicking with Congressmen and the KCIA was a highly prized letter from the Korean government. Ahn Kwang Suk of the R.O.K Office of Supply notified American rice exporters that "Mr. Tongsun Park has once again, as in the past, agreed to serve as an intermediary." The letter went on to say Tongsun's service would be required for all rice business with Korea. It meant that Americans could not sell rice to Korea without paying an agent's commission to Tongsun Park.

The U.S. Department of Agriculture took one look at the letter and informed the rice sellers that the government would not finance any sales involving Tongsun Park. Agriculture explained that the Korean government itself had, in effect, disqualified Tongsun, since a bona fide sales agent representing the seller could not be someone forced on the seller by the buyer, in this case a foreign government. This was a blow to Tongsun. It could cut him and the Korean influence campaign out of the expected rake-off, since the bulk of rice sales at that time was under the Food for Peace program, which was financed by the U.S. government. After consulting with KCIA Director Lee Hu Rak, he informed the Agriculture Department he was withdrawing as sales agent. The Korean government then offered, though did not require, a company named Dai Han Nong San as selling agent. There was no objection from the Americans. The sales were transacted and commissions were paid to Dai Han Nong San at its Washington bank account, which had been opened by Tongsun so he could get the money as planned for Congressmen, Korean politicans, and himself.

Agriculture Department investigators had no idea that Tongsun Park ended up getting the commissions. It was not due to their not trying to find out more about him. When Tongsun first became the rice-selling agent, they had run name checks on him. The agencies queried were the FBI, the CIA, the Office of Naval Intelligence, army intelligence, and air force intelligence. The only information turned up was from the CIA, which reported a Tongsun Park being connected with the George Town Club but, inexplicably, nothing else. Unknown to Agriculture at that time, there was another file in one of the intelligence agencies

containing a report that said Tongsun was under KCIA control
and had acquired the rice agency by having Prime Minister
Chung Il Kwon make the arrangements with Kim Hyung Wook,
the KCIA director.

In 1972, before and after Tongsun formally withdrew as rice
agent, the Agriculture Department again investigated him because of persistent rumors that he was working for the Korean
government. Investigator George Blake wanted to get access to
his income tax records but found that he avoided having to pay
taxes by spending only six months a year in the United States.
Tongsun refused to show Blake any of his own records, and the
Agriculture Department had no authority to subpoena. Amaz-
ingly, another name check by the intelligence agencies yielded
nothing negative.

An unfortunate irony of Washington bureaucracy is that
even when information is abundant, the offices in need of it
sometimes get left out. Such was George Blake's lot. Having received nothing to support the rumors about the rice trade, he
closed Agriculture's second probe in January 1974. Yet by that
time, the FBI, the Department of Justice, and the intelligence
agencies had information reporting that the KCIA controlled the
rice trade and used it to raise operating funds; that the KCIA
controlled Tongsun Park; that Prime Minister Chung had shared
in Tongsun's take from the rice commissions; that the KCIA had
received correspondence concerning rice sales from Congressmen
Gallagher and Hanna and Louisiana Governor Edwards; that
Congressmen Gallagher and Hanna had received payments from
Tongsun Park from money made in the rice deals; and that Congressman Gallagher had urged President Park to put Tongsun
Park in charge of both the rice sales and the influence campaign
in the United States.

Much of the information in 1971 and 1972 had made it as
far as Henry Kissinger and John Mitchell, with no effect. The
rest was found in intelligence files by the Koreagate investiga-

tions in 1977. It had been lying there all those years. No one ever paid any attention.

"UNLIKE OTHER PRESIDENTS, I do not intend to interfere in the internal affairs of your country." Richard Nixon was giving Prime Minister Kim Jong Pil the signal he wanted: a green light for Park Chung Hee to go ahead with his dictatorial new Yushin system.

Kim was in the United States to represent Korea at the memorial service for President Truman. One week earlier, he had been at Park Chung Hee's hastily scheduled fourth inauguration on December 27, 1972, midway through Park's third four-year term. Park had been careful to use the outward forms of democracy to put an end to what was left of democracy in Korea: drafting a new constitution, getting it approved through a national referendum, getting himself elected under the new constitution, and electing a new National Assembly. That way the rest of the world would have less to complain about. And Nixon wasn't complaining.

To Park, Nixon was a big improvement over John Kennedy. He had had to give in to Kennedy because neither he nor Korea was strong enough then to do otherwise. For ten years he had been plagued by the institutions of democracy the Americans insisted on. The way the United States and the other rich countries ran things was not the way he wanted to run Korea. If he practiced their form of democracy, he could not be certain of remaining President as long as he wished. He not only thought he was the only man capable of holding the nation together against the threat from North Korea; he also feared he could not stay alive unless he remained President.

Through the years, the threat from the North was Park's ready explanation for tightening his control over the people, whether he was arresting political opponents, closing universities, or declaring a state of national emergency. In 1972, however, he faced a unique situation. For the first time, North and South Korea were negotiating for the peaceful reunification of Korea. The two governments issued a joint communiqué on July 4 promising to work together toward reunification and agreeing not to defame each other or undertake armed provocations. A special South-North Coordinating Committee was set up. A wave of hope spread across South Korea, and Park Chung Hee rode a crest of popularity.

The communiqué had been partly the result of KCIA Director Lee Hu Rak's secret trip to Pyongyang to meet Kim Il Sung. The iron discipline of Kim's dictatorship made a deep impression on Lee. He returned to Seoul distressed because the people in the South were not paying Park as much respect as the North Koreans accorded Kim Il Sung. This must be corrected, he said. Unless the South were as tightly controlled as the North, he told the President, Kim Il Sung would have a decided advantage over Park in the process of reunification.

The promises of the July 4 communiqué came to naught. The North-South dialogue stalemated and eventually talks were broken off. But Park Chung Hee heeded Lee Hu Rak's advice. During a cabinet meeting only three days after the communiqué, he warned against "excessive optimism, hasty judgment, and excitement" caused by the contacts with the North. He called for greater efforts to keep Communist ideology from infiltrating South Korean society. On September 2, he followed with a policy statement to the National Assembly that stressed the need to reorganize the nation's internal system to deal with competition from the North. In the same statement, he introduced a new rationale: tightening the reins was necessary also to "eliminate the side effects" of South Korea's extraordinary economic growth, meaning that expectations for individual liberty were getting too high. Ironically, more dictatorship was to be the South Korean people's reward for what they thought had been political as well as economic progress.

On October 17, President Park announced his Yushin (revitalizing) Reforms. He imposed martial law, dissolved the National Assembly, and forbade political activity except for persons selected to propagandize for the Yushin Reforms. He scheduled a national referendum on a new draft constitution and declared that if it was not approved "we will be permanently dropped out of the future progress of world history." According to the government's election records of the referendum on November 21, 91.9 percent of all eligible persons voted, and 91.5 percent voted to approve Yushin.

The day Yushin went into force, December 27, 1972, a parallel event was taking place in North Korea. A new constitution was adopted there by the Supreme People's Assembly, elevating Kim Il Sung's title from "Premier" to "President."

The Yushin constitution gave Park Chung Hee unlimited power. There is no direct election of the President, nor any limit on the number of terms he can serve. Park wanted to make sure there were no more challenges from strong opponents like Kim Dae Jung in the 1971 election. The constitutionality of laws is determined by a presidential committee rather than the Supreme Court. The President appoints one-third of the members of the National Assembly and he can dissolve the Assembly whenever he wishes. The Assembly can meet no more than 150 days per year because, the government said, in the past the Prime Minister and cabinet ministers "were deprived of valuable time needed to perform their official duties by being kept at the National Assembly to answer repetitious questions." The President's most sweeping power comes from Article 53: he can issue emergency decrees on any subject whenever, in his judgment, there is threat of a national crisis. Park proudly labeled his new system "Korean-style democracy."

President Park did not hesitate to use his power to issue emergency decrees. Religious leaders, including Catholic Bishop Tji Hak Soon, were imprisoned for criticizing the government.

The famous poet Kim Chi Ha was first sentenced to death, then resentenced to life in prison. In 1978, his sentence was commuted to 20 years. Hundreds of student protesters were jailed in 1974 under a decree authorizing the death penalty for missing classes. The students were not executed, but on April 9, 1975, eight men were hanged for allegedly belonging to a "People's Revolutionary party." Similar charges against the eight had been dropped ten years earlier when three of the four prosecutors assigned to the case resigned because they refused to be involved in a groundless case.

Although Nixon promised not to interfere with Yushin, a State Department spokesman during a press conference made it clear that the U.S. government did not think Park's new system was warranted in view of South Korea's economic strength, support from allies, and already stable government. Outside the Nixon administration, reactions were stronger. American newspapers and prominent scholars were very critical, as were some members of Congress. Opposition to Yushin was notably outspoken in the Korean community in the United States. Korean-Americans issued declarations, staged protest demonstrations, and organized groups such as the Korean Congress for Democracy and Unification.

Park Chung Hee was extremely sensitive to the criticism in the United States. An unfavorable image there could endanger the support he needed from the mighty ally. Prior to Yushin, Park's influence campaign had been geared to convincing Congress to approve military aid and oppose further troop reductions. Now he had to add an entire new dimension to the campaign: convincing Americans that Yushin was justified. Since the media, intellectuals, and the Korean community were causing new trouble, more attention to those sectors was needed. The KCIA was assigned to take charge of the new task. Park's advisers assured him that although the Korean lobby in the United States was still in good shape, more manpower would be used to maintain a favorable image for him. Tongsun Park and the Moon organization were to continue with their ongoing projects.

By the end of 1972, a major propaganda drive was under way in the United States. A group of Korean-Americans were brought to Seoul in December and instructed to work to improve Park's image. Some were told to prevent antigovernment Koreans from organizing. One ran a Korean-language newspaper supported with KCIA money. Another got funds for radio and television propaganda. Others were assigned to influence American journalists. Free trips to Korea for journalists were offered and sometimes accepted. In the academic world, the KCIA subsidized General Kang Young Hoon at the rate of $88,000 a year for his Research Institute on Korean Affairs in Silver Spring, Maryland.

Harvard University was given special attention because of the impact of critical statements by prominent professors Edwin Reischauer and Jerome Cohen. Dr. Alexander Juongwon Kim, a researcher and law student at Harvard, reportedly was paid by the KCIA to influence scholars. He approached a well-known professor of East Asian affairs with a suggestion that the professor arrange for a cover story in *Time* or *Newsweek* on President Park. The professor said that would be impossible. Kim said he was sure the professor could do it and the Korean government would be grateful enough to pay him $50,000. The professor refused and ended the conversation.

The Park regime's efforts to "create a pro–R.O.K. atmosphere" on campuses resulted in arranging for the Korean Traders Scholarship Fund to make a $1 million grant to Harvard in 1975. During the mid-seventies, smaller grants were made directly by the government or through the traders association to the University of California at Berkeley, Columbia University, George Washington University, the University of Hawaii, and Western Michigan University.

The KCIA, experienced at controlling the people at home,

issued orders to control Koreans in the United States. Yang Doo Won, the station chief in Washington, instructed his agents around the country to squelch opposition to Yushin. Korean residents' associations were infiltrated, and elections for officers were rigged. Those who criticized Park Chung Hee were branded Communists. Retired Admiral Lee Young Woon, a motel operator in the Los Angeles area, was offered $100,000 to stop his opposition activities. In Washington, when Chung Sung Nam began speaking out, the regime retaliated against his relatives in Korea. His brother in Seoul told him to stop irritating the government because interrogations and warnings by the KCIA had become more than he could stand. Kim Woon Ha of Los Angeles and Song Sun Keun of San Francisco were publishers of anti-Park Korean community newspapers. After refusing the KCIA's offers to buy them off, advertisements from local Korean businesses stopped, forcing Song to close his newspaper. As his political activities continued, so did harassment from the KCIA. He later testified under oath that a KCIA officer in San Francisco, Limb Man Sung, became so enraged that he attempted to run his car into Song's car one night.

Park Chung Hee and the KCIA were discovering that phase two of the influence campaign was more difficult than phase one. The first phase was simple and lucrative in comparison. Tongsun Park was bribing Congressmen, and Congress was approving the money for military aid. Whether passage of the aid bills was due to Tongsun's efforts or not, he had excellent connections in Washington, and Korean officials were making money from his rice deals. From the Moon organization, Korea was getting some good publicity out of the Little Angels, and Moon was winning the minds of thousands of young Americans for Korea. But persuading people in the United States to love Yushin was a tough job. The KCIA could not handle it alone. The entire Korean Embassy would have to be mobilized for the task.

KCIA station chief Yang Doo Won briefed the Embassy officers in a series of secret meetings in the spring of 1973. He set forth the plan to silence criticism of Yushin and buy American support by targeting Congress, the executive branch, the media, academia, religious circles, business, and the Korean community. It was too much for Lee Jai Hyon, the Embassy's chief spokesman, so he defected. Three times during a period of several months in 1973 after he left the Embassy, Lee was interviewed by FBI agents in the Washington area and in Illinois. He described the Korean government's influence campaign as revealed to him at the Embassy meetings, but was left with the impression that the agents never grasped the importance of it. In fact, they never even filed reports on their conversations with Lee.

The FBI agents' inattention fit the general pattern. The FBI also did virtually nothing with the State Department's 1973 request to investigate KCIA harassment of Korean-Americans. While the Embassy meetings mapping the influence campaign were in progress, Henry Kissinger and his staff were ignoring an intelligence report that the Park regime had ordered Ambassador Kim Dong Jo and the KCIA station chief to prevent Kim Dae Jung, Park's opponent in the 1971 election, from meeting with American officials during his stay in Washington. That was only a couple of months after Richard Nixon promised not to interfere with Yushin. By the time of Nixon's meeting with Kim Jong Pil early in 1973, Yushin had already been exported to the United States to coerce Park's critics into silence.

"Because of abusive KCIA activities," said Kim Woon Ha, the Los Angeles newspaperman, "Los Angeles is not U.S. territory to Korean-Americans; it has become rather a territory of South Korea."

AN ALL-DAY 300-mile motorcade in his honor was not what John Nidecker had in mind when he went to Korea. As a special assistant to President Nixon, he had been invited by the Korean government to represent the United States at the Korean Presidential Prayer Breakfast in May 1974. He had been responsible for some of the arrangements for national prayer breakfasts in Washington, and it was he who had seen to it that Sun Myung Moon sat as far as possible from the head table. He was in Korea to attend a religious event, but his hosts had mounted a political extravaganza to show the Korean people that the Park regime and the Nixon administration were on very close terms. The motorcade wound its way from Seoul to Pusan, escorted by each provincial police force, stopping at each city so Nidecker could be feted with a welcoming reception, meeting the mayors and governors.

His suite at Seoul's Chosun Hotel was a floral grotto. He was showered with gifts: paintings, jewelry, carvings, lacquerware, and a decorative plaque with an engraved inscription from his principal host, Park Chong Kyu, the director of the Presidential Protective Force. The most impressive gift was an ancient stone wine server said to be 2,400 years old. Because of its obvious value, he surrendered it to the State Department when he returned to Washington and it was later bought by a museum in Illinois for $10,000.

Escorts, Nidecker thought, were all right when you needed them. But it was almost impossible to get away from Row Chin Hwan and his two ubiquitous helpers. From their own rooms next to Nidecker's suite they could hear the lock click in his door and be out in the hall with him before he reached the elevator. After the first day or so, Nidecker learned how to close the door quietly without making the lock click. There was no place special he wanted to go, but at least it was nice to be able to go downstairs and walk around the lobby on his own.

It soon became apparent why they tried so hard to be with him at all times. They wanted to steer him away from the wrong people. One of those was Cardinal Stephen Kim. Nidecker was making a point of talking to religious leaders because he was interested in Christianity in Korea and in their attitudes toward Moon and the Unification Church. The Park regime did not want bad reports on Moon going back to the White House during Moon's Project Watergate, nor did it want Nidecker to hear the criticism of Park's dictatorship that so often came from Christian leaders.

Arriving at Cardinal Kim's office at Myongdong Cathedral, Nidecker was told by his escort that the meeting would have to be short because of a very important appointment coming up next. Nidecker went inside alone and tried to talk to the Cardinal, but the escort kept sending messages saying to hurry up for the next appointment. The Cardinal's conversation was inhibited because he obviously realized what the escort was up to. Nidecker finally asked not to be interrupted with messages. Cardinal Kim opened up and said a number of his priests were being arrested for criticizing the government.

When Nidecker arrived for the important next appointment with Park Chong Kyu, he was kept waiting for about twenty minutes. His talk with Park had little substance.

The prayer breakfast was a splendid affair with President Park in attendance. Cardinal Kim was seated about as far from the head table as Nidecker had put Moon at Nixon's prayer breakfast. Some of the other Christian leaders Nidecker had met were not even invited. He had composed a pleasant five-minute statement to be given just before the benediction, with an ending that said President Nixon had asked him to urge the Korean people to "Listen to God." Row Chin Hwan, his chief escort, was not pleased when he saw what Nidecker had written. He had expected Nidecker to deliver a statement from President Nixon to President Park. Korean newspapers had already reported that he had brought with him a special message from Nixon to Park. Nidecker was unwilling to invent one, so when it came time for his statement the master of ceremonies merely announced that Nidecker had brought greetings from the American President. The benediction was pronounced and the prayer breakfast was over.

Just before Nidecker left for the airport to return to the United States, a smiling man handed him a sealed white envelope, wished him a safe journey home, and said several times, "Don't open it until you get on the plane." On the face was written, "Bon Voyage—Park Chong Kyu." Nidecker stuffed it in his coat pocket, got in his car, and departed for Kimpo Airport with motorcycle escorts. With Row Chin Hwan sitting next to him, he could not take the envelope out of his pocket. So he tore off a corner to get a glimpse inside and saw American money. At the airport he managed to break free from the organized farewell and picture-taking for a few seconds to hand the envelope to Alan Krause, his escort from the American Embassy. All he had time to say was, "Take this and look at it when you get back. Give it to the Ambassador."

He was glad to be on the plane at last. His fellow passengers were glad, too. The government had held the plane for an hour so Nidecker and President Park could say good-bye. The farewell meeting had not taken place, however, because Park was playing golf. When the plane landed in the United States, Nidecker phoned Alan Krause at the Embassy in Seoul and got a message that startled him. The envelope had contained $10,000 in cash. Ambassador Habib was returning it to Park Chong Kyu.

The Korean government apparently thought Nidecker still had some potential for influencing even though he had declined the generous good-bye gift. Within a month, Row Chin Hwan came calling at the White House bearing more gifts. There was a painting for General Haig, a set of pearls for Mrs. Haig, pearls and earrings for Mrs. Nixon, pearls and earrings for Rose Mary Woods, and pearls, earrings, and perfume for Mrs. Nidecker.

Since Park Chong Kyu had been such a gracious host in Seoul, would Nidecker be so kind as to look after Park during his visit to Washington a few months hence? Nidecker said his varied White House assignments were too unpredictable—he really couldn't commit himself. Row dropped the subject, and Nidecker was relieved. He had had quite enough of Park Chong Kyu. He mailed the gifts back to Row's office in Korea.

A few days later, Row Chin Hwan was back again. He wanted to help the White House with the 1974 congressional elections. Would Nidecker serve as the intermediary for some cash contributions to candidates for Congress? Just draw up a list of preferred candidates and Row would provide from $5,000 to $10,000 for House seats and from $10,000 to $20,000 for Senate seats. He could go as high as $30,000 for the Senate seats most important to the White House. Nidecker declined, saying it would be both improper and illegal. Gracefully, he got rid of Row as quickly as possible and made a point of never seeing him again.

By the time Park Chong Kyu visited the United States in January 1975, there was a new American ambassador in Seoul. Richard Sneider had arrived the previous August. He knew Park Chong Kyu had tried to bribe an aide to the President of the United States with $10,000 in cash, but he went out of his way to ensure that Park had an interesting schedule in the United States by requesting appointments for him. After Park returned to Korea, Sneider wrote to an American professor: "I consider what you have done for Park to be very much in the interest of both his country and ours and want to send you my personal thanks for responding so enthusiastically to our request for assistance."

Sneider did complain to Korean officials about Row Chin Hwan, though. He also tried a positive tack: to praise persons who he thought disdained gift-giving tactics with Americans, such as National Assembly member Lee Bum Jun and her hus-

band, Park Chung Soo. But not long before Sneider started praising them, they had in fact traveled to Washington to offer free
trips to Korea and honorary degrees to Congressmen, their
wives, and their staff.

IT WAS ALL a matter of what was considered important in Washington. The Korean influence campaign was not on the list of priorities. Even if the Koreans sometimes strayed beyond the
normal bounds of lobbying, the thinking went, they were viewed
as basically harmless. To most officials who saw snippets of the
influence campaign, it was a tempest in a teapot, a small friendly
nation making a big unnecessary fuss. Nixon and Kissinger were
preoccupied with earth-shaking issues. The FBI was busy track-
ing Communists. And so it went. Whether intended or not, ignoring the influence campaign had the effect of permissiveness
because the Koreans encountered no one to stop them. That was
the way it had looked to Ambassador Porter in Seoul in 1971,
when he knew little more than that Tongsun Park and Radio of
Free Asia were connected with the KCIA. He learned years later
that even in 1971 Washington knew a great deal more. But nothing ever seemed to happen.

8

Three Who Stood in the Way:
Ranard, Habib, Fraser

THE TOP LEVEL of the State Department, too, was preoccupied with priorities dictated by Kissinger. Between 1970 and 1974, the highest official working full time on Korea was Donald Ranard, director of State's Office of Korean Affairs. The unofficial title for this job is "country director." Those who hold such jobs are all senior Foreign Service officers, most at the top pay grade. On an abbreviated organizational chart, their level is near the top, next after the Secretary of State and an assistant secretary for a regional bureau. In reality, the distance between a country director and the Secretary of State is much greater. If Ranard followed each in-between step, as a good Foreign Service officer should, the journey from his sixth-floor office to the Secretary on the seventh floor would take him to one of three Deputy Assistant Secretaries of State for East Asian and Pacific Affairs, then to the Assistant Secretary, an Undersecretary, the Deputy Secretary, and finally, the Secretary of State. The separation was compounded by the fact that there are thirty-five country directors, some fifty-four deputy assistant secretaries, and nineteen assistant secretaries altogether.

Nor did Ranard spend all his time on guard duty against a

growing Korean conspiracy in the United States. All he was able to see was bits and pieces here and there. And he already had his hands full with other assignments. He was responsible for handling all diplomatic communications between the State Department and Ambassador Porter's Embassy. Before sending instructions to the Embassy in Seoul, he had to coordinate with any office in the State Department and any agency in Washington interested in the subject at hand. He was also the main contact between the Korean Embassy and the State Department.

In spite of all the bureaucratic drawbacks, Ranard was in a key position to take initiatives, and he did. While those at the top may have been permissive, Ranard was not.

Ranard was an experienced professional, respected highly by his colleagues. In style, he was tougher than most diplomats. What appeared to his superiors as stubbornness may have accounted for his never becoming an ambassador. During the sixties, he had been deputy ambassador in both Burma and Australia. He was no newcomer to Korean affairs, having served at the Embassy in Seoul as counselor for political affairs from 1959 until 1962. When he took over the Korea desk at the State Department in the spring of 1970, the first problem he faced was Nixon's troop cut.

It was obvious the Koreans were carrying their fight against the troop cut beyond the negotiating table. Ranard could see that the people engaged in the fight were not all regular government officials. There was Tongsun Park scurrying about Capitol Hill, lavishly entertaining Congressmen, rushing to Seoul to accompany congressional visitors. There was Moon's man, Bo Hi Pak, getting President Park to send letters for Radio of Free Asia to sixty thousand Americans at the height of the troop withdrawal frenzy and while military aid for Korea was pending in Congress.

Ranard knew more than that about Tongsun and Pak. The USCIA had told him they were lobbying for the Korean government under KCIA control. They were part of some stepped-up

Korean lobbying plan aimed at the troop reduction and the promised $1.5 billion in military aid. Ranard did not have details, but he was suspicious. The situation warranted following closely, so he started a separate file for reports relating to it.

Proper lobbying definitely had its place, he felt. There would be nothing wrong with diplomats and visiting R.O.K. officials urging Congressmen to support the Korean position. Other Koreans and Americans could lobby, even full time, as long as they were duly registered as agents of a foreign government. Ranard knew the Korean and American governments both wanted Congress to approve the money to modernize the R.O.K. armed forces; he was committed to it himself. It was far too important a job to put in the hands of the likes of Tongsun Park and Bo Hi Pak. He decided to say something about it to the Korean Embassy.

Like Porter in Seoul, Ranard raised the subject obliquely. He could not come right out and say he had intelligence information reporting that Tongsun and Pak were working for the KCIA in Washington. He told the Korean diplomats they would be better off if they confined lobbying activities to Embassy officers. As the weeks wore on with no change, he began mentioning Tongsun Park by name. The replies he got were weak. Obviously, it was a very sensitive subject. The Koreans would not go so far as to agree that Tongsun should not be lobbying. Rather, they said, it was difficult for the Embassy to deal with Tongsun because he had important contacts in Seoul. Ranard got the impression they looked upon Tongsun as an interloper.

In January 1971, Ranard got his first glimpse of the kind of contacts Tongsun had. He went out to Dulles Airport to welcome Chung Il Kwon, who had just stepped down as Prime Minister. Ambassador Kim was there along with other officers from the Embassy. Tongsun was there, too. By this time Ranard had heard from Ambassador Porter that Tongsun had offered $1,000 to Congressman Broomfield in Seoul earlier that month. Ranard

decided to put away diplomatic niceties and say what he really
thought. Alone with the Embassy's political counselor for a moment, he said, "This man is poison, and the sooner you people
come to realize that and get rid of him, the better off you will be."

When Chung Il Kwon deplaned a few minutes later, he was
openly delighted to see Tongsun.

About a week later, Ranard's office received a request from
Tongsun. He was asking for an appointment with Secretary of
Defense Laird for Chung Il Kwon. It irked Ranard that Tongsun
was the one making the request, but quite apart from that he saw
no reason why a former Prime Minister should get to see the Secretary of Defense. It was enough, Ranard thought, that he meet
with Secretary of State Rogers as already arranged. Everyone
knew Chung's visit had been designed to make the Park regime
look good for the upcoming presidential election in Korea. Ranard turned down Tongsun's request and informed the Defense
Department. He later learned, to his surprise, that Chung had
met with Laird anyhow by going through some Congressman. At
the time, Ranard did not know the Congressman had been William Minshall, a member of Tongsun's charmed circle.

Ranard and Ambassador Porter each thought the other
should handle the problem of Tongsun. They agreed Tongsun's
activities had to be curtailed. Because Ranard found the Korean
Embassy powerless to stop Tongsun, he thought Ambassador
Porter should get tough with the leaders in Seoul. Perhaps Tongsun could be permanently recalled to Korea. But Porter found
the Korean government unwilling to do anything and felt Tongsun should be stopped in Washington, where his activities were
going on. Both positions were understandable. Ultimately, the efforts of both men were frustrated.

THE FILE in Ranard's office on Tongsun and Bo Hi Pak was getting thicker.

Unable to accomplish anything at his level in Washington or at Porter's in Seoul, Ranard became convinced an investigation was in order. It was he who initiated the State Department's request for an investigation of Radio of Free Asia by the Justice Department. He was strongly supported by Winthrop Brown, Deputy Assistant Secretary of State and former ambassador to Korea. Brown had been concerned about ROFA since 1966 when Bo Hi Pak got it started under KCIA auspices. He had always worried that ROFA's shady finances and KCIA ties could lead to a scandal involving prominent Americans. The request for an investigation was strengthened by Senator Fulbright's interest. The Senator had criticized the State Department for not keeping a closer watch over organizations propagandizing for foreign governments in the United States. He had cited ROFA as an example.

The information State gave Justice was compiled by Ranard. He was hoping for a full investigation of all improper Korean lobbying. His information memo in June 1971 included everything he had at the time, not only about ROFA, but also Tongsun: ROFA collecting money from unsuspecting Americans while using free broadcast facilities in Korea through the KCIA; ROFA using the names of distinguished Americans without their knowing; President Park's letter to sixty thousand Americans initiated by Bo Hi Pak; the Korean Cultural and Freedom Foundation as a propaganda and money-raising front for Moon; Tongsun's ties with the KCIA and his activities as an influence peddler, including the attempt to bribe Congressman Broomfield.

The Justice Department and the FBI certainly had enough to work with. With that much information, a serious investigation could have prevented the Koreagate explosion that came five years later. They ignored the Tongsun material, interviewed Bo Hi Pak once, and dropped the case.

The full investigation Ranard sought never happened. Although it had been initiated in the name of the Undersecretary of State and conducted in the name of the Attorney General, neither considered the matter important enough to pursue further. All Ranard was able to accomplish, therefore, was what he did on his own. He warned Congressmen about their names on the ROFA letterhead. Congressmen Paul Findlay, Samuel Stratton, Roger Zion, and Senator Winston Prouty discovered they were listed on the ROFA Advisory Council without their ever having consented. They had their names removed.

Ranard had also become aware of another troublemaker: Kim Kwang. In November 1970 Kim was touring East Asia asking American embassies for briefings on sensitive subjects and using his position on Congressman Gallagher's staff as an entrée. Ranard saw to it that Kim got no more than unclassified general briefings. Around the same time, the American CIA told Ranard that Kim Kwang apparently had a working relationship with the Korean CIA. Ranard also knew he was a Tongsun man. Kim Kwang obviously fit into the overall lobbying picture, blurry as it was to Ranard at the time. He added a folder marked "Kim Kwang" to his special file and waited for further developments.

He got some solid, very serious information in late June of 1971. It came not from the CIA, but from an even more sensitive intelligence source. The report said the KCIA had been instructing Kim Kwang to rig Gallagher's hearings in favor of the Park government's position.

Now, Ranard believed, he had a chance to do something about Kim Kwang. He invited some intelligence officers to his office to discuss the matter. They agreed the information indicated a problem but asked if Ranard had seen the previous sensitive report on Kim Kwang. He had not. He felt a little embarrassed. Perhaps the other report had been overlooked in the heavy flow of documents crossing his desk every day. He adjourned the meeting and scheduled a second one so he could go back and do his homework.

A search of his office files failed to turn up any other recent report on Kim Kwang. That meant it had never been sent to him. In the meantime, the intelligence officers had been doing some checking after Ranard's first meeting. At the second meeting they said they had instructions not to discuss the matter any further. They indicated it was being handled at a higher level.

Fine, Ranard thought, that's exactly where it should be handled. Something this serious deserved the attention of Henry Kissinger and Secretary of State Rogers. That was the way Ranard viewed it even without knowing the other intelligence report said Kim Kwang had paid Gallagher for information the KCIA wanted.

The intelligence report on Kim Kwang was in fact passed upward. It reached Kissinger and Attorney General Mitchell on July 16, only to be ignored. Having been cut off, Ranard was unaware of that development, but something happened about the same time that made him realize Kim Kwang was still riding high.

Speaker Albert's big congressional delegation to Korea was coming up in August. Ranard had been working on the arrangements for the trip with Harry Cromer of the House Foreign Affairs Committee staff. Toward the end of July, Cromer asked Ranard to come up to the Hill for a talk about which staff members should accompany the delegation. They met in the Rayburn Building with Roy Bullock, chief of staff of the Foreign Affairs Committee. Cromer and Bullock said Speaker Albert was planning to take Suzi Park Thomson of his staff and Gallagher had asked that Kim Kwang also be included in the delegation. Suzi was an American citizen, they noted, while Kim Kwang was not. Did Ranard have any views on including Suzi and Kim in the delegation?

Ranard was forbidden to tell them about the sensitive intelligence he had seen on Kim Kwang. There had not yet been any hard intelligence on Suzi, but he and Ambassador Porter suspected she was connected with the KCIA. He told them it would be inappropriate to take Suzi or Kim and in Kim's case, very inappropriate.

For Bullock and Cromer it was a question only of whether Kim should go, since Gallagher was a member of the Foreign Affairs Committee. There was nothing they could do about Suzi. She worked for the Speaker. They tried to block Kim, but Gallagher was determined to take him and had Speaker Albert's support. Albert called Secretary of State Rogers, who knew nothing about the issue. Rogers asked Assistant Secretary Marshall Green to handle it. Green, having been briefed by Ranard and knowing Ambassador Porter's feelings, called Albert to say he and Porter thought it would be inadvisable for Kim to go. Gallagher then called Green, insisting he knew Kim better than anyone else and "would pledge my soul and honor on Kim's integrity."

Albert changed sides in the face of the State Department's objections. Gallagher had to give up but he was not happy about it. The trip to Korea with an important congressional delegation would have given Kim the kind of recognition he wanted in Seoul. All Gallagher could do now was try to salvage Kim's reputation. He told Assistant Secretary Green that although he was withdrawing his request in the interests of harmony, he did not want any slurs made on Kim's character. He asked Green to convey that to Speaker Albert as well, which Green did.

It had been Ranard's only success after a year of Korean lobby-watching.

IN AUGUST 1971, Ambassador Porter was appointed chief U.S. negotiator at the Paris peace talks on the Vietnam War. His successor as ambassador to Korea was Philip Habib, another outstanding diplomat and one of the best-loved men in the Foreign Service. People liked Habib even if they disagreed with him.

With that quality, he could afford to be blunt, which he often was. His subordinates never complained about the enormous amount of work he required of them, because he was even more demanding of himself. In Seoul, he suffered a major heart attack, yet he plunged back into his work as if nothing had happened and kept going until another attack almost killed him in 1977 when he was Undersecretary of State. His ethical standards were equally rigorous. He believed the United States should stand for something decent.

Habib came from a poor Lebanese family in Brooklyn. Foreign Service colleagues affectionately called him "the Arab rug merchant." His dedication to fighting for what he believed in led to a prolonged collision with Graham Martin, the ambassador to South Vietnam. Martin saw himself as a kind of "Super Ambassador" who should deal directly with the President of the United States and ignore everyone else. As Assistant Secretary for East Asia in the mid-seventies, Habib's actions made clear he thought Martin was wrong about both his position as ambassador and U.S. policy in Vietnam. When the angry Martin tried to pull rank on the people working for Habib, Habib defended them.

Gregarious in every way, he had the gift of gab. He could not just sit quietly while someone else did all the talking. Once, when an admiral was briefing some Congressmen on the situation in Vietnam, Assistant Secretary Habib could not resist adding comments along the way whenever the admiral's information was incomplete. He was irrepressible, as always. After the briefing, Habib's aide scolded, "Phil, what's wrong with letting the admiral have his dog-and-pony show? Can't you keep your mouth shut?"

As soon as he got settled in Seoul in the fall of 1971, Habib said, "My nose told me" that Tongsun was up to no good. Habib was expert at picking up a scent, but he also had help from others. In Washington for briefings before he took up his post in Korea, he had heard Defense Secretary Laird say Tongsun's lobbying was a nuisance. The other officers in the American Embassy knew a lot from Ambassador Porter's experience with the problem of Tongsun. It did not take Habib long to come to his own strong conclusions. Tongsun was always in and out of town, commandeering visiting Congressmen and cavorting with high Korean officials. Knowing Porter and Ranard had tried and failed to get the Korean government to do anything, Habib was not optimistic. If his power with the Korean government was limited, at least he had complete control over his embassy. He would quarantine Tongsun. At a staff meeting, he issued an order that no one from the Embassy was to have anything to do with Tongsun. They were not to accept his invitations or receive him in their homes or offices. "He's a Korean government agent," he told them.

Later, when Habib went out to Kimpo Airport for the arrival of Otto Passman on one of his visits, there was Tongsun in a group of waiting Korean officials. Habib walked over to Chung Il Kwon, who was then Speaker of the National Assembly. Pointing to Tongsun, he said simply, "If he stays, I go."

Tongsun left the airport, but most of Passman's time in Seoul was spent with him. They moved about town in a limousine Tongsun had outfitted with a small American flag flying from the front bumper, supposedly a prerogative of the American ambassador. Habib fumed.

Tongsun was painfully aware of Habib's boycott. It was bad enough that he couldn't walk into the American Embassy to announce his latest triumph whenever he wanted to; it was worse that the boycott was generally known in Seoul. His reputation for influencing Americans was suffering. Maybe he could get at the problem from the Washington end by working on Ranard. He knew Ranard was not a fan, but why not try to cultivate him? It seemed worth an effort.

Ranard got a phone call from Tongsun. Mr. and Mrs. Ranard were cordially invited to dinner at Tongsun Park's home. Among the guests would be Senator Birch Bayh and Senator Ernest Hollings. Ranard said thanks but he couldn't make it.

"Oh, that's too bad," said Tongsun. "How about lunch at the George Town Club sometime soon?"

Sorry, that wouldn't be possible either, Ranard replied.

Tongsun insisted he had to talk to Ranard. "Well, then," said Ranard, "you'll have to come by my office." They made an appointment.

Tongsun appeared right on time. The problem was Ambassador Habib, he explained. The Ambassador had cut him off from the Embassy and was telling people he was connected with the KCIA. It was hurting his good name. He came from a respected family in Korea. He was a graduate of a fine American university and had a number of distinguished friends in the United States going back many years. Louise Gore, the American ambassador to UNESCO, was one of the oldest. What Ambassador Habib was doing to him was unfair. Couldn't Ranard do something to change Habib's attitude?

Ranard responded with aplomb. "Ambassador Habib is a very knowledgeable person on Korea and I respect his judgment. I will leave the running of the Embassy to him."

Habib and Ranard had known each other for years. It was Habib who had succeeded Ranard as political counselor at the Embassy in Seoul in 1962. While neither was able to put a stop to Tongsun in their respective positions, he was a frequent subject of correspondence between them. Periodically Habib wrote "Dear Don" letters to keep Ranard informed of Tongsun's doings in Seoul. He reported Tongsun's interjecting himself into congressional visits, paying Passman's hotel bill, running around with high KCIA officials, and "doing his damnedest to get around me." Some Congressmen, Habib wrote, had complained that Tongsun used extortion tactics to get his high rake-off from rice sales. All Congressmen were being advised by Habib to stay away from Tongsun. When Hanna had asked him to make friends with Tongsun, Habib had replied he would be glad to do any reasonable thing for the Congressman but that was out of the question. One of Habib's letters referred to Tongsun as "the slob."

In 1973, Ranard began getting complaints from Korean-Americans about harassment by the KCIA. He knew Park Chung Hee's Yushin dictatorship had caused division in the Korean community. He was astonished to learn how deep it was and that the KCIA was making it worse. Opponents of Yushin told him about threatening phone calls in the middle of the night. At a conference of Korean scholars in St. Louis, the KCIA had tried to keep the critics quiet with threats. The KCIA's most spectacular effort was directed against Kim Dae Jung, President Park's opponent in the 1971 election, who had come very close to beating Park in spite of the government's massive use of money from Americans, Japanese, and Koreans. Before his defeat, Kim had correctly predicted that if Park Chung Hee won, he would not allow another real presidential election. In 1973 he had been denouncing the Yushin dictatorship during extensive travel in the United States and Japan. Kim had become the hero of the anti-Yushin Koreans. KCIA agents followed him wherever he went, using local Koreans to harass him.

Kim Dae Jung had been scheduled to make a speech at the International Student Center in San Francisco on May 18, 1973. While the event was still in the planning stage, the Korean Consul General, Yun Chan, tried to order a stop to the plans. Yun told Song Sun Keun, one of Kim's supporters, that the speech must be canceled because he would not allow any meetings for Kim Dae Jung in San Francisco. Song replied that as an American citizen he would not take orders from the Korean government. The plans for Kim's rally proceeded.

A KCIA officer from Los Angeles arrived at the rally accompanied by ten burly karate experts carrying ketchup and eggs in brown paper bags. These were supposed to be thrown at Kim Dae Jung when he began to speak, but the bags were taken by police stationed at the entrance. As Kim started speaking, the karate experts and the KCIA officer began shouting and jeering, and one, Rhee Min Hi, tried to climb on the stage to silence Kim. He was subdued by Kim's bodyguards. The San Francisco police removed Rhee from the building and restored order. Before they left, KCIA officer Bae Young Shik identified himself as a diplomat and told the police, "This meeting is for Koreans and we will take care of it ourselves."

It was appalling to Ranard that the KCIA seemed to feel free to coerce people in the United States as if they were in Korea. He gave the FBI the information he had about the harassment and requested an investigation. The FBI checked its field offices in New York, San Francisco, and Washington, and interviewed some of the people who had filed harassment complaints. The 1973 investigation of harassment was as unproductive as the investigation of Radio of Free Asia had been in 1971. The FBI came up with no more information than Ranard had provided to begin with.

The worst was yet to come for Kim Dae Jung. His overseas activities had become intolerable to Park Chung Hee. Many thousands of Koreans in the United States and Japan were rallying around Kim as he denounced the dictatorship, calling Park a "generalissimo." He was being received by high officials of the American government. He was about to begin a year as a research fellow at Harvard University. Park's attitude toward Kim was close to paranoia.

In mid-afternoon on August 8, 1973, the KCIA kidnapped Kim Dae Jung from his suite at the Grand Palace Hotel in Tokyo. Drugged, he was taken to Osaka by car and transferred to a high-speed Korean boat the next day. Tied down with weights, he heard his KCIA captors planning to throw him overboard. He began saying final prayers.

In Japan, instant public uproar had followed Kim's disappearance. The Japanese government called for his safe return. The U.S. government also issued a strong statement drafted by Ranard. In Seoul, Ambassador Habib made forceful appeals to the Korean government. On board the boat, Kim heard an aircraft approach very near. At once, he was untied and fed. Five days after his disappearance in Tokyo, he turned up on a street near his home in Seoul. The Park regime denied any part in the Kim Dae Jung affair. Three days later, he was arrested on charges of violating election campaign laws.

There was never any doubt that the KCIA did the kidnapping. Japanese police found a KCIA officer's fresh fingerprints in Kim's room. Men seen going down the hotel elevator with Kim were identified as KCIA officers. An American CIA investigation in Seoul traced the plot to the KCIA.

A major crisis in Korean-Japanese relations ensued. The Japanese government was in a quandary. The press and the public were screaming about the violation of Japanese sovereignty by Korea. The evidence was there; it was clear the KCIA had done it, but the kidnappers were foreign government officials beyond the reach of Japanese law. And the Korean government was denying everything. Within the Japanese government, some officials argued for a tough stance to force the Park regime into accounting for the kidnapping. Tokyo did cool its relations with Seoul for several months. However, Japan's economic interest in Korea was worth billions. Important also to some Japanese politicians were the substantial kickbacks they had been getting from the Park regime. Eventually it was decided to sweep the matter under the rug with a diplomatic settlement ignoring the KCIA's role.

Seeing what the KCIA had done in Japan, the State Department's concern about harassment in the United States became more urgent. Ranard's superiors agreed to his recommendation that the Korean Embassy be told to transfer KCIA station chief

Yang Doo Won out of the United States. Yang was seen as the man behind the surge of harassment. His presence had become a bone of contention in the Korean community and an embarrassment to the American government. William Porter, now Undersecretary of State, called in Ambassador Kim and told him Yang Doo Won had to leave the country. After a respectable interval for face-saving, the Korean government sent him home in January 1974.

Ranard's special file on Korean lobbying and influencing had grown steadily thicker since he had started it more than three years before. This was only his second success after many tries. Throwing the KCIA station chief out was unprecedented in Korean-American relations, but Ranard was mistaken to expect it would make the KCIA behave better in the future.

KOREA HAD taken plenty of heat from Japan over the Kim Dae Jung kidnapping. All the Park regime had been able to do was lie about complicity in the incident and say Japan was being unfairly critical. There had been nothing to posit for a counterattack against Japan. Then on August 15, 1974, the Koreans found an issue they could use. President Park's wife was shot to death in Seoul in an attempt to kill the President. The assassin, Mun Se Kwang, was a Korean who lived in Japan. The Korean government blamed Japan because Mun, who was pro–North Korea, had been allowed to leave Japan and go to Korea. The issue was perfect for Korean-Japanese controversy because Madame Park personally had been very popular in Korea and almost half the Koreans living in Japan had pro-North sympathies. For years the Park government had complained about Chosen Soren, the big pro–North Korean organization in Japan. Japan, being a free country, had allowed the organization to exist.

Now the Korean government was demanding that Japan accept responsibility for the killing of Madame Park and issue a formal apology. Japan refused. Anti-Japanese demonstrations, stage-managed by the Korean government, raged in Korea for weeks. Paid protesters in front of the Japanese Embassy hacked off the ends of their little fingers with kitchen knives. Diplomats fled when a crowd broke into the Embassy building.

Japanese Prime Minister Tanaka had scheduled a visit to the United States in September. It was to be his first meeting with President Gerald Ford. Ranard learned that the Korean government intended to use the Tanaka visit to bring the controversy over Madame Park's death to the United States. Intelligence reports told him the KCIA was planning anti-Japanese demonstrations in Washington, Los Angeles, San Francisco, and New York. He pondered for two days over how to deal with the new big problem. As in the past with Tongsun's activities, he could not let the Koreans know he had secret information obtained from within their government.

Then he got a call from Julie Moon on September 13. Julie, a feisty anti-Park journalist who always had an enormous amount of information, said KCIA officers from the Embassy were trying to organize demonstrations in Washington against Tanaka's forthcoming visit. Ranard thanked Julie, unable to tell her how important her call really was. He now had corroboration outside the intelligence reports.

He called Minister Pak Keun, the Korean ambassador's deputy, whom he had known for several years. Ranard said he understood the Korean government was organizing demonstrations in connection with Tanaka's visit to the United States. He advised calling off any such activities.

"But, Don, what you've heard just isn't true," replied Minister Pak.

Ranard laid it on the line. "Look, this is not a negotiation," he said. "I know about it; you know about it. The smartest thing would be to call it off. These demonstrations would be the dumbest thing you could do."

There were no demonstrations.

Ranard retired from government service in the fall of 1974. Habib had suggested he stay on longer, but he was ready to leave after twenty-seven years as a Foreign Service officer. For one, he and Kissinger had different brands of foreign policy. More and more, Ranard had become dismayed over Kissinger's low priority for human rights in countries like Korea. Ranard's colleagues knew this, and some of his superiors were not sorry to see him go. He had been rocking the boat.

Four years of Korean lobby-watching inside the State Department yielded Ranard only three successes. He hindered Tongsun's Capitol Hill operation by shutting Kim Kwang out of Speaker Albert's delegation to Korea. He dealt a blow to the KCIA by forcing the station chief out of the country. And he stopped some KCIA demonstrations. It was not until the Koreagate investigations began that he found out his third success had hit the other main element in the influence campaign: the Moon organization, which reportedly had been paid by the KCIA to carry out the demonstrations. Each of his successes had made a dent in one of the three pillars of the influence campaign. But one man in the State Department was not enough to prevent Koreagate while the rest of Washington kept looking the other way.

THE MERE SUGGESTION of congressional hearings to look at human rights in South Korea was shocking to the Park regime. Yushin had caused a lot of bad press in the United States, divided the Korean community, and prompted criticism from some respected professors. To deal with these problems the Korean government had mounted phase two of the influence campaign. With the Nixon administration quiet about Yushin, the challenge to Park's image had come from outside the U.S. government. Hearings by a subcommittee of the House of Representatives could change that.

As soon as word got out that the Subcommittee on International Organizations was planning to hold public hearings on the human rights issue, Minister Pak Keun of the Korean Embassy went to meet the subcommittee chairman, Congressman Donald Fraser of Minnesota.

The Koreans had never had any dealings with Fraser. The Embassy's closest friends on his committee, Foreign Affairs, had been Congressmen William Broomfield, Edward Derwinski, and Lester Wolff. And Tongsun had had Gallagher, but he had not been reelected after his indictment two years before. Fraser had not caused any problems for the Koreans. They knew of him only as a strong supporter of foreign economic aid who had not objected to military aid for Korea.

Pak Keun found Fraser to be a soft-spoken man who let him do the talking. Pak said his Embassy was surprised to learn about the Congressman's plans. Since Congress rarely held hearings on Korea, and the United States was a close ally, he said, the Embassy would like to have been able to consult with the subcommittee while the hearings were being planned. Perhaps there was still time for that. Had a definite date been set?

Fraser said yes, a date had been set, Tuesday of the following week. A public notice was due to be released.

Pak asked if it might be possible to postpone the hearing to allow some time for consultations.

Witnesses had already agreed to come on the scheduled date, Fraser explained, so it would be very difficult to reschedule. He gave Pak a list of the witnesses.

Fraser had no idea he had become a major concern in a Korean influence campaign. He knew nothing of Korean lobbying. When an invitation to a dinner party came a few weeks later from a Mr. Tongsun Park, Fraser's secretary, Elsie Wonneberger, sent the Congressman's regrets because he had never heard of Tongsun and had another engagement anyhow. Tongsun's party would not have interested him if he had gone. Tongsun might not particularly have enjoyed Fraser either. People meeting him for the first time couldn't believe he was a politician. Basically a very shy person, Fraser avoided the social circuit, preferring quiet evenings at home with his family, where he liked to tinker with gadgets—Heathkits, broken washing machines, model airplanes with motors. He was probably the only Congressman who carried a tool kit with him on official business overseas, just in case anything broke down along the way.

Congressman Lester Wolff, who differed with Fraser on Korea and other issues as well, said he considered Fraser to be one of the brightest members of the House. Fraser was known for his liberalism, innovative ideas, and intelligence. All three of those traits brought him into frequent conflict with Wayne Hays of Ohio, the powerful and nasty chairman of the House Administration Committee. Once, when Hays became annoyed with one of Fraser's aides, he crossed the man's name off the House payroll for that month. In response, Fraser forced Hays into a debate on the House floor by stopping House business with repeated quorum calls. Hays backed down and the aide got his salary after three destitute weeks. If Hays's ploy had succeeded, it would have set a precedent whereby Hays could have fired any House committee employee he did not like. When reporters asked Speaker Albert for his position on the matter, the Speaker said he always made a point of never getting into a fight with Wayne Hays.

Fraser and the Korean government had been on a collision course for a long time, although neither knew it. Starting in August 1973, Fraser's subcommittee had already held nineteen hearings on human rights and foreign policy before turning to Park Chung Hee's Yushin dictatorship. Originally, his goal had been to get the United States to give more support to human rights work in the United Nations, but he had recognized another problem as more urgent: the United States was giving too much support to anti-human-rights forces. He had learned about Yushin from American human rights lawyers, church leaders, and professors such as Harvard's Edwin Reischauer.

The point of impact for Park Chung Hee and Fraser was the main hearing room of the House Foreign Affairs Committee on July 30, 1974. The hearing had been planned for a smaller room where the subcommittee usually met. The interest generated by the announcement had been so great that the location was changed and police were asked to be on hand to control the crowd.

Before the witnesses could begin, the committee's Korean lobby spoke up. Congressman Broomfield took Fraser to task for criticizing the Park government and not having a "more balanced" slate of witnesses, and submitted an eight-page paper prepared by the Korean Embassy. He then urged that the following week's hearing include Father Moffett, an American missionary working in Korea who just happened to be seated in the audience. Congressman Wolff, saying he had heard of Moffett's great knowledge, seconded Broomfield's recommendation and offered another priest as well, Father MacFadden. Fraser said he would be glad to accommodate the Congressmen's wishes.

Testimony from the witnesses then began. New York attorney William Butler represented Amnesty International. He had recently completed a study in Korea on the Yushin system. Butler described mass arrests, prolonged detention without trial, and other denials of due legal process, constant surveillance by the KCIA, unlimited power in the hands of President Park, and torture of political prisoners. Among several accounts of torture, he described what happened to Soh Sung, a student at Seoul National University:

> . . . a handsome young man when he entered prison . . .had a badly burned face and body when he was brought to court.

His ears and eyelids had disappeared and his fingers adhered together. It was necessary for him to sign a record by using the imprint of his toe. The Korean government explains this obvious change of appearance by saying that he fell into burning oil on a stove.

Acting Assistant Secretary of State Arthur Hummel stressed the United States' commitment to defend South Korea. But he also conceded, in surprising detail, that Yushin was a very tightly controlled system. It was the strongest human rights testimony Fraser had ever heard from the State Department. Hummel's statement had been written by Donald Ranard and one of his officers on the Korea desk, Ed Kelley.

After the second day of hearings, Fraser received written statements from several Congressmen for placement in the published record. That is common practice in Congress. What surprised Fraser was the detailed knowledge of Korea some of the Congressmen showed. Apparently somebody had done a lot of studying. Three years later, Fraser read two federal grand jury indictments and found the statements had been the product of Tongsun and Hanna.

Fraser could not bring himself to vote for $238 million in military aid to Korea in 1974. He had sat through two days of human rights hearings. He had heard Yushin pro and con from twelve witnesses. In a long talk in his office, he had heard Ambassador Hahm Pyong Choon argue for the Park regime. Fraser could not accept the notion that the United States should pay South Korea to become more like North Korea. If South Korea were moving in a democratic direction, he was fully prepared to support $238 million or even more if it seemed needed. But Prime Minister Kim Jong Pil had just said the Park regime expected to stick with Yushin for at least six years more.

When the Foreign Affairs Committee took up the foreign

aid bill in the fall, Fraser offered an amendment eliminating almost all military aid to Korea. It was narrowly defeated after heavy lobbying by the State Department and the Korean Embassy. For the first time in his career, Fraser announced he would vote against the foreign aid bill when it came before the full House on December 18. Undersecretary of State Carlyle Maw came to Fraser to negotiate. Fraser's advocacy during House floor debate had always been important for getting foreign aid bills passed. Maw knew that if a few other liberals followed Fraser's lead this time, the entire bill would be defeated. They reached a compromise: an amendment to be offered by Fraser, cutting Korea by $93 million because of violations of international human rights standards. With the two sides reconciled, the House adopted the measure by voice vote.

The Korean government was stunned. It was the only time Korea had ever been singled out for a cut in military aid, and the reason was human rights. One man, acting by himself, had dragged President Park through the mud in public hearings. Not satisfied with that, it seemed, he had slashed almost $100 million out of the military modernization program, which was already behind schedule because of annual worldwide cuts in American military aid.

It was not the *amount* of military aid that was important; it was *symbolism*. The image of the Park government was what counted—in South Korea, in the United States, and in North Korea. That was why the reason for the aid cut was so painful. While Fraser was negotiating with the State Department, the Korean government had decided it would be better to take an even deeper aid cut if the human rights language could be removed from the amendment.

It had all happened in the space of four months. In that short time, Fraser's individual action had devastated both fronts of the influence campaign: military aid in Congress and the image of Yushin. Fraser had never even heard of Tongsun's payoffs, the free trips to Korea, Moonie demonstrations for the KCIA, the Korean Cultural and Freedom Foundation, KCIA harassment, and all the rest. At the end of 1974, the influence campaign and Humpty Dumpty had a lot in common.

NOT QUITE as unaware as Fraser, Phil Habib was also taking a step toward Koreagate. In August 1974 he had finished his tour as ambassador to Korea with feelings of irritation and frustration over Tongsun's antics in particular and Korean lobbying in general. Now that he was back in Washington as Assistant Secretary of State, there might be an opportunity to do more.

Some months earlier, while still ambassador, he had been in Ranard's office talking about Tongsun. Something just had to be done in Washington about the problem, Habib had said earnestly.

Ranard threw it back at him. "Goddamnit, Phil! You wrote those letters about him. You've got the commission from the President. You go to the White House!"

Habib had pounded his fist on Ranard's desk and said, "All right, then. Leave it to me!"

He needed more than his letters and suspicions to take to the White House. He would have to catch the Koreans red-handed with something recent. With the Koreans upset over Fraser, very likely something could be going on. The best way to find out would be to have the intelligence services keep an extra-close watch.

The information he got in February 1975 showed the Korean government was trying to bribe certain Congressmen. It was more specific than anything Habib had seen before. He rushed to Kissinger's office only to find it empty. In the excitement of his discovery he had forgotten Kissinger was out of town.

Upon returning a few days later, Kissinger was beset with

the irrepressible Habib. Kissinger had ignored the intelligence report about bribery of one Congressman: Gallagher. Habib's new information indicated bribery of more than one. That made a difference to Kissinger; he decided to tell President Ford.

When Gerald Ford was briefed about Habib's information in February 1975, the Korean influence campaign was well into its fifth year of buying and renting Congressmen. This was apparently the first time anyone had told the President of the United States.

Besides Kissinger, who had known about the bribery since 1971, one other top White House official knew something about the influence campaign: press secretary Ron Nessen. But Nessen's knowledge was slight, and he had nothing on bribery. He had learned through U.S. intelligence channels that Tongsun Park and Bo Hi Pak were working for Korean intelligence and that the Koreans had targeted him for cultivation. Presumably, they thought he might be susceptible because his wife was Korean.

Habib had succeeded in alerting the President, but his February information was not enough for Ford to act on immediately. It implied attempts to bribe, but not actual passing of money. Since the information was inconclusive, the President ordered a close watch for further developments. Habib asked for more intelligence reports and waited.

IN MAY AND JUNE, Fraser held five more human rights hearings. Although the KCIA reportedly had stopped torturing political prisoners, the overall situation in Korea had not improved. Under Fraser's military aid amendment, President Ford could have given Korea an extra $20 million if he felt the Park regime had begun to observe human rights. Ford had made no such ruling, and the full $93 million cut stood. In Korea, however, Prime Minister Kim Jong Pil had told the people the extra $20 million was on the way.

Fraser had visited Korea for five days in late March. The government had tried to fill his schedule with social events and military briefings as they had been doing for years with Tongsun's crowd. He had wanted to meet some students and former National Assemblymen who claimed to have been tortured, but the government had rounded them all up before he arrived. Prime Minister Kim Jong Pil had promised Fraser no one would be arrested or interrogated for talking to the Congressman, but two days after Fraser left Korea, the Reverend Kim Kwan Suk and the Reverend Park Hyon Kyu were thrown in jail for several months. During the fourth afternoon of the visit, the cabinet deliberated over whether to persuade President Park to meet with Fraser. It was decided not to try; Park Chung Hee was furious over what Fraser had done.

Until Lee Jai Hyon testified at the hearing on June 10, Fraser had assumed that, except for the kidnapping of Kim Dae Jung in Japan, KCIA repression was confined to Korea. But Lee described heavy-handed tactics by the KCIA to silence Park Chung Hee's critics throughout the United States and said there was an elaborate plan to "buy off, seduce, and intimidate" both Americans and Koreans.

Lee's testimony necessitated widening the scope of inquiry. Fraser's focus had been on what the United States should do about relations with the Park government in the face of human rights violations in South Korea. The allegations Lee made pointed to an extra dimension in the United States, comprised of repression, corruption, and violation of national sovereignty. It seemed to Fraser the Justice Department was the agency to do something about it.

Fraser's letter of June 12 to Attorney General Edward Levi asked for an investigation of all illegal activities alleged by Lee Jai Hyon. The response two months later enclosed a useless list of Americans registered as agents of the Korean government: lawyers, trade consultants, and public relations men. As for the request for an investigation, John Davitt, chief of Justice's Internal Security Section, wrote, "I will advise you of any developments which occur."

Nothing occurred.

If Justice won't do anything, then Congress should, Fraser felt toward the end of 1975. By that time, he had more to go on than the Lee Jai Hyon testimony alone. Lee's appearance had emboldened the Korean community. Fraser's office was deluged with allegations against the KCIA. Finding the House Judiciary Committee uninterested in an investigation, he decided to try doing it himself.

IN OCTOBER, Phil Habib got the intelligence he had been waiting for. It was much more definite about bribery in Congress than the February material. It went to President Ford through Kissinger. The President ordered it turned over to the Attorney General. Habib, State Department legal adviser Monroe Leigh, and White House counsel Philip Buchen made the arrangements necessary for transmitting the supersensitive intelligence material. In November, it was delivered to Acting Attorney General Robert Bork. It had taken an order from the President to get Justice to move.

Meanwhile, Fraser was completely unaware of these events and that Justice had become interested after seeming to have brushed aside his 1975 inquiries. In 1976 the Fraser subcommittee held five hearings in a series called "Activities of the Korean Central Intelligence Agency in the United States." Two names kept popping up wherever Fraser looked: Tongsun Park and Sun Myung Moon.

KCIA harassment was clear and unarguable. But Tongsun and Moon were the mystery men. Fraser and his investigative staff—only two people at that time—did not yet have access to intelligence reports. It appeared to them that Tongsun and Moon were working for the Korean government in positions subordinate to an all-powerful KCIA. It was a simplistic notion, though not bad for that early stage of the game. Later they were to learn more sophisticated truths: that the KCIA, while powerful, was one of several factions skillfully manipulated by Tongsun and Moon; and that Tongsun and Moon could take directions without staying subordinate to the KCIA in everything they did.

Fraser's mini-investigation of 1976 shed some light on clouded mysteries. He had heard rumors that unnamed Congressmen had taken bribes, but he was hoping it wasn't true and he knew his subcommittee had no jurisdiction on the subject. A lot was learned in other areas from knowledgeable witnesses willing to testify, such as Donald Ranard (retired from the State Department) and former Moonies. But Fraser had important questions to ask Tongsun and Bo Hi Pak, and they were not of a mind to talk voluntarily.

The power of subpoena is the only way to compel witnesses. In late August 1976, Fraser obtained authority to issue subpoenas for his investigation by a vote of the House International Relations Committee. It was the first time in the committee's 150-year history that subpoena power had been granted.

A few days after the committee vote, Fraser had a visitor from the Justice Department. Paul Michel introduced himself as the person handling the Korean investigation. By this time, Fraser knew that Justice had started doing some investigating, but his information was sketchy.

Michel was very interested in what Fraser intended to do with his subpoena power. Of course the subcommittee could do as it wished, he noted, but if Fraser subpoenaed Tongsun Park it might upset the approaches Justice was making to Tongsun. Michel explained he hoped to get Tongsun's cooperation without a subpoena.

Fraser felt relieved to hear they were on to Tongsun. He told

Michel he did not want to do anything to upset Justice's investigation. Later, however, he would like to be able to question Tongsun himself if possible.

There would be no problem with that, Michel assured, if the Congressman could wait a few weeks, perhaps three or four.

For the next month and a half, Fraser's staff made follow-up phone calls to Michel. Just a little while longer, he kept saying, and he would be finished with Tongsun.

On September 30, Tongsun fled to London without giving Justice any useful information or being questioned by Fraser.

Koreagate

A NEW NATIONAL scandal erupted on Sunday morning, October 24, 1976, when the *Washington Post* was delivered. SEOUL GAVE MILLIONS TO U.S. OFFICIALS, read the front-page banner headline.

The story opened with, "A ring of South Korean agents directed personally by South Korean President Park Chung Hee has dispersed between $500,000 and $1 million yearly in cash gifts and campaign contributions." Tongsun Park and unnamed KCIA officers were identified as the main agents. An accompanying story described his rice agency. On page 2, there were pictures of Congressmen Hanna, Gallagher, and Broomfield, and Governor Edwards. The *Post* had obtained copies of six checks from Tongsun to Hanna for a total of $22,500. A cryptic remark was quoted from Gallagher's tax evasion trial, a mention of his "Korean friend." The story carried Broomfield's denial of ever accepting $1,000 from Tongsun. Edwards, though, admitted his wife had received $10,000.

Within a month, "Koreagate" had become a household word, the bastard descendant of Watergate in the family of Washington corruption.

For more than a year, there had been stories in the newspapers suggesting suspicious activities by Koreans. As a result of Fraser's 1976 hearings and some investigative reporting, the public had been reading allegations about Tongsun, Moon, Suzi Park Thomson, and the KCIA, with less certain references to Congressmen. The nearest the press had come to putting it all together was a *New York Times* story in October by Richard Halloran that described a South Korean "extra-diplomatic lobby" under the KCIA. The focus was on the intent of the Korean government. It was a concept similar to Fraser's, too broad-based to sweep people off their feet.

At the *Washington Post*, reporters Maxine Cheshire and Scott Armstrong had been concentrating more narrowly on the names and numbers of Congressmen involved. That was why their story on October 24 was such a blockbuster. The scandal that erupted had crystal-clear definition. Cheshire and Armstrong had reduced the disparate information to one central proposition: Congressmen had been bribed by Tongsun Park for the Korean government. From that time forward, people wanted to know just three things: How many Congressmen were bribed? Who were they? What would be done about them?

Citizens wrote Congressmen demanding that the scoundrels be ferreted out and punished. At the same time, they wondered whether their own Congressman was on the Korean take, too.

Republicans saw the scandal as the Democrats' Watergate. They were quick to point out that almost all of Tongsun's pals had been Democrats. And among those who had been favored by Tongsun were House leaders, including O'Neill, Brademas, and McFall.

For months, there was a spate of Koreagate stories in the newspapers. Some editors thought it would rank with Watergate as a political upheaval. Although the reporting uncovered many important facts about the influence campaign, speculation ran amok about how many Congressmen were involved. The *New York Times* first said ninety were being investigated, then estimated later that 115 might be implicated, based on a counting of Congressmen who had traveled to Korea or attended Korean parties. In January 1977, Senator Howard Baker played the numbers game on NBC's *Meet the Press*. About fifty members of Congress apparently had been bribed, he said. That was news to the Koreagate investigators.

In March, columnist William Safire used Baker's figure to spin a tale of his own. Claiming inside knowledge of intelligence from the National Security Agency, he assumed erroneously that Kissinger had found forty to fifty Congressmen accepting Korean bribes in 1974 and 1975. He also said Kissinger had kept the bribery news from President Ford in order to use it himself for blackmailing the House leadership. What Safire wrote was pure fiction. He was shooting at two favorite targets—Henry Kissinger and the Democrats. Safire proclaimed that the corruption could be put down only with "the slamming of cell doors behind one out of every ten Congressmen." But since the Korean investigation was "President Carter's first cover-up," he said, justice would not be meted out. (In 1978, Safire was to adjust the count to "13 of our most powerful Congressmen," who belonged "behind bars"; he did not explain what had happened to his earlier high figure.)

The numbers game raised public expectations too high. It gave Congress a worse beating than deserved. Once people heard forty, fifty, or a hundred Congressmen might be involved, they expected just as many culprits to be caught. Anything less was seen as a whitewash.

Equally regrettable about the Koreagate press was its failure to probe Moon's activities. There were news stories reporting congressional findings that Moon had ties with the KCIA, but Moon was a distant second to the press's fixation on the bribing of Congressmen. As a result, most Americans never knew the Korean influence campaign had an element much more destructive to society than Tongsun.

Moon's cult, lying to people in the streets, was making more money in three months than Tongsun made in six years from rice commissions. While Tongsun was wrecking a few congressional careers, Moon was wrecking thousands of families. Tongsun lobbied by charming people at parties, but Moon had young Americans pledging to die for him and Korea at his command.

SPEAKER CARL ALBERT was not among those returning to Washington for the 95th Congress in January 1977. There was speculation on Capitol Hill that Koreagate was at least part of the reason he had decided to retire. His longtime interest in Suzi Park Thomson and Susan Bergman could have scandalized the Speaker's position had he remained in office.

Moonie Susan Bergman, one of Master's congressional "PR sisters," had continued her regular visits to Albert when he arrived for work in the morning. The Speaker welcomed Bergman even after the newspapers began writing about his relationship with her.

The newspapers had written quite a bit more about Suzi Park Thomson. For years, Maxine Cheshire had noticed that Suzi had been doing some big entertaining for a congressional secretary with a salary of less than $15,000. Suzi hosted parties for Congressmen at her apartment, in the recreation room of her apartment building, and at restaurants. The number of guests varied from five or six to more than two hundred. Speaker Albert often attended, as did KCIA officers. Her escorts to functions at the Korean Embassy included Albert, Congressman Hugh Carey, and Congressman Lester Wolff. Cheshire also knew Suzi had traveled to Korea with Congressmen several times, at the expense of either the Korean or the American government.

Every observer of the diplomatic social scene saw a lot of Korean lobbying in the early seventies, and it seemed to Maxine Cheshire that Suzi was the central figure. Cheshire had a hunch there was a spy story in Suzi's affairs. It seemed all the more so when she discovered one of the essential ingredients of spy adventures: sex. California Congressman Bob Leggett was involved with three women at the same time. One was Suzi. Leggett was maintaining two households, one for his wife and one for his first mistress. Both women had children fathered by Leggett. His second mistress, Suzi, had her own place.

In February 1976, a Cheshire story said the Justice Department was investigating Leggett and Congressman Joseph Addabbo of New York, another close friend of Suzi's, for possibly having accepted payments from the Korean government.

Teamed with Scott Armstrong, Cheshire went to Leggett in search of a connection between Suzi and Korean intelligence. He was mortified over their knowledge of his secret personal life but insisted Suzi had nothing to do with the KCIA.

Leggett's virility seemed matched by his candor in answering Armstrong's questions. As a member of the Armed Services Committee, did the Congressman keep classified material in his office? Yes. Did he take it home with him? Yes. Did he stop at Suzi's on the way? Yes. Each time Armstrong asked a question about Leggett's work, Cheshire would ask one about his personal life. Most annoying of all to the Congressman was Cheshire's poke at Suzi's real age. Leggett insisted she was thirty-one. Cheshire produced proof from United States Immigration: Suzi was forty-five.

The story appeared on the front page of the *Post* on July 18, 1976.

Carl Albert kept Suzi in his employ for all six years he was Speaker despite John Mitchell's 1971 warning about her connections with the KCIA. He even weathered the newspaper stories about Suzi and Leggett. During his last year in office, she had appeared before a grand jury five times to answer questions about the alleged payments to Leggett and Addabbo, and about her parties and travels with Congressmen and her ties with the KCIA.

Details of Suzi's role in the influence campaign were to be revealed by the House Ethics Committee. The Ethics investigators found that the KCIA began funding Suzi's entertaining when she started working for Albert in 1971. The influence campaign itself had begun only four months earlier. Suzi's suitability as an agent must have been obvious to the KCIA. She had the social flair and connections of a Tongsun Park, and the sex appeal of a Moonie "PR sister."

Colonel Lim Kyuil and Kim Sang Keun of the KCIA had the job of delivering cases of liquor to Suzi for her congressional parties. Besides the liquor, the KCIA was paying Suzi $300 to $400 per party. But, like Tongsun, Suzi seemed more interested in lobbying for herself than for Korea. High-powered subsidized party giving was fun. KCIA people were always free to come, since they were footing the bill. But she usually planned her own parties, making her own guest list without waiting for the KCIA to tell her who should be invited.

Colonel Lim Kyuil didn't like it that way. Suzi was hard to control. She was always asking for more liquor than he thought she should be getting. There was nothing he could do about it, though. Suzi was a pet of Ambassador Kim Dong Jo's wife. She claimed to be a relative of Mrs. Kim.

During office hours Suzi was a more conscientious agent. She often briefed Ambassador Kim over the phone before his lobbying trips to Capitol Hill. When the Embassy invited Congressmen to parties, she would urge them to attend and notify the ambassador's secretary which ones had agreed to go. After Kim returned to Korea, she served Ambassador Hahm also. When Hahm was lobbying against Fraser's human rights hearings in

1974, Suzi asked Congressman Gerald Wiggins to introduce the ambassador to Congressman Morris Udall. On August 2, Udall met with Hahm, but made a statement against the Park regime for the hearing three days later anyway.

How much Speaker Albert knew or cared about Suzi Park Thomson's work as a subsidized Korean agent is not known. At least one of his official acts, though, raises questions about whom he was representing himself.

In September 1976 the House was set to vote on a resolution about Korea. It had been approved unanimously by the International Relations Committee. That was unprecedented for the committee, because Congressmen Fraser and Derwinski had always been at odds on Korea. But, in this case, the two antagonists had actually teamed up to write the resolution. The resolution critized *both* Koreas: North Korea first, for murdering two American army officers with axes; and South Korea for sending eighteen prominent persons to prison for signing a statement in favor of a peaceful return to democracy. Approval by the full House seemed a foregone conclusion. After some lobbying by the Koreans, Speaker Albert took the resolution off the House schedule. He said it was "too controversial."

BY SPRING OF 1977, Koreagate had spawned five investigations.

At the Department of Justice, the Public Integrity Section of the Criminal Division was trying to determine whether persons under United States jurisdiction appeared to have broken laws and, if so, to present evidence of indictable offenses to a grand jury. Justice's investigation, under Paul Michel, had been wandering around in the dark since early 1976. Along the way, Tongsun had skipped the country after Michel persuaded Fraser not to subpoena him, and Suzi Park Thomson had been pointedly unhelpful as a grand jury witness.

Michel was tight-lipped in dealings with the press and congressional investigators. It was also his style to give the impression of knowing more than he did know. When the scandal broke in the newspapers, the *Washington Post*'s sources at Justice had become concerned that Maxine Cheshire and Scott Armstrong perhaps had more information than Justice's own investigators. An embarrassing situation for federal investigators but ideal for reporters. Cheshire and Armstrong were able to bargain for more information for their stories. After Tongsun's departure, however, the Justice Department got a big break: Tongsun's ledgers and written reports to the Korean government. The documents had been found in Tongsun's house when it was seized on a tax lien. Unlike the material Justice had gathered from intelligence agencies, Tongsun's own papers could be used as evidence in court. The Justice Department chose to confine its work to the question of payoffs to Congressmen, centering on Tongsun's activities, as the press was doing. Habib's vigilance on congressional bribery had induced action from Justice after five years of doing nothing.

But Justice continued to look the other way when it came to Moon. Habib had tried to do something about that, too. In May 1976 he had asked Justice for an investigation to determine whether Moon, Bo Hi Pak, and several Moon front groups should be required to register as agents of the Korean government. Justice's response played right into Moon's hands. Justice refused to investigate because it said there was no prima facie evidence that Moon's organization was not a bona fide church. Besides, the response noted, there had already been an investigation. That was the "investigation" in 1971 when Justice dropped State's case against Radio of Free Asia after one interview with Bo Hi Pak.

The second investigation was that of the House Ethics Committee, whose formal name was the Committee on Standards of Official Conduct. It undertook to discover whether Congressmen, their staffs, or their families had violated the House ethics code by accepting gifts or favors from agents of the South Korean government. If the committee found violations, it could make recommendations for the full House to vote on, such as censure, reprimand, or deprival of committee membership or chairmanship. The Ethics Committee had jurisdiction only over sitting members of the House (the Justice Department, however, was investigating both past and present members).

The press and public interest groups such as Common Cause voiced doubts about the Ethics Committee's suitability to probe Koreagate. Many people tended to view the committee as lethargic. The reason was its reputation for going easy on erring Congressmen. Most members of the committee, like Chairman John Flynt, were from an "old boys network," seen as loath to crack down on their colleagues. The gentle wrist-tapping the Ethics Committee had given Florida Congressman Bob Sikes for corrupt business dealings was not a good precedent for cleaning up a bribery scandal.

When the scandal first broke, Chairman Flynt had not felt a need to act. The Justice Department was investigating; let them deal with it. But the newspapers kept harping on Korean payoffs. More than usual, Congress had become an object of cynicism, suspicion, and ridicule. In December 1976, Cartoonist Paul Conrad of the *Los Angeles Times* showed the Capitol dome decorated with Christmas stockings; the caption said, "The stockings were hung by the chimney with care, in hopes that Tongsun Park soon would be there."

By the end of the year, Ethics Committee staffers John Swanner and Jay Jaffee had convinced Flynt that the scandal would not "just go away." Flynt approved their recommendation for a full investigation with a special staff.

Philip Lacovara was chosen to head the investigation, with the title of special counsel. Having served during Watergate as assistant special prosecutor under both Cox and Jaworski, Lacovara had a reputation as a tough investigator. His appointment in January did a lot to offset people's doubts that Chairman Flynt and the committee would try to get to the bottom of the scandal.

By December, Fraser had also concluded he should do more. The staff of two that handled his 1976 hearings on the KCIA was not enough. The more he had investigated, the more he had found. Allegations kept mounting steadily. He decided to ask for authority by which he could investigate all aspects of the Korean influence campaign other than bribery of Congressmen.

The Fraser investigation had the widest scope as to subject matter and the least power to take action on its findings. As part of the House International Relations Committee, the Fraser Subcommittee looked at the effects of the influence campaign on relations between the United States and South Korea. The name of the probe reflected the foreign affairs focus: the Investigation of Korean-American Relations. The investigation sought to identify improper or illegal activities in the conduct of relations, such as awareness and tolerance of questionable Korean activities by the U.S. government, extortion of American companies by the R.O.K. government, ties between the Moon organization and the R.O.K. government, and KCIA penetration of American media, business, academia, and the Korean community in the United States.

Fraser had been the first to investigate what was to become Koreagate, having started in 1975 after hearing Lee Jai Hyon describe a many-faceted KCIA conspiracy. Fraser and Habib were the catalysts, but the ground Fraser plowed was vast. To most people, his work seemed amorphous, although he made a number of important findings.

The Senate Select Committee on Ethics provided the fourth investigation. It had a mandate corresponding to that of the House Ethics Committee; that is, to determine whether Senators, their staffs, or families had violated the Senate code of ethics by accepting gifts or favors from Korean government agents. It was the Senate's good fortune, however, that Tongsun had busied himself mostly with the House.

The Senate Select Committee on Intelligence, which formed the fifth probe, had the reputation of acting as watchdog over the CIA. Its earlier investigations had exposed unsavory CIA activities from assassination plots to experimentation with LSD. The Committee's Korean investigation was more pedestrian. It examined what U.S. intelligence agencies did with respect to improper Korean activities. Realizing other allied countries might be behaving the same as the Koreans, the committee undertook the project as a case study of the activities of intelligence services from friendly countries in the United States.

THE HOUSE ETHICS COMMITTEE ran into big trouble not long after getting under way, causing a crisis of confidence that resembled the effects of Nixon's "Saturday night massacre" during Watergate.

Philip Lacovara had approached his new job with enthusiasm. It offered intriguing legal and political challenges. At the same time, he felt some trepidation over whether the Ethics Committee could exert the kind of leadership needed. The investigation could bog down in a crisis of will, an innate inability to take action against sitting Congressmen. But he was encouraged by what Chairman Flynt had said to him when they first talked. "We'll give them the best damn investigation they ever had!" Angered by the press skepticism, Flynt had been defiant. That was a good sign to Lacovara.

Hiring a staff was the first test of the autonomy Flynt had promised Lacovara. Flynt never interfered. In late May, Lacovara's staff of about twenty-five was on board. Offices were located in a specially renovated section on the fifth floor of House Annex 2, a large building at the foot of Capitol Hill used for many years to house the FBI's national fingerpint file. The Fraser investigation had its offices across the hall. A Capitol policeman stood guard twenty-four hours a day at the head of the corridor.

For some time, Lacovara had been troubled by the attitude of the then Assistant Attorney General for the Criminal Division, Benjamin Civiletti. Civiletti seemed to be trying to protect Justice's investigation by keeping Lacovara at arm's length. Civiletti apparently shared the widespread doubts about Congress's being able to conduct a hard-nosed probe of the bribery scandal. Lacovara needed a lot from the Justice Department, especially access to certain witnesses and documentary evidence. At first, Civiletti would not even outline what Justice had. Lacovara had requested access to Kim Sang Keun, formerly the KCIA's number two man at the Embassy, who had defected to Justice officials in November 1976. Civiletti was refusing to let the Ethics investigators talk to Kim.

Without more cooperation from the Justice Department, Lacovara felt he would be handicapped. At his suggestion, Chairman Flynt sent a letter to President Carter asking for help. The letter brought about a meeting between Flynt and Attorney General Griffin Bell in June. Civiletti was with the Attorney General, and Flynt had brought in Ethics Vice-Chairman Floyd Spence, Lacovara, Chief Counsel John Nields, and the Ethics Committee's permanent staff director, John Swanner.

The brief meeting featured a swapping of old stories between fellow Georgia lawyers Bell and Flynt. Civiletti described a document found in Tongsun Park's house that listed Congressmen with dollar amounts next to their names. Attorney General Bell regarded the list with suspicion. He did not think all those Congressmen had accepted money. As names were mentioned, Bell would exclaim that he knew the man in question too well to imagine his being on the take. Bell urged caution. Irreparable harm could be done to members of Congress if public hearings were held, he said.

With Flynt echoing Bell's sentiments right down the line, Lacovara found himself wondering if this meant suspect Congressmen were to get clean bills of health simply by being well regarded by the Attorney General and the chairman of the Ethics Committee.

The meeting was altogether unsatisfactory as far as Lacovara was concerned. Bell and Flynt were soft-pedaling, and Justice refused to give Ethics the information requested or allow an interview with Kim Sang Keun.

In mid-June, the newspapers published names of some persons the Ethics Committee had voted to subpoena. Flynt hit the ceiling. Lacovara had no idea how the papers had gotten the information; it could have come either from a member of the committee or from the staff. Flynt ordered Lacovara to return all classified material to the executive branch immediately. He forbade further contact with intelligence agencies. But Lacovara had no classified material to return. The intelligence agencies would not give him any unless Flynt signed the agreements they had negotiated with Lacovara for the purpose of authorizing access for the Ethics Committee's investigation. Flynt had not gotten around to signing the agreements before and he was refusing to sign them now. The leaking of names of persons subpoenaed was a matter unrelated to the agreements with the intelligence agencies. Therefore, the CIA remained ready to furnish classified material if the chairman of the Ethics Committee would just sign. Flynt would not hear of it.

Things were getting bogged down. What wasn't bogged down was entangled. It was exasperating for Lacovara and his staff. Early in July, he wrote Flynt a memo, sending copies to all members of the Ethics Committee. Various problems, he asserted, had put the investigation behind by as much as six weeks.

Committee meetings had rarely been held or even called. A stack of subpoenas had been left unauthorized. Sworn depositions could not be taken because committee members could not be found to preside. And the chairman was not backing the effort to get cooperation from the State Department and the CIA.

It was a bad time for Lacovara to take his planned two-week vacation in England. Flynt had agreed to the vacation, but Lacovara had come to realize there was some risk involved in spite of the understanding. He departed with his family, believing Flynt was capable of firing him by making something big out of the vacation.

In London, Lacovara got a phone call from one of his Washington law partners with some bad news. The confidential memo to Flynt had been leaked to the newspapers by two members of the Ethics Committee. Flynt was saying Lacovara had no room to complain when Lacovara himself had taken off on a vacation.

Lacovara placed a call to Flynt to say he regretted the leak and had had no desire for a confrontation.

That was difficult to believe, growled the chairman. Flynt was upset about the leak, but he seemed madder about what the memo had said to begin with. He upbraided Lacovara for insubordination, telling him he was always acting as if he were an independent special prosecutor. Lacovara said he would return to Washington right away for a talk. Flynt hung up.

As he prepared to go home, Lacovara mused about Flynt's "special prosecutor" theme. The chairman was always playing on it. It was clear to Lacovara and the staff that Flynt thought the Watergate generation of young attorneys was a bunch of smart alecks. Flynt was from the old school. The Watergate kind of deep digging and probing was not for him, and he didn't like Lacovara and company trying to force it on him. In Washington, Flynt was calling Lacovara "a spoiled brat" who expected to have his own way on "every damned frivolous demand he made."

The next day, July 15, news from Lacovara's law partners was much worse. Flynt had taken to leveling a grave charge. He was accusing Lacovara of padding pay vouchers with more hours than he had worked and saying he would request an investigation by the General Accounting Office. That was the limit for Lacovara. Obviously, basic trust was out the window. There was no longer any reason to go home and talk to Flynt. Lacovara quit.

If he had talked to Chief Counsel John Nields before resigning, he later felt, he might have tried to salvage something with Flynt. His departure demoralized the staff. With the investigation already in a quagmire, Lacovara had been the hope for getting things moving.

An avalanche of criticism fell on Flynt. House Republicans, joined by junior Democrats, urged President Carter to appoint a special prosecutor, Watergate-style, which would take the investigation out of Flynt's hands. Common Cause called for the removal of Flynt as Ethics Committee chairman, as did some Congressmen. The press railed against him. Unruffled by the attacks, Flynt continued denouncing Lacovara, and said of the chairmanship, "I never expected to win any popularity."

Flynt got Lacovara off his back, but his own wings were then clipped by Speaker O'Neill. The Speaker had initially backed Flynt in an effort to show that the regular system in the House could produce a thorough investigation under Flynt's chairmanship. That would change. After Lacovara left, Flynt never had any real power.

THE INTERCOM buzzed in Leon Jaworski's office in Houston, interrupting a meeting with a client. His secretary said Speaker O'Neill was calling from Washington. Jaworski pressed the blinking button on his phone and greeted the Speaker.

O'Neill's tone was urgent. "I can't even begin to describe how badly public confidence in Congress is sliding. We have to satisfy the people that the House will investigate the Korean bribery scandal thoroughly. You are the only person the people know and trust enough. We need you to take the special counsel's job."

It sounded like Watergate all over again. Jaworski remembered a call four years before from General Alexander Haig at the White House. Haig too had described a serious crisis of public confidence, the "Saturday night massacre." Haig too had said Washington had to have Leon Jaworski.

Jaworski's reservations about O'Neill's appeal were similar to those he had felt when Haig called. He doubted he would have enough independence and he didn't see why another qualified person could not be found.

"I'm not interested in the kind of situation Lacovara had," he told the Speaker. "I don't want to bow to the chairman of the Ethics Committee."

"It's not the chairman who's calling you," O'Neill stressed. "I'm calling you."

House Majority Leader Jim Wright was also on the line. A fellow Texan, he had known Jaworski for many years. "Leon," he pleaded, "there's nothing we could ask you to do that's more important than this."

Jaworski said he needed time to think it over. He would call them back the next day.

He then placed a call to Peter White, an attorney with the Washington office of his law firm, Fulbright and Jaworski. He told White about the conversation with O'Neill and Wright, and asked him what he thought. White said it seemed like a no-win proposition. For a man like Jaworski, he thought, this offered no gain; he could only lose. Still, White conceded, Koreagate was an important matter, and getting involved would surely be "a great adventure."

O'Neill and Wright did not wait for Jaworski to call back the next day. They called him.

He told them his conditions. As with Watergate, he insisted on guarantees of independence.

O'Neill was forthcoming. "I'll take anything to the Floor you want. If you can't get it from the committee, we'll get it for you."

O'Neill and Wright ironed out the conditions over the next two days. They talked to Flynt in Washington and to Jaworski by telephone. By July 22, agreement had been reached. The conditions of Jaworski's service as special counsel to the House Ethics Committee were unprecedented for congressional staff: he could deal directly with the Speaker of the House on any matter; the committee would authorize any subpoena he requested; only the full House of Representatives had the right to discharge him; and he served without salary.

Jaworski's appointment changed public attitudes overnight. Because of Watergate, Jaworski's name had a magical effect. People believed if anybody could expose the Congressmen bribed by Koreans, Jaworski could. The press was euphoric. The *Washington Post*'s lead editorial cheered "the return of Leon Jaworski."

Since he planned to continue living in Houston, Jaworski needed someone to sub for him on the days he was not in Washington. He chose Peter White to be deputy special counsel. The two men had not worked together closely before, but he had always regarded White as a very bright and personable young attorney who knew his way around in the government. Jaworski was to find White's service indispensable. And at the end of their Koreagate association, he said White was "absolutely the best choice I could have made."

Speaker O'Neill and Majority Leader Wright were to come through on every request Jaworski made. Minority Leader John Rhodes also proved "100 percent agreeable" to his work. Jaworski's big problems in Koreagate were Chairman Flynt and the Korean government. He could get around Flynt's dilatory foot-dragging by taking important matters directly to the Speaker. But ultimately he was to find there was no way to overcome the intransigency of the Korean government.

FRASER'S INVESTIGATION also met with disaster in the early stages. It had its origins in his interest in General Kim Hyung Wook, former director of the KCIA. For more than a year, beginning early in 1976, Fraser had urged Kim Hyung Wook to come out of seclusion and tell what he knew about the KCIA in the United States. However, Kim preferred living quietly with his family in Alpine, New Jersey, on the fortune he had accumulated while serving as a top official in Park Chung Hee's government. He had lost his power in 1969 in a clash among political factions vying for Park's favor, but he still had his money. He had settled into self-imposed exile with his family, bodyguards, and a Mercedes-Benz, spending his time gambling, playing golf, and writing his memoirs. He never lost hope for the day when he would return home to run Korea. Park Chung Hee, his former mentor and collaborator in the 1961 coup, had become an object of hatred for allowing his own fall from power. Kim had been talking candidly about the KCIA on a confidential basis, but he refused to go public.

Jimmy Carter's plan to withdraw all American ground troops from Korea changed Kim's mind. He expressed his views against Carter's policy to reporter Richard Halloran and lifted his embargo on information about the KCIA. The front-page New York Times story on June 5, 1977, quoted Kim as saying that KCIA operatives in the United States included Tongsun Park, Sun Myung Moon, Bo Hi Pak, Suzi Park Thomson, and President Park's son-in-law, Han Byung Ki, who had been South Korea's deputy ambassador at the United Nations. Kim said President Park should take the blame for the Korean scandal and resign.

Having finally gone public, Kim agreed to appear as a witness at one of Fraser's hearings. On June 22, he testified that as KCIA director he had arranged for Tongsun Park to become the middleman for American rice sales to Korea and had transferred $3 million in government money to American banks to help Tongsun get loans for the George Town Club. Park Chung Hee was a tyrant responsible for all of Korea's problems, Kim charged.

Long before the story in the *New York Times*, President Park had feared Kim Hyung Wook might do something like this. As Koreagate heated up in 1976 and 1977, it became increasingly important to keep Kim quiet. The best way to assure this would be to get him to return to Korea. Park wrote an effusive letter praising him for "remarkable achievements" that would be "everlasting in our history" and inviting him to come home for a good talk about old times. KCIA Director Kim Jae Kyu also asked him to "come back to the fatherland and work together hand in hand as in the old days." When these overtures failed, Park tried to get him out of the United States by offering an ambassadorship to Mexico or Brazil, whichever Kim chose.

When the *Times* story appeared, the Korean government denounced Kim publicly as a traitor. Behind the scenes, however, the government worked harder to appease him. Something had to be done about his scheduled appearance at Fraser's hearing.

First, ex-KCIA officer Baek Tae Ha and Yoo Yung Soo, a friend of Baek and Kim, tried to talk him out of it. Then Park Chung Hee dispatched Minister without Portfolio Min Byung Kwon from Seoul to New Jersey. Min, whom Kim had known since boyhood, brought along a gift of Korean delicacies made by Park's daughter. His mission was to put three propositions to Kim: Don't testify, move to another country, or have Fraser's hearing postponed for two weeks to allow time to remove "poisonous" statements from his written testimony. The government had given up trying to keep him quiet about the KCIA; the bot-

tom line now was to prevent damaging remarks about President
Park. They were willing to pay him not to reveal his knowledge
of things in Park's past, like what he might say on the murder of
a *kisaeng* girl (geisha), her involvement with Park and other government luminaries, the sending of her baby boy to Japan. Also,
an apology would be appropriate for the remarks he had already
made in the *Times* article, Min said.

Kim began drafting a letter of apology to Park, then stopped
suddenly.

"Since he didn't send a letter, why should I send a letter?"
he shouted. "Does he think I can be appeased with hors
d'oeuvres?"

Kim flew into a fit of rage over the government's calling him
a traitor. He threatened to tell the Fraser Subcommittee that Min
had been sent by Park to cajole him. Minister Min gave up and
returned to Seoul.

Even after Kim testified, the government persisted, trying to
buy his promise not to make further attacks. The efforts were
more than a gesture. Kim Hyung Wook still had not spilled the
worst of what he knew about Park Chung Hee.

At the Korean Consulate General in New York, Sohn Ho
Young was responsible for coordinating the task of appeasing
Kim Hyung Wook. His public title was Consul in Charge of Security, but actually he was the KCIA station chief for New York
and eleven northeastern states. Since transferring from the Houston consulate, his work had become concentrated entirely on the
Kim Hyung Wook project. He was disgusted with it. While the
Korean people were being told by the government that Kim was
a pro-Communist traitor and a thief for taking $1 million out of
the country illegally, the government had ordered Sohn to have
him silenced with flattery or bought off. Sohn was also supposed
to vilify Kim in the New York Korean community, the aim being
to isolate him from his friends.

When the negotiations with Kim collapsed, Sohn got an unexpected order transferring him back to Seoul. It was too early for a routine transfer. He had been in New York only eight months. No explanation was given. Sohn was certain he would get the blame for failure to reach an agreement with Kim and he would be punished for it. He had a wife and two children to think about. He would defect.

A trusted friend suggested contacting Fraser. On September 14, Sohn and wife drove to Washington and checked into the Colonial Arms motel in suburban Rockville, Maryland. Fraser's investigators met with him in his room the following morning. He asked for protection so he could remain in the United States and he was prepared to provide information to the investigation if Fraser could help him.

Interpreting the conversation, Ed Baker conveyed to him, in Korean, Fraser's willingness to get U.S. government protection in exchange for his cooperation. Fraser would need a couple of days for the necessary arrangements, such as a place for the Sohns to live in hiding. Sohn said he would prefer to make the break the following Tuesday, the twentieth. Since he was already packing his household effects for the transfer back to Korea, no one at the office would suspect anything. He had made a point of not resisting the sudden transfer. On Tuesday, he would call from a pay phone in Tenafly, New Jersey, and identify himself as Lee Chung Shik. That would mean everything was set. Then he and his family would proceed to Washington.

Fraser approved the plans when the investigators returned to Capitol Hill at two o'clock. He directed that until Sohn had arrived safely in Washington, the other members of the subcommittee should not be informed except for Congressman Edward Derwinski, the senior Republican on the subcommittee.

The staff briefed Derwinski at 4:15 P.M.

By five o'clock, the KCIA had learned that one of its officers in New York, unnamed, was about to defect.

It was not until one o'clock the next afternoon that Fraser's investigators found out from Paul Michel of the Justice Department that the KCIA had been tipped off.

They feared for Sohn's life. Sohn must be warned, assuming he was still free. The phone call to his home would have to be handled very carefully by Ed Baker, speaking in Korean.

His wife answered.

"How is your husband, Mrs. Sohn? This is the man you met yesterday morning."

"Oh, he's fine. He went to the office today. I expect him back in an hour or so."

There had been no plans for Sohn to go to work that Friday. Monday was the day he was supposed to make an appearance at the office.

Fraser called in the FBI. Sohn's family would have to be picked up immediately. Agents in New Jersey were rounded up to go to the home. All they could do for Sohn himself was to wait. Nothing could be done at the Korean Consulate, since it was outside American jurisdiction. Someone suggested flying one of Fraser's investigators to New York to stand outside the consulate with FBI agents and identify Sohn if he emerged in KCIA custody. But first, another call to his wife.

"Has your husband come home yet?"

He hadn't. It was already 3:30 P.M., and she had expected him earlier. But there was nothing unusual about his going to the office, she said. Shortly before noon, he had decided to go clean out his desk.

"Mrs. Sohn, listen to me carefully. Some Americans will arrive at your house in a few minutes. Please do as they ask. Don't worry; we sent them. They will help you."

Around four o'clock, the FBI called to say they had arrived at Sohn's house. They were there with the wife and children, still waiting for him. Fraser's staff, consumed with worry about what the KCIA might be doing to Sohn, stayed huddled around the telephone. At five forty-five, the FBI called again. Sohn had come home unaware that anything had gone wrong. He and the family had left with FBI agents immediately and were on their way to Washington.

About thirty minutes later, a squad from the KCIA arrived at Sohn's residence and knocked on the door. No one was home.

At the time of the defection, Fraser did not know who the KCIA's informer was. On September 19, he requested the Justice Department to investigate the breach of subcommittee security. The FBI interviewed all persons with knowledge of Sohn's contacts with the subcommittee, especially the subcommittee members and staff. The case was then presented to the Koreagate grand jury. On September 28, the press reported that Sohn had defected and was cooperating with Fraser. For the time being, the problem of the security breach remained secret.

Then the press got wind of it. On October 28, the *Washington Star* ran a front-page headline banner: "Did Congressman Tip Off KCIA Defection?"

A detailed story by Jerry Landauer, picked up from the *Wall Street Journal*, reported that federal investigators suspected Congressman Derwinski of informing the KCIA that one of its officers was about to defect and cooperate with the Fraser investigation. Immediately after Sohn's defection, the article said, the State Department, the CIA, and the Defense Department concluded unanimously that someone from the Fraser Subcommittee—either a Congressman or a staff member—had tipped off the KCIA, and that, after interviewing a number of persons and evaluating other evidence, Derwinski emerged as the principal suspect. The evidence had been presented to a grand jury, but an indictment of Derwinski was in doubt, reportedly because the hardest evidence was sensitive intelligence material reporting a telephone conversation between Derwinski and Korean officials. For national security reasons, the government would not divulge such material or even acknowledge that it existed.

Congressman Lee Hamilton told the press that someone

close to Justice's investigation had informed him Derwinski had called the Korean Embassy immediately after learning the defection plans of a KCIA officer stationed in New York. Hamilton was a member of the Fraser Subcommittee and chairman of a special House Ethics subcommittee that also investigated the Derwinski-Sohn affair.

Derwinski denied that what he did was wrong. He said he called the Korean Embassy regularly and had frequent contacts with Korean officials. Giving the impression he was being nailed for something quite innocuous, he speculated that U.S. intelligence could have intercepted a secret Korean Embassy cable, which might have said: "Our friend Ed Derwinski is on a committee that is shielding a defector and he's going to help us find out about it."

Derwinski claimed he was being accused merely because he was a friend of Korea: "I'm not the culprit in this thing. . . . Because of my consistent support for South Korea and my skirmishes within the committee," he surmised, "I wind up as suspect No. 1 because of guilt by association."

The Justice Department investigators sought indictment of Derwinski under a provision in federal statute on obstruction of justice. The law prohibits acts to "influence, intimidate or impede" a witness in a congressional investigation. The maximum penalty is five years in prison and a fine of $5,000. Derwinski later said that when he was called before the grand jury in November, he refused to answer questions, citing the "speech and debate" clause of the Constitution, which grants members of Congress immunity from prosecution for certain activities in the course of official duties. He took the position that even if he was involved, he could not be prosecuted. Had he answered questions and, in so doing, had he lied, he could have been prosecuted for perjury.

Derwinski had a special dislike for South Korean defectors.

He had made that clear at a Fraser hearing two years before the Sohn affair. After Lee Jai Hyon bared the details of the KCIA's secret plan to seduce American officials and manipulate policy toward Korea, the mere mention of Lee's name made Derwinski livid. When a list of prospective consultants for Fraser's investigation was proposed to Derwinski in 1977, he objected only to Lee Jai Hyon. It was understandable from Derwinski's perspective. He was a sincere supporter of a steadfast American commitment in Korea. South Korea was an ally under threat of attack by a belligerent Communist foe. While much of the rest of the world was moving toward accommodation with Communist nations, South Korea remained staunchly anti-Communist. Derwinski was the same way. He knew the current of the times was against him, but, without a trace of bitterness, he consistently called for full support of anti-Communist causes and governments. When racists or dictators were criticized, Derwinski put aside his personal distaste for some of their policies and courageously defended them if they were strong anti-Communists.

Korean defectors were a menace to him because their information was the hardest to refute. If what Lee Jai Hyon said were proved true, the anti-Communist government of South Korea was in for big trouble in the United States. Derwinski probably perceived this more clearly than anyone, long before the Korean influence campaign became a major scandal.

Derwinski's name never appeared in any of Tongsun Park's ledgers. Accepting bribes would be wholly out of character for him. He stood in sharp contrast to the Congressmen on the take from Tongsun. He was one of the few members of Congress who could voice all-out support for Park Chung Hee at the height of Koreagate without having his motives questioned. He had opposed Fraser at every turn: the human rights hearings, the military aid cut, the investigations. If he was capable of informing on Sohn Ho Young, he did so for what he saw as the greater good of avoiding further erosion of American support for the South Korean government.

The Koreagate grand jury was unable to indict Derwinski because the intelligence information could not be used as evidence. A special sealed report was filed with United States District Judge William Bryant. According to the *Washington Post*, it stated that the jurors were convinced Derwinski was guilty. On the grand jury's recommendation, Judge Bryant passed the report on to the House Ethics Committee for further investigation. The committee did consider the report for several months but closed the case without taking disciplinary action. The evidence outside the intelligence information was insufficient.

The Derwinski-Sohn affair crippled the Fraser investigation for six months. The Departments of State, Justice, Defense, and the CIA stopped providing classified material to the subcommittee because of the unresolved breach of security. The investigation had relied heavily on intelligence reports and other secret documents from those agencies. Work on some important subjects came to a standstill with the cutoffs. A major series of hearings scheduled for October could not be held until the following March. After months of painstaking negotiations with agencies, access to classified material was resumed in February on a carefully controlled basis.

When the grand jury finished its work without returning an indictment, Derwinski proclaimed to the world that he had been vindicated. In November 1978, he was elected to Congress for his eleventh term by a large majority.

Inviting Tongsun Back

AFTER A comfortable six months at London's Claridge Hotel, Tongsun bought a townhouse in the fashionable Mayfair area in the early spring of 1977. Leaving the Claridge with bills unpaid, he had his new place redecorated and furnished anew. As always, he spared no expense. His London image was garnished with a Rolls-Royce, and he added a country home. He had acquired membership in three exclusive clubs, where he often played the tables in the company of a lovely lady or discussed business with new friends.

Tongsun was not only doing what came naturally; he was following his lawyer's advice. From Washington, William Hundley had told him to keep a high profile to deflate suggestions he was a fugitive. When Tongsun left for London, Hundley had said he should wait it out there until things cooled down in Washington. Bill Hundley had a reputation as an astute lawyer for famous guilty men. Among his clients was John Mitchell. He went about his work with a congenial and disarming manner. At the Justice Department, where he had been an official several years earlier, he was respected and liked.

At the time of Tongsun's exit from the country in September

1976, Hundley had surmised correctly that Justice did not have much hard evidence. It had also been clear the investigators at Justice did not believe what Tongsun was telling them. After one interview with Tongsun, an irate Paul Michel had said to Hundley, "Don't even bother to bring that guy over here again if he can't come up with a better story!"

Hundley really couldn't fault Michel for feeling that way. He knew it had not been a very good story. Tongsun had answered the investigators' questions by saying how nice it was that he had so many good friends in Washington. He had assured them the only reason he spent so much time with Congressmen was that he liked them. He had denied ever making payments to Congressmen, acting surprised that anyone could think such a thing. Yes, there had been that one cash gift to Governor Edwards's wife Elaine. There was no way he could get around that, since it had already been conceded by Edwards in public.

After Tongsun left the country, things got hotter instead of cooling down. The press had made the difference. With Tongsun denying the charges from the safety of London, the Justice Department was taking the heat. Paul Michel's investigation was beginning to look foolish as the newspapers came out with more and more Koreagate revelations. Some of the information for the stories obviously was coming from leaks inside Justice, the result of dissent among investigators about Michel's cautious bureaucratic approach. Ever since his work on Bebe Rebozo's affairs during Watergate, Michel had been regarded by many as a less than zealous prosecutor.

BY EARLY 1977, the Koreagate grand jury had heard testimony from former KCIA Director Kim Hyung Wook and Kim Sang Keun, the first defector from the KCIA. But what they said was limited regarding Tongsun's dealings with Congressmen. A big break came in March when the Internal Revenue Service seized

Tongsun's house and let the Justice Department have the documents that were found. An inventory was done with the help of Jay Shin Ryu, a disenchanted former employee of Tongsun's. Diaries and ledgers were located. Along with evidence the investigators already had, such as Tongsun's puffed-up list seen at the Anchorage airport, they were able to begin separating fact from fiction.

Michel and Civiletti, his boss, were determined to get Tongsun back. They needed him to give testimony that could be used to prosecute those Congressmen they were now convinced had been paid off. By the time Tongsun moved into his Mayfair townhouse, however, Bill Hundley had told Michel he would not be returning. He had decided to stay in London permanently. For several months it had been pretty obvious Tongsun had abandoned the idea of living in Washington. He had liquidated his American assets after the Internal Revenue Service imposed a tax lien. Tongsun was hardly of a mind to return for a possible grand jury indictment, subpoena from Congress, or both.

Michel was not interested in prosecuting Tongsun. There was a national uproar about Congressmen taking bribes from Korean agents. Getting the guilty Congressmen was what mattered, and Tongsun was the key. Michel even hesitated in using the threat of indictment to bargain with Hundley for Tongsun's cooperation. Instead, he stressed an offer of immunity from prosecution. He just wanted Tongsun to come back.

Hundley refused the invitation. When Tongsun departed, Hundley had assured Justice he would return if requested. Hundley had gone further by saying he himself could accept service of a subpoena for his client. Michel was angry at the refusal. But Hundley was mad at Michel over the way Justice had obtained the documents from Tongsun's house. Without a warrant or notice to Tongsun, Justice had subpoenaed the Internal Revenue Service, which gladly turned them over.

Predictably, there were grumblings in Congress over the Justice Department's failure to get anywhere with Tongsun. Philip Lacovara, then still running the House Ethics Committee's investigation, believed there was enough evidence to indict Tongsun. In the summer of 1977, three members of Congress complained to Attorney General Bell. Representatives Elizabeth Holtzman and Jerome Ambro got the impression the Attorney General was neither determined nor well informed about the case. He told them he was concerned Tongsun might become "another Vesco"—a rich fugitive businessman. There was not enough evidence to indict Tongsun, Bell said, so to indict solely to have him extradited would be wrong. Congressman Bruce Caputo, a maverick junior member of the Ethics Committee, was a constant critic of the government's handling of the Korean investigation. He wrote Bell stressing the need to have Tongsun extradited and criticizing the Attorney General for failing to indict him. In an August letter replying to the three Representatives, Civiletti warned that an indictment or formal written interrogatories might force Tongsun to leave London for shelter in Korea, a country with whom the United States did not have an extradition treaty.

As the criticism mounted, Attorney General Bell told members of Congress the White House had entered the picture. Through diplomatic efforts, it was hoped the Korean government would make Tongsun available for questioning in London

AT THE STAFF LEVEL, investigators from both the Ethics Committee and the Fraser Subcommittee were in London in August inquiring about Tongsun. Paul Michel was unhappy about that. He did not want others talking to Tongsun before the grand jury got his testimony. When Robert Bermingham of the Ethics Committee staff went to London in early August, Tongsun and his colleagues made themselves unavailable. Michael Hershman,

Fraser's deputy staff director, visited Tongsun's office unannounced on August 19. He identified himself and asked to see Peter Bartholemew, an American employee. After a few awkward moments in which the receptionist called in another employee, Hershman was told Bartholemew had returned to Seoul with Tongsun.

The move had been sudden. Tongsun did not even tell Hundley until he reached Tokyo for a change of planes. He called to say he had to go to Korea because his mother was very ill. He planned to return to London in ten days, so Hundley should not be concerned. Hundley believed Tongsun intended to do as he said, if he could. The Korean government, however, might have some say in the matter. Korea and the United States were the two countries to stay out of, Hundley had always felt. For the time being, England seemed ideal. Tongsun had agreed. But Hundley knew Tongsun would not hesitate to go to Korea if his mother needed him.

Paul Michel was incensed. Tongsun had gotten away again and it was all over the newspapers. Again Tongsun was saying he would only stay ten days; he had made similar statements when he left Washington almost a year before. The diplomatic efforts to question him in London were down the drain. Each time Tongsun relocated, he got farther away, both in miles and in legal reach. Civiletti and Michel had worried that an indictment would scare him into going back to Korea. Now he had gone without even being indicted.

An indictment now became the number-one priority. Within a week, it was drawn up, approved by the grand jury, and sealed on August 26. It was all done in strictest secrecy so Tongsun would not know. Michel acted as if he actually thought Tongsun would go back to London; Hundley had relayed Tongsun's promise to return in ten days and Michel believed it. Hundley was asked to fly to London and talk to Tongsun about coming to

Washington. The Justice Department even dispatched Thomas Henderson, chief of the Public Integrity Section, to London to make arrangements for dealing with Tongsun on his expected return.

At a press conference in Seoul on August 25, Tongsun made it clear that a year of Koreagate had not mellowed him: "I always enjoy the company of political figures and that happens to be my hobby," he explained benignly. Since a hobby is a personal pursuit, any suggestion that he was connected with the Korean government was "absurd." As for travel plans, he had no intention of returning to Washington to "subject myself to that kind of injustice and mistreatment."

A literal reading of those remarks told Michel only that a willing return to the United States was not in the offing; London had not been ruled out. Michel hoped Tongsun would go there and walk into the trap of a secret indictment.

The indictment did not stay secret very long. There was a leak to the press on September 1. When made public in full by the U.S. District Court on September 6, it was found to contain thirty-six counts against Tongsun. It charged conspiracy for the rice-political payoff scheme, bribery, illegal campaign contributions, mail fraud, racketeering, and failure to register as an agent of the KCIA. Details spanning nine years of Tongsun's complex political and social life were revealed. Twenty-three Congressmen and four Senators were named, including those alleged to have received gifts or contributions and those who put Hanna's and Tongsun's written statements into the record of Fraser's 1974 hearings. (Attorney General Bell said that mentioning the congressional names did not necessarily mean they were all suspected of breaking the law.) Named as unindicted co-conspirators were Hanna (also described as a KCIA agent) and former KCIA directors Kim Hyung Wook and Lee Hu Rak.

In Seoul, Tongsun told reporters the indictment was a "total surprise." He cast the issue in personal terms. He was hurt. "I can't tell you how much I was disappointed." As he saw it, America had let him down after he had done so much good.

The indictment angered Hundley and left him puzzled. He wondered why Justice had waited until Tongsun was in Korea to indict him. In a press interview, Hundley noted Tongsun had been "in an extraditable country for a year moving freely about, and they return the indictment when he's in one without a treaty." Hundley's advice to Tongsun was to "stay put" until what was happening in Washington was clearer. Tongsun really had no say in the matter. The Korean government was not about to let him go anywhere.

Among the staff at the House Ethics Committee's investigation, the way the Justice Department had handled Tongsun was more than puzzling. To some it had been "sheer buffoonery." They were referring to the London-Seoul travel problem and the indictment. But those issues had only worsened the Ethics investigation's already existing exasperation with Justice. Slow to act on Tongsun, Justice had been just as slow to cooperate with Ethics. The Attorney General and Civiletti had promised cooperation, but Paul Michel kept hoarding information and withholding documents, apparently hoping to safeguard any cases the Department might bring.

The competition among investigations was counterproductive and embarrassing. Some witnesses would tell one congressional committee what another committee was doing. In other cases, investigators from Ethics and the Fraser Subcommittee both were able to discover Justice did not know as much as Michel had made it seem.

GETTING TONGSUN back became a bigger priority than ever. With him indicted and in Korea, it was now a direct government-to-government issue between the United States and South Korea.

That created a dilemma for the Carter administration. Carter had made a campaign promise to withdraw all American ground troops from Korea. It had been one of the first decisions he made about changes in foreign policy. A month before his inauguration he had told a group of Senators and Congressmen his position was firm. The idea ran counter to conventional thinking at the State Department and the Pentagon, and it was foursquare against what the Park government wanted. Any talk about troop withdrawal came at the worst time as far as Park was concerned, no matter what the time.

When Jimmy Carter entered office, there were three big Korean issues: troop withdrawal, Koreagate, and human rights. Candidate Carter had said, in connection with troop withdrawal, "It should be made clear to the South Korean government that its internal oppression is repugnant to our people and undermines the support for our commitment there." Nevertheless, Carter's State Department hoped to proceed on three separate tracks. That approach proved impossible. The issues became hopelessly entangled. The Park government stonewalled on Koreagate. That made Congress reluctant to approve money for military aid to compensate for the troop withdrawal. Carter had to slow down his timing for the plan. Human rights ended up on the back burner.

President Carter had written to Park Chung Hee asking for Tongsun's return to the United States, offering full immunity from prosecution if Tongsun testified about the Congressmen involved. The day after the press reported Carter's initiative, Korean Foreign Minister Park Tong Jin announced his government's rejection of the offer. The decision to testify could be made only by Tongsun himself, Minister Park said, adding that Tongsun was "strongly opposed to the idea." A Blue House aide angrily charged the United States with demanding that the Korean government (the same government that abducted Kim Dae Jung from Japan) "kidnap" Tongsun and "deliver him bound and gagged."

Congressman Les Aspin, who had met with President Park a few days before the rejection announcements, said Park, when asked to return Tongsun to the United States, had "smiled and said to us, 'But we wouldn't want to violate his human rights, would we?' "

Never one to do things in an ordinary way, Tongsun made an unusual approach of his own. His girlfriend of several years, Tandy Dickinson, lived down the hall from Attorney General Bell in Washington's Watergate South apartments. One night in mid-September there was a knock on Bell's door. It was a woman who said Tongsun Park was calling from Seoul and wanted to talk to him.

"You must be kidding," exclaimed Bell. The woman said it was for real.

Bell wondered for a moment whether he was being set up. He decided to go with the woman. He shouldn't pass up the chance, since Tongsun was a fugitive and might want to surrender.

She led him to Tandy Dickinson's apartment. Dickinson, who was talking to Tongsun on the phone, handed it to Bell when he came in.

"Mr. Attorney General? Hello, this is Tongsun Park. I've heard so many good things about you. Everyone says you are a very fair man. I want you to know I love the United States and I'd like to get my troubles worked out."

Tongsun then asked Bell to talk to Bobby Lee Cook, a prominent Georgia lawyer, about the case. Tongsun said he knew Cook and understood the Attorney General did too.

Bell didn't want to say much. Without a lawyer present to represent Tongsun, he felt he really should not be talking to him. "But you already have an attorney, Mr. Park," replied Bell. "It's not proper for me to continue talking with you unless Mr. Hundley is involved."

The conversation ended with Tongsun urging the Attorney General to contact Bobby Lee Cook.

Bell remembered Congressman John Flynt's having mentioned something about Cook a week or so earlier. Flynt had heard Cook might also be representing Tongsun. Cook had not contacted the Justice Department, though. Bell decided to call Cook and ask about it.

Cook said he, too, had received a phone call from Seoul. Tongsun had asked if he would make some "preliminary inquiries." Since Cook knew the Attorney General, Tongsun had reasoned, it might be helpful if Cook were to sound him out. Tongsun had seemed to be trying to get a clearer picture of what he was up against in Washington. Cook had never met Tongsun and was not familiar with the details of the case. He told the Attorney General he was not representing Tongsun officially and felt somewhat at a loss about what to do, if anything.

Nothing came of it. Trying to get at the Attorney General through an old Georgia acquaintance was typical of Tongsun, however. It was his stock in trade to play on friendships. His greatest successes had always come that way. He used Hanna on other Congressmen and Korean officials. He had used Edwards for closing in on Passman. It was not surprising that he would think the Attorney General could be softened up, too.

ON SEPTEMBER 27, the grand jury indicted Hancho Kim, an American citizen living in the Washington area. KCIA defector Kim San Keun had testified to having delivered a total of $600,000 to Hancho Kim in 1974 and 1975. The money, made in two payments over a nine-month span, was to be given to Congressmen. It had come from Yang Doo Won at KCIA headquarters in Seoul. The Hancho Kim operation was part of phase two of the influence campaign, aimed at redressing the dictator image President Park had gotten. Kim Sang Keun said the scheme was hatched at a meeting Hancho Kim and Yang Doo Won had had with President Park.

"Operation White Snow," as it was called, was complete with secret code names. Yang Doo Won was "Catholic Father." Hancho Kim was "Dr. Hamilton." Security was tight. Even Kim Sang Keun's boss in Washington, the station chief, was not told. But "Patriarch," President Park, was kept informed and satisfied. Hancho Kim reported by telex directly to "Catholic Father" in Seoul. (During the same period, the KCIA set up direct telex communications with Tongsun, too, in an operation called "Ice Mountain.")

"White Snow" was an attempt to thwart Fraser's human rights activities. It was supposed to stave off further damage after his hearings in July and August 1974. In September 1974 the KCIA gave Hancho Kim $300,000. He was to use it for five members of the House Foreign Affairs Committee; they were called the "Advance Guard." In June 1975, Hancho Kim got another $300,000. Again, it was for the "Advance Guard." Fraser was causing more trouble with hearings. There was an even more urgent reason for the KCIA to be concerned this time. Lee Jai Hyon had just told Fraser's subcommittee, in public, about the KCIA's secret plans for the influence campaign.

Paul Michel had other information to corroborate Kim Sang Keun's story. Copies of telex messages were subpoenaed from RCA telecommunications. Michel knew how and where to look. From prior experience working for the Senate Intelligence Committee, he was aware that for many years the National Security Agency had monitored RCA's telex traffic through an operation of its own called "Shamrock."

Hancho Kim was supposed to have been a successor to Tongsun as an agent of influence to wine, dine, and bribe Congressmen. By 1975, Tongsun had been getting too well known and too controversial to suit the KCIA. Hancho Kim turned out to be an even less dependable agent than Tongsun. At least Tong-sun did pay off some Congressmen. But Hancho Kim's rip-off of the KCIA had been total. He spent it all on himself. Like Tong-sun, he was always overextended. But Tongsun was a rich man. Kim was not. The two $300,000 payments were the only large windfalls he ever had, and he went on a spending spree, paying cash for a new Cadillac Fleetwood Brougham. He paid off long-overdue debts owed at department stores, banks, furniture stores, and his children's private school. In a civic gesture, he donated $10,000 to Findlay College in Ohio, which he had attended for one semester many years before. The college gave him an honor-ary degree and set up the Hancho Kim Far Eastern Center. Like Tongsun, he was good at puffing up reports to the KCIA. He claimed to have been responsible for getting Congressmen to visit Korea. In an April 1975 report, he said he had "got together with Secretary of State Kissinger, and met with President Ford."

Kim Sang Keun simply took Hancho Kim's word about the meetings, the trips, and paying money to the "Advance Guard." Except for Congressman Tennyson Guyer, who was a friend, Hancho Kim apparently was not even acquainted with the others on the list he himself had made. There is no evidence that Han-cho Kim ever used any of the $600,000 for Guyer or for any oth-er "member" of the "Advance Guard" (Congressmen Guy Vander Jagt, Benjamin Gilman, Larry Winn, and Robert Lago-marsino). Therefore, he could not be charged with bribery. In-stead, Hancho Kim was indicted for conspiracy to defraud the United States, lying to a grand jury, and income tax evasion.

Former Congressman Hanna's turn for an indictment came next. For some time prior, the Justice Department had been try-ing without success to construct a bribery count against Hanna. The missing link was found by an attorney on the Ethics Committee staff, Martha Talley. During a deposition with her in mid-September, Hanna had slipped and let out that he had expected 25 percent of the rice commissions in return for helping Tongsun. Hanna's lawyer, Charles McNelis, immediately realized the implications of what his client had said. He asked the Ethics Committee not to pass it on to the Justice Department, since Congress is not required to share its confidential information with the executive branch. Ethics informed Justice, however, and on October 14, Hanna was indicted. His was the first congressional indictment.

Justice's knowledge of what Hanna had done was extensive. The indictment contained forty counts, charging bribery, conspiracy, mail fraud, and failure to register as a foreign agent (the first time in history a Congressman had been charged with acting as an agent of a foreign government). McNelis commented, "It's a good thing spitting on the sidewalk isn't a Federal offense or they would have thrown that in!"

LEON JAWORSKI DECIDED to hold some public hearings for the Ethics Committee in October. He was irked by Seoul's attitude toward the scandal. It was another cover-up like Watergate, only more difficult because a foreign government was doing the covering up. He could not do anything about the planners—President Park and others. He wanted Tongsun, though, and felt the same way about former Ambassador Kim Dong Jo; both had given money to Congressmen. Both Jaworski and the Justice Department had the responsibility of dealing with the guilty Congressmen. Testimony from Tongsun and Ambassador Kim was essential for doing that job. Since the United States and South Korea were friends, Jaworski felt the Park government should make Tongsun and Kim available for questioning. He was after Congressmen, not Koreans, but needed those two Koreans to furnish the evidence. Since he had neither of them, he decided on hearings, which might apply some useful pressure on South Korea by laying out the details of the bribery operations.

From the first announcement of the hearings, Jaworski prodded the Korean government. He complained that "full exposure of the facts . . . does not seem achieveable without the unrestricted cooperation of the government of South Korea."

He went further by making a veiled threat: "It is quite incongruous for us to extend . . . aid when reciprocal cooperation in this important investigation is not forthcoming." Congressman Bruce Caputo, the gadfly of Koreagate, was ahead of Jaworski by several weeks. In early September, he had tried for a drastic chop in aid to Korea for not returning Tongsun. The Caputo amendment had been defeated. Speaker O'Neill and Jaworski were not ready to go that far yet. Better to try other things first, they thought.

The Ethics Committee's October 1977 hearings attracted the media in full force. The room was packed with camera equipment, reporters, and spectators. Public Broadcasting Service carried the proceedings live.

The three days of hearings made an orderly exposé of the bribery schemes. Jaworski started off on October 19 with evidence on Ambassador Kim Dong Jo. Lee Jai Hyon was there to tell the story of the ambassador's stuffing envelopes with hundred-dollar bills, putting them in his attaché case, and going off to Capitol Hill in 1973. Lee had given that account in public twice before, once for Fraser in 1975 and again on television in 1976. This time there was someone to back it up. Nan Elder, Congressman Larry Winn's secretary, testified that in September 1972, Ambassador Kim had left an envelope full of money for the Congressman. They money was returned.

Kim Hyung Wook told how, as director of the KCIA, he had gotten Tongsun started as the rice sales agent in 1968. Customs inspector Dennis Hazelton described his encounter with

Tongsun at the Anchorage airport. Details of Hancho Kim's "White Snow" operation and "Ice Mountain" were given by Kim Sang Keun, supported by former Tongsun employee B. Y. Lee.

Since the Koreagate press had been saturated with news about Tongsun, Jaworski viewed the hearings as a means of showing the public that Kim Dong Jo was equally important. But it would take more than hearings and appeals from Leon Jaworski to make the Park regime listen. On a special mission to Seoul, Civiletti and Michel had reached a stalemate in negotiations over Tongsun. Jaworksi thus asked for the help of the full House of Representatives. At his initiative, a resolution was passed on October 31 calling on the Korean government to cooperate "fully and without reservation" with the investigations. The vote was 407–0.

The mood in Congress was getting nasty. The Carter administration, still trying to keep the issues separate, wanted Congress to take up a request for $800 million in military aid for South Korea. House International Relations Committee Chairman Clement Zablocki favored the proposal on its own merits. But after taking a sampling of his colleagues' feelings, he quickly concluded it would probably go down in flames if acted on now. If it were to succeed at all, it would have to be later under better conditions. By the end of October, Zablocki had announced his committee would not consider the aid request for the time being.

No matter how hard they tried, the leaders in Seoul could not wish Koreagate away. The cumulative effect of pressures in the United States brought about a change of mind in December. An agreement was reached. Tongsun could be questioned by the American government, first in Seoul, then in the United States. If he testified truthfully, the Justice Department would have his indictment dismissed. A lie detector could even be used.

The saving grace for the Park regime was that Tongsun would not be required to answer questions about his dealings

with South Korean government officials. The government made
sure he understood that point well before it entered into the
agreement. The Justice Department had no particular problem
with the condition. They needed Tongsun for his information
about payments to Congressmen. As far as ties with the government were concerned, there was already plenty of evidence. It
had been proved long before that he was a Korean agent.

Hundley had had a lot to do with bringing the Koreans
around. First he got a good immunity deal for Tongsun. Then he
convinced Tongsun it would be best to come back and talk. The
Korean government had been hardest to persuade. At first,
Hundley's suggestions had produced an angry reaction. But that
was before the pressure from the United States intensified.

At the time of the December agreement, the Korean government was still holding out against Tongsun's appearing in Congress. The unpredictability of Congress had always worried the
Seoul leaders. Individual Congressmen might ask Tongsun any
question under the sun, or leak secret testimony to the press. The
December agreement had left the question unresolved. The Koreans intended that he testify only in court. They hoped to satisfy
Congress by letting Jaworski and the Senate Ethics Committee
counsel, Victor Kramer, sit in during the interrogation in Seoul.

Jaworski would have no part of it. He did not want the Korean government to think it had done him any big favors. He
would question Tongsun at a hearing of the Ethics Committee
and no place else. He was responsible for finding whether Congressmen had violated the ethics code, and he would do the job
the way it was supposed to be done.

Secretary of State Vance and Attorney General Bell both
urged Jaworski to go to the Seoul interrogation. It might be the
Ethics Committee's only chance with Tongsun, they warned, if
the Koreans refused to let him testify in Congress.

That was a risk Jaworski was willing to take. His ace in the hole was Congress and the public. Anytime he wanted to, he could appear on *Meet the Press* and say that State and Justice were obstructing Congress's efforts to get the guilty Congressmen. He was thinking about doing just that. He thought the government's concentration on Tongsun was wrong. Kim Dong Jo was at least as important. To his mind, the agreement with Korea should cover both men. But the Carter administration was taking it step by step. The diplomats were saying if Jaworski didn't embrace the agreement, the Koreans would consider it ungrateful for their compromise, and refuse to cooperate anymore.

The idea was that half a loaf is better than none. Jaworksi saw it as less than half a loaf. Not only were they not pressing for Kim Dong Jo along with Tongsun, they were settling for less than all of Tongsun. Questions about his connection with the Korean government were to be taboo, thereby depriving the investigators of testimony from Tongsun about his being an agent and, perhaps, other relevant workings of the influence campaign.

Once more, Bell pleaded with Jaworski to go to Seoul. Again Jaworski refused, but said he would not interfere with their plans. "I won't stand in your way. Go ahead," he told Bell.

Bruce Caputo, on his own, decided to attend as an observer. Jaworski favored the idea. The Ethics Committee could benefit by having a member there to listen. The Senate Ethics Committee sent Dan Swillinger, the deputy special counsel.

The interrogation of Tongsun in Seoul began on January 13, 1978. For the sake of appearance, the Korean government pretended to interrogate also. The agreement with the United States had carried the words "mutual prosecution" in the title. Everything was perfectly balanced. Next to the table for the American prosecutors was one for the same number of Korean prosecutors. The head Korean prosecutor had the same rank in the Ministry of Justice as Civiletti had in the Justice Department. The KCIA matched numbers evenly with the FBI agents present. Tongsun

sat at the witness table flanked by Hundley on the left and his
Korean lawyer, Moon In Ku, on the right. The sessions were
closed to the public.

The first day began with a few minutes of questioning by the
Korean prosecutors. This exercise served to keep Tongsun mindful not to cross the boundary line into the forbidden area of his
connection with the government.

The Americans' turn took up the rest of the day. Paul Michel sounded serious and to the point. After reminding Tongsun
he had taken an oath to tell the truth, Michel put the first question:

"Now isn't it the truth, from a period of about the late 1960s
through about the middle of the 1970s you made substantial payments to numerous American Congressmen?"

Tongsun did not say yes. He asked a series of questions
about what Michel meant and gave a few half-finished answers.
It was part of the dodging game he played all day. Specifics were
glossed over with generalities. He tried to cast his story in terms
of personal friendships and detached observations. A typical
Tongsun answer was to say buddies in Congress would hit him
up for a few bucks now and then.

Each time Tongsun responded with a generality, Michel
sharpened the question and confined it to a single issue. Soon
Tongsun was filling in details of how much went to which Congressmen. But it was a long and drawn-out process. Answers
were calculated to give only as much as Tongsun thought the
Americans knew. The information from his diaries and ledgers
made it hard for him to fudge. He was infuriated that they had
been confiscated from his house in Washington.

Michel's questions concentrated on the charmed circle. Hanna had been his closest friend in Congress, Tongsun said, both a
"brother" and a "business partner." Concerning Passman, Tongsun said they got together because of a shared interest in collect-

ing watches. By the end of the day, however, Michel had been able to get him to admit making large payments to Hanna, Passman, Gallagher, and Minshall.

At 4:30 P.M., Michel announced, "We have reached the completion of one small phase of the overall interrogation, and we have reached an appropriate point to do some polygraph examination." As the session adjourned, Tongsun was led away to the lie detector.

He hated the polygraph more than anything. It robbed him of his defenses. It reduced the charmer to a biological organism. Being hooked up to that machine was humiliating. The whole world knowing about it was awful. What hurt the most, though, was for his mother to know. The polygraph made him look like a crook. He certainly didn't think he was. Even if everyone else thought he was a crook, he did not want his mother to see it that way.

In absentia, Tongsun's mother was a big influence in the interrogation room. Day after day, when Tongsun began to wax slick with his storytelling, Michel would warn, "Mr. Park, if you keep telling us this stuff, we'll have to use the polygraph." Upon hearing that threat, his song would modulate into a different key. Mother must always believe her boy was telling the truth.

The press descended upon Congressman Caputo whenever he emerged from one of the interrogation sessions. He reported that Tongsun's answers to questions were useful and seemed to be truthful. Caputo refused to give names of Congressmen. Civiletti and Michel avoided the press, but they welcomed having Caputo serve as point man as long as he kept his comments discreet.

Caputo felt less of a welcome from Ambassador Sneider. The ambassador was polite, but it appeared he would have preferred that Caputo—a harsh critic of the Park regime's noncooperation—had stayed in Washington. (Fraser had fared worse, with Sneider intervening directly in his investigation. Sneider had counseled the president of an American oil company not to cooperate with Fraser and to ignore a subpoena if one came. He had taken it upon himself to urge Fraser's investigators to disregard some information he learned they had picked up. They followed up on the lead anyway and uncovered one of the most substantial cases of the Korean government extorting money from American companies.)

The Seoul interrogation went on for thirteen days. Tongsun's veracity was tested by the polygraph three times, and he passed. With methodical care, Michel had drawn volumes of information out of him. During off-hours, relations between Tongsun and the people from the Justice Department had been minimal. The American prosecutors kept him at arm's length, much to his disappointment. It was not his way of dealing with people. The prosecutors would never let him be himself around them. The reporters were different. Tongsun hosted a party for them.

Tongsun's testimony led to the indictment of Otto Passman on March 31 for bribery, conspiracy, and fraud. He was accused of using his position to pressure the Korean government into buying American rice, and then persuading the departments of State and Agriculture to finance the sales with Food for Peace credits. The indictment said Passman's service had gained him $213,000 from Tongsun. On April 28, Passman was indicted again, this time for failing to pay taxes on the money received from Tongsun.

It had not been clear from Tongsun's testimony what Passman might have done with the money. The Justice Department and the House Ethics Committee, working together again, had become convinced that most of it seemed to have gone into Otto's passion—watches and jewelry.

Passman's attorney in Washington, Jim Hamilton, conveyed the Justice Department's urging of a guilty plea. Passman, weakened in his old age, almost agreed. He said he did not think he was guilty, but it seemed the prosecutors probably could convince a jury he was. Bolstered by his friend Marion Edwards, the governor's brother, Passman decided to hold firm. It was a matter of the old man's honor. Louisiana lawyer Camille Gravel, Governor Edwards's attorney, was called in. Together he and Hamilton were able to improve Passman's prospects considerably. They convinced a federal judge to consolidate the two indictments. Once that was done, the judge had to agree to move the trial to Louisiana because in tax cases, the defendant is entitled to be tried in his home jurisdiction.

The Justice Department had been cleverly outmaneuvered by Passman's lawyers. His chances before a hometown jury would be much better than in Washington. In Louisiana there were many who did not frown on a politician's helping himself to certain opportunities in public office as long as he was doing a good job for the people back home.

THE PARK GOVERNMENT kept Tongsun in Korea until the end of February 1978. The sticking point had been testimony in Congress. Jaworski was adamant, though, and he had the Carter administration supporting him. The Koreans finally agreed that Tongsun could be questioned by the House and Senate Ethics Committees. But if Fraser insisted on having him, the whole deal would be off. For years, the mention of Fraser's name had infuriated Park Chung Hee. The KCIA had spent $600,000 alone for Hancho Kim to try to stop Fraser. And Fraser's main investigatory interest lay in the forbidden area: Korean government activities.

Speaker O'Neill asked Fraser to forgo issuing a subpoena to Tongsun. Fraser consented, with the understanding he might exercise his option during Tongsun's expected second trip to the United States. He had been ready to subpoena Tongsun in 1976, more than two and a half years before. He was not investigating bribery, though, and would not stand in the way of those who were.

Tongsun stayed busy during his March and April visit to the United States. On the one hand, there were the grueling grand jury sessions and the closed meetings of the House and Senate Ethics Committees. On the more pleasant side, there were evenings at the George Town Club, dates with Tandy Dickinson, yachting on Chesapeake Bay, and socializing in the Middleburg, Virginia, fox-hunting country.

He made his congressional public speaking debut in front of cameras on April 3. The occasion was his first open session with the House Ethics Committee. He beamed his remarks beyond the committee to the television audience:

Instead of reading any prepared language rhetoric type of statement, what I wanted to do with the committee and the American public, I felt that I will just come into their living room and more or less have a little chat.

In his heyday, Tongsun had thought he was "the male Perle Mesta." Now he was a victimized Horatio Alger:

Some American periodical called me a swindler, which caused my mother to have a stroke, and from which she hasn't recovered since. Some people have even said what I have done in Washington was mysterious, at least, and constituted illicit activities. But I want to tell you what I have done in Washington I like to say constituted an American success story on a small scale.

Tongsun was right. The irony of his story is that he had learned the lessons of America too well. They had combined neatly with his driving motivation for recognition. He was no master spy or black villain. He was shrewd but affable, a minor corruptor of public ethics. He had been able to buy off about 1 percent of the members of Congress, certainly far fewer than the total number of corrupt people in government. A lot of others he simply conned. The way he had pulled it all off had been a marvel.

Sitting before the cameras at a congressional hearing, he was far more than the man-about-town and behind-the-scenes operator he had been. He was a superstar.

The cameras were there again when he stepped off a Korean Airlines jet at Seoul's Kimpo Airport on April 17. At home, the newspapers had made him a kind of folk hero—a successful Korean boy treated unfairly by his American friends. He reassured his waiting public by saying, "There is nothing to worry about. They must be grateful for my testimony."

II

Kim Dong Jo:
The Still-Untold Story

PARK CHUNG HEE'S government could always say, as it did, that the influence campaign was merely "the so-called Tongsun Park lobbying case." Tongsun was the fall guy. He was pushed out front in an effort to hide what the government had done. He was the logical one to take the rap. American newspapers had uncovered more about him than any of the others.

Deceit had been a basic technique of the campaign's protagonists all along. Covering up the campaign required relying even more heavily on deceit. The Park regime lied about Tongsun's assignments: he was just doing his own thing. Likewise, Moon, Suzi Park Thomson, and Hancho Kim had nothing to do with the government, the story went. When Fraser released the U.S. government intelligence reports about the 1970 Blue House planning meetings, spokesmen for President Park denied the meetings had ever taken place. What Fraser was doing was insulting to the South Korean President, they declared, but not surprising in light of the Congressman's persistent "anti-Korean bias." They reacted the same way when Fraser published the KCIA's 1976 plan for influence peddling, despite the initials of high KCIA officials on a copy of the Korean original.

Tongsun, Moon, Suzi, and Hancho Kim at best had shown mixed loyalty to the KCIA. Obviously, they were in the influence campaign mostly for what they could get for themselves. For Tongsun, it had been money and recognition. For Moon, it had been more personal power. For Suzi, it had been money and liquor to throw big parties. For Hancho, it had been a new Cadillac. But they were faithful to the government's cover-up position when they denied being Korean agents. It was also the best way of trying to save their own necks. Moon went the furthest. He claimed the Korean government had actually been *persecuting* his movement through the years. His proof was Ambassador Hahm Pyong Choon's 1975 complaint about Moon demonstrations at the United Nations. Telling that story frequently, the Moonies conveniently leave out the sequel: After the ambassador complained, the KCIA director in Seoul ordered the Embassy to stop interfering with Moon. The instructions were to cooperate with Moon because he was looked upon as a positive factor for building good relations between South Korea and the United States.

Throughout the cover-up, President Park made the most of the technicality that Tongsun, Moon, Suzi, and Hancho were not regular full-time government officials. He could tell his American ally they were not working for the government and ignore evidence to the contrary. With Ambassador Kim Dong Jo it was different.

An ambassador is a government's chief representative in a foreign country. Since the regime could not get around that fact, it was decided to pretend he had never made payments to Congressmen and to claim diplomatic immunity from questioning by Americans.

Handing out envelopes stuffed with money to Congressmen had not been the only unpraiseworthy act in Kim Dong Jo's career. During the decades when Korea belonged to Japan, people had to go along with the colonial masters in order to get along at all. There were varying degrees of collaboration, though. Kim Dong Jo's father had owned a rice mill near Pusan. He could not be faulted for staying on good terms with the Japanese to keep the license he had to have to operate his business. The Japanese thought him loyal enough, and the son bright enough, for Kim Dong Jo to be admitted to Kyushu Imperial University, which was government owned and one of the best in Japan.

Collaboration offered political opportunities. Kim Dong Jo was never a man to let one pass. He was motivated by more than economic necessity. As a Japanese police official during World War II, he carried out secret assignments that included spying on Koreans. Hundreds of thousands had been brought to Japan to work in the war industries. Informers like Kim Dong Jo helped control the resistance. With police identification papers, he was able to travel freely between Japan and Korea. His service had been loyal enough to get him a big promotion before the end of the war. The Japanese made him chief of the administration section for the provincial branch of the government's Materials Control Corporation in his home area. There, it was his job to ration food and other provisions for Koreans. His decisions on behalf of Japan affected the daily lives of thousands of Korean families.

After Korea was liberated from Japan, Kim Dong Jo got a job with the U.S. military government. A fellow ex-collaborator from his hometown, who had a high government position, had arranged something for him in the provincial government, again controlling supplies. In the late 1940s Kim landed a spot in the Foreign Ministry of the Syngman Rhee government. Advancement took him all the way to vice-minister of foreign affairs before he fell into disfavor and left the government.

Park Chung Hee's military takeover brought Kim Dong Jo back. He presented himself to Kim Jong Pil, the mastermind of

the coup and founding director of the KCIA. At that time Kim
Jong Pil was in the process of setting up the Democratic Republican party, so he hired Kim Dong Jo as foreign affairs adviser to
the party. After a period as president of Korea's export promotion organization, he was sent to Tokyo to be his government's
chief representative. When Korea and Japan concluded a treaty
in 1965, Kim Dong Jo became the Republic of Korea's first ambassador to Japan. There, he acquired a notorious reputation
among Korean residents as a bag man who made payments to
Japanese politicians and businessmen. He also extracted large
payments to his government from Korean residents in Japan by
threatening political disfavor.

Kim Dong Jo had been slated to be ambassador to West
Germany after Japan. The assignment did not satisfy him. Washington, the top foreign post, was what he wanted. After a personal plea to Park Chung Hee and some help from Kim Jong Pil, he
became ambassador to the United States in November 1967.

In Washington, Kim was both knowledgeable in his job and
popular around town. He and his wife entertained quite a bit.
They did it well. Both were cordial: he with a good sense of humor and she with charming manners. Kim Dong Jo had a fine instinct for where power lay in Washington. Perceiving the limits
on the State Department's clout, he worked hard at cultivating
persons from the White House, the Pentagon, and Congress. He
knew Seoul would measure his success in terms of how much aid
Korea got and how conscious Washington was of the North Korean threat as portrayed by the Park regime. He was well funded.
In addition to regular allowances for entertainment and personal
expenses, there was a special lobbying fund at his disposal. He
did not have to account for it. What he did with the money was
his own business. Between 1967 and 1969, the fund reportedly
amounted to over $1 million.

As President Park's chief representative, Kim Dong Jo considered himself the chief lobbyist as well. Persuading politicians was his province. So was the bestowing of cash gifts. If anyone else did it, it should be at his direction. That was the way things had been in Tokyo and he intended it to stay the same in Washington. Tongsun was an intolerable usurper. Darting about like a misguided missile, he was undercutting everything Kim was trying to do with Congressmen. Again and again, Kim had complained to Seoul about Tongsun, but Tongsun had the right backers in Seoul. There was nothing he could do to control the usurper. Kim Dong Jo therefore went about paying Congressmen quietly on his own.

After six years as ambassador to the United States, Kim returned to Seoul in December 1973 to become Minister of Foreign Affairs. Already well accustomed to passing out money to American politicians, he did not stop just because he was no longer ambassador. He was at it again at a conference of honorary Korean consuls in Washington in October 1974. Two honorary consuls, Donald Clark of Atlanta and Dwight Hamilton of Denver, acknowledged being given $3,000 each. They distributed the money to the campaigns of pro–Park Chung Hee candidates in the 1974 congressional elections, as Kim requested.

Kim Dong Jo's wife was enlisted in the cause, too. A visit to Korea in October 1975 by some Congressmen and their wives afforded another chance for handing out white envelopes. One evening around midnight, Lucille de la Garza, wife of a Texas Congressman, heard a knock on her door at the Chosun Hotel. She was surprised to see Mrs. Kim Dong Jo at such a late hour.

The two women exchanged greetings in the doorway. The telephone rang and the Congressman answered it. As he began talking on the phone, Mrs. Kim took an envelope out of her black handbag, handed it to Mrs. de la Garza, and said good night.

Mrs. de la Garza showed her husband the envelope full of hundred-dollar bills when he got off the phone. He was no stranger to cash from Koreans, having accepted a campaign contribution from Tongsun and reported it at the time as required by law. But this was different. De la Garza knew Mrs. Kim was the wife of a Korean government official. He had thought Tongsun was only a private businessman. The money was returned to Kim Dong Jo the next day with a request that it be donated to a certain Catholic school. (Three weeks later in Washington, Congressman de la Garza received a letter from the school thanking him.)

Mrs. Kim made at least one other call that night. Carol Myers invited her inside the room but declined the envelope when it came out of the handbag. Mrs. Kim did not want to take no for an answer so the envelope exchanged hands several times, confusing Mrs. Myers. When they finally said good night and closed the door, Mrs. Myers turned around and discovered the envelope on the dresser. She ran down the hall with it, but Mrs. Kim was not there. In the morning her husband, Congressman John Myers of Indiana, returned the money.

There were other congressional couples in the visiting delegation, but the de la Garzas and the Myerses are the only ones who said anything about such visits from Mrs. Kim Dong Jo.

The pattern of Kim Dong Jo's activities was clear from the evidence Leon Jaworski had. There was no question that Kim Dong Jo made a practice of passing out cash. But Jaworski's evidence of actual money offers came from three Congressmen—Winn, Myers, and de la Garza—who had turned it down. One would have to be extremely naïve to believe that in six years as ambassador and two years as foreign minister, a man of Kim Dong Jo's demonstrated habits had made only three offers of money to Congressmen. What happened to the other envelopes Lee Jai Hyon had seen in the attaché case? Lee had seen only one stuffed attaché case, and that was in 1973. What about the previous five years the Korean government had given the ambassador money for that purpose? Jaworski was no fool. He knew there were Congressmen who had not said no to Ambassador Kim's generosity. He had been hired by Speaker O'Neill to find out who they were. Those who had taken money from Tongsun may not have known he was a Korean government agent, but that could not be the case with the ambassador.

Although almost all Congressmen filled out Ethics Committee questionnaires, and sworn depositions were taken from thirty-five, none were telling on themselves. There was only one way to find them. Jaworski had to have Kim Dong Jo talk under oath.

Providing Tongsun had been quite enough as far as the Korean government was concerned. But Jaworski was making a lot of noise about the former ambassador, and ever since Watergate, Americans tended to listen when Jaworski said something. The Koreans needed a good legal argument to reinforce the stone wall. They found it in the Vienna Convention on diplomatic privileges. Under the convention, foreign diplomats may not be subpoenaed by the government of the country where they are stationed. They are immune from compulsory process. Both the United States and South Korea were parties to the Vienna Convention. The Park regime would use international law to justify the cover-up.

Speaker O'Neill and Jaworski met with the current ambassador, Kim Yong Shik, on January 31. They were told Tongsun could be made available to the Ethics Committee. Because of diplomatic immunity, however, it would be impossible to produce Kim Dong Jo.

The general dispute over Kim Dong Jo was well known by the time Jaworski appeared on *Meet the Press* on February 5. Responding to a question by Richard Halloran of the *New York Times*, Jaworski explained his position:

HALLORAN: Aren't you asking the Korean government to violate diplomatic immunity by making former Ambassador Kim available to you?

JAWORSKI: No, we are not asking for anything along that line. What we are really asking for is voluntary assistance and voluntary cooperation. It is what I would term is the norm in the extension of comity as between nations, comity under international law. They have received many favors from us. All we are asking them to do is help clear up a scandal that has hurt a very important institution of our government.

Since the Koreans had made the issue a diplomatic one, Jaworski took the opportunity of a national television appearance to apply some pressure on the White House. He called on President Carter and Secretary of State Vance to pry Kim Dong Jo loose from Seoul.

At the President's cabinet meeting the next day there was a lot of discussion about Jaworski and Kim Dong Jo. Jaworski had a point, but so did the Koreans. Vance pointed out that the Vienna Convention benefited American diplomats no less than South Korean. If the State Department backed Jaworski's position, he argued, any nation on earth could feel entitled to question American ambassadors under oath. It was no comfort to Vance that Jaworski realized that. On *Meet the Press* he had gone so far as to say, "I think if the shoe were on the other foot I would say we owed it to South Korea to do exactly what we are asking South Korea to do." It was all right for Jaworski to say that; he was not Secretary of State. Quite a few countries had been known to complain about American ambassadors from time to time.

Members of the cabinet were strongly in favor of South Korea's producing Kim Dong Jo voluntarily. The South Koreans were not volunteering, however. If they yielded under pressure from President Carter, that would make it even less voluntary. And Vance believed Jaworski's position was contrary to the Vienna Convention to begin with. The President agreed with Vance.

Jaworski and Vance were old friends. "I'm trying to get the

facts, Cy," he said at a meeting in the Secretary of State's office. "If this thing can't be unraveled, then I'll have to tell the American people, and let them conjecture from then on."

Vance did not want Jaworski making any public statements suggesting he had kept the truth from being known. He chided Jaworski for taking advantage of the Secretary of State's delicate position in the matter. Vance, too, wanted the bribery mystery solved. But he could not espouse Jaworski's interpretation of the Vienna Convention. The most he was willing to do under the circumstances was to have the State Department serve as honest broker between the Ethics Committee and the R.O.K. government.

In March, Jaworski—through the State Department—let the Koreans know he would ask for nothing further if he could have testimony from Kim Dong Jo. That was disheartening to Fraser, because he was interested in working with Jaworski to get Kim Ki Wan, an important former KCIA officer. Both investigations wanted to talk to Kim Ki Wan, and his representatives had said he wished to leave Korea and cooperate. Kim Dong Jo was more crucial, however.

A month later, Ambassador Kim Yong Shik made an offer to Speaker O'Neill. Kim Dong Jo would be willing to "clarify" things over the telephone with Speaker O'Neill. The Speaker rejected the offer: in an investigation for disciplinary action against Congressmen, informal testimony was worthless. He and Jaworski agreed a telephone talk would be no more useful than an interview Kim Dong Jo had given *Newsweek* a few weeks earlier. Kim had denied everything.

Jaworski had a more liberal offer for the ambassador on April 25. Kim Dong Jo would not have to come to the United States. The questioning could be in any country other than Korea. Kim and Jaworski did not even have to be in the same room. The questions and answers could be done in writing. The one requirement was that Kim Dong Jo take an oath to tell the truth.

It was the oath that was totally unacceptable to the Koreans. Administering an oath would be imposing a requirement on Kim Dong Jo that, they argued, violated the Vienna Convention.

Having made no gains with concessions, O'Neill and Jaworski escalated. They decided it was time to use foreign aid as leverage on Korea. A resolution was drafted and introduced; it threatened to cut off all nonmilitary aid if Kim Dong Jo were not made available. The only pending nonmilitary aid was for Food for Peace credits and the Peace Corps.

The resolution would have to be considered at a hearing by the House International Relations Committee. Jaworski found the committee's chairman, Clement Zablocki, reluctant, but on O'Neill's insistence, he agreed to hold a hearing and co-sponsor the resolution. Despite Jaworski's fears—during a recess, he commented, "I'm making it as tough for them as I can, but it isn't like Watergate"—the committee approved the resolution unanimously.

When the measure came before the full House on June 1, O'Neill made a supporting speech from the floor, in a rare departure from custom.

"We will not tolerate evasive responses in the face of such a serious matter!" he vowed to the applause of his colleagues. He recounted the 54,000 lives and $11 billion the United States had spent on Korea and issued a warning: "Let there be no doubt that the consequences will be great if the Republic of Korea refuses to cooperate!"

The House passed the resolution by a vote of 321–46.

In Seoul, the Park regime seemed unmoved by either the rhetoric or the resolution. Officials at the Foreign Ministry said South Korea could get along easily without the Food for Peace and the Peace Corps. It was the uncomradely gesture they resented. Smiling at his American friends, one official said, "It is an insult. It amounts to blackmail."

South Korea did not budge, so the House carried out its

threat on June 22. An amendment sponsored by Majority Leader
Jim Wright eliminated $56 million worth of aid. That did not
make any difference either. The Korean position stayed the same.

Jaworski had by now modified his insistence on testimony
under oath. "Comparable means of assuring reliability" would be
satisfactory, such as having the Korean government attest to the
truthfulness of Kim Dong Jo's testimony. He was turned down
again. A last-ditch effort was made late in July. Speaker O'Neill
asked that President Park agree to meet in Seoul with two members of the Ethics Committee—Floyd Spence and Lee Hamilton—to try to resolve the impasse. The offer was rebuffed.

Jaworski saw no point in going on. Virtually every avenue
had been traveled. He had even gone outside official channels
and asked Tongsun's lawyer, Bill Hundley, to appeal to the Koreans. They had listened to Hundley about Tongsun, but Hundley was unable to make a dent in the stone wall around Kim
Dong Jo. The only thing Jaworski had not tried was a cut in military aid. He was unwilling to do that. Tampering with military
aid was something he was against personally, and he doubted the
House would support it anyhow.

On July 28, Jaworski announced he was resigning as special
counsel to the House Ethics Committee. He said that without
Kim Dong Jo's testimony, "we have certainly come to a place
where the investigation must come to a close. There is nothing
else we can do."

The Korean government, he concluded, "wants to suppress
what the facts are."

EVEN BEFORE JAWORSKI LEFT, the newspapers had begun calling Koreagate a flop. The scandal had fallen far short of the
press's own speculation that as many as a hundred or more Congressmen might be nailed for accepting payoffs. The evidence was
indicating that Tongsun's payments in the upper five-figure and

six-figure range went only to the four members of the charmed circle, none of whom was still in Congress. His smaller transactions with some thirty other Congressmen and Senators appeared to have been legal in a technical sense. The big question of whom Kim Dong Jo paid off seemed unanswerable.

Ethics Committee Chairman Flynt shed no tears over Jaworski's departure. Independence for a committee counsel was alien to his experience. Through many years in Congress, he had become accustomed to staff people who took orders and were seen but not heard. That was the way things were supposed to be on the Hill. Although the Korean investigation made it different, Flynt stayed the same. All along, Flynt apparently resented being overshadowed by the large figure Jaworski cut. Petty squabbles erupted at closed meetings of the committee. Flynt became piqued over the plan to have Jaworski make an opening statement before the television cameras at the committee's first hearing in October 1977. At one point, he had even refused to attend the hearing. The two men each made opening statements, but Jaworski's got more coverage. It was Jaworski's investigation as far as the press was concerned.

From Jaworski's perspective, the bribery scandal was an issue too critical to allow foot-dragging by Flynt. It was hard to get the chairman even to call committee meetings, he discovered. Flynt's help was almost never there when Jaworski needed it. Having the chairman support the amendment to cut off economic aid was essential, but Flynt did not want to vote for the measure.

"Not once have you spoken on the House floor on our behalf," said an exasperated Jaworski.

"Well, what about you? You're always dealing with the Speaker instead of the chairman of your committee," retorted Flynt.

"It was the Speaker who brought me in, not you," Jaworski reminded him.

There was a lengthy pause before Flynt grudgingly replied, "All right, I'll support the amendment."

It had always grated on Flynt that everyone knew O'Neill had stepped in to hire Jaworski himself in order to restore credibility to the Ethics Committee's investigation. Bitterness over that fact smoldered throughout his relations with Jaworski. With Jaworski gone, Flynt reemerged from obscurity. He proclaimed a new breakthrough immediately. Word had come from the Korean government through the State Department, he announced on August 3, to the effect that Kim Dong Jo "would supply new and concrete factual information regarding his financial transactions with members of Congress." The Ethics Committee decided to respond to South Korea's overture.

The agreement Flynt entered into was one already considered and rejected by Jaworski in previous months: questions and answers in writing not under oath. Still, after the Korean rebuffs on everything else, Jaworski had himself come to believe such written interrogatories might be worthwhile as a first step if the Korean government attested to the truthfulness of the answers. Chairman Flynt and the new American Ambassador to Korea, William Gleysteen, were under the impression Seoul would meet that condition.

Twenty-two subdivided questions were sent by the Committee to Kim Dong Jo on August 19, 1978. He replied on September 18 with a long letter and eight attached comments. The Ethics Committee took the position, by vote, that Kim's response was "totally unsatisfactory and insulting." There was no "new and concrete" information as promised. The committee judged the answers to be neither truthful nor complete. Flynt's balloon had burst. There had been no breakthrough, nor was there to be one in the remaining weeks of the investigation. The committee concluded it would be fruitless even to ask the Korean government for more information on anything.

Kim Dong Jo's response had swept aside all the evidence with a blanket statement: "Regarding the repeated questions in your questionnaire about my monetary offers, I would like to state that I never offered or attempted to offer any money directly or indirectly to any U.S. Congressman or other public officials."

His letter was a lecture to the investigators. They had no "objective evidence," he declared, and whatever information they had was "one-sided." The committee had damaged the image of the R.O.K. government by making an "unfounded claim" that there was a plan to corrupt Congress. He described himself as a wonderful ambassador and cited a 1972 *Newsweek* article that, he said, had listed him as "one of the five most efficient" in Washington.

THE ETHICS COMMITTEE was never to get the real story from Kim Dong Jo. It had Tongsun's story, though, and was able to decide which Congressmen should be disciplined for accepting his largesse. They were in the nickel-and-dime category compared to the charmed circle.

In October, the committee found three sitting Congressmen—all California Democrats—guilty of misconduct. Censure by the House was recommended against Edward Roybal for lying under oath and converting to his personal use a $1,000 campaign contribution from Tongsun in 1974. The committee recommended reprimands (a lesser condemnation) in the cases of John McFall and Charles Wilson. McFall was found to have failed to report campaign contributions totaling $4,000 from Tongsun in 1972 and 1974. Wilson was found to have denied falsely that he received a wedding gift of $1,000 cash from Tongsun in 1975.

The full House acted on the committee's recommendations by reprimanding all three Congressmen. The penalty for Roybal was lowered from censure after he asserted he was being singled out because he was a Mexican-American. Censures and reprimands express the House's disapproval of a member's conduct. They do not limit his privileges or official activities but do affect his reputation.

The committee found no violation of the ethics code in the campaign contributions Tongsun made to the other sitting Congressmen: John Brademas, Eligio de la Garza, Thomas Foley, John Murphy, Melvin Price, Frank Thompson, and Morris Udall. It was not improper for them to accept the money (as long as it was reported as required) because it was received before 1975, when contributions from foreign nationals became illegal, and because there was no proof that they had known Tongsun was a foreign government agent.

"Tip" O'Neill, who had been an important target for Tongsun, was found to have done nothing improper. The Ethics Committee's investigative report on O'Neill, however, suggested he used poor judgment in accepting Tongsun's party hospitality.

Although the committee had no jurisdiction over ex-members of Congress, it wanted to find out as much as possible about the scope of Tongsun's activities. Based on testimony from Tongsun and other evidence, the committee had reason to believe Tongsun had given $10,000 to Nick Galifianakis of North Carolina in 1972, and $1,000 to John Rarick of Louisiana in 1974. Both denied under oath they had received the money. A federal grand jury, after considering the Ethics Committee's information, indicted Galafianakis for perjury in April 1979. Rarick was not indicted, however, because the grand jury determined that when he testified before the Ethics Committee, the oath had not been properly administered. Galafiankis got off on a similar technicality. Because correct procedure had not been followed in taking his testimony, a federal court dismissed the indictment.

Other Korean payments to Congressmen in 1974 and 1975,

apparently made in reaction to Fraser's hearings and military aid cut, were discovered by U.S. intelligence. The money reportedly was passed by Foreign Minister Kim Dong Jo while visiting the United States or by Embassy officers such as Colonel Lim Kyuil. Without mentioning names, the Ethics Committee said that, according to intelligence, the Korean government had paid four Congressmen in four-figure amounts and planned to pay two others in five-figure amounts.

Intelligence reports usually are not admissible as legal evidence, even when they are records of telephone conversations or cable transmissions. In order for the Ethics Committee to make formal findings, there had to be live witnesses to corroborate the other evidence. Neither the Justice Department nor the Ethics Committee had been able to file charges against Congressman Derwinski because there had been no available witness to the tip-off on Sohn Ho Young's defection from the KCIA. Likewise, the Ethics Committee could not proceed against the other Congressmen named in intelligence reports.

In large part, the Park regime's cover-up succeeded. No regular official of the government ever admitted doing anything improper. A few defectors did, but they were labeled by the Korean government as liars and traitors. The only person to admit anything with the government's blessing was Tongsun. Kim Dong Jo got by with being remembered as the mystery man who stuffed money into envelopes, packed them in his attaché case, and headed for Capitol Hill.

Kim Dong Jo's many destinations on Capitol Hill probably will never be known. But there are Congressmen who must get up every morning thankful for the stonewalling Park regime.

The congressional bribery investigations can be expected to have a good long-term effect. When the probe ended, there was a new attitude of vigilance on the Hill regarding foreign lobbying. The scandal seemed to have had a sobering effect. Those who took money were likely to think twice before doing it again. Those who didn't felt stronger deterrence.

The Ethics Committee did all it could with what it had. Nothing it could have done would have met the expectations raised by the press. The investigation did not catch all the crooked Congressmen, but it was not from lack of trying. When it came to an imperfect close, Congresswoman Millicent Fenwick had a fitting comment.

"We may have brought forth a mouse," she said, "but it was an honest mouse."

Dueling with the Moonies

"HE'S WHITE, Baptist, and from Georgia. Does that make President Carter a member of the KKK?" blared the heavy boldface type at the top of Bo Hi Pak's signed full-page ad in the June 30, 1977, *Washington Post*. Of course that didn't make the President a Klansman, the statement went on, any more than the Reverend Moon should be considered a KCIA agent just because he is yellow, anti-Communist, and from Korea. The Koreagate scandal had created a national climate of guilt by association wherein all things Korean had become suspect, Pak wrote. Moon was the most victimized man in America. And the main victimizer was Congressman Fraser, who was trampling on Moon's right to religious freedom.

It didn't seem that way to Fraser. He had started out by investigating KCIA activities in the United States and found evidence that the Moonies had been paid by the KCIA to stage an anti-Japanese demonstration in Washington. He broadened his investigation to cover all relations between the United States and South Korea and found evidence that Pak had collected money for Unification Church activities by telling American contributors it was for Radio of Free Asia. He was astonished by the extent of swindling and illegality suggested by the evidence. It seemed as if there was a Moon front group for every purpose. Because one of Moon's groups was a church, he stipulated that religious beliefs were to be left alone. He told his staff and the public that the investigation was looking into political and business activities only, in search of ties with the Korean government; freedom of religion was inviolable under the First Amendment.

What Fraser failed to take into account was that to Moon there was no distinction between political, business, and religious activities. It was all religion. Fraser should have studied the Divine Principle.

To assert Master's position authoritatively, the Moon organization hired outstanding legal talent. Moon's own attorney was Charles Stillman of New York. Bo Hi Pak retained John Bray and Frank Lilly of one of Washington's largest firms: Arent, Fox, Kintner, Plotkin and Kahn. The Unification Church was represented by the firm of Melrod, Redman and Gartlan. Former Watergate prosecutor Richard Ben-Veniste, along with Michael Golden, handled most of Melrod, Redman and Gartlan's work for the church.

For a time, the church had a very important defender in the media: columnist Jack Anderson. Anderson was on the board of the Diplomat National Bank and served as its chief spokesman. In two very angry letters, he called Fraser's probe of the $1 million Moonie investment in the bank "a witch hunt." His association with the bank, he stated, had come as a result of his interest in the Asian-American community. After discovering what the Moonies were up to, Anderson resigned in November 1976 and expressed regret over attacking Fraser. His correspondence with Fraser had been "intemperate," he now said.

Fraser was subjected to a nationwide propaganda barrage during the summer and fall of 1977. The Moonies were determined to stop the investigation. Letters went out to thousands of lawyers, clergymen, and politicians—including every Senator and Congressman. Unification Church president Neil Salonen made personal calls on Congressmen. He and others held press conferences and appeared on local television. They even went after Fraser's wife and children. His wife, Arvonne, was described as a fanatical left-wing feminist whose job at the State Department put her in a conflict of interest with her husband in Congress. They tried to make something sinister out of Fraser's daughter's participation in an anti–Vietnam War demonstration at the University of Minnesota.

Not surprisingly, the smear campaign was counterproductive. Fraser's office received hundreds of letters backing him up in response to Moonie pleas to stop him.

GETTING MOONIES to testify at hearings required more than a subpoena. It took a lot of legwork as well.

Neil Salonen called on Fraser unexpectedly in May 1976, the day after the *New York Times* reported for the first time that the subcommittee was investigating Unification Church activities. The *Times* story had it all wrong about links with the Korean government, he said, so he wanted to clear up any misunderstanding Fraser might have had about the church.

Fraser said he was concerned about apparent illegal KCIA activities in the United States and had received information that the Unification Church might be involved.

The information could not be true, Salonen assured him, because the church did not engage in political activities.

"What about the Freedom Leadership Foundation?" Fraser asked.

Salonen explained that the Freedom Leadership Foundation and the Unification Church were two different organizations. He was president of both, but neither was political in any way. The church was religious and the foundation was educational. To avoid further misunderstanding, he wanted to leave some reading material for the Congressman. One of his colleagues stacked books on the table.

Fraser thanked him and asked, "Would you be willing to appear as a witness at one of our subcommittee hearings?"

Salonen said he would.

The subcommittee staff sent a letter formalizing the request. A different Salonen replied. He reiterated his "earnest willingness" to provide information about the Freedom Leadership Foundation but professed surprise at being invited to testify at a hearing on KCIA activities. "I am quite certain that I would be unable to contribute anything to such a hearing." Two days earlier, Bo Hi Pak had made a similar reply to a similar letter.

It was about a month later that the International Relations Committee granted Fraser the authority to subpoena witnesses. With an authorized subpoena in hand compelling Salonen to testify, two Fraser investigators went to the Moonie office on Connecticut Avenue in mid-September. They had tried to schedule an appointment, but Salonen and Unification Church lawyer Richard Ben-Veniste had given them the runaround for several days. They identified themselves at the door and climbed the stairs to the lobby on the second floor. No, Mr. Salonen wasn't in. No one could say when he would return, since he was very busy preparing for the church's "God Bless America" rally to be held at the Washington Monument the next night. The investigators said they would wait. No, they would have to leave because the office was private property. They left, although they were aware that Salonen was in his office at that moment talking to a newspaper reporter. They had timed their visit to coincide with an appointment the reporter had told them was scheduled.

There was a possibility Salonen would go to Pershing Square, where there was to be a gathering to promote the rally. They waited there for over an hour among Moonies gaily costumed to look like Betsy Ross and George Washington. They were getting exasperated and decided to try the office once more. This time, they took along a United States marshal. The Moonies were adamant. The marshal couldn't even get inside the front door. The subpoena for Salonen was served on the doorman.

Later that day, Ben-Veniste called Fraser to say that Salonen was now willing to testify voluntarily. Fraser agreed to regard the subpoena as not having been served.

FOR CHURCH PEOPLE, the Moonies had some strange allies. One was a man calling himself Walter Riley; his real name was Clyde Wallace. Riley was a convicted felon who had been in and out of jail several times over a period of more than twenty years. He ran a business in the National Press Building called The Spy Shop; it specialized in selling electronic bugging equipment. But he described himself primarily as a journalist. His acquaintance with Bo Hi Pak was through his Korean wife, who had known Pak while both were working at the Embassy in the early sixties.

Riley was a trader in information. Until he realized there was no gain in it for him, information flowed freely to Fraser's investigators. Some of his stories were far-fetched, like the one about a nationwide ring of Korean call girls run by the KCIA. He also claimed the Moonies held him in high esteem, often soliciting his views on decisions affecting church policy.

On some matters, what Riley said was backed up by evidence found later. He was correct in his observation that Bo Hi Pak and Neil Salonen were often at odds with each other and that although Salonen had the title of church president, it was Pak who had the power.

On June 18, 1976, *CBS News* reported that Moonies owned about half of the total stock in the Diplomat National Bank. The following day, Bo Hi Pak met in his office with Riley and church leaders Neil Salonen, Michael Runyon, and Cha Han Joo. According to Riley, Pak said he was worried because a lot of cash had been brought in from Japan, Germany, and Korea for him to use to buy bank stock in the names of thirteen low-ranking Moonies. If Fraser brought out their names, his role, and the source of the money there could be trouble over possible violations of law.

Salonen was described by Riley as concerned about the potential for embarrassment to the church but without Pak's personal dilemma, since he considered his own investment to be legitimate.

Draw up some phony promissory notes, Riley suggested; at least that would make it seem the thirteen people were genuine investors in their own right. It wouldn't solve the problem of the foreign source of the funds though. The meeting ended with no decision.

After passing Moonie secrets to the Fraser investigators for a while, Riley saw that switching sides could be more to his advantage. Fraser's people had nothing to offer him and, besides, Fraser wasn't tough enough on Communism. Riley wrote an article for publication that claimed a defector from Polish intelligence told him the Russians had identified Fraser as "an agent of influence in the Soviet intelligence network." Although Riley concedes the Moonies had asked him to do such a story to offset the Congressman's theme of ties between Moon and the KCIA, he insists it was not written for them. However, the only American paper known to have carried his story was Moon's *News World*. In the Korean press, it was a front-page item during a visit to Seoul by Fraser's investigators in December 1977.

Riley's appetite was whetted. He was getting some attention as a journalist. So he bore in on Fraser. Going through several years of staff pay records, he discovered a Fraser employee had been paid for several months' work in a lump sum instead of once a month for each month. He played it up as a major payroll scandal. Then he came up with what he called "reverse Korean pay-offs." The five outside consultants for the investigation were said to have been paid off by Fraser, through their contracts with the subcommittee, for appearing as witnesses at hearings in previous years—a kind of bribe with a deferred payment. Riley continued to make phone calls to Fraser's investigators, asserting that since he was a reporter they should talk to him. At one point he even told them he was thinking about writing that Fred Rayano, a former New York police official on the Fraser staff, had tapped his telephone. Riley thought he had made the big time as an investigative reporter, but it was only a moment in the sun, courtesy of the Moonies.

IF CONGRESS were to make a list of the ten all-time most difficult hearing witnesses, Bo Hi Pak's name would probably be on it. He declined to testify voluntarily in 1976. The following year he refused even an informal staff interview. A subpoena was authorized and served after protests from his lawyer. He then appeared before the subcommittee in a closed session and answered only two questions: What is your name? What is your address? The rest he refused, invoking freedom of religion, freedom from self-incrimination, and diplomatic immunity (having been a Korean Embassy official in the early sixties). The subcommittee obtained a federal court order conferring immunity from prosecution on Pak and compelling him to answer the subcommittee's questions.

Then Bo Hi Pak began to perform.

His forty-page opening statement at the first hearing on March 22, 1978, consumed more than an hour. The Reverend Moon's divine work had been severely damaged by Fraser's "unfounded, vicious attack," he declared.

> You nailed Reverend Moon's name and the Unification Church to the cross. You crucified us. Reverend Moon and

I prayed as Jesus prayed: "Father, forgive them for they know not what they do."

But even Jesus did not have to deal with the *New York Times*. Today our job is infinitely more difficult because of papers like the *New York Times* who have crucified Reverend Moon on a worldwide level.

His answers to questions were as indirect as his opening statement was direct. In the course of two hours, though, he did acknowledge paying $3,000 in KCIA money to a Japanese Moonie who made some anti-Communist speeches in Korea. The KCIA gave him the cash in Washington. He took it to Korea, the woman came from Japan to meet him there, and he paid her.

At the first public hearing, Fraser allowed Pak four times the customary fifteen minutes for opening statements. No other witness had consumed so much of the subcommittee's time in that way. The opening statements were critically important to Pak, however. They were the only saving grace in an otherwise intolerable humiliation of the Unification Church. At the second hearing, three weeks later, Fraser announced that the questioning would begin at the outset. Pak's attorney, John Bray, asked that Pak be given fifteen minutes for another opening statement. Fraser agreed. Pak launched a tirade of righteous indignation, heedless of the time limit.

PAK: I myself cannot tolerate any longer this outrageous action. Mr. Chairman, in my last testimony I brought to—

FRASER: Colonel—

PAK: (continuing)—your attention the innocent suffering of members of the Unification Church throughout the world.

FRASER: Colonel, we have run well past the 15 minutes.

PAK: Yes, Mr. Chairman. I plead with you. Let me finish. There are just a few more pages to go. I definitely would like to finish and speak to the American people.

FRASER: How many pages are you referring to?

PAK: I am talking about six pages.

FRASER: Colonel, I am sorry. That would take another 12 minutes. At our last hearing, in checking the record, half of the time was taken up by your opening statement.

PAK: Particularly—

FRASER: I know that you have made copies available to the press, and we will put the entire statement in the record.

PAK: I would like to stay here longer, Mr. Chairman, even up to midnight. Let me have 5 more minutes to continue and finish my statement. Particularly, it is very important for me emotionally, the last part of this statement, because it involves the character assassination on my moral character and on my leader, Reverend Moon. I cannot go on without telling you and the American people and let me have 5 or 6 minutes.

FRASER: Colonel, we will give you time at the end to finish reading the statement if you like, but I think now we do need to proceed with the questions. I had hoped that in the more than 15 minutes you had picked out the most important parts, and I hope that is what you have done.

PAK: The most important is coming from this time on.

If Fraser started asking questions, Pak vowed, he would answer by continuing to read his statement. Bray implored Fraser to let him go on. All right, Fraser said, six more minutes.

The time pressure and the fervor of the prepared text made Pak emotionally supercharged. Fraser was "an instrument of the Devil" for spreading lies about Moon.

PAK: Have you ever been interested in the truth?

FRASER: Colonel, I think under our arrangement now we have come to the end of your time.

PAK: I would like to finish just the conclusion, sir.

FRASER: What are you proposing now?
PAK: Give me one minute, sir.

Nonstop, he went on with the diatribe at accelerated speed. His voice became louder and louder. How did history remember Nero and Julian the Apostate? As the great persecutors. "And so history might remember Donald Fraser, if it remembers him at all."

He waved his arms vehemently. Near the breaking point, his voice trembled as he shouted with tears in his eyes: "You may get my scalp, Mr. Chairman, but never my heart and soul! My heart and soul belong to God! The Lord is my shepherd. Even though I walk through the valley of the shadow of death, I fear no evil, for Thou art with me!"

Finished at last, he buried his head in his arms on the table and sobbed loudly. The audience sat in shocked silence. Fraser said nothing. The sound of Pak's crying echoed in the hearing room. Bray consoled him.

After about two minutes, Pak raised his head and calmly announced, "Mr. Chairman, I am ready sir. Thank you."

Fraser questioned with patience that to his staff seemed almost as exasperating as Pak's answers. A simple question like "When did you first get to know the Japanese woman?" Fraser quietly rephrased no less than seven times, each time getting a different indefinite answer. (The woman in question was a Moonie, Fumiko Ikeda, to whom Pak had admitted paying the $3,000 in KCIA money.) But few committee chairmen had ever had to deal with someone like Bo Hi Pak, forever contradicting, evading, and prolonging point after point. The process of getting information out of him seemed interminable.

Pak said the money he used for buying stock in the Diplomat National Bank came from the "Unification Church Pension Fund International," which, according to his prepared statement, had been formally established by him in 1971 because Moon wanted to set up a family assistance program for elderly church members. Under questioning, Pak did not know how much money was in the fund, where it was kept, whether it was ever deposited in a bank, or what happened to it. He then retreated by saying the fund was set up informally and loosely and he wasn't sure how it got its name. Using subpoenaed financial records, Fraser showed that Pak had brought $223,000 in cash from Japan to the United States in the early 1970s. Pak said he borrowed the money in several installments from a Japanese church member, Mitsuharu Ishii, but was not sure when or where, or how many loans there were. He could not recall any written records. At a subsequent hearing, he produced three promissory notes he had drawn up a few weeks before.

Pak's denunciation of Fraser reached its peak at the third hearing, on April 20. Walter Riley's fable about Fraser and the Soviet KGB was the springboard for a string of insults. Fraser was "a traitor, a second Benedict Arnold, an enemy of this Nation and all free nations." He was an enemy of Korea and America for giving aid and comfort to the Communist cause.

"Worse, you have become God's enemy because God is counting on Korea and America and leaders like Reverend Moon to turn the tide against the satanic forces of communism."

There was hope even for Fraser, though. Pak admonished: "Repent, for the Kingdom of Heaven is at hand!"

Fraser proceeded with questions as if nothing had happened.

The Moonies were enraged by the media coverage of Fraser's investigation. Pak lodged a written complaint that television cameras were present at the hearings without his consent. Yet he declined to exercise his right not to be photographed. The reason was that some of the cameras were all right, while others were not. Fraser allowed Moonie cameramen from One Way Productions to film the hearings even though they were not accredited to the House TV gallery. Pak made good use of the films. He put together an anti-Fraser TV documentary, starring himself. It was shown in Korea during prime time, making Pak a national hero. Among the viewers was Tongsun Park, who said he was repulsed.

WITH THE BENEFIT of hindsight, Fraser investigators Ed Gragert and Marty Lewin wish they had driven past the Unification Church building without stopping that afternoon in February 1978.

They were on their way back to Capitol Hill after the person with whom they had scheduled an interview had failed to show up. At 16th Street and Columbia Road they noticed the Unification Church emblem atop a building where some construction work appeared to be under way. Lewin remembered reading somewhere that the Unification Church had purchased what was formerly a Mormon Church building. Why not go in and ask for a tour? They weren't expected back at the office for a while anyway. Inside, the receptionist, a young woman, greeted them. What a lovely building, they commented, and Lewin mentioned his interest in church architecture. Would they like to have a tour of the building? Sure, if possible. They signed the guest register, as requested by the receptionist, giving names and addresses. After a few minutes, a man appeared to show them around. An adjoining meeting hall and the sanctuary were in the process of renovation. They commented on the interesting stained-glass windows depicting Mormon theology. The guide offered to show the downstairs area and invited them to a meeting that night, but they declined, thanked him, and left.

Two months later, after one of Bo Hi Pak's performances before the subcommittee, Gragert and Lewin were standing together chatting with spectators in the hearing room. A man approached Lewin and asked if he had said he was an architect when he visited the Unification Church.

No, answered Lewin.

At the same time, a woman was asking Gragert if he remembered her. No, he didn't. "I'm the receptionist at the Unification Church," she said smiling. "Hello again."

Lewin, recognizing the woman, greeted her.

The man asked Lewin, "Didn't you just tell me you had never been to the Unification Church building?"

"No," replied Lewin. "You asked if I had said I was an architect and I said no."

The woman invited them to come back again for a full tour of the church at their convenience. They thanked her.

After two more months, on June 22, Bo Hi Pak held a press conference. He had just given his final testimony for Fraser on the preceding day.

"Today, I would like to announce that the Unification Church and I have jointly filed a massive lawsuit for $30,000,000 against Congressman Donald M. Fraser and his investigators, Mr. Edwin H. Gragert and Mr. Martin Lewin, on the grounds of conspiracy to violate and deprive the Unification Church and me of our constitutional rights."

The suit charged Fraser with attempting to "deceive and trick" Bo Hi Pak with questions at hearings, and for making illegal payments to other witnesses for testimony adverse to the church, Pak, and the Korean government. The effect of Fraser's action, the suit stated, was to impede Pak's projects and cause a severe reduction in financial contributions to the church. Gragert and Lewin were accused of conducting an illegal search of the church building at Fraser's direction, posing as architects. The suit demanded $30 million in damages and a court injunction to halt the investigation.

For Pak, the legal action marked "a day of vindication for all the powerless, all the unpopular, and all the oppressed." The Moonie newspaper, the *News World*, editorialized indignantly: "How many other surreptitious entries were attempted? Would the subcommittee go so far as to use illegal wiretaps, electronic surveillance, and other deceptive techniques?"

Fraser, Gragert, and Lewin were in good company. The Unification Church also filed against the *New York Times* for $45 million, the New York State Board of Regents for $28 million, and the *Times* of London for $20 million. The Moonies made a practice of frivolous lawsuits. Although dismissal was generally a foregone conclusion, lawsuits could and sometimes did have the effect of tying up defendants' time or intimidating persons from taking on the Moonies. Fraser's staff found many opponents of the Moon organization reluctant to cooperate with the investigation out of fear of lawsuits or other personal harassment.

BO HI PAK, as ever the quintessential Moonie, intended to serve as a shield for Moon. Fraser's volumes of interviews, KCFF files, financial records, and intelligence reports were highly damaging to Moon's image. But he must not allow Fraser to drag Master into the hearing room as he had been. If necessary, he would be the sacrificial animal at Fraser's pagan rite. That would be his ultimate act of service to God and Moon. Pak would lay down his very life to avoid having Master degraded by public interrogation.

With so much evidence pointing to Moon, however, Fraser reluctantly concluded he should be questioned. After the ordeal with Bo Hi Pak, he dreaded the prospect of going through something worse with Moon. Moonie intransigence had caused the investigation to spend much more time on the Moon organization than planned. Other important matters were not getting the attention they deserved.

Moon's lawyer, Charles Stillman, turned down Fraser's request that Moon be questioned informally by the staff. Stillman then made a counteroffer. Moon would consider a request to meet informally with Fraser and the other Congressmen on the condition they come to his estate on the Hudson, and that they conduct the meeting "in a manner befitting the dignity of a spiritual leader." Fraser was not at all interested in making a pilgrimage to Belvedere for an audience with the new Messiah. The subcommittee had already issued a subpoena for Moon, and Fraser was prepared to use it. He informed Stillman that Moon had two weeks to agree to answer questions voluntarily. If he still refused, Fraser intended to serve the subpoena. Moon would then be required to appear as a witness at a hearing scheduled for June 13.

Two days before the two weeks were up, on May 13, 1978, Moon flew to London on the Concorde using a false name. Like Tongsun Park two years before, he skipped the country when things got hot.

Bo Hi Pak was furious over Fraser's suggestion that Moon's exit had anything to do with the subpoena deadline. The Reverend Moon had long planned to carry his personal missionary work to Europe, Pak insisted. The reason for going at that time was to officiate at a mass marriage of 180 church couples in England. As for the subpoena, Master would fight it in the courts when he returned. Moon might consider accepting the subpoena under one condition: that Fraser also subpoena Pope Paul, Billy Graham, Oral Roberts, and the heads of the Baptists, Jews, Methodists, and others. Moon never returned for the announced battle. He remained abroad, in England and Korea, until November 1978, one week after Fraser's investigation ended.

FRASER WAS NOT the only one closing in on the Moonies. The Korean Cultural and Freedom Foundation had been barred from soliciting contributions in New York after 1976. The State Social Welfare Board had discovered that less than 7 percent of the funds collected by KCFF for the Children's Relief Fund could have been used for that purpose. The public was told that money was needed urgently to save the lives of 350,000 children who were facing "terminal forms of malnutrition" in Southeast Asia. Contributions were to be used to buy emergency supplies of blood plasma and food. The Children's Relief Fund appears to have been more an exercise in image-building than a drive to raise funds for the cult's coffers. An audit showed that Bo Hi Pak himself got $26,000 each year, while the bulk of contributions in 1975, $920,000, was paid to the Richard A. Viguerie Company, a professional fund-raising firm, for handling the mail solicitations. Another $58,000 went to the Associated Public Relations Council of Washington, owned by Donald Miller, who was also the executive director of KCFF

In September 1977 the Securities and Exchange Commission charged Bo Hi Pak with securities violations for having bought 43 percent of the stock of the Diplomat National Bank in the names of eighteen persons. Pak had, by that time, gotten rid of most of the stock. He was able to have the SEC complaint settled by consent decree whereby he was enjoined from committing future violations of the kind he had been charged with. But by 1979 the SEC had found more evidence of lawbreaking. This time, the Unification Church International, whose president was Bo Hi Pak, was charged with violating anti-fraud laws in a scheme to gain control of the bank. The Moonies, true to form, retaliated with a motion to dismiss the charges, accusing the SEC of "selective prosecution." It was rejected by the judge. As before, the charges were settled by consent decree: no finding of guilt, no public disclosure of the evidence; rather, a promise not to acquire bank stock "by means of untrue statements of material facts or omissions." In a statement to the press on July 6, Pak, claiming he had contersued the SEC, said he was pleased to have a settlement out of court because, "It is certainly not the desire of the Unification Church International to cause the SEC to spend further public monies to pursue or defend this case."

Pressure from the Immigration and Naturalization Service between 1973 and 1978 forced more than three hundred foreign Moonies to leave the United States. They had violated the terms of their visitor visas both by overstaying and by working in profitmaking businesses, which was consistent with Moon's plan to use missionaries to "open avenues of commerce" around the world. Because of the fund raising, immigration authorities turned down the cult's petitions to reclassify the aliens as religious trainees so they could stay much longer. That position was upheld by the courts, though the process dragged on for more than five years while the cult's lawyers took advantage of every opportunity for delay.

In 1978 the New York State Board of Regents denied accreditation to Moon's theological seminary in Barrytown after finding numerous administrative irregularities.

At least two local governments have refused to give the Moonies a free ride on taxes. New York City and the village of Tarrytown, New York, rescinded tax exemption for certain properties. The cult, insisting its buildings were used solely for religious purposes, fought back with appeals that were still pending in 1979.

A WELL-USED THEME of the Moonies was that Fraser was persecuting them in order to boost his chances of becoming a United States Senator. Actually, Minnesota voters cared little about his Korean investigation. They were concerned about issues like inflation and the boundary waters canoe area in northern Minnesota. All through his career, Fraser knew foreign affairs activities didn't get him elected. If anything, the investigation made him stay in Washington while he could have been in Minnesota facing his aggressive and well-financed primary opponent. The Moonies made a point of not absenting themselves from the primary campaign, though. Michael Smith of the Freedom Leadership Foundation went to Minnesota and organized a group of Moonies to help his opponent. Every poll predicted Fraser would win the Democratic primary hands down. He lost by a narrow margin of votes, which the press attributed to a large Republican crossover for his opponent.

Hearing the news in Korea, Moon was jubilant. He preached a sermon declaring that God made Fraser lose the election because he had defied the will of Heaven and tried to turn Korea into another Vietnam.

American Moonies had been indoctrinated to believe everything that happened to Fraser "was instructed by Father." Now Father's prophecy was being fulfilled. God's enemy was being punished. They were mindful of Moon's vows of vengeance, like the one in a sermon on "Indemnity and Unification":

> So far the world can be against us and nothing has happened. Now when they are against us then they are going to get the punishment. So from this time ... every people or every organization that goes against the Unification Church will gradually come down or drastically come down and die. Many people will die—those who go against our movement.

The instrument of the Devil was drastically coming down. Five days after the election, Fraser's house was set on fire. It is not known who was responsible.

The Menace

AMERICA WAS an ideal place for Park, Moon, and Tongsun to operate. As an ally, South Korea was not suspected of subversion. The U.S. government was watching the Soviet KGB, not the Korean CIA. All three men were able to manipulate at will.

American institutions are vulnerable to such people. In an open society such as this, any view can be expressed. If it sounds convincing, people will believe it. The halls of Congress are open to foreign government officials, businessmen, or evangelists from whatever country. If the country was Korea, they were always welcome because of the long friendship with the United States. Throughout this country, the agents of the Korean influence campaign could come and go as they pleased. Some people believed what they said. Some accepted money from them. Some were intimidated by them. Some became controlled by them.

President Park's KCIA forced unsubmissive Koreans out of business in the United States. His political party extorted money for him from American businessmen in Korea. Money was offered to get Park's picture on the front page of *Time* or *Newsweek*. The KCIA's written plans targeted about a hundred American leaders for "manipulation" or "co-opting." Agents such as Moon and Tongsun bribed Congressmen or prepared Americans to die for Korea. It was a great boondoggle for Moon and Tongsun. In the land of big money and big power, they made both.

President Park benefited less from the influence campaign than did Tongsun and Moon. That is ironic, since the objective of the Blue House planning meetings in 1970 was to get more American support for the R.O.K. government. At that time, Park and his advisers were overreacting to changes in U.S. policy, as usual. Nixon and Kissinger were absolutely determined to protect South Korea from another war with the North. Park knew that. He had nothing to worry about on that score, if that was his main concern.

There had to be another reason for Park's extreme anxiety. It can be seen in the thrust of his personal political maneuvers. In 1969 he railroaded a change in the constitution to allow him to run for another term. After he was reelected, Park declared martial law for several months. Then, in 1972, he dumped the old constitution and replaced it with a new one giving him unlimited powers. Under the Yushin system, he can remain President as long as he wishes without being bothered by elections.

The influence campaign was designed to get maximum American support to help keep Park Chung Hee in power.

American Presidents did support Park's government, but not as a result of the influence campaign. They did it for the traditional reason: to ensure stability for U.S. strategic interests. The many visits of Congressmen to Korea, however, yielded Park some benefits. In Korea, the regime's propaganda created public impressions that the Americans were with him all the way. In the United States, some of the opposition in Congress to the Carter troop withdrawal plan undoubtedly could be traced to the Park regime's expert orchestration of congressional visits in the past.

The failures of the influence campaign outweigh the successes, though. The campaign gained Park nothing he could not have gotten without all the skulduggery. His country was one that Americans were quite willing to support under normal circumstances. Exposing the campaign in 1976 brought two years of the most strained relations the two allies ever had. As for military aid, the campaign seems not to have had a positive effect during its heyday. Except in 1974 and 1976, Congress did not even make a separate decision on how much aid Korea would get. That was done by the State Department and the Pentagon after Congress had approved an overall amount for all countries together, which included the extra aid Nixon had promised the Koreans. Each year Congress had cut the overall figure, but this was not aimed at Korea, though Korea got less than planned as a result. Congress just wanted to trim military aid in general. The lobbying and payoffs had been virtually irrelevant.

In 1974, when Congress did vote on aid for Korea separately, Park lost. Fraser's amendment denied $93 million for the most humiliating reason: suppression of human rights. Phase two of the influence campaign—enhancing Park's image in the United States—clearly had not succeeded.

Fraser tried for another cut in 1976, but the House defeated his amendment. The State Department and the Korean Embassy had argued strongly against a second cut. There was no evidence of improper persuasion. Tongsun and the KCIA apparently were not instrumental in the lobbying.

The end of the scandal afforded a chance for re-warming relations between Seoul and Washington. Two years had gone by without Park having a meeting with the new President of the United States. That had never happened before. Park had never had a face-to-face talk with the man who intended to take all American ground troops out of Korea. He had wanted to meet Jimmy Carter from the beginning. If a summit meeting was held during Koreagate, Park could say it was proof of what he had been maintaining all along: that the "so-called Tongsun Park case" really was not a serious problem with Washington.

Carter did not fall for that. He had an extra reason for holding Park off anyhow. He wanted Kim Dae Jung freed. Park resisted. Not only did he resent Carter trying to force him to let a political prisoner go; it was also important to him that his most influential political prisoner stay in jail. After Koreagate had quieted down, he yielded. On December 27, 1978, Kim was released. The release opened the way for a Carter-Park meeting. It was set for the end of June when Carter was to be in the area for the Tokyo summit meeting of the heads of the industrial powers.

It worried Park that his visitor was a President known to be a human rights advocate. The regime prepared for Carter's coming by announcing that human rights was not expected to be on the agenda, placing Kim Dae Jung under house arrest, and threatening to prosecute persons who made "disrespectful statements" about President Park to the Carter party.

Human rights was on Carter's agenda, nonetheless. In his only public statement while in Seoul, which was televised live with translation into Korean, he said he believed South Korea's economic progress "can be matched by similar progress through the realization of basic human aspirations in political and human rights." He had talks with rights leaders Cardinal Kim and the Reverend Kim Kwan Suk, and the president of the opposition New Democratic Party, Kim Young Sam. There was a line about human rights in Carter's and Park's concluding joint communique, a first for any meeting between an American President and the head of a repressive government. Before leaving, Carter had Secretary of State Vance inform the press that he had requested the release of over one hundred political prisoners by name. Although Carter's human rights initiatives surpassed anything done by his predecessors during visits, the results were not encouraging. The Korean press was not allowed to report the American call for release of prisoners, and the newspapers downplayed the talks with religious and opposition figures as no more than "shooting the breeze." Park's release of eighty-six prisoners on July 17, hardly a sign of liberalization, seemed designed only to placate Carter. For Koreans, he promised the full force of Emergency Measure Number 9, the catch-all edict for throwing people in jail. Two days after freeing the eighty-six, Park issued a stern warning to those who favored changing the constitution "by demanding what is called 'the restoration of democracy.' " Ready, as ever, with a list of perils to justify prolonging the dictatorship, he added a new item, "the national security problem following the recent Korea-U.S. summit conference." In every other context, the regime was hailing the Carter visit as a major triumph for Park Chung Hee.

The new "security problem" Park cited was the rejection by North Korea of his and Carter's proposal to convene three-way talks aimed at reducing tensions and reunifying the Korean peninsula. A hostile North Korea proved once again to be the best thing Park had going for himself. By joining Carter in the proposal, he appeared reasonable to the Americans. Rejection of the proposal strengthened his case for staying firmly in power and insisting on full support from the United States. No time was lost in taking advantage of North Korea's intransigence. The day after Park's warning, National Assembly Speaker Paik Too Chin said North Korea's response was "unmistakable evidence that it is seeking to invade South Korea." Therefore, there could be no freedom for dissent, which he equated with "communistic activities," because "anti-Communism is the blood vessel of our survival."

To Park's further satisfaction, on July 21 Carter ordered a halt to the planned withdrawal of American troops because U.S. intelligence had discovered a sizable buildup of ground forces by

North Korea. Although troop withdrawal, with a delay until 1981 at the earliest, remained an American policy goal, the Korean government called the halt a "virtual nullification" of the policy.

With American military support holding firm no matter how he ruled, Park's crackdowns grew bolder. The headquarters of the opposition New Democratic party was raided at 2:00 A.M. on August 11 by some one thousand policemen and KCIA plainclothes agents; 172 unemployed women textile workers and 26 New Democratic party legislators were forced out of the building with tear gas and clubs. Many were injured and one woman was killed. The U.S. State Department called the action "excessive and brutal."

Park's next target was the president of the New Democratic party, Kim Young Sam, who had been criticizing Park regularly since winning his post in May. After some court maneuvers to deprive Kim of the party position, Park had him expelled from the National Assembly on October 4. The method was, by now, a characteristic one: Members of Park's party convened not in the Assembly chamber but in an underground conference room with a heavy police guard to keep the opposition out. In protest, Washington immediately recalled Ambassador Gleysteen from Seoul, an unprecedented move that shocked Korean leaders. The remaining opposition Assembly members, newly galvanized, then resigned their seats en masse on October 13. By the 18th, the government had imposed martial law on Pusan, South Korea's second largest city and Kim Young Sam's home district, in an attempt to quell anti-government demonstrations. In 1960, Pusan had been a starting point for the demonstrations that brought down Syngman Rhee's government.

Within the establishment there were those who began to feel Park Chung Hee had gone too far. Some of the generals and members of the ruling party privately viewed the expulsion of

Kim Young Sam as a great blunder. With apparently no thought of getting rid of the President or overhauling the regime, they did favor somehow pulling back at least to the way things were before Kim was ousted.

From an unexpected quarter came the most extreme measure. On October 26, Park Chung Hee was shot to death across a dinner table by his host, KCIA Director Kim Jae Kyu.

That the assassin should be, of all people, the director of the KCIA, was astonishing. So was Kim Jae Kyu's reported motive: disagreement with Park's heavy-handed treatment of dissenters. The KCIA had always been Park's personal instrument of control. The death of the President at the hands of the director threw the agency into a demoralized state, its future uncertain. Whatever Kim Jae Kyu's power goals, they came to naught. The generals refused to join him and he was jailed along with his alleged accomplice, Blue House aide Kim Kye Won (himself a former KCIA director). That the leaders of the establishment now seemed to favor liberalization was encouraging, since they had so long supported Park's president-for-life drive. There emerged an immediate consensus among them that the Yushin constitution would not be suitable for the post–Park era. The government of Acting President Choi Kyu Ha, who had been Park's figurehead Prime Minister, spoke in support of revising the constitution, releasing persons imprisoned under Emergency Measure Number 9, and holding a presidential election under a new constitution.

Kim Jong Pil, founding director of the KCIA and early ally of Sun Myung Moon, reappeared as a major power contender. Two weeks after the assassination, he was chosen unanimously to succeed Park as head of the Democratic Republican party (of which he was also the founder). In a public show of conciliation, he paid a courtesy call on opposition party chief Kim Young Sam. Both men aspired to the presidency, as did former Prime Minister Chung Il Kwon and Kim Dae Jung, who was released from house arrest. Opposition leaders, suspecting attempts by Park's clique to rig the future system for its own benefit, denounced the government plan to retain the Yushin system for the interim.

Hard-line generals moved to shut the opening political door just six weeks after Park was killed. In what looked very much like a military coup, sixteen army leaders were arrested and replaced with men trusted by Major General Chon Too Hwan, head of the Army Security Command and his power-behind-the throne, Major General Roh Tae Woo. With Chon in control, the United States could find itself thrown back to a situation not unlike 1961 when Park Chung Hee seized power: takeover by an autocratic general backed by a Kim Jong Pil-type mastermind, neither of whom was noted for close ties or sympathies with America.

A poll conducted by the Gallup institute in 1979 showed the American people's support for South Korea was at its lowest point ever. Only 21 percent said they believed U.S. forces should be sent to Korea in the event of another war there. In a 1978 survey, conducted by Potomac Associates, South Korea ranked low on a list of which countries Americans considered it was important to get along with, and was regarded as less reliable a friend of the United States than Japan or India among Asian nations.

Americans who have soured on Korea because of the scandal should reconsider. Deceitful men like Park Chung Hee, Sun Myung Moon, and Tongsun Park are not all Korea has to offer. The Korean people have proved themselves among the most capable in the world. They have achieved an economic miracle in only a few years. South Korea is far too important a country for the United States to reject. It is no longer the pitiful poverty case it was in the 1950s. It is a growing industrial nation and an important trading partner with the United States. Growth of democracy could have a chance with Park gone. South Korea still has a belligerent foe in North Korea. Park Chung Hee's self-serving exaggerations aside, Americans can believe their own leaders' assessment that North Korea is dangerous. And it should not be forgotten that the United States bears a very large responsibility for what has happened in Korea for the past thirty-five years, both good and bad.

The kind of government South Korea has had makes many Americans reluctant to give support. Park Chung Hee betrayed his American ally by setting up the Yushin dictatorship. It has caused suffering for Koreans and trouble with the United States without strengthening South Korea's security. On one point Yushin was completely successful: it kept Park in power, safe from all opponents, until he was struck down by one of his own men.

TONGSUN DID extremely well by the influence campaign while it lasted. Korea's interests may have been poorly served, but not his own.

When it was all over, he had some regrets. The scandal had caused so much notoriety and taken so much of his time, he said, it kept him from making about $20 million more from his businesses. And he had missed the Washington social life. Tongsun remained undaunted, though. His enterprises in Korea and the Middle East were still flourishing. He thought a political career in Korea should be the next step for him. Preposterous as that seems after the disaster he brought the South Korean government, it is not unlike Tongsun. He never says "never."

With the dismissal of his indictment in August 1979 under the immunity agreement, Tongsun was once again free to come and go in this country.

The charmed circle, no longer charmed, is out of Congress. Hanna chose not to run for reelection in 1974 and went to prison in 1978 for conspiracy to defraud the United States. Repentant, he entered the federal penitentiary at Maxwell Air Force Base, Alabama. There, the former Democratic Congressman made friends with a Republican with whom he had been at odds during another scandal, John Mitchell.

Comparing Watergate and Koreagate, Mitchell insisted there was nothing similar between the two.

"Oh yes, there is, John," Hanna rejoined. "Down here, we're both in the same camp!" Mitchell let out with a gutsy laugh of the kind Watergate TV viewers never heard.

Passman, after being indicted, had asked not be tried at all because of advanced age and failing health. A judge turned down the request after a court-appointed doctor examined Passman. Awaiting trial, he steadfastly insisted he never accepted money from Tongsun.

"Seventy-eight years down the drain." Passman lamented, viewing the charges as the ruination of his life. "I stood for everything good. I was a Grand Mason. Only a hundred were ever chosen. Now the only thing I have to look forward to is the grave."

As things turned out, he had a great deal to look forward to. On April 1, 1979, Passman was acquitted on all charges after a hometown jury deliberated only 90 minutes.

While his trial was going on, Passman was seen each morning arriving for breakfast in a Cadillac, walking briskly in and out of a hotel without a cane. For the courthouse arrival, he traveled by Chevrolet and made his way inside by leaning on his lawyers and a cane. Central to his defense was a claim that he had been an unwitting tool in a plan devised by Governor Edwards, Gordon Dore, and Tongsun. After the favorable verdict was announced, the defense team joined together in song and dance for all to behold, chanting, "The Governor made me do it! The Governor made me do it!" Passman, in equally high spirits and having abandoned the cane, said the next day, "I've made an amazing recovery since last night."

Grover Connell, Tongsun's rice dealer and sometime ally with Passman behind the scenes against Tongsun, was indicted in

April 1978 for lying to a grand jury about his dealings with Tongsun. After Tongsun had proved to be an unconvincing witness in the Passman trial, the charges against Connell were dropped in April 1979.

No convictions resulted from Tongsun's testimony. Hanna, the only Congressman to go to jail, had pleaded guilty. Comparing his plight to Passman's happy ending, he said his guilty plea looked foolish in retrospect. In May 1979 he was released from prison for good behavior after serving one year of a two-year sentence.

Two members of the charmed circle emerged from Koreagate with no legal problems to worry about. By the time Tongsun came back to testify in 1978, it was too late to do anything to Gallagher and Minshall. They could not be prosecuted because the five-year statute of limitations had run out. Leaving Congress in 1974, Minshall was working in Washington in 1979 as head of a lobbying concern, Congressional Associates. After Gallagher served his sentence for income tax evasion, he went back to New Jersey to be a middleman for sales between American and foreign companies. In late 1976, before the statute of limitations had expired, Paul Michel of the Justice Department had backed off even from having Gallagher questioned by the grand jury. That was shortly after Michel had let Tongsun slip through his fingers and at at time when he had quite a bit of material on Gallagher.

Michel became Associate Deputy Attorney General in 1978.

Hancho Kim, supposedly intended as the KCIA's successor to Tongsun, was convicted in May 1978 for conspiracy and lying to a grand jury. He never paid Congressmen a penny of the $600,000 the KCIA gave him. In July 1979, he began serving a six-month sentence after being placed on probation for a separate tax conviction and obtaining dismissal of an indictment for contempt of Congress.

Congressmen Joseph Addabbo and Robert Leggett, whom the Justice Department began investigating in early 1976, were not indicted. Only three months after Assistant Secretary of State Habib had succeeded in getting a Justice probe under way, their names were the first to surface in public as being suspected of receiving Korean payments. The Koreagate investigations came up with no admissible evidence, and intelligence reports were insufficient. In 1979, Addabbo became chairman of the House Defense Appropriations Subcommittee. Leggett survived his 1976 election contest in spite of public revelations about his tripartite love life, which included Suzi Park Thomson. Ending his congressional career in 1978, he became president of the Joint Maritime Congress, which lobbies the government.

There were no job offers in Congress for Suzi Park Thomson after Speaker Albert retired. In 1977, she announced she was opening a catering service in Washington, explaining that since giving parties was what she was best known for, she might as well try to make a living out of it.

In the Senate, where Tongsun had been less active, the Select Committee on Ethics found substantial contributions to the election campaigns of "at least seven Senators," but that none had been guilty of violating the ethics code. Senator Birch Bayh of Indiana was criticized for "neglect" of his duties by stating in writing twice that he had neither received nor been offered more than $35 from Tongsun. There was "substantial credible evidence" of a $1,000 contribution. Also, Tongsun had given a party in Bayh's honor that cost $3,800. One Senator, the late Allen Ellender of Louisiana, had himself credited Tongsun, along with Passman and Governor Edwards, with convincing him to change his vote to favor an amendment for military aid to Korea in 1972. But there was no evidence that Ellender did so as a result of any contribution, actual or promised.

For all the fuss about a scandal big enough to rival Watergate, the results were meager indeed.

In the spring of 1979, less than six months after the bribery investigations, it appeared as if Koreagate might have a successor. The House Ethics Committee began a preliminary probe into allegations of influence-buying by South Africa and Iran.

THE FUROR over congressional bribery obscured the menace of Moon in the United States. That, too, was a tragedy.

That Moon was a part of the Korean government's influence campaign is a point well established. He was one of its three main elements along with the KCIA and Tongsun's operation in Congress. His Korean Cultural and Freedom Foundation and his Washington minion, Bo Hi Pak, were listed for lobbying at President Park's Blue House planning meetings in 1970. He planted "PR sisters" in Congressmen's offices. His agents promoted Korean interests in Congress. He organized a political demonstration for the KCIA in 1974. A component of the Moon organization was included in the KCIA's written plan for operations in the United States for 1976. In that year, President Park himself still considered Moon useful.

Even without the documented ties to the influence campaign, common sense says the Korean government would consider it more than a little helpful that Moon had thousands of obedient American youths cheering and praying for Korea every day and believing Korea was God's chosen nation. Quite an investment in future American support for Korea.

It was Moon's good fortune and America's misfortune that no evidence was found that Moon bribed a Congressman. Petty as payments would be compared to the damage Moon has actually done to society, the Justice Department and the newspapers might then have thought he was a major problem. Bribery is not Moon's racket, though. To bribe is to *give* money. Moon *takes* money. He takes it by the millions every month.

The Korean scandal missed the mark by a mile. Most people who followed the scandal did not even know Moon had anything to do with the Korean influence campaign. It was all about pay-

offs to Congressmen. That made news. Tongsun's little escapade
is over. But Moon is still riding high.

Exposing the influence campaign brought down some Korean agents and Congressmen, perhaps including Speaker Carl Albert. But not Moon. He always told the cult he was bigger than
the KCIA, Korea, the United States, even "better" than God. So
far, his record on those points is pretty good.

He needed the KCIA's blessing to get going in Korea. He
got it by way of cult members close to Director Kim Jong Pil.
The Korean government became indebted to him because of the
Little Angels' propaganda bonanza. The doors to big business
were therefore opened to him. Contracts for manufacturing
weapons followed. Moon became a multimillionaire in Korea. In
the meantime, Bo Hi Pak was lining things up for Master on the
American end. He got powerful Americans to support Moon's
front, the Korean Cultural and Freedom Foundation, pretending
it had no connection with Moon. The cult needed money, so Pak
ripped off Americans with Radio of Free Asia, helped by KCIA
Director Kim Hyung Wook.

President Park and his influence planners may have thought
they were using Moon for Korea. What they may not have realized was how much Moon was using Korea for himself. Korea
was the Adam country but only because it gave birth to him. He
treats all governments, just as he treats all people, with contempt. People are mere stepping stones to the throne he claims
God promised him. The path he treaded to power must be paved
with important people. Dwight Eisenhower "paid his bill" by
having his picture taken with Moon, and lending his name, un-
suspectingly, to the Korean Cultural and Freedom Foundation.
The annual "International Conference for the Unity of Sciences"
is important enough for Moon to spend half a million dollars
bringing scientists from all over the world. The subsidized scholars' mission is to make Moon look good and develop unified
thinking that "will be the leading ideology of the world." Back in

their home countries, scholars are supposed to do things "which will enable us to direct the world policies toward the same goals." Well paid, many scholars return to Moon's jamboree year after year, unaffected by public exposure of his hidden purposes.

When skeptics suggest something less than noble motives behind the science conferences, the cult answers with one of Moon's ready-made turnabout questions: "Do they really think that such eminent scientists and scholars are so foolish as to allow themselves to be so used?"

Moon's track record suggests either the world is dumb enough, or he is smart enough, to get what he wants. Certainly he is contemptuous enough to believe both.

For Moon, President Park's influence campaign was just a part of his own influence campaign. Tongsun's idea was similar, but he was successful on a much smaller scale. Moon was not as dependent on the government as Tongsun and Suzi Park Thomson. By the time the government's campaign collapsed in scandal, it had already served him well. He no longer needed it. He was firmly established in the United States, the land of big money and big power.

He did not come through Koreagate unscathed by bad publicity. The controversy over Moon in America led the Park regime to make some unfriendly gestures for appearance's sake. As late as the end of 1977, however, one of Moon's companies was negotiating over a Korean government weapons contract in the United States.

Politically, Moon was in a weaker position than before Koreagate. He still had his cult, though, with plenty of money and members. He concentrated on expanding the business empire and tightening discipline.

The business empire afforded Moon more direct control than the unwieldy arena of politics. The companies belong to the Family. Father runs the Family. There is no such thing as dissent against Father in the cult. In some ways, the business empire is like a huge, multinational corporation. Its scope extends from selling flowers to making antiaircraft guns. Profits could be shifted from place to place for tax advantages or new investment: among companies, among countries, or between taxable and tax-exempt components of the Moon organization. People could be shifted in the same way, whenever it suited Father.

Moving people around the business empire has another advantage. It offers great training for the all-purpose militant society Moon is preparing for. He is developing highly skilled slaves. Not surprisingly, the quality of work is quite high. Opportunities for advancement are there, too. A capable member of the cult can graduate from peddling candy in supermarket parking lots to being a shipbuilding executive. There is no salary incentive, though, since the money goes back into the cult. But that is no big problem. Moon knows how to use the money best for building a better world. It all has its appeal to bright people in their twenties under Moon's control.

Where Moonies go into business, they are formidable. Fishermen in Gloucester, Massachusetts, have tasted the stiff competition. Things have not been the same since the Moonies came to town with apparently unlimited money and almost unpaid manpower from the cult.

The cult has answers to criticisms of its business involvement. Members of the Unification Church are getting "spiritual training" working in church businesses. To single out the Unification Church for criticism is unfair, says Bo Hi Pak. He and other leaders of the cult like to claim what they are doing is no different from the business dealings of the established churches. Their favorite analogy is the Catholic Church and its huge holdings.

The analogy crumbles in the most cursory comparison of the Pope and Catholic businessmen with Moon and the Unification Church. When young girls have not met the day's fund-raising quota, the Pope does not leave them at bars at 3:00 A.M. to hawk for money. Moon does. Catholic businessmen are not required to turn over almost all their earnings to the church. Moonies are. The Pope does not directly control church investments. Moon does. The Pope does not tell Catholics to lie in order to make money for the church. Moon does. There are many different Catholic views about business in the world. There is only one Moonie view.

Deprogramming, the ritual death of over 900 members of the People's Temple in Guyana, and the report of the Fraser Subcommittee have resulted in tighter discipline inside Moon's cult and more militancy toward the non-Moon world. Deprogramming is the process of talking someone out of cult control. Past associations are reawakened and the person begins to think for himself again. Obviously, this is the most serious kind of subversive threat to Moon. Many hundreds of persons have been deprogrammed. The success rate is about 95 percent. Using those retaken by Moon, the cult has succeeded in legal action against some of the deprogrammers. The reason is that cult members are at first held against their will by parents and deprogrammers.

The large number of members lost through deprogramming is a big concern to Moon. Not only has he lost them; many of them are working actively against him now. Preventive measures have been taken. Deprogrammers are described as depraved persons. Moonies are being told that deprogrammers will rape them or beat them, or that parents will put them in an insane asylum. Cult leaders have given instructions that if a member knows he is being led to a deprogramming, he should try to commit suicide by being run over by the car. That way, Moon would be served with double justice: the member would not have failed Father, and the parents or deprogrammers would be charged with killing. If there is no chance for a car suicide before the member is taken home, he should go into the bathroom and slash his wrists.

Moonie phobia over defectors spawns actual violence, as Brett Blaze learned when he returned to pick up his clothes and van after leaving the cult in August 1979. The Moonies, one of them holding a gun, refused to let him have his van. Blaze and his five companions got into their car, vowing to go to the police. As they pulled away from the curb, Scott Powell, Virginia state director of the Unification Church, ordered Mark Boitano to shoot. One bullet hit a front tire. Another pierced a door, but no one was injured. Powell and Boitano were arrested and charged with both shooting into an occupied vehicle and using Blaze's van without authorization. A Moonie official told reporters that the occupants of the car were to blame: Powell and Boitano only wanted to flatten the tires so "the criminals could not get away."

The Guyana mass deaths horrified the nation into greater cult consciousness. The Moonies downplayed the connection. They insisted they are a church, not a cult. Massachusetts Moonie chief Aidan Barry pooh-poohed the whole thing, saying, "It's like crying 'Wolf, Wolf' . . . when the real wolf is Communism." The Moonies were helped by apparently well-meaning established church leaders such as Dr. James E. Wood, executive director of the Baptist Joint Committee on Public Affairs. At Senator Robert Dole's public congressional meeting on the cults on February 5, 1979, Wood objected to any use of "pejorative" words like "cult" because they are not nice.

The Fraser Report of October 31, 1978, gave detailed evidence of lawbreaking by the Moon organization. Also included was a description of Moon's involvement in the influence campaign. Moon and Pak have never conceded a Korean influence campaign existed, much less their own participation in it. Instead, they mirrored the Park regime's position that the whole thing was a matter of Tongsun Park acting all on his own. The Moonies published a response to the Fraser Report. It did not even refer to many of the findings.

Before the report, cult members had already been programmed to believe Fraser was a Communist and an instrument of the Devil. It was easy, then, to program responses to outsiders who mentioned the report. Fund raising at the Newark Airport, Kathy Brown knew what she was supposed to say. She was beautiful except for the zombielike, glassy look in her eyes. Softly and sweetly, she said, "They have no proof. It's all lies."

She was asked about Fraser's house being set on fire. "We don't have to do things like that," she replied. "God punishes those who go against him. Why waste your life thinking negative thoughts? We are doing beautiful things for the world."

Thinking for oneself is a very painful thing for a Moonie to do. Father removes pain by removing thought.

At Senator Dole's hearing there was testimony about the physical condition of Moonies. Joe Alexander was affiliated with a rehabilitation center for former cult members in Tucson, Arizona, until lawsuits forced it to close down. He said: "We have seen and helped, during rehabilitation, girls having their menstrual cycles for the first time in months and years. We have seen and helped young men whose beards have stopped growing while in the cults."

Those statements brought laughter from the hundred or so Moonies packed into the hearing room. At other times and with other speakers, they yelled, "Garbage!" or "Liar!"

Shelley Turner remembers what Moonie leaders told girls like herself who missed their period for many months. They said it was fine; it meant being "pregnant with God." It was a good enough explanation for Shelley while she was in the cult. Four years after leaving, though, she still had the problem.

There is a Moonie explanation for everything.

Lying. One of the central tenets of the faith is the Doctrine of Heavenly Deception. Good must deceive evil. The non-Moon world is evil. It must be lied to so it can help Moon take over. Then it can become good under Moon's control. In the Bible, Jacob lied to Isaac. God rewarded Jacob by making him the father of the nation of Israel. Closer to home, you lie to little children about Santa Claus and the Easter Bunny until they are old enough to understand, don't you?

"Zombie" eyes. A sign of deep spirituality, unity with Father. Members are encouraged to use mirrors so they can watch the transfixed gaze develop.

Lack of sleep and food. If the spirit is strong, the body will be strong. If the body is weak, it is because of "spiritual problems."

Killing parents. They might try to destroy Master. There is no choice between the life of a "flesh" father and Moon; Master's work must go on. Anyway, parents who don't believe in Moon belong to Satan and must die.

Suicide. Better to die faithful to Father than be a living "Judas."

All these things are taught in the name of religion, a belief in God according to the gospel of the "Reverend" Moon. Inside the cult, mind control is used to make it convincing. Outside, free-thinking people balk. Moon has an explanation for that, too: the power of Satan. Again, the cult believes him, but it isn't enough for dissenters in the non-Moon world.

The non-Moon world, being of Satan, lives under the laws of Cain. Constantly, they get in Moon's way. One law, however, is very useful. It makes it possible to try to get around all the others. The First Amendment to the Constitution guarantees freedom of religion. As long as Moon says everything the cult does is religious, he can claim the protection of the First Amendment.

The advantages of using the First Amendment were seen early. Before Moon moved to the United States in 1971, he and his small band of followers realized the operation would have the most flexibility if it was called a church. Businesses, political activities, and tax-exempt status could be protected. Moon was dubbed "Reverend" in 1969. In 1970 the name "Unified Family" was changed to "Unification Church." Organization and goals stayed the same. Only the name was changed, for its "effect on the institutions of society." A cult publication explained, "The name implies respectability and stability."

Since Moon's invasion of America began, he has marched forward steadily behind the First Amendment shield. Calling himself "Reverend" and his operation a church early enough, Moon put the burden of contrary proof on the non-Moon world. His beliefs are protected fully by the First Amendment. He insists his actions are, too. His beliefs cover everything. No matter what the cult does, therefore, it is claimed to be an exercise of religious belief.

In the non-Moon world, Fraser conducts an investigation. He wants to find out if the Moon organization's political and business activities are part of the Korean influence campaign. At first, he has only allegations that the Moonies acted as unregistered agents of a foreign intelligence service, the KCIA. The Moonies can believe in God as they choose, but they ought not to violate the law in the process, he thinks. He is amazed at what he finds: evidence that the Moon organization has violated laws on banking, immigration, taxes, currency control, charity fraud, arms export control, and foreign agents registration.

To the Moonies, everything Fraser did from start to finish violated their freedom of religion. Since they claim everything they do is religious, Fraser had no right to question what they do. The cult's published comment on the Fraser Report says it well: "Its objections to the activities of the followers of Rev. Moon are fundamentally objections to their religious beliefs."

Moon apparently thinks his "religious beliefs" are a special license to break laws. The new Messiah is above the laws of Cain. Whatever contempt Moon has for the laws of the United States, he sees fit to hide behind the First Amendment to the Constitution. That raises questions for the non-Moon world about the meaning of freedom of religion:

Does freedom of religion give Moon the right to violate

the Thirteenth Amendment to the Constitution, which outlaws slavery?

Did freedom of religion give Moon the right to be paid secretly by the KCIA to carry out a plot to throw eggs at the Japanese ambassador and disrupt an official visit of the Prime Minister of Japan?

Does freedom of religion give Moon the right to smuggle large amounts of money into the United States?

Did freedom of religion give Moon the right to try to take over an American bank in violation of banking laws by buying half the bank's stock secretly with cult money?

Did freedom of religion give Moon the right to smuggle hundreds of aliens into this country under the guise of "students" or "religious trainees" so he could put them to work full-time in his businesses?

Does freedom of religion give Moon the right to evade taxes by transferring large amounts of money from one cult member to another, calling it a loan?

Did freedom of religion give Moon's minion, Bo Hi Pak, the right to collect $1 million from Americans under the guise of a "Children's Relief Fund," and then use 93 percent of the money to pay public relations men?

Did freedom of religion give Moon and his cult the right to negotiate, as an unregistered agent of the Korean government, for the manufacture and export of M-16 rifles?

Does freedom of religion give Moon the right to infiltrate the offices of Senators and Congressmen with covert agents who report details of personal lives to the cult for its special card file?

Did freedom of religion give Moon the right to refuse to answer questions about these activities before a subcommittee of Congress?

The Fraser Report recommended a federal task force to investigate the Moon organization for lawbreaking. Evidence of systematic violation of laws appears in the report. But a subcommittee of Congress is neither a law enforcement agency nor a court. It can only investigate and legislate. The Fraser Subcommittee did not recommend making any new laws to deal with the Moonies in the areas investigated. It found evidence that the Moon organization had violated many existing laws. What the subcommittee called for was for law enforcement and regulatory agencies to do their jobs, specifically the Department of Justice (including the FBI, the Antitrust Division, and the Immigration and Naturalization Service), the Treasury Department, the Securities and Exchange Commission, the Federal Reserve Board, and the Internal Revenue Service.

Past attempts at investigating Moon activities by each of those agencies alone had been piecemeal, inconclusive, and without the benefit of pooled information. That worked to Moon's advantage every time. It is one of the pitfalls of Washington bureaucracy. That was why the Fraser Subcommittee recommended a coordinated effort by an interagency task force.

After the Fraser Report and the Guyana tragedy, there was still no indication that any such investigation would begin.

The American system is ill-equipped to deal with Moon. He knows this and benefits from it. He can break some laws and use others for protection. By perverting freedom of religion, he can keep thousands of people in brainwashed captivity while he intimidates and manipulates the non-Moon world. He hurls lawsuits at those who offend him, whether parents of cult members or the *New York Times*. He has Nobel laureates feeding his ego and prestige by attending his conferences. He has high-principled civil libertarians and churchmen rallying to his defense.

Moon also has held the Department of Justice cautiously at bay for years. In 1976, Undersecretary of State Habib had asked for an investigation of the Moonies under the Foreign Agents Registration Act. Justice refused even to take a look, since the Moonies called themselves a church.

It was still hands off in 1977. On July 29, Assistant Attorney

General Civiletti, in a letter to a Congressman, wrote, "It has been our experience that members of these religious sects are apparently competent, consenting adults." He decided to do nothing because to take brainwashing seriously "would seem to require a finding that the members' religious beliefs were false." The United States government believed brainwashing was real enough in the Korean War. Apparently that was different because Communists were doing it to American soldiers. When Moon does it in the name of God he gets away with it.

Attorney General Griffin Bell added confusion to his Department's caution. After the deaths in Guyana, he said, "I don't know what a cult is. I'm a Baptist. Maybe that makes me a member of a cult." Then two months later, on February 2, 1979, he said he believed Patty Hearst had been brainwashed.

AN OPEN SOCIETY must let totalitarians have their say. If the Nazis are able to march down the street, and the Communists can publish their *Daily World*, then Moon has the right to tell people God wants him to take over the world. Likewise, others are entitled to criticize what he says. Not so, says Moon.

Hundreds from his cult were shipped to Washington to protest Senator Dole's information meeting on the cult phenomenon. Outside the Senate Office Building, they waved signs proclaiming "Senator Dole, this is a witch hunt." Inside, Neil Salonen took the stand and told the Senators and Congressmen what the Moonies thought about the meeting.

This very proceeding itself violates the spirit of the First Amendment and violates the rights of believers which the First Amendment was designed to protect. It will have a chilling effect on the free exercise of those beliefs.

George Swope, a Baptist minister, gave a different view of congressional inquiry into church activities:

> Members of the Congress, I tell you frankly, if you receive hundreds of accusing letters from parents of young adults who have joined the Baptist denomination, and if you receive hundreds of statements from young adults who have left the Baptists alleging mind control, the potential for suicide and murder, illegal immigration and financial practices, and other destructive physical and psychological activities, I feel it would be your duty to establish a task force to investigate those allegations against my own denomination.

PRESIDENT PARK CHUNG HEE's illegal Korean influence campaign was waged for almost six years before it was stopped. Henry Kissinger knew bribery and espionage were going on in 1971. It was four years before he did anything. House Speaker Carl Albert learned Suzi Park Thomson was connected with the KCIA in 1971. He kept her on his staff for five more years. In 1971 the FBI knew Congressmen Hanna and Gallagher were in Tongsun's pay. They were left alone. That same year, the Justice Department and the FBI ignored the evidence that the Moon organization was working for the Korean government. Eight years later, they still had done nothing about Moon.

Sun Myung Moon is the flourishing survivor of the scandal. The Attorney General continues to be deceived by Moon's perversion of religious freedom, even after the horror of the People's Temple. Some civil libertarians and leaders of established churches likewise play into Moon's hands. As for the major newspapers, they have yet to take the offensive with the kind of investigative reporting that uncovered so much in Watergate and the payoffs in Koreagate.

What will it take to bring the menace of Moon into account

with the law? The dictatorship and slavery he is building cannot survive in this country. But too often justice moves slowly.

The People's Temple had its retreat at Jonestown in the Guyana jungle. Off the coast of South Korea, Moon is said to have an island. Members of the cult are told that is where Father will take them when the world moves against him.

There is no central lesson to be learned from Koreagate, no one deficiency that can be identified and corrected to safeguard the future. The elements were too diverse for that. The influence campaign fed on neglect by leaders of our government, inadequate law enforcement, the greed of politicians, gullibility to con men, the alienation of youth, and family disunity. These are foibles all too familiar to Americans.

NOTES

Abbreviations of Frequently Cited Sources

KI Report: Investigation of Korean-American Relations, Report of the Subcommittee on International Organizations, Committee on International Relations, U.S. House of Representatives, Washington, Oct. 31, 1978, 447 pages.

SIO-I: Activities of the Korean Central Intelligence Agency in the United States, Part I, Hearings before the Subcommittee on International Organizations, Committee on International Relations, U.S. House of Representatives, Washington, March 17 and 25, 1976, 110 pages.

SIO-II: Activities of the Korean Central Intelligence Agency in the United States, Part II, Hearings before the Subcommittee on International Organizations, Committee on International Relations, U.S. House of Representatives, Washington, June 22, Sept. 27 and 30, 1976, 87 pages.

KI Part 1: Investigation of Korean-American Relations, Part 1, Hearings before the Subcommittee on International Organizations, Committee on International Relations, U.S. House of Representatives, Washington, June 22, 1977, 75 pages.

KI Part 3: Investigation of Korean-American Relations, Part 3, Hearings before the Subcommittee on International Organizations, Committee on International Relations, U.S. House of Representatives, Washington, Nov. 29 and 30, 1977, 209 pages.

KI Part 4: Investigation of Korean-American Relations, Part 4, Hearings before the Subcommittee on International Organizations, Committee on International Relations, U.S. House of Representatives, Washington, March 15, 16, 21, 22, April 11, 20, and June 20, 1978, 721 pages.

KI Part 5: Investigation of Korean-American Relations, Part 5, Hearings before the Subcommittee on International Organizations, Committee on International Relations, U.S. House of Representatives, Washington, June 1, 6, and 7, 1978, 227 pages.

KI Part 7: Investigation of Korean-American Relations, Part 7, Hearings before the Subcommittee on International Organizations, Committee on International Relations, U.S. House of Representatives, Washington, June 22, 1977, July 20, 1978, Aug. 15, 1978, 92 pages.

KI Appendix: Investigation of Korean-American Relations, Appendixes to the Report of the Subcommittee on International Organizations, Committee on International Relations, U.S. House of Representatives, Washington, Oct. 31, 1978, 2 volumes, 1,523 pages.

House Ethics Report: Korean Influence Investigation, Report of the Committee on Standards of Official Conduct, U.S. House of Representatives, Washington, Dec. 1978, 218 pages.

House Ethics Part 1: Korean Influence Investigation, Part 1, Hearings before the Committee on Standards of Official Conduct, U.S. House of Representatives, Washington, Oct. 19, 20, and 21, 1977, 581 pages.

House Ethics Part 2: Korean Influence Investigation, Part 2, Hearings before the Committee on Standards of Official Conduct, U.S. House of Representatives, Washington, April 3, 4, 5, 10, and 11, 1978, 1,157 pages.

Senate Ethics Report: Korean Influence Inquiry, Report of the Select Committee on Ethics, U.S. Senate, Washington, Nov. 1978.

Senate Ethics Part 1: Korean Influence Inquiry, Executive Session Hearings before the Select Committee on Ethics, U.S. Senate, Washington, March 14, 15, 16, 17, 22, 23, and April 10, 11, 27, 1978, 857 pages.

Senate Ethics Part 2: Korean Influence Inquiry, Hearings before the Select Committee on Ethics, U.S. Senate, Washington, May 1978, 1,273 pages.

PROLOGUE

Page

1–8   Based on interviews with Lee Jai Hyon; also his testimony before the Fraser Subcommittee, June 10, 1975, published in *Human Rights in South Korea and the Philippines: Implications for United States Policy,* Committee on International Relations, U.S. House of Representatives, Washington, 1975, pp. 177–185.

1 HIS EXCELLENCY

11–17   Interviews with Korean and American scholars of Korea, including one who is a native of Kumi, Park Chung Hee's hometown; *Area Handbook for South Korea,* U.S. Government Printing Office, Washington, D.C., 2nd ed., 1975, pp. 7–30; *KI Report,* pp. 13–18.

11   Figures on casualties in the 1919 independence movement are attributed to "Korean sources" in *Area Handbook for South Korea,* p. 22.

14   The American occupation authorities' apprehensions about dealing with noncollaborator Koreans was such that even before American forces landed in Korea, steps had been taken to shut out the noncollaborator, non-Communist Koreans. General John Hodge, the U.S. commander, had told the Japanese to maintain order because he was fearful of Communist influence. When he arrived at Inchon, Japanese soldiers with bayonets were holding back a large Korean welcoming crowd. Two of the welcomers were shot.

17   Kim Jong Pil: As a student at Seoul National University immediately after World War II, Kim had been active as a leftist demonstrator against the policies of the U.S. military government. Two or more of his brothers collaborated with the Communist invaders in 1950.

18–23   Details of Park's coup d'état: interviews with former Korean and American government officials; *Sub Rosa,* by retired CIA officer Peer De Silva, Times Books, New York, 1978, pp. 172–188.

23–24   Establishment of the KCIA: *KI Report,* pp. 22–23, 89.

24–27   Corruption in Park Chung Hee's government: *KI Report,* pp. 226–235.

24   Shoul Eisenberg: According to the U.S. Embassy in Seoul, Eisenberg was reported also to have obtained contracts in Korea by paying commissions of as much as 25 percent to members of President Park's staff (*KI Report,* pp. 228, 251).

26   President Park paying off politicians with money kept in his office: *KI Report,* p. 234.

27   East Berlin spy case: The West German government strongly objected to the kidnappings as a violation of national sovereignty; aid to South Korea was suspended and diplomatic relations were nearly severed. Even the Korean ambassador to Bonn, a former general and foreign minister, reportedly was harassed and tortured by the KCIA in connection with the incident. (Professor Gregory Henderson.)

27–29   Economic development under Park Chung Hee: *KI Report,* pp. 158–207.

29   Corruption, militarism, and dictatorship under Park Chung Hee: interviews with Korean and American scholars and former government officials.

2 THE LORD OF THE SECOND ADVENT

Commentary on Moon's theology was derived from *The Divine Principle* (a publication of the Unification Church), Moon's speeches to his followers published for internal use by the cult under the title of *Master Speaks,* and interviews with former Moonies, including some who were instructors in the Divine Principle.

31   "You are the son I have been seeking": *Master Speaks,* Feb. 23, 1977 (*KI Appendix* C-227).

32   "The reason why Jesus died was because he couldn't have a bride": *Master Speaks,* Dec. 27, 1971 (*KI Appendix* C-207).

35   "Rumors reached the American Embassy": Interview with officer of the U.S. Embassy, Seoul, during the late fifties.

35   Moon's arrest by South Korean police in 1955: *KI Report,* p. 353. Also, a leading Seoul newspaper reported that, "According to the investigative reports, he did not follow military conscription procedure and also overstated his age at 43 rather than 36. [The reports said] it was found that he illegally imprisoned [a 22-year-old female student] for three days and forced her to adopt the new religion." (*Dong A Ilbo,* July 6, 1955.) A week later, the newspaper said "evidence of some seven incidents of adultery with female adherents has come to light" but that prosecution could not proceed unless husbands filed complaints. Five followers of Moon were also reported to have been arrested (*Dong A Ilbo,* July 14, 1955). A Korean criminal court record shows that on November 21, 1955, Moon was found "not guilty" of violating the military draft law.

36   "The writer of this note is a man of heavenly mission": *Master Speaks,* Dec. 27, 1971 (*KI Appendix* C-207).

37   "Moon teaches that lying is necessary": *Master Speaks,* March 16, 1972.

37   "snatched her out of the Satanic world": *Master Speaks,* Sept. 22, 1974 (*KI Appendix* C-221).

38   "Before Moon grants permission . . . to marry": *Master Speaks,* Nov. 17, 1974 (*KI Appendix* C-223).

38   "Four of his early followers": U.S. government intelligence and confidential interviews (*KI Report,* pp. 354, 363).

38–40   Kim Jong Pil and the Unification Church: interviews with former Korean and American government officials; *The Doomsday Cult,* by John Lofland, Irvington Publishers, New York, 1977, pp. 227–229; Kim's 1962 U.S. itinerary (*KI Part 4,* pp. 687–695); CIA report dated Feb. 23, 1963 (*KI Part 4* Supplement, pp. 458–459); *KI Report,* pp. 354–355. University of California sociologist John Lofland, who was a confidant of the San Francisco Moonies during the early 1960s, described the meeting with Kim Jong Pil in his book, referring to Kim as "the Director" and the Moonies as "the DP's," meaning "Divine Principle." At the meeting, according to Lofland, Kim said he had "great sympathy" with the Moonies. "He could not help them openly in Korea, but he would secretly give them a hand whenever possible. . . . In any event, after the meeting with the Director, the DP's possessed an important sense of being secretly near the center of power in Korea." Three months after the San Francisco meeting, the CIA filed an "unevaluated" intelligence report from Seoul that said Kim Jong Pil had "organized" the Unification Church and "has been using the church . . . as a political tool." When the report was published by the Fraser Subcommittee in 1978, it was denounced by the Moonies as inaccurate, since Moon founded the Unification Church in 1954. The subcommittee recognized that "the term 'organized' as used in the report is inaccurate to the extent that it is equivalent to 'founded' or suggests that Kim Jong Pil began the Moon movement." However, the subcommittee found "a great deal of independent corroboration for the suggestion in this and later intelligence reports that Kim Jong Pil and the Moon Organization carried on a mutually supportive relationship, as well as for the statement that Kim used the UC for political purposes." Also, the Fraser investigators learned that a Korean-speaking U.S. official had heard Kim use the words "organize" and "utilize" in reference to the Unification Church.

40   Bo Hi Pak's devotion to Moon: Pak's testimony (*KI Part 4,* pp. 156, 436); Robert Roland's testimony (*SIO-II,* pp. 14–16).

40–42   Relations between Robert Roland and Bo Hi Pak: interviews with Roland; Roland's testimony before the Fraser Subcommittee (*SIO-II*, pp. 14–16).

42   The Little Angels as one of hundreds of Moon front groups: Neil Salonen, president of the U.S. Unification Church, testified that the Little Angels and the church "may share the same founder, but otherwise there is no connection." The Fraser subcommittee concluded, however, that "there is essentially one 'Moon Organization,' " based on evidence that Moon exercises control over the many entities with which his name is affiliated (*KI Report,* pp. 332–334). For further details about the Little Angels, see *KI Report,* pp. 324, 359–361.

42–43   Pak's application for tax-exempt status for the Virginia Unification Church, April 1963, and Ambassador Chung's letter: *KI Part 4,* pp. 697–719.

43   The Korean Cultural and Freedom Foundation as a Moon front group: findings of the Fraser investigation (*KI Report,* pp. 355–359, 361–362; *SIO-II,* p. 16).

43–44   Bo Hi Pak's release from the South Korean army to head Moon's foundation: Pak's testimony (*KI Part 4,* p. 471).

44   Bo Hi Pak's use of former Korean Ambassador Yang You Chan and influential Americans: *KI Report,* pp. 357–359.

44   Program of the first annual banquet of KCFF: *KI Supplement to Part 4,* pp. 420–423.

45   "Eisenhower 'paid his bill in full' ": *KI Report,* p. 348.

46   "KCIA Director Kim Hyung Wook expedited the issuing of passports": testimony of Kim Hyung Wook (*KI Part 1,* pp. 27–28).

46   South Korean government favors to the Little Angels: *KI Report,* pp. 359–361.

46   Using the Little Angels to bring money into the U.S.: Pak testified that the 18 million yen was brought to him by the "Little Angels Co., on travelling tour. . . . Whether they divided the money, many people brought it in as individuals, I do not know. . . . Probably (the company manager) reported it or not reported it. . . . So it can be regarded he thought that was perfectly all right because so many people coming." (*KI Part 4,* pp. 297–298.)

46   "we have laid the foundation to win the embassy personnel": *Master Speaks,* Jan. 30, 1973 (*KI Appendix* C-211).

47   The Little Angels' booking agent was Daniel Ben Av of Los Angeles (*KI Report,* p. 360). The foundation's board chairman was Charles Fairchild, who left the organization in 1977 after discovering Bo Hi Pak's unauthorized borrowing of money and that the

foundation was controlled by the Moon organization (*KI Report,* pp. 361–362).

47   "Satan will attack by saying that Reverend Moon is exploiting these children for his own glory": *The Director's Newsletter,* a Moon publication, Oct. 17, 1973 (*KI Report,* pp. 360–361).

47   "one of the most daring undertakings against the communists": Radio of Free Asia fund-raising letter, March 18, 1966 (*KI Supplement to Part 4,* p. 454).

47–53   Radio of Free Asia: Bo Hi Pak's testimony (*KI Part 4,* pp. 183–187); Lawrence Mays's sworn deposition (*KI Part 4,* pp. 598–635); unpublished sworn deposition of Kim Chong Hoon, former executive director of ROFA; interviews with former Korean and American government officials; documents in *KI Supplement to Part 4;* and *KI Report,* pp. 357–359. Of additional interest is Lawrence Mays's account of an approach to him by Bo Hi Pak in the spring of 1978, when Pak was compelled to testify before the Fraser Subcommittee. He said Pak asked him to keep quiet about Radio of Free Asia, first offering a contribution to Mays's planned congressional election campaign, and then threatening to use the story about the $10,000 bad check against Mays in public.

53   Radio of Free Asia and the KCIA: According to a U.S. intelligence report of Aug. 10, 1966, the KCIA had been given the task of "working out proposal for reestablishment of Radio Free Asia," partly as a result of a request from Yang You Chan in Washington (*KI Part 4 Supplement,* p. 461). An intelligence report dated March 14, 1967, stated, "ROK CIA pushed it strongly behind the scenes. The Seventh (Psywar) Bureau of ROK CIA monitors the programs and activities of ROFA." (*KI Part 4 Supplement,* p. 462).

53   "secretly his 'Divine Principles children' ": *New Age Frontiers,* a Moon publication, June 15, 1965 (*KI Report,* pp. 324–325).

54   "someday they will realize that I am truly the most noble and precious VIP that ever came to America": *Master Speaks,* Feb. 16, 1975 (*KI Appendix* C-224).

54–55   The 1970 World Anti-Communist League conference in Japan and former Moonie Allen Tate Wood's meetings with Moon in Seoul: Wood's testimony before the Fraser Subcommittee (*SIO-II,* pp. 20–21); interview with Wood; subsequent investigation by the Fraser Subcommittee.

3 THE CHARMER

56–59   Early life of Tongsun Park: interviews with acquaintances of
Tongsun Park.

59   "a citizen of the free world": *Senate Ethics Report,* p. 25.

59   Introduction to Presidents Johnson and Park: interview with the
interpreter for the meeting.

60   Tongsun's arrest by the KCIA for pretending to be a relative of
President Park: Kim Hyung Wook's testimony (*KI Part 1,* pp.
19–20).

61   Establishment of the George Town Club: interview with a former
employee of Tongsun Park.

62–73   Tongsun's early dealings with Congressman Hanna: interviews
with Hanna, Dec. 1978.

62   "John, you are entitled to the recognition": Hanna quoted from
interview.

66   "Kim had then arranged a transfer of $3 million": Kim Hyung
Wook's testimony (*KI Part 1,* p. 21). In other testimony, Kim said
he remembered being told the money was transferred and that
Tongsun got the loans (*House Ethics Part 1,* pp. 106–107). The
bank, Philadelphia National, has no record of either happening, although two of its officers told investigators that Tongsun had said
the Korean government would either deposit or withdraw a large
amount, depending on whether the bank agreed to Tongsun's loan
request (*House Ethics Report,* p. 11).

66–67   Tongsun's and Hanna's meeting with KCIA director, August
1968: Hanna's testimony (*House Ethics Part 2,* pp. 238–242); Kim
Hyung Wook's testimony (*House Ethics Part 1,* p. 110).

68   "everything was taken care of": Kim Hyung Wook's testimony
(*Senate Ethics Part 2,* p. 1104).

69–70   William Wurster: Wurster's testimony before the House Ethics
Committee (*House Ethics Part 1,* pp. 123–128).

70   "Frankly, gentlemen, I would like to help you": Robert Freeland's testimony before the House Ethics Committee (*House Ethics
Part 1,* p. 142).

71–72   "other business operations": *Senate Ethics Report,* p. 26.

74   "If my friends want me to help sell their surplus rice": *In the
Matter of John McFall,* Report of the Committee on Standards of
Official Conduct, U.S. House of Representatives, Washington,
D.C., July 1978, p. 166.

75   "intelligence information underscoring the urgent need for the
appropriation": Passman quoted in the *Congressional Record,* Dec.
8, 1969.

75–76   "We now have money in the foreign aid bill": House Ethics Committee report on Congressman McFall, July 1978.

76   "the members of our delegation to Korea": Letter from Hanna to Prime Minister Chung Il Kwon, Dec. 11, 1969 (*House Ethics Part 2*, p. 394).

76   Tongsun's relations with the KCIA under Kim Hyung Wook: Kim Hyung Wook's testimony (*Senate Ethics Part 2*, pp. 1098, 1602).

77   "He was my agent": *New York Times*, June 5, 1977.

4 THE ORIGINS OF THE INFLUENCE CAMPAIGN

78–79,   Interviews with Ambassador Porter; Porter's testimony before
80,   the Fraser Subcommittee (*KI Part 4*, pp. 36–72).
90–91,
93–94

79–80   Commentary on the seizure of the USS *Pueblo*: based on *KI Report*, pp. 55–57.

80   "Defense Minister Kim Sung Eun . . . complained to Lieutenant General Robert Friedman": interview with General Friedman.

80   "Foreign Minister Choi Kyu Ha told reporters": *New York Times*, Feb. 3, 1968, p. 8.

80   "There was no doubt in Lyndon Johnson's mind": Johnson's memoirs, *The Vantage Point*, Holt, Rinehart and Winston, New York, 1971, p. 536.

81   Benefits to South Korea from the Vietnam War: *KI Report*, pp. 53–54, 174–177.

81–82   The Vance mission: *KI Report*, p. 57; "Confidence in U.S. Has Ebbed in Seoul," by Richard Halloran, *New York Times*, Feb. 16, 1968, p. 32.

83   Early South Korean interest in starting an arms industry: *KI Report*, pp. 74, 76–78.

84   Park Chung Hee's preference for Humphrey over Nixon: interviews with former Korean government officials, including former KCIA Director Kim Hyung Wook. Reportedly, Park believed he was backing the winner, his experts on American politics having told him Humphrey would be elected.

85   "The weak can be rash; the powerful must be restrained": Secretary of State Rogers quoted in the *Korea Herald*, April 18, 1969.

85–89   Park's plans for a third term and the meeting with President Nixon in San Francisco: interviews with former Korean and American government officials; Porter testimony (*KI Part 4*, pp. 38–39); *KI Report*, pp. 60–61.

88   Kissinger's memory of the Nixon-Park meeting in 1969: In testimony before the Fraser Subcommittee, Kissinger said he could not remember which sessions he attended or whether troop withdrawal was discussed (*KI Part 4*, p. 240).

88   Park's use of the 1969 meeting with Nixon to benefit the amendment for a third term: A U.S. Embassy officer, in a confidential interview, called it an example of "slick diplomacy." In July, right after the importance of Park's purported special relationship with the United States was underscored by news of the upcoming meeting with Nixon, Park raised the stakes in the third-term bid by announcing he would resign if the amendment was not approved in a nationwide referendum. Two days before the San Francisco meeting, the *New York Times* (Aug. 19, 1969) described Nixon as "careful to avoid any hint of political support for President Park in the South Korean leader's effort to amend his country's constitution. . . ." Nixon's only personal reference to Park was in the joint statement issued at the end of Park's visit, when Nixon cited "remarkable progress" under Park's leadership (Department of State Bulletin, Sept. 15, 1969, at *KI Appendix* C-14, p. 223).

89   "You won't believe this": interview with John Court.

92   The "J Factor" and payments to Park's election campaigns by U.S. corporations: *KI Report*, pp. 247, 240–258. In 1975, B. R. Dorsey, Gulf Oil chairman, testified that Gulf paid $3 million to the ruling party of South Korea in 1970 (*KI Appendix* C-156, p. 790). Responding to a questionnaire from the Fraser Subcommittee, Caltex Petroleum conceded its role in the transfer of $4 million in 1971 (*KI Report*, pp. 243–244). The subcommittee identified four other American firms in apparent examples of extortion by the Park government during the 1970s: American Health Facilities International; Hohenberg Brothers International, a subsidiary of Cargill, Inc.; GATX Corporation; and Union Oil of California (*KI Report*, pp. 244–252). The subcommittee also published information that suggested Gulf had made an undisclosed payment of $1 million to Park's election in 1963. The sources were testimony by former KCIA Director Kim Hyung Wook that the payment had been made, and a description by a Gulf executive of the company's first payment in Korea. The description uniquely fits the circumstances surrounding the 1963 election but the Gulf executive insisted the first political payment was made in 1966, not 1963 (*KI Report*, p. 232).

93–94   Negotiating the troop withdrawal: interviews with former State
' Department officials; Porter testimony (*KI Part 4*, pp. 45–50); testimony by Donald Ranard (*KI Part 4*, pp. 74–78).

93   "the Koreans were getting far too good a financial deal": This view was held by Defense Secretary Melvin Laird, as well as other U.S. officials (*KI Report*, p. 65).

94–95   The Park-Agnew meeting: interviews with former Vice President Agnew, General Dunn, and other American officials; Porter testimony (*KI Part 4*, pp. 48–50); Ranard testimony (*KI Part 4*, pp. 76–78); *KI Report*, pp. 66–67.

96–98   South Korean plans for the influence campaign: interviews with former Korean and American officials; published summaries of U.S. intelligence reports (*KI Part 4*, pp. 52, 59, 135, 137); narrative in *KI Report*, pp. 33–35, 124–129, 365.

97   "the Research Institute on Korean Affairs, a R.O.K. government front operation": General Kang, head of the institute, reportedly said President Park personally gave him the initial money to set up the institute. The Fraser investigation found that Kang and Korean Embassy officials laundered at least $173,954 in R.O.K. government money for the institute by giving cash to individuals who would then make contributions with checks for the same amount (*KI Report*, pp. 290–293). The 1976 KCIA Plan estimated its annual operating expenses for the institute to be $88,000 (*KI Part 3*, p. 133). When Kang returned to Korea permanently in December 1976, he told several persons it was because the outbreak of Koreagate made it impossible to keep the institute open (*KI Report*, p. 292).

98   Conference for the Development of Free Institutions: incorporation papers and accompanying documents (*KI Appendix* C-55, pp. 402–420).

5 TONGSUN AND HIS CONGRESSMEN

99   Tongsun and Moon compared: The Koreagate investigations found no evidence of noteworthy collaboration between Tongsun and the Moonies. Their dealings with the Korean government apparently were separate. For a short period during the mid-sixties, Tongsun was a member of the board of the Korean Cultural and Freedom Foundation, presumably voted to the board because he was a prominent Korean in Washington. Both Tongsun and the

Moonies invested heavily in the Diplomat National Bank. But the Fraser Subcommittee found no collusion between Tongsun and the Moon organization in the stock purchases (*KI Report,* p. 385).

99–101   Conference for the Development of Free Institutions: Tongsun Park's testimony (*Senate Ethics Part 1,* pp. 102, 170, 305); *KI Report,* pp. 34, 125.

100   "Let us be generous": letter from Speaker McCormack to all members of the House, March 13, 1970 (*KI Appendix* C-55, p. 411).

100–101   Kim Kwang: *KI Report,* pp. 101, 125–126.

101   Contribution by check to twenty-five Senators and Congressmen in 1970: Tongsun's testimony (*House Ethics Part 2,* pp. 21–30); unpublished transcript of Seoul interrogation of Tongsun.

101–102   Tongsun's October 1970 reports to the KCIA: found in Tongsun's house by federal investigators and published in *House Ethics Part 2,* pp. 995–1019.

103–106   Interest in Congressmen Minshall and Gallagher: Tongsun's testimony (*House Ethics Part 2,* pp. 85–87); *House Ethics Report,* pp. 31–34, 55–57; *Senate Ethics Part 2,* p. 1568; unpublished transcript of Seoul interrogation of Tongsun, vols. 7 and 11; confidential interviews.

107   "kicking the hell out of the United States foreign aid program," "tens of thousands of fat cats": Passman quoted in *Washington Post,* April 1, 1978.

107   Passman's travels and "consultants": testimony of Donald Richbourg, Passman's subcommittee staff director, who traveled with him (*House Ethics Part 2,* pp. 315, 319–320).

108   Foreign aid and West German prophylactics: *Washington Post,* April 1, 1978.

108   "The greatest President in the history of the United States": statement by Passman heard by the author at a hearing of Passman's subcommittee in 1974.

109–114   Interviews with Governor Edwards, Congressman Passman, and others.

113–114   "greetings from President Nixon," "It will be touch-and-go": "Interview with Otto Passman," *Rice Journal,* Sept. 1971, pp. 3–4.

114–115   Financing the rice deal: *KI Report,* pp. 212–214.

115   "promised that he would not reduce": from a report relating to Passman that was seized from Tongsun's house (*House Ethics Part 2,* p. 1041).

116   "You are no longer acceptable": unpublished transcript of Seoul interrogation of Tongsun Park.

116   "This isn't just acting as a friend": Hanna's testimony (*House Ethics Part 2,* p. 247).

117   Hanna's letter to KCIA Director Lee Hu Rak: *House Ethics Part 2*, pp. 407–409.

117   "She tried to tell her husband": interview with Hanna.

117–118   Letters from fourteen Congressmen to President Park: *House Ethics Part 2*, pp. 411–432.

118   Hanna's personal letter to Tongsun: *House Ethics Part 2*, pp. 435–436.

118   Lunch with Gallagher, July 29, 1971: *House Ethics Part 2*, p. 926.

119   Payment to Gallagher, Aug. 3, 1971: *House Ethics Part 2*, p. 798.

120–121   Hanna and Tongsun in Seoul, Nov. 1971: Hanna's testimony (*House Ethics Part 2*, pp. 249–252); interviews with Hanna.

121   Letters from Edwards, Ellender, and Holifield: Hanna's testimony (*House Ethics Part 2*, p. 249); *House Ethics Part 2*, pp. 442, 446–447).

121–122   Gallagher's letter to Park Chung Hee, Nov. 1971: *House Ethics Part 2*, pp. 1045–1048.

122   Payment from Tongsun, Nov. 1971: *House Ethics Part 2*, p. 802; *House Ethics Report*, p. 33.

122–123   Conditions of reinstatement as rice agent: *House Ethics Report*, pp. 18–19.

123      $5,000 payment to Gallagher, Jan. 1972: unpublished transcript of Seoul interrogation of Tongsun; *House Ethics Report*, p. 33.

124   Offer of money to the Edwardses; interviews with Governor and Mrs. Edwards; *House Ethics Report*, p. 35. The House Ethics Committee determined that Tongsun, without giving money directly to Edwin Edwards, delivered a total of $25,000 to Mrs. Edwin Edwards and Marion Edwards, the governor's brother (*House Ethics Report*, pp. 34–37).

125–127   Accommodation between Tongsun and Passman: testimony of Gordon Dore (*House Ethics Part 2*, pp. 185–188); interview with Dore; Tongsun's testimony (*House Ethics Part 2*, pp. 54–55); interview with Passman; *House Ethics Report*, pp. 40–41.

126   "There is no security on this earth": quotation from Tongsun's diary, Jan. 17, 1972 (*House Ethics Part 2*, p. 725).

127   "I feel that I now know you": telegram by Passman, Jan. 24, 1972 (*House Ethics Part 2*, p. 463).

127   Luncheon in Seoul: interviews with Passman and Edwards; Tongsun's testimony (*House Ethics Part 2*, p. 55); Gordon Dore's testimony (*House Ethics Part 2*, p. 188).

128   Passman's messages to Seoul urging Tongsun's return to the United States: *House Ethics Part 2*, pp. 466–472.

129   Gallagher's letter to KCIA Director, March 1972: *House Ethics Part 2*, p. 1049.

129   Kim Hyung Wook carrying messages to the Korean government for Tongsun: Kim Hyung Wook's testimony (*House Ethics Part 1*, pp. 113–114).

129   "Riviera": Tongsun's diary (*House Ethics Part 2*, p. 474).

129   R.O.K. Office of Supply letter to Connell: *House Ethics Part 2*, p. 475.

129   KCIA payment of damages to Tongsun: Tongsun's testimony (*House Ethics Part 2*, pp. 79–80); Jay Shin Ryu's testimony (*House Ethics Part 1*, pp. 191–192). The money came from a Zurich account in the name of Kang Sung Tae, an aide to Park Chong Kyu.

129   Tongsun's diary entries for March 28–29, 1972: Tongsun's testimony (*House Ethics Part 2*, p. 81); *House Ethics Part 2*, p. 730.

130   Passman's press release: *House Ethics Part 2*, p. 479.

130   Visit to St. Francisville, La.: interviews with Edwards and Passman; Gordon Dore's testimony (*House Ethics Part 2*, p. 189); *House Ethics Report*, pp. 41–42.

131   Hanna's draft letter to President Park: found in Tongsun's house by federal investigators; there is no evidence as to whether it was sent or not (*House Ethics Part 2*, p. 530).

131   Passman's letter to President Park: *House Ethics Part 2*, p. 1095.

131–132   Minshall's letter to the KCIA, June 22, 1972: *House Ethics Part 2*, p. 526.

132–133   "Tongsun's six-month report card," known as the "T. S. Report": *House Ethics Part 2*, pp. 684–704.

133   Money to CREEP through Minshall and MacGregor: *House Ethics Report*, p. 56.

134   John Richardson: unpublished transcript of Seoul interrogation of Tongsun; interview with Tongsun.

134–135   Relations between Tongsun and Senator Hubert Humphrey: Tongsun's testimony (*Senate Ethics Part 1*, pp. 30–44).

135   "Gallagher had long been suspected of having ties with organized crime": *Life* magazine, in an article entitled, "The Congressman and the Hoodlum," said Gallagher "time and time again has served as the tool and collaborator of a Cosa Nostra gang lord, Joe Zicarelli," of the Joe Bonanno family. The story alleged, in part: that Gallagher had interceded against police interference with Zicarelli's gambling operations; that a convicted gangland killer, Kayo Konigsberg, said he had removed the body of Barney O'Brien, a small-time loan shark, from Gallagher's basement on orders from Zicarelli; and that Gallagher had denied any wrongdoing in connection with Zicarelli. (*Life*, Aug. 9, 1968.)

135–136   Tongsun's diary entries: For April 3, 1973, "Passman 50 agreed

4/11" (*House Ethics Part 2,* p. 597); for April 5, "Met Grover at New York, 80 A.S. 150 Ber" (*House Ethics Part 2,* p. 598); for April 9, "Left Kennedy for Bermuda, Arrived Bermuda, Met Bank Official, 150, 130-in cash, 75, 50, 2, Left Bermuda, Returned to DC" (*House Ethics Part 2,* p. 599); for April 11, "Delivered 75 + 50 + 2 to P" (*House Ethics Part 2,* p. 600); also Tongsun's testimony (*House Ethics Part 2,* pp. 91–92).

136–137   Incident at the Anchorage airport: testimony of Dennis Hazelton (*House Ethics Part 1,* pp. 168–181).

138   "Commander-in-Chief of the impeach Nixon movement": quotation from report seized from Tongsun's house by federal investigators (*House Ethics Part 2,* pp. 1031–1032).

138   "in the bedroom of TSP": *House Ethics Part 2,* p. 1034.

139   "economic development may be achieved": *House Ethics Part 2,* p. 1032.

139   Tongsun's claim that O'Neill requested he make payments to Congressmen and their wives: *House Ethics Part 2,* p. 1031; Appendix to *House Ethics Report,* pp. 162–171.

140   Tongsun's conversation with Hubert Humphrey: interview with Tongsun.

140   Tongsun and Hanna generating statements for Fraser's hearings: interview with Hanna; Hanna's testimony (*House Ethics Part 2,* p. 257); the statements were published in *Human Rights in South Korea: Implications for United States Policy,* House Foreign Affairs Committee, Washington, 1974, pp. 153–161, 168–169; Hanna's letters to President Park and KCIA Director Shin (*House Ethics Part 2,* pp. 634–642).

141   Fund-raising party for Congressman John Brademas: Tongsun's testimony (*House Ethics Part 2,* pp. 104–105); *House Ethics Report,* p. 150.

141   Birthday parties for Congressman O'Neill: Tongsun's testimony (*House Ethics Part 2,* p. 106); *House Ethics Report,* pp. 163–164.

141   "a letter to President Ford about 'the destruction of democracy in South Korea' ": the letter was drafted by the author (*Human Rights in South Korea: Implications for United States Policy,* House Foreign Affairs Committee, Washington, 1974, p. 191).

141   Passman's antipathy toward Tongsun: interviews with Edwards and Passman.

141   "one of the most brazen individuals that ever lived": quote from Passman's letter to Grover Connell, July 9, 1974 (*House Ethics Part 2,* p. 630). Interestingly, Tongsun used the same word to describe Passman, but in a more positive vein. Testifying before the House

Ethics Committee in 1978, Tongsun said, "I felt that I had finally found somebody powerful enough and brazen enough to protect my interest, and I was very grateful to Mr. Passman" (*House Ethics Part 2,* p. 94).

142   "tremendous cooperation": quote from Passman's cablegram to Tongsun, July 12, 1974 (*House Ethics Part 2,* p. 631).

142   St. John's Maritime: Gordon Dore's testimony (*House Ethics Part 2,* pp. 199–200); Joseph Alioto's testimony (*House Ethics Part 1,* p. 137).

142–143   Howe suicide: *Washington Post,* April 11, 1975; *Maxine Cheshire, Reporter,* by Maxine Cheshire with John Greenya, Houghton-Mifflin, Boston, 1978, pp. 221–225.

6 MINIONS AND MASTER

144   "$300 million": *Master Speaks,* Nov. 17, 1974 (*KI Appendix* C-223).

144–145   Description of the kind of person Moon succeeds in taking in: interviews with former Moonie leaders, including Steve Hassan.

145–146   "Moon taught a clear strategy for attracting prospective converts": *Master Speaks,* "On Witnessing," Jan. 3, 1972.

146–148,
151–153,
156,
161–164,
181   Chris Elkins: interviews with Elkins.

147   "Your whole body": *Master Speaks,* April 14, 1974 (*KI Appendix* C-216).

147   "You must live with me spiritually": *ibid.*

148   "You will rearrange the mechanisms within yourself": *Master Speaks,* Jan. 1, 1973.

148   "your mind is my mind": *Master Speaks,* April 14, 1974 (*KI Appendix* C-216).

148   "$800,000": interview with ex-Moonie leader Allen Tate Wood, who ran the candle factory in Upper Marlboro, Maryland.

148   "The three functions": interview with ex-Moonie leader Gary Scharff.

149   "Moon: Would you prefer to sleep seven hours": *Master Speaks,* Sept. 22, 1974 (*KI Appendix* C-221).

149   "Cult members should commit suicide": Allen Tate Wood's testimony, June 22, 1976 (*SIO-II*, p. 21); interviews with former Moonies; "Mass Suicide Possible in Moon Church, 3 Say," *New York Times*, Feb. 20, 1979, p. D-14.

149–150   Deaths of Moonies: *New York Daily News*, June 7, 1976; *New York Times*, August 24, 1976; *Detroit News*, August 16, 1979; *New West* magazine, January 29, 1979, p. 63; interviews with police officials and former Moonies.

150   Health problems: interviews with ex-Moonies; *Crazy for God*, by Christopher Edwards, Prentice-Hall, Englewood Cliffs, N.J., 1979, pp. 82–92.

151   "Among Moon's tour trophies": *Day of Hope in Review*, Part 1, published by the Unification Church, 1974.

151–152   "Moon was standing on a mountainside in Korea": interviews with ex-Moonies giving Moon's story of the origins of the support campaign for President Nixon.

152   "full-page Watergate statements": *Day of Hope in Review*, Part 1, published by the Unification Church, 1974.

153   Moonie preparation for the Christmas Tree Lighting: interview with Gary Scharff who was a member of the "Horse Team."

153   "A White House aide": John Nidecker, in testimony before the Fraser Subcommittee, June 1978 (*KI Part 5*, pp. 15–16).

154   "We stopped the world for him": "From Korea with Love," by John D. Marks, in the *Washington Monthly*, Feb. 1974.

154   "power clique": interviews with ex-Moonies identifying the core of Moonie leadership.

154   Moon's comments on racial talents: *Master Speaks*, July 29, 1974 (*KI Appendix* C-218).

154–155   "Dr. Joseph Kennedy": *KI Report*, pp. 340–341.

155   "He . . . urged the President 'not to knuckle under to the pressure' ": *Day of Hope in Review*, Part 1, published by the Unification Church, 1974.

156   "This is the equivalent of the Roman Emperor": *Master Speaks*, Feb. 14, 1974 (*KI Appendix* C-214).

156   "the Unification Church and the White House . . . can be very close places": Ibid., Feb. 14, 1974.

156   "David Martin": interview with Chris Elkins.

156   "his wife's permanent visa": *KI Report*, p. 402.

157   "Congressman Richard Ichord": interview with former House Speaker Carl Albert.

157   "Senator Strom Thurmond": *KI Report*, p. 402.

157   "PR Sisters" and "many good-looking girls": *KI Report*, p. 342;

Master Speaks, Dec. 29, 1971 (*KI Appendix* C-209); untitled speech by Moon, May 7, 1973 (*KI Appendix* C-321); interviews with ex-Moonies, one of whom reported having visited the Washington Hilton suite and being shown photos of Congressmen and Moonie girls with their arms around each other.

157   "She was Japanese, as it should be": In *Master Speaks,* July 26, 1974, Moon said, "Eve has been working really hard in places like this, and in the future everybody will follow this pattern."

157   "one for the diplomat" presumably means one to function as a diplomatic persuader in a Senator's office.

157   "The Speaker wasn't interested": interview with former House Speaker Carl Albert.

157   Susan Bergman's telephone conversations with Albert: interview with an ex-Moonie who was present on both occasions.

158   Barrytown: Not to be confused with Tarrytown; Moon has large facilities for training at both villages on the Hudson.

158   "Park Chung Hee viewed him as an asset": interviews with former Korean and American government officials.

158   President Park's letter to ROFA contributors: *KI Part 4,* p. 185. After American officials complained about the letter, Bo Hi Pak obtained a letter from Senator Strom Thurmond to the effect that the State Department had no objection to "courtesy contacts" by heads of foreign states with American citizens. Although this letter did not say whether the State Department was referring to the ROFA mailing, Bo Hi Pak claimed the letter vindicated his role in the mailing (*KI Report,* p. 365, *KI Part 4,* pp. 187–188).

158   Donald Miller's book: *KI Part 4 Supplement,* p. 468; *KI Report,* p. 365.

159   Bo Hi Pak as a conduit for Prime Minister Chung Il Kwon to send money to the United States: *KI Report,* p. 366.

159   Moon's anti-Communist training center: *KI Report,* p. 352.

159   Manufacture of military weapons: *KI Report,* pp. 83, 326, 352.

160   "He reminded the cult": *New Hope News,* a Moon publication, April 21, 1975; *KI Report,* p. 342.

160–161   Project Watergate, activities in Congress, role of Rabbi Korff and Bruce Herschenson in the three-day prayer fast: interviews with former Moonies.

161   "Failure to lift Nixon up": interview with Gary Scharff.

161–162   Chris Elkins and the egg-throwing plot: *KI Report,* pp. 343–345; Elkins's testimony before the Fraser Subcommittee, Sept. 27, 1976 (*SIO-II,* pp. 44–49).

162–163   "According to intelligence reports": declassified summaries of intelligence reports and testimony by Kim Sang Keun (*KI Part 5,* pp. 71–72). The intelligence summary, approved for public release by the originating agency, said, in part: "The head of the Washington KCIA arranged with Reverend Moon's group for demonstrations in front of the Japanese Embassy and the White House. The KCIA had used Moon and members of the Unification Church to stage rallies in the United States in support of Korean government policies and aims, and on at least one occasion Moon received KCIA funds for that purpose. Due to State Department objections, the planned anti-Japanese rallies had to be called off at the last minute by the KCIA chief through one of Reverend Moon's subordinates. The thousands of dollars already expended on the aborted demonstrations had to be written off to good will."

163–164   Chris Elkins's political activities while a Moonie: testimony of Chris Elkins (*SIO-II,* pp. 45, 46, 51–53).

163–164   "If we can turn three states of the United States around": *Master Speaks,* Mar. 24, 1974 (*KI Appendix* C-215).

164   "Some day, in the near future": *Ibid.*

164–168   Based on interviews with ex-Moonies, including Steve Hassan.

165   Tully's wife: ex-Moonie Steve Hassan recalled Moonie leader Takeru Kamiyama having described her as "a crazy fanatic."

165   "if leaders had a slave mentality themselves": Elaborating on this point, ex-Moonie Steve Hassan said that by taxing leaders with impossible goals, Moon endeavored to suppress the ego that might emerge if goals were accomplished. Early in 1975, Moon levied a requirement on Kamiyama to recruit three thousand new members. Hassan's quota for the Flushing, New York, center was four hundred. Neither goal came near being met. After an all-out effort, Hassan's group was able to bring in only about thirty.

166   "appalled by the individuality he saw" and "Germany, where people 'were trained in totalism' ": *Master Speaks,* Jan. 3, 1972.

166   Showing Hitler Youth films: interviews with ex-Moonies.

168   Annual gross from street fund raising: Former Moonie leader Allen Tate Wood gave a higher estimate than Steve Hassan. After testifying in the Manhattan Supreme Court in connection with a case involving the Unification Church's tax-exempt status, Wood said on the basis of 2,000 Moonies fund raising every day, the average per person is $150 to $300, for an annual gross of $109.5 to $219 million (*New York Post,* May 16, 1979).

168–175   Moon's business activities: *KI Report,* pp. 325–332, 372–376; confidential interviews.

169–170   Moonie interest in the Diplomat National Bank: Findings regarding stock purchased with Moonie money are based on sworn testimony and subpoenaed bank records (*KI Report,* pp. 377–378); loans to Bo Hi Pak (*KI Report,* p. 382); ruling by Controller of the Currency (letter at *KI Appendix* C-252); $7 million in Moonie transactions (*KI Report,* p. 382).

169   "that the currency will be freely coming back and forth" and "an international bank": *Master Speaks,* Feb. 16, 1975 (*KI Appendix* C-224).

170   "to guide the academic world": *Master Speaks,* Feb. 16, 1975 (*KI Appendix* C-224).

172–173   M-16 rifle negotiations: *KI Report,* pp. 367–368, 83; *KI Appendix* C-34–39, 41–45.

173   Moon's plans to buy the Empire State Building, Ford Motor Company, and Pan American World Airways: *Master Speaks,* Nov. 22, 1974; interview with a former Moonie leader.

175   " 'Reverend Moon is far better than me, the Heavenly Father' ": *Master Speaks,* July 31, 1974 (*KI Appendix* C-219).

175   The "petty" laws of the United States: notes taken by a Unification Church member at a meeting with Moon in Barrytown, N.Y., June 1, 1977. The subject of the discussion was the newspaper, *News World.*

176   International movement of Moonie funds: *KI Report,* p. 337; the Fraser Subcommittee said "there was massive evidence that (the Moon organization) had systematically violated" U.S. currency laws (*KI Report,* p. 388).

176   Visas: *KI Report,* pp. 335–336; summary of Immigration and Naturalization Service investigations of Moon (*KI Appendix* C-212).

176   "never received KCIA money": testimony of Bo Hi Pak (*KI Part 4,* p. 666).

177   "Unification Church Pension Fund International": Pak's testimony (*KI Part 4,* p. 308); *KI Report,* pp. 380–381.

177   "a New York judge": George D. Burchell, Justice of the Supreme Court of New York, Westchester County, in a ruling on a tax dispute between the Village of Tarrytown and the Unification Church, August 14, 1979.

177   Bad press as a "lightning rod," and "the quickest strategy to take over the rest of the world": *Master Speaks,* Feb. 23, 1977 (*KI Appendix* C-227).

178   Moon organization's closeness to the R.O.K. government: *KI Report,* pp. 351–355; interviews with government officials, present and former. An unexplained hint of ties with the KCIA came, surprisingly, from an attorney for the Unification Church, Michael Gold-

en. During a conversation with one of Congressman Fraser's investigators on Nov. 4, 1977, Golden said in response to a question about his client, "You know who makes the decision. It's made in the Korean CIA office."

178   "begging for our opinion and actions": *Master Speaks,* Sept. 22, 1974 (*KI Appendix* C-221).

178   Gary Scharff: interviews with Scharff.

179   " 'I'm the son of God before being your son,' " and " 'I want to be a member of the Unified Family' ": *Master Speaks,* Nov. 17, 1974 (*KI Appendix* C-223).

179   "Your utmost enemy is in your family": *Master Speaks,* Feb. 14, 1974 (*KI Appendix* C-214).

179–181   Steve Hassan: based on interviews with Hassan.

181–186   Wendy Helander: confidential interviews.

184   "a young man from the Unification Church": *New Haven Journal-Courier,* Feb. 23, 1976.

186   Neil Salonen's comment on the lawsuit: *New Haven Register,* June 20, 1978.

7 WASHINGTON LOOKS THE OTHER WAY

189–192   Based on Ambassador Porter's testimony before the Fraser Subcommittee (*KI Part 4,* pp. 36–74).

192–195   Commentary on Henry Kissinger is based on his testimony before the Fraser Subcommittee (*KI Part 4,* pp. 238–250); interviews with U.S. government officials, present and former.

193   A summary of the July 16, 1971, intelligence report on Gallagher is in *Activities of Friendly Foreign Intelligence Services in the United States: A Case Study,* Report of the Senate Select Committee on Intelligence, Washington, June 1978, p. 16. For corroborative commentary on Gallagher, Kim Kwang, and the intelligence report, see *KI Report,* pp. 134–135.

193   Kissinger's inattention to Korea: In his memoirs, Kissinger refers to South Korea only in passing: two sentences (both footnotes, pp. 398, 986) and mention of the name six other times for comparing or listing allies. (*White House Years* by Henry Kissinger, Little, Brown and Company, New York, 1979.)

193   Kissinger's knowledge of Korean lobbying and bribery: In his testimony before the Fraser Subcommittee, Kissinger said he had no recollection of having seen the intelligence reports dated Sept.

30, 1971, Nov. 24, 1971, and Feb. 3, 1972. When intelligence did reach him, he boasted, his action led to exposing the illegal deeds of Korean agents and Congressmen: ". . . indeed, this whole investigation started because I turned over the names that came to our attention in 1975 to the Attorney General . . ." (*KI Part 4,* p. 245). Subcommittee investigators were intrigued by an enigmatic comment by Kissinger that while apparently not having seen the three intelligence reports, he did recall something about "this one Congressman who was later indicted" (*KI Part 4,* p. 243). Months after Kissinger's testimony, the subcommittee discovered a fourth and earlier intelligence report that Kissinger had seen on July 16, 1971; it was about bribery and espionage involving Congressman Gallagher (who was indicted in 1972 on a tax charge). This finding raises questions about Kissinger's truthfulness when he testified that "in early 1975, . . . I had thought of the Korean activities in terms of lobbying" until he was shown "some sensitive intelligence information that indicated that there might be some attempt not to lobby but to bribe Congressmen" (*KI Part 4,* p. 247).

193–194   Nixon, Kissinger, and the National Security Council: A career CIA officer, who served as director of Intelligence and Research at the State Department during the early Nixon years, wrote that Kissinger "came to use the NSC apparatus and the intelligence community as his private staff rather than as supporting staff for the President." (*Secrets, Spies, and Scholars: Blueprint for the Essential CIA,* by Ray S. Cline, Acropolis Books, p. 202.)

194–195   Sanitized versions of Hoover's "eyes only" letters: Sept. 30, 1971 (*KI Part 4,* p. 553); Nov. 24, 1971 (*KI Part 4,* p. 555); Feb. 3, 1972 (*KI Part 4,* p. 557); for commentary, see *KI Report,* pp. 131–132.

195   "that the Blue House had been involved in contributing several hundred thousand dollars to the Democratic party": Refers to information received by two U.S. intelligence agencies regarding Hubert Humphrey's 1968 campaign for President. The Fraser Subcommittee investigated the report by questioning the intelligence officers who had collected the information, Humphrey campaign officials and aides, former KCIA Director Kim Hyung Wook, and Tongsun Park. Also, financial records of the campaign were reviewed. No conclusion could be reached as to whether a contribution had been made, although there were strong indications the Korean government intended to contribute. Tongsun Park said he recalls rumors about contributions of from $100,000 to $400,000 (*KI Report,* pp. 132–134).

196–197   Attorney General Mitchell and the Hoover letters: Mitchell's testimony before the Fraser Subcommittee (*KI Part 4*, pp. 143–147); interviews with former House Speaker Carl Albert.

197   FBI consideration of a national security wiretap on Gallagher: sanitized version of Sullivan-Soyars note to Hoover (*KI Appendix* C-60); commentary (*KI Report*, pp. 135–136).

197–198   Investigation of Radio of Free Asia initiated by the State Department in 1971: *KI Report*, pp. 129–130, 137–140.

198   Pak's claim that he had been proven innocent: his testimony before the Fraser Subcommittee (*KI Part 4*, p. 166).

198–199   Letter from R.O.K. Office of Supply to Grover Connell: *KI Part 4*, p. 561; *House Ethics Part 2*, p. 475.

199–200   Department of Agriculture inquiries about the rice agency and Tongsun's ostensible withdrawal as agent: commentary (*KI Report*, pp. 143–144); documents (*KI Part 4*, pp. 560–566).

201   "Unlike other Presidents": interview with former U.S. government official; *KI Report*, p. 39.

201–203   Park Chung Hee and the Yushin policy: interviews with former Korean and American government officials; *KI Report*, pp. 38–41.

203   "Yushin [revitalizing] Reforms": "Revitalizing" is the Park regime's own translation of the word. "Yushin" means "restoration, renovation" according to the *New Korean–English Dictionary*, compiled by Samuel E. Martin, Lee Yang Ha, and Chang Sun Un, Minjung Seogwan, Seoul, 1968. In Japan, the same Chinese-derived word was used as the name for the movement for restoration of the Emperor's power in 1868.

203   "were deprived of valuable time": official comment in *Draft Amendments to the Constitution of the Republic of Korea*, Korean Overseas Information Service, Seoul, 1972, p. 10.

205   "A group of Korean-Americans were brought to Seoul": *KI Report*, pp. 145–146.

205   Dr. Alexander Juongwon Kim: *KI Report*, pp. 145–146, 310.

205–207   KCIA harassment and intimidation of Korean residents in the United States: interviews with Korean-Americans and former Korean government officials; *KI Report*, pp. 93–96, 402–403.

205   "create a pro–R.O.K. atmosphere": quoted from the 1976 KCIA Plan for Operations in the United States (*KI Part 3*, p. 133).

205   Korean grants to American universities: *KI Report*, pp. 263–284.

206   "a KCIA officer . . . tried to run his car into Song's car": Song Sun Keun testified that Consul Limb Man Sung of the KCIA tried to smash into his car, in which he was seated, after an argument the night of March 4, 1976. Chung Tai Bong, a friend of Song's, made a sworn statement saying Limb told "Mr. Rhee and me that he had

tried to kill Song by running him down in front of the San Francisco consulate" because "Limb's work in northern California had been exposed and thus hampered" by Song. Korean officials, responding to press inquiries about the incident, said no KCIA agents were stationed in San Francisco (*KI Part 5*, pp. 90–92, 216, 209).

207   "Lee was interviewed by FBI agents": interview with Lee; *KI Report*, p. 148.

207   "Henry Kissinger and his staff were ignoring an intelligence report": *KI Report*, p. 146.

207   "Because of abusive KCIA activities": Kim Woon Ha's testimony before the Fraser Subcommittee (*SIO-I*, p. 17).

207–211   John Nidecker's 1974 visit to Korea: Nidecker's testimony (*KI Part 5*, pp. 13–31; documents at pp. 121–145).

211–212   Ambassador Sneider: Sneider's testimony before the Fraser Subcommittee (*KI Part 5*, p. 45); documents (*KI Part 5*, pp. 164–165; *KI Part 3*, pp. 55–56).

212   Among those offered trips or degrees by Lee Bum Jun and Park Chung Soo were Congressman Fraser, Mrs. Fraser, and the author.

8 THREE WHO STOOD IN THE WAY: RANARD, HABIB, FRASER

213–220,   Donald Ranard: Based on Ranard's testimony before the Fraser
226–227   Subcommittee (*SIO-I*, pp. 66–82 and *KI Part 4*, pp. 74–106); interviews with Ranard and other former American and Korean government officials.

219–220   State Department suspicions of Kim Kwang and Suzi Park Thomson: *KI Report*, p. 131; State Department memorandum entitled "Congressional Trip to East Asia: Congressman Neil Gallagher's Request that Kim Kwang Accompany Him, August 5, 1971" (*KI Part 4*, pp. 516–517).

220–221   Ambassador Habib: interviews with associates of Habib and the author's acquaintance with him.

223–224   Habib's "Dear Don" letters: *KI Part 5*, pp. 151–163.

224–225   Disruption of Kim Dae Jung's rally in San Francisco: *KI Part 5*, pp. 79–87.

225–226   KCIA kidnapping of Kim Dae Jung: U.S. government reports; interviews with Kim Dae Jung and present and former U.S. officials; testimony by Donald Ranard before the Fraser Subcommittee (*SIO-I*, p. 78).

226–227   State Department action to remove Yang Doo Won, alias Lee

Sang Ho, from the United States: testimony of Donald Ranard (*SIO-I,* p. 14); testimony of Ambassador Richard Sneider (*KI Part V,* pp. 46–47); a State Department memorandum, dated Aug. 17, 1973, said, "We have concluded that while the present R.O.K. CIA chief remains in Washington, he will continue to be a source of contention in the Korean community and embarrassment to the U.S." (*KI Part V,* pp. 166–167).

228   Ranard's action to stop KCIA demonstrations: Ranard's testimony (*SIO-I,* pp. 75–76); interview with Ranard.

230–235   Congressman Fraser: the author participated in all the events described.

230   "his committee, Foreign Affairs": the name of the committee was changed from Foreign Affairs to International Relations in 1975, then back to Foreign Affairs in 1979.

231   "one of Fraser's aides": the aide was the author.

231   "the speaker had said he always made a point": *Washington Post,* Aug. 16, 1972.

232–233   Fraser's 1974 hearings: *Human Rights in South Korea: Implications for United States Policy,* Committee on Foreign Affairs, U.S. House of Representatives, Washington, 1974.

235–236, 238   Habib's actions in 1974 and 1975: *KI Report,* pp. 152–153, 156–157; interviews with Habib and Ranard; Kissinger's testimony (*KI Part 4,* pp. 247–248).

236   Ron Nessen: *It Sure Looks Different From The Inside* by Ron Nessen, Playboy Publishers, Chicago, 1978, p. 45; *KI Report,* p. 110.

237   Fraser's visit to Korea in 1975: the author accompanied the Congressman.

237–238   Fraser's letter to Attorney General Levi, and John Davitt's reply: *Human Rights in South Korea and the Philippines: Implications for United States Policy,* Committee on International Relations, U.S. House of Representatives, Washington, 1975, pp. 453–454.

239–240   Paul Michel's visit to Fraser's office: the author was present.

9 KOREAGATE

241   In Korea, the Park regime imposed a total ban, lasting several months, on media reporting of the scandal. Copies of *Washington Post* articles were confiscated from passengers arriving at the Seoul airport. At a special press conference for foreign reporters only, Lin

Bang Hyun, spokesman for President Park, called the *Post* stories "malicious, sensational reporting" and denied that President Park or the Korean government ever had anything to do with Tongsun Park. (*Washington Post,* Oct. 27 and 28, 1976.)

241   *New York Times* columnist William Safire is credited with having coined the term "Koreagate." With the suffix "gate" signifying political scandal in Safire's lexicon, he had dubbed a French scandal "winegate" and in 1979, the allegations about the finances of the Carter Warehouse constituted "Cartergate." The Korean press, understandably, never took to "Koreagate," but in 1978, a Seoul housing scandal involving government officials was called "apartmentgate."

242   "extra-diplomatic lobby": *New York Times,* Oct. 2, 1976. When the *Washington Post,* the *Times*'s arch-rival for major national news, broke the big Koreagate story on October 24, the *Times*'s head office took the Washington bureau to task for getting scooped. The Washington bureau countered by telling the head office to get editor Gerald Gold "off his ass," insisting Gold was responsible for sitting on Halloran's story for two months, eliminating its most explosive information, and burying it on page 6.

243   The *New York Times*'s estimates of numbers of Congressmen involved: On October 28, 1976, the headline on a story by Nicholas Horrock read, "Inquiry Focused on Ninety Congressmen," based on Tongsun's 1973 list seen by the Anchorage customs inspectors. Richard Halloran's story of July 11, 1977, said, "Now it appears that at least 115 . . . were involved." Both articles appeared on page 1.

243   Senator Baker's *Meet the Press* appearance: *Washington Post,* Jan. 24, 1977.

243   William Safire's columns: "The Back Channel" (*New York Times,* March 10, 1977); "The Year's Cover-Up" (*New York Times,* July 20, 1978), which said, "Devotees of successful criminal cover-ups should doff their hats reverently to" Speaker O'Neill, Benjamin Civiletti of the Justice Department, and Leon Jaworski.

245   Suzi Park Thomson and Congressman Leggett: Thomson describes the relationship in some detail in her book, *Suzi: The Korean Connection,* Condor Publishing Co., Westport, Conn., 1978, pp. 279–282.

245   News story on Justice Department probe of Congressmen Leggett and Addabbo: *Washington Post,* Feb. 19, 1976.

246–247   Suzi Park Thomson and the KCIA: According to former KCIA officer Kim Sang Keun, Suzi had close relations with station chief Kim Yung Hwan (who also delivered liquor to her) and Colonel

Lim Kyuil, the KCIA's liaison with Congress. Kim Sang Keun recalls stopping by Colonel Lim's apartment one night and leaving hurriedly when he discovered Suzi was visiting. Suzi's bank savings deposits rose sharply in 1971 when she began working in Speaker Albert's office, contrasting with frequent check-bouncing before. In 1975, deposits totaling almost $5,400 were unaccounted for on her income tax return. The 1976 KCIA Plan describes her as a person utilized in the past and intended for future utilization (*House Ethics Report*, pp. 96–98).

247   Speaker Albert and the 1976 resolution on Korea: A newspaper account of Albert's shelving of the resolution said, "Albert has been considered a major congressional ally of South Korean President Park Chung Hee. An aide to Albert, Suzi Park Thomson, was granted immunity earlier this month to testify before a grand jury probing allegations that House members have accepted bribes from the South Korean government" (*Washington Post*, Sept. 23, 1976).

247   "Justice's investigation ... had been wandering around in the dark since early 1976": Attorney General Bell, commenting on the state of the probe when he arrived in Washington, said, "I was astonished to find that there really wasn't much of an investigation going on, only a few lawyers looking into allegations, most of which were being seen in the news" (Speech by Attorney General Griffin Bell, Los Angeles, Dec. 7, 1978).

248   Habib's inquiry to the Justice Department about Moon in 1976: *KI Report*, p. 156.

251–258   Problems in the House Ethics Committee's investigation: interviews with Philip Lacovara, Leon Jaworski, Peter White, John Flynt, and members of the committee staff.

254   "a spoiled brat": *Washington Star*, July 16, 1977.

254   "every damned frivolous demand": *Washington Star*, July 17, 1977.

255   "I never expected ... popularity": *New York Times*, July 19, 1977.

258   Kim Hyung Wook living in New Jersey on a fortune accumulated while KCIA director: Kim admitted having brought $2.6 million into the United States and having received $750,000 in political party funds while at the KCIA (testimony of Kim Hyung Wook, *KI Part 7*, pp. 28–29). The Fraser Subcommittee said, "In January 1978, General Kim was arrested and convicted on a guilty plea of smuggling $64,000 into the United States from Europe. Shortly after that arrest, the subcommittee also learned that $16,000 in payments to Porkchop (listed in Tongsun Park's ledgers) were payments made to Kim.... There were indications in bank

memoranda that Kim's fortune might have amounted to as much as
$15 to $20 million in United States and foreign bank accounts; that
he maintained $4 to $6 million in offshore time deposits managed
by his New York bank; that he continued to bring funds out of Korea through the use of friends' business bank acounts . . . as late as
June 1977." (*KI Report,* pp. 423–424.)

259   Kim Hyung Wook's testimony before the Fraser Subcommittee:
KI Part 1, pp. 4–69.

259   Passage from President Park's letter to Kim Hyung Wook: *KI
Part 1,* p. 16.

259   KCIA Director Kim Jae Kyu's letter to Kim Hyung Wook: *KI
Part 3,* p. 72.

259–260   The Korean government's overtures to Kim Hyung Wook: testimony of Sohn Ho Young (*KI Part 3,* pp. 82–92); interviews with
Sohn; KCIA messages (*KI Part 3,* pp. 190–205).

260   "the murder of a *kisaeng* girl": Former KCIA Director Kim
Hyung Wook testified that Chung In Sook, a woman known for
"sexual involvements with many high-ranking officials," had a son
whose father was rumored to be President Park or Prime Minister
Chung Il Kwon. The government said the killer was her elder
brother, and he was convicted, but Kim Hyung Wook doubted his
guilt (*KI Part 7,* p. 57). An investigative story in the *Washington
Post* stressed indications that Chung Il Kwon was the father, that
the brother was not the killer, and that the government was extremely sensitive about the entire issue ("Korea's 'Geisha Girl'
Scandal," by Selig S. Harrison, *Washington Post,* Feb. 14, 1971). In
an interview with Fraser's investigators, Kim Hyung Wook said
that following the 1970 murder when rumors had reached a consensus that Chung Il Kwon was the father, Mrs. Chung had said this
was impossible because her husband had had a vasectomy. A year
before Kim's 1978 testimony, KCIA defector Sohn Ho Young had
told investigators the KCIA feared Kim might give Fraser information that would link President Park to the killing.

260   "Since he didn't send a letter": KCIA document obtained from
Sohn Ho Young, *KI Part 3,* p. 199.

261–263   Defection of Sohn Ho Young: the author was a participant.

262   "His wife answered": Heightening the anxiety over the safety of
Sohn and his family, there was a delay of more than an hour before
the staff was able to communicate with Mrs. Sohn, who spoke almost no English. Ed Baker, the only speaker of the Korean language on the staff at the time, had been stuck on the subway during
a breakdown.

263   "reportedly because the hardest evidence was sensitive intelligence": A news article said, "How the American authorities got their information is not clear, but one possibility, according to sources familiar with the case, is that Government intelligence agencies monitored telephone conversations between Mr. Derwinski and Korean representatives. . . . Informed sources indicated that the National Security Agency, which undertakes highly sophisticated electronic surveillance, had produced the information" (*New York Times,* Oct. 29, 1977).

263–264   "Congressman Lee Hamilton told the press": *Chicago Tribune,* Oct. 29, 1977.

264   "He said he called the Korean Embassy frequently": during the week of Sohn's defection, Derwinski said, he was on the phone with Korean officials "almost daily" to talk about an upcoming conference in Bulgaria, but he "never mentioned Sohn" (*Chicago Tribune,* Dec. 7, 1977).

264   "Our friend Ed Derwinski": Derwinski quoted in the *Chicago Tribune,* Dec. 7, 1977.

264   "I'm not the culprit": Derwinski quoted in the *New York Times,* Oct. 29, 1977.

264   "Derwinski later said that when he was called before the grand jury": According to the press, Derwinski "conceded that he had deliberately concealed from reporters his appearance before the grand jury. At the time, he said, he was acting on the advice of his lawyer, Thomas Kennerly" (*Chicago Tribune,* Dec. 7, 1977).

264   "he refused to answer questions. . . . even if he was involved, he could not be prosecuted": *Wall Street Journal,* Dec. 7, 1977.

266   "that the jurors were convinced Derwinski was guilty": *Washington Post,* Dec. 6, 1977.

266   "The committee . . . closed the case without taking disciplinary action": press release, Committee on Standards of Official Conduct, U.S. House of Representatives, Oct. 14, 1978; *Washington Post,* Oct. 15, 1978.

10 INVITING TONGSUN BACK

267–273, 279–280, 282–283   Based on interviews with U.S. government officials, members of Congress, lawyers, and investigators, in addition to the author's participation in some of the events.

270   Letters between members of Congress and the Justice Department in summer 1977: *Washington Post,* Aug. 11, 1977.

271   "Hundley believed Tongsun": He was quoted as saying, "In view of the circumstances, the illness, I would certainly expect that he would just go visit his mother for a few days and then depart unhampered" (*Washington Post,* Aug. 19, 1977).

272   Tongsun's statements to the press in Seoul: *Washington Post,* Aug. 25, 1977.

272   Tongsun's indictment leaked to the press: *Washington Star,* Sept. 1, 1977.

272   Release of the indictment by U.S. District Court: *Washington Star,* Sept. 6, 1977.

273   "in an extraditable country for a year": Hundley quoted in the *Washington Star,* Sept. 2, 1977.

274   "It should be made clear to the South Korean government": Jimmy Carter quoted from a June 1976 campaign speech (*KI Report,* p. 71).

274   "strongly opposed to the idea": *New York Times,* Sept. 9, 1977.

274–275   "President Carter had written to Park Chung Hee"; "A Blue House aide angrily charged"; Congressman Aspin's meeting with Park: *Washington Star,* Sept. 8, 1977.

275–276   Attorney General Bell's telephone conversation with Tongsun: *Washington Post,* Jan. 16, 1978.

276   Indictment of Hancho Kim: *Washington Post,* Sept. 28, 1977.

277–278   Hancho Kim, "White Snow," "Ice Mountain," and "Shamrock": *House Ethics Report,* pp. 61–83; *House Ethics Part 1,* p. 47.

278–279   Indictment of Richard Hanna: *Washington Post,* Oct. 15, 1977.

279   "It's a good thing spitting on the sidewalk isn't a Federal offense": Charles McNelis quoted in the *Washington Star,* Oct. 15, 1977.

280   "full exposure of the facts" and "It is quite incongruous": Jaworski quoted in the *Washington Post,* Sept. 30, 1977.

280–281   Testimony at House Ethics Committee hearings, Oct. 1977: Lee Jai Hyon (*House Ethics Part 1,* pp. 20–31); Nan Elder (*House Ethics Part 1,* pp. 15–20); Kim Hyung Wook (*House Ethics Part 1,* pp. 102–122); Dennis Hazelton (*House Ethics Part 1,* pp. 168–181); B. Y. Lee (*House Ethics Part 1,* pp. 75–90). House resolution calling on Korea to cooperate with the investigations: *New York Times,* Nov. 11, 1977.

283–286   Interrogation of Tongsun in Seoul: unpublished transcript of interrogation and interviews with lawyers and congressional persons present.

285   In January 1978, Tongsun's mother reportedly warned him not to go to the American Embassy to sign the immunity agreement as planned, fearing a plot to capture him. She avoided Hundley and was said to believe he was an American government agent intent on damaging her son's legal position. Others in the family were less protective of Tongsun. His older brother Ken had become disgusted with Tongsun's penchant for getting into trouble. Ken's wife was quoted as having said the best thing to do with Tongsun would be to drive him up to the middle of the demilitarized zone between North Korea and South Korea, and leave him there.

286   Indictments of Otto Passman: *Washington Post,* March 30, 1978 and April 29, 1978.

286–287   Legal moves on behalf of Passman: Interviews with lawyers representing Passman and the Justice Department.

287   Fraser's agreement not to subpoena Tongsun: the author was a participant.

288   Quotes from Tongsun's public appearance before the House Ethics Committee: *House Ethics Part 2,* pp. 11–12.

289   "There is nothing to worry about": Tongsun quoted in the *Korea Herald,* April 18, 1978.

11 KIM DONG JO: THE STILL-UNTOLD STORY

290   "the so-called Tongsun Park lobbying case": frequently stated by the Korean press; quoted by Fraser (*KI Part 4,* p. 1).

290   R.O.K. government denies Fraser's findings on the Blue House meetings: Korean government spokesman quoted in the *Washington Post,* March 17, 1978.

291   Ambassador Hahm's complaint about the Moonies and the response from the KCIA: *KI Report,* p. 347; declassified summaries of U.S. intelligence reports (*KI Part 5,* pp. 77–78); Bo Hi Pak's testimony (*KI Part 4,* pp. 168–169).

292–294   Background on Kim Dong Jo: interviews with former Korean Embassy officers.

294   "Kim Dong Jo therefore went about paying Congressmen": *House Ethics Report* (p. 86) refers to "Kim Dong Jo's penchant for distributing cash to U.S. politicians": *House Ethics Part 1,* p. 24; *House Ethics Part 1,* pp. 15–18.

294   Kim Dong Jo's payments to honorary Korean consuls: *House Ethics Report,* p. 86.

294–295   Mrs. Kim Dong Jo's attempted payments to wives of Congress-men: testimony of Mrs. Kika de la Garza (*House Ethics Part 1*, pp. 90–94); testimony of Mrs. John Myers (*House Ethics Part 1*, pp. 97–98); *House Ethics Report*, p. 86.

296–300   Jaworski gave details of his efforts to obtain Kim Dong Jo's testimony in a written statement issued in his name by the House Committee on Standards of Official Conduct, Aug. 2, 1978.

297   "the President's cabinet meeting": confidential interviews.

297   "countries . . . complain about American ambassadors": One such country was South Korea at the height of Koreagate. Former Ambassador Porter, in a CBS interview on April 6, 1978, gave the impression that the United States may have been using listening devices on the Blue House before he became ambassador. This set off an uproar in the Korean National Assembly with demands that Porter be called to Korea to testify, just as Congress was demanding that Korea produce Ambassador Kim Dong Jo. The State Department reacted firmly in the negative.

299   "Jaworski found the committee's chairman . . . reluctant": interview with Jaworski.

299   "I'm making it as tough for them as I can": Jaworski quoted in a column by Mary McGrory, *Washington Star*, May 24, 1978.

299   O'Neill's statements on the House floor: *Congressional Record*, June 1, 1978.

299   "It is an insult": Korean official quoted in the *New York Times*, June 2, 1978.

300   "we have certainly come to a place": Jaworski quoted in an article on his decision to resign, *Washington Post*, July 28, 1978.

301–302   Relations between Jaworski and Flynt: confidential interviews.

302   "would supply new and concrete factual information": *House Ethics Report*, p. 92.

302   House Ethics questionnaire for Kim Dong Jo: *House Ethics Report*, pp. 183–186.

302   "totally unsatisfactory and insulting": language adopted by the House Ethics Committee (*House Ethics Report*, p. 93). Lee Jai Hyon rated special uncomplimentary mention in Ambassador Kim's response to the Ethics Committee. It was Lee who had fired the opening shots of Koreagate in 1975 by testifying about the KCIA's plans and the Ambassador having stuffed envelopes with money as he departed for Capitol Hill. The Ambassador said Lee had always been an "opportunist" who "did his best to offer false loyalty to the fatherland." (*House Ethics Report*, p. 217.) The Ambassador failed to mention that he himself had suggested Lee de-

fect in 1973 rather than submit to grilling by the KCIA.

302–303   Kim Dong Jo's reply to the questionnaire: *House Ethics Report,* pp. 204–218.

303   *Newsweek* article in 1972 about Kim Dong Jo: A survey by the magazine listed "the five finest" ambassadors to be Dobrynin of the Soviet Union, Rabin of Israel, Ushiba of Japan, Kim of South Korea, and Bogdan of Romania. The article, observing that the U.S. government "has fallen all over itself giving Korea money and weapons," credited Ambassador Kim with having "helped the process enormously," and said he "understands the centers of power in Washington better than most Westerners." (*Newsweek,* Dec. 18, 1972.)

303–304   Disciplinary and other findings of the House Ethics Committee: *House Ethics Report,* pp. 57–59, 135–171. In addition to the three Congressmen found guilty of misconduct, a fourth had been charged by the Committee in a statement of alleged violation. After public hearings, Edward Patten of New Jersey was found not guilty of misconduct in connection with a $500 contribution from Tongsun.

305   Intelligence reports identifying additional Congressmen as having accepted Korean payments: *House Ethics Report,* p. 87.

306   "We may have brought forth a mouse": Congresswoman Fenwick quoted by reporter Charles Babcock in the *Washington Post,* Oct. 9, 1978.

12 DUELING WITH THE MOONIES

307   "He's White, Baptist, and from Georgia": full-page newspaper advertisement (*Washington Post,* June 30, 1977).

308   "It was all religion": In a memorandum to the Fraser Subcommittee, Moon's lawyer, Charles Stillman, stated, "The members of the Unification Church view everything which Rev. Moon thinks, says and does as a step toward fulfilling his religious mission. All aspects of his life are bound up with, and dominated by, his theology" (*Our Response,* published by the Unification Church, New York, 1979, p. 175). Preaching to his followers, Moon said, "We must have an automatic theocracy to rule the world. So, we cannot separate the political field from the religious. . . . Separation between religion and politics is what Satan likes most" (*Master Speaks,* May 17, 1973, at *KI Report,* p. 314, and *KI Appendix* C-

212). On economic matters, Moon said, "This system should eventually prevail so overwhelmingly, that ... people ... will buy according to centralized instructions. What kind of system of thought or economy can function to give these centralized instructions? Religion is the only system that can do that" (*Master Speaks,* Jan. 2, 1972, at *KI Report,* p. 315, and *KI Appendix* C-210).

309   "the *New York Times* reported ... the subcommittee was investigating": "Moon's Sect Pushes Pro-Seoul Activities," by Ann Crittenden, *New York Times,* May 25, 1976; also published in *Science, Sin, and Scholarship: The Politics of Reverend Moon and the Unification Church,* Irving Louis Horowitz, editor, MIT Press, Cambridge, Mass., 1978, pp. 176–191.

310   "A different Salonen replied": Salonen's letter to the author, June 17, 1976 (*SIO-II,* p. 620); Bo Hi Pak's letter to Congressman Fraser, June 15, 1976 (*SIO-II,* p. 61).

310   "Two Fraser investigators went to the Moonie office": the two were Richard Mauzy and the author.

311   Criminal background of Clyde Wallace, also known as Walter Riley: *KI Report,* p. 371; FBI records.

311–312   Meeting about the source of investment funds for the Diplomat National Bank, June 19, 1976: Salonen and Pak both testified that a meeting took place in Pak's office. Salonen said there was a discussion about the money for the bank investments having come from foreign countries; he refused to give further details because, he said, a lawyer was also present, which established the protection of attorney-client privilege. Pak said the source of the investment money was not discussed, although he acknowledged Riley was there "trying to make some useful suggestion to deal with the press" (*KI Report,* pp. 383–384; *KI Part 4,* p. 338).

312   Walter Riley's story labeling Fraser a Communist agent: *KI Report,* p. 371; Pak's testimony, April 20, 1978 (*KI Part 4,* pp. 256–257).

312   "a Fraser employee had been paid ... in a lump sum": Fraser said one year's salary ($7,400) was paid in two lump sums in February and March 1978, in order that one of his eighteen authorized staff positions could be kept open for a summer intern. Paying employees in advance is prohibited by a federal statute, but the prohibition had not been included in the administrative regulations of the House of Representatives. When Fraser discovered his error after Riley's research of staff pay records, he refunded the advance money to the House and put the employee on a regular monthly pay basis (*Washington Post,* June 27, 1978).

313   "reverse Korean payoffs": column written by Walter Riley (*Our*

Response, published by the Unification Church, New York, 1979, p. 189); a Seoul newspaper headline read, "Rep. Fraser Bribed Five For Anti-Moonies Data" (*Korea Herald,* June 22, 1979); Pak's statement to the press, June 22, 1978 (*Our Response,* pp. 192–193).

313–314   Exchanges between Fraser and Pak during hearings: Pak's testimony (*KI Part 4,* pp. 160, 202–203, 207–208).

316   "When did you first get to know the Japanese woman?" Pak's testimony, April 11, 1978 (*KI Part 4,* pp. 210–211). According to Pak, Yang Doo Won of KCIA headquarters sent him $3,000 in Washington with a request that he pay the full amount to Mrs. Ikeda (whose real name is Yasue Erikawa) in consideration of travel and other expenses she incurred while speaking at some rallies in South Korea in 1975. Pak claimed he then went to Korea in February 1976 and asked Mrs. Ikeda to come from Japan to meet him there, whereupon he persuaded her to accept the money. A Unification Church publication later said, "Mr. Pak had simply done a personal favor for an old army friend; that is all," referring to General Yang, Assistant Director of the KCIA (*Our Response,* p. 103). Describing the transaction in his testimony, Pak said, "It is a beautiful story" (*KI Part 4,* p. 212).

316   "Unification Church Pension Fund International": Pak's testimony, June 20, 1978 (*KI Part 4,* pp. 308–315). After investigating the Moonie investments in the Diplomat National Bank, the Fraser Subcommittee "was unconvinced that such a fund was ever established or used for that purpose" (*KI Report,* p. 385). The Securities Exchange Commission and the Federal Reserve Board tried to question the thirteen persons in whose names Pak had purchased bank shares. Some could not be found, while others refused to testify on Fifth Amendment grounds. "Those who did respond did not support Pak's testimony before the subcommittee" (*KI Report,* p. 381).

317   "$223,000 in cash from Japan": Pak's testimony, April 20, 1978 (*KI Part 4,* p. 295).

317   "three promissory notes drawn up a few weeks before": Pak's testimony, June 20, 1978 (*KI Part 4,* pp. 321–323, 325, 327–328).

317   "a traitor," "a second Benedict Arnold," "Repent": Pak's testimony, April 20, 1978 (*KI Part 4,* pp. 255–260).

318   "Among the viewers was Tongsun Park, who said he was repulsed": interview with Tongsun.

318–319   Visit to the Unification Church by Ed Gragert and Martin Lewin: interviews with Gragert and Lewin. For the Moonie version, see *Our Response,* pp. 29–30, 137–140.

319   Announcement of Moonie lawsuit against Fraser: Pak's state-

ment to the press, June 22, 1978 (*Our Response*, pp. 190–198).

319–320   "How many other surreptitious entries were attempted?": editorial (*News World*, May 18, 1978).

321   "in a manner befitting the dignity of a spiritual leader": from conversations with Moon's attorneys.

321   "Moon might consider accepting the subpoena": Pak's statement to the press, June 22, 1978 (*Our Response*, pp. 196–197).

321–322   Barring the Korean Cultural and Freedom Foundation from solicitation in the State of New York: *Washington Post*, Feb. 21, 1977.

322   Bo Hi Pak and the Securities and Exchange Commission: *KI Report*, p. 385; *Washington Post*, July 7, 1979.

323   Moonie immigration problems: summary of investigations by the Immigration and Naturalization Service (*KI Appendix* C-212).

323   "open avenues of commerce": *Master Speaks*, Feb. 16, 1975 (*KI Appendix* C-224).

324   "was instructed by Father": 1978 lecture notes by a Moonie who left the cult in 1979.

324   "So far the world can be against us and nothing has happened": *KI Report*, pp. 315–316; *Master Speaks*, Feb. 14, 1974 (*KI Appendix* C-214).

324   The fire at Congressman Fraser's home in Washington: Mrs. Fraser and her daughter, Jeanne, left the back door unlocked when they went next door for dinner with friends. Returning home within about thirty minutes to do her schoolwork, Jeanne discovered a fire raging from the bottom of the three-story unencased stairwell. An investigation by the fire department concluded that the fire had been set with solvent poured on the floor, and that had it gone undiscovered for another fifteen minutes, the house could not have been saved.

13 THE MENACE

328   "disrespectful statements": *Dong A Ilbo*, Seoul, June 27, 1979.

328   "can be matched by similar progress": *Korea Herald*, July 1, 1979.

329   Carter-Park communique: *New York Times*, July 2, 1979.

329   "shooting the breeze": *New York Times*, July 3, 1979.

329   "by demanding . . . 'the restoration of democracy' ": *Korea Herald*, July 20, 1979.

329   Remarks of Speaker Paik Too Chin: *Korea Herald,* July 21, 1979.

330   Details on the assassination of Park Chung Hee: *New York Times,* Oct. 30, 1979.

332   "A poll conducted by the Gallup institute": *Korea Herald,* July 15, 1979. The poll had been done by Gallup for *American Public Opinion and U.S. Foreign Policy, 1979,* John E. Reilly, editor, Chicago Council on Foreign Relations, Chicago, 1979.

332   "a 1978 survey": *The United States and Korea: American Attitudes and Policies* by Ralph N. Clough and William Watts, Potomac Associates, Washington, 1978.

333   "When it was all over, he had some regrets": interview with Tongsun Park, July 1978.

334   "Oh, yes there is, John": interview with Richard Hanna and John Mitchell, December 1978.

334   "Seventy-eight years down the drain": interview with Otto Passman, December 1978.

334   Behavior and tactics of Passman and his lawyers during the trial: interview with a reporter who covered the trial.

335   Hanna's comment after the Passman trial: *Washington Post,* Mar. 29, 1979.

336   Suzi Park Thomson announces the opening of a catering service: *Washington Star,* Dec. 9, 1977.

336   Findings of the Senate Ethics Committee: *Senate Ethics Report,* pp. 2, 77, 124.

337   "A component of the Moon organization was included in the KCIA's written plan": The component is the Freedom Leadership Foundation. The KCIA Plan was published in English and Korean by the Fraser Subcommittee (*KI Part 3,* pp. 107–138).

338   Moon's International Conference for the Unity of the Sciences: As soon as the Fraser investigation was over, thus terminating its subpoena power, Moon returned to the United States in time to appear at his seventh "Unity of the Sciences" conference, held in Boston, Nov. 24–26, 1978.

338   "will be the leading ideology of the world," "which will enable us to direct the world policies toward the same goals": *Master Speaks,* Jan. 30, 1973 (*KI Appendix* C-211). For further description of the science conference as a Moon tool, see *KI Report,* pp. 321–322.

339   "Do they really think that such eminent scientists": *Our Response,* published by the Unification Church, New York, 1979, p. 55.

339   "one of Moon's companies was negotiating over a Korean government weapons contract": *KI Report,* pp. 326–328, 371, 366–369; *KI Appendix* C-34–39, 41–45.

341   "The success rate is about 95 percent": interviews with deprogrammers.

341   "he should try to commit suicide by being run over by the car": interviews with former Moonies.

341–342   Shooting incident in Norfolk, Va.: *Washington Post,* Aug. 22, 1979.

342   "It's like crying 'Wolf' ": comment to Boston television reporters by Aidan Barry, Nov. 22, 1978.

342   "Cult" as a pejorative word: testimony of James Wood at an information meeting, "The Cult Phenomenon in the United States," U.S. Senate, Washington, Feb. 5, 1979.

343   Kathy Brown: conversation with the author, Newark Airport, Feb. 6, 1979.

343   Joe Alexander: testimony at Senate meeting on the cult phenomenon, Washington, Feb. 5, 1979.

343–344   "There is a Moonie explanation for everything": interviews with former Moonies, including Shelley Turner and Steve Hassan.

345   "A cult publication explained": *New Age Frontiers,* Jan. 1971 (*KI Report,* p. 318).

345   "Its objections to the activities": *Our Response,* published by the Unification Church, New York, 1979, p. 123.

346–347   The Fraser Subcommittee's recommendations are in *KI Report,* pp. 390–392.

348   "It has been our experience": the full text of Assistant Attorney General Civiletti's letter is in *Our Response,* pp. 270–271.

348   "I don't know what a cult is": Attorney General Bell at a press conference in Los Angeles, Dec. 7, 1978.

348   "he said he believed Patty Hearst had been brainwashed": appearance by Attorney General Bell on ABC's *Good Morning, America,* Feb. 2, 1979.

348–349   Neil Salonen and George Swope: testimony at Senate meeting on the cult phenomenon, Washington, Feb. 5, 1979.

350   An island off the coast of South Korea for Moon's last stand: interviews with former Moonies.

INDEX

Addabbo, Cong. Joseph, 245, 335, 336
Agnew, Spiro, 94–95, 96
Ahn Kwang Suk, 198
AID, see United States Agency for International Development
Albert, Cong. Carl, 72, 121, 138, 157–158, 194, 196, 219, 220, 231, 336, 349
  Korean influence campaign, 244–247
Alexander, Joe, 343
Alioto, Mayor Joseph, 68
Allott, Gordon, 132
Ambro, Cong. Jerome, 270
American Rice Company, Houston, 72
American Youth for a Just Peace, 163
Amnesty International, 232
Amory, Robert, 198
Anderson, Jack, 308
Arizona, University of, 146
Armstrong, Scott, 242, 245, 248
Asian and Pacific Affairs, House Subcommittee on, 106
Aspin, Cong. Les, 275

Bae Young Shik, 225
Baek Tae Ha, 259
Baker, Ed, 261, 262
Baker, Sen. Howard, 243
Barry, Aidan, 342
Bartholemew, Peter, 271
Bayh, Sen. Birch, 223, 336
Bayne, Junette, 150
Bayonne, N.J., 105
Bell, Griffin, 252, 253, 270, 275, 276, 282, 348
Ben-Veniste, Richard, 186, 308, 310, 311
Berger, Samuel, 23
Bergman, Susan, 157
Bermingham, Robert, 270
Bernstein, Dr. Joel, 28
Blake, George, 200
Blaze, Brett, 341–342
Boitano, Mark, 341
Bork, Robert, 238
Brademas, Cong. John, 58, 141, 242, 304
Bradley, Tom, 151
Brainwashing, 347–348
Bray, John, 308, 314, 315, 316
Bressler, Charles, 61

Broomfield, Cong. William, 102, 191, 230, 232, 241
  Tongsun Park and, 108
  and U.S. military aid to South Korea, 75
Brown, Kathy, 343
Brown, Winthrop, Amb., 51, 52, 191, 198, 217
Bryant, William, 266
Buchen, Philip, 238
Bullock, Roy, 219, 220
Bundy, William, 44
Burke, Adm. Arleigh
  KCFF and, 44–45
Burma Oil of Britain, 72
Butler, William
  testimony before Fraser subcommittee, 232–233
Byrd, Sen. Harry, Jr., 102

California Rice Growers Association, 68, 70, 72, 74, 77
Caltex, Petroleum, 92
Capehart, Sen. Homer, 44
Caputo, Cong. Bruce, 270, 283, 285
Carey, Cong. Hugh, 244
Carroll, Lt. Gen. J. E., 39
Carter, Jimmy, 151, 252, 255, 258, 297
  human rights in Korea, 328–329
  and U.S. troop withdrawal from Korea, 274, 326–330
Catholic Church, 340
CDFI, see Conference for the Development of Free Institutions
Celler, Cong. Emanuel, 111
Central Intelligence Agency (CIA)
  KCIA and, 23–24
  Korea and, 19, 22, 251, 253, 254
Chang Do Young
  Park coup and, 18
Chang Myon, 24, 26
  Park coup and, 18–19, 21, 22, 23
Cheshire, Maxine, 242, 244–245, 248
Choi Kyu Ha, 80, 331
Choi Sang Ik, 39
  Moon and, 154

Chung Il Kwon, 14, 15, 43, 49, 59, 60, 63, 65, 67, 74, 76, 77, 91, 93, 104, 115, 178, 222, 331
  and Korean influence campaign, 96–7, 190–192, 216
Chung Sung Nam, 206
Civiletti, Benjamin, 252, 269, 271, 273, 284, 348
Clark, Donald, 294
Cleveland, Ohio, 103
Cohen, Jerome, 205
Collegiate Association for the Research of Principles, 164
Colt Industries, 173
  rifle plant for South Korea, 83
Combined Intelligence Research Center, 24
Committee to Re-elect the President (CREEP), 133
Common Cause, 255
Conference for the Development of Free Institutions (CDFI), 98, 99–101
Congress (U.S.)
  Koreagate, 247–266, 325–327, 333–337
  Tongsun Park influence peddling and, 101–143, 189–212, 241–248, 258–260, 281–289
  see also Park, Tongsun; names of committees, Congressmen, Senators
Congressional Associates, 335
Connell, Grover, 115–116, 128, 135, 141, 142
  indictment dismissed, 334
Conrad, Paul, 249
Conrad, Richard, 184, 185
Cook, Bobby Lee, 275, 276
Corcoran, Tom, 59
Coulter, Gen. John
  KCFF president, 52
Court, John, 89
CREEP, see Committee to Re-elect the President
Cromer, Harry, 219, 220

Daly, Bill, 149
D'Ambry, Robert, 61
Davitt, John, 238
Defense Ministers Conference
(R.O.K.–U.S., 1971), 104
De la Garza, Cong. Eligio, 294–295,
304
De la Garza, Lucille, 294
Democratic Republican party (Park's
party), 52, 63, 86
organized, 25
Deprogramming defined, 341
Derwinski, Cong. Edward, 230, 247,
305
obstruction of justice charge, 264–
266
and Sohn Ho Young defection, 261,
263
support for South Korea, 264–266
De Silva, Peer, 19, 21, 22
Dickinson, Tandy, 275, 288
Diplomat National Bank
Moon organization and, 169–171,
308, 311, 316, 322
Dole, Sen. Robert
public congressional hearings on
cults, 342–343, 348
Dore, Gordon, 125, 126, 130, 142, 334
Dunn, Gen. John, 95

East Berlin spy case, 27
Edwards, Chris, 150
Edwards, Cong. Edwin, 109, 124, 127,
130, 132, 241, 334, 336
Tongsun Park and, 110
Edwards, Elaine, 124, 268
Edwards, Marion, 287
Eisenberg, Shoul, 24
Eisenhower, Dwight D., 44, 45, 53,
336
Elizabeth II, Queen, 45
Elkins, Chris
as Moon convert, 146–148, 151,
152, 153, 156, 161–164, 181
Ellender, Sen. Allen J., 121, 131, 132,
336

Enton, Paul, 61
E-Systems Corporation, 72
Ethics Committee (House)
Koreagate investigation, 248–250,
251–258, 336
Kim Dong Jo investigation, 295–
303
public hearings, 279–281
Tongsun Park and, 304
Ethics Select Committee (Senate)
Koreagate investigation, 250–251,
336

FBI, *see* Federal Bureau of Investigation
Federal Bureau of Investigation (FBI),
262, 349
and KCIA harassment of Koreans
in America, 225
Korean influence campaign and,
192–198
Fefferman, Dan, 152, 164
Fenwick, Cong. Millicent, 306
Findlay, Cong. Paul, 218
Findlay College (Ohio), 278
Five Star Navigation, 71
FLF, *see* Freedom Leadership Foundation
Flowers, Cong. Walter, 140
Flynt, Cong. John, 249, 250, 251–255,
258, 276, 301–302
Foley, Cong. Thomas, 304
Food for Peace Program, 64, 65, 76,
90, 114, 199, 286, 299
Ford, Betty, 142
Ford, Gerald, 46, 141, 162, 228, 243
Korean bribery of Congressmen,
236–238
Foreign Affairs
Nixon article, 84, 85, 87
Foreign Affairs Committee (House),
105
Foreign Operations Subcommittee
(House)
Passman and, 106–107, 111
Fraser, Arvonne, 309

Fraser, Cong. Donald M., 7, 8, 171,
    176, 177, 247
  defeat for reelection and burning of
    home, 323–324, 343
  International Organizations Sub-
    committee (Fraser subcommit-
    tee), 230
    hearings on human rights and
      Korean aid, 7–8, 139–141, 142,
      277
    hearings on KCIA activities in
      U.S., 238–240
    investigation of Moon and Unifi-
      cation Church, 307–324, 342–
      347
    Koreagate investigation, 250,
      258–266, 285–286, 287–288
    Pak testimony, 313–318
    Tongsun Park hearings, 230–
      231, 238–240
  in Korea (1975), 237
  military aid to Korea, 230–240, 327
  personal characteristics, 231
  and Sohn Ho Young defection,
    262–263
  Unification Church lawuit against,
    319–320
Fraser Report, 342–347
Freedom Leadership Foundation
    (FLF), 5, 54, 55, 161–162, 163,
    309, 323–324
Freeland, Robert, 68–70
Friedman, Gen. Robert, 80
Fulbright, Senator, 75

Galifianakis, Nick, 304
Gallagher, Cong. Cornelius, 100–101,
    102, 118, 123, 125, 128–129,
    135, 140, 241, 285
  FBI memos on, 193–196
  income tax evasion, 335
  indictment of, 230
  KCIA and, 218
  and Korean influence buying, 105–
    106, 193–196, 335, 349
  Korean trip, 219–220

George Town Club, 61–63, 101, 125,
    130, 133, 134, 141, 288
"George Town Club of Seoul," 69
Georgetown University
  School of Foreign Service, 57–58
Giannastasio, Bill, 182
Gilligan, John, 151
Gilman, Cong. Benjamin, 278
Gleysteen, Amb. William, 302, 330
Goldberg, Arthur, 79
Golden, Michael, 308
Gore, Louise, 59, 61, 223
Gragert, Ed, 318–320
Gravel, Camille, 287
Green, Marshall, 20, 21–22, 220
Guam Doctrine, 86–87
Gulf Oil Co., 26, 92
Gutman, Jeremiah, 186

Habib, Philip, 134, 135, 210, 248
  and Korean influence peddlers,
    220–224, 238, 335, 347
  Tongsun Park and, 235–236
  U.S. Ambassador to R.O.K., 220
Hahm Pyong Choon, 138, 177–178,
    246–247
  Fraser subcommittee hearings on
    human rights, 233
Haig, Gen. Alexander, 89, 210, 256
Haldeman, H. R., 86
Halloran, Richard, 242, 258, 296
Hamilton, Dwight, 294
Hamilton, Jim, 286–287
Hamilton, Cong. Lee, 263–264, 300
Han, Bud (Han Sang Keuk), 38
Han Hak Ja
  marriage to Moon, 37
Han Hyohk Hoon
  defection to U.S., 5–6, 7
Han Sang Kil, 38
Hanna, Cong. Richard, 102, 224, 233,
    241, 285
  indictment of, 278–279
  Korean trips, 63–64, 65–68, 72–73,
    76
  prison sentence, 333–335

Tongsun Park and, 61–63, 77, 100, 116–124, 140–141, 194, 349
named co-conspirator in Tongsun indictment, 272
U.S.–Korean rice deal, 61–72 and U.S. military aid to South Korea, 74, 75, 76
Hannah, Dr. John, 114–115
Hapdong news agency, 27
Hassan, Steve
Moon convert case, 166–168, 179–181
Hayes, Patrick, 44
Hays, Cong. Wayne, 231
Hazelton, Dennis, 136–137
Hearst, Patty, 348
Helander, Wendy
Moon convert case, 181–186
Henderson, Gregory, 19, 21, 22
Henderson, Thomas, 272
Herschenson, Bruce, 160, 161
Hershman, Michael, 270–271
Ho Ho Bin, Mrs., 36–37
Holifield, Cong. Chet, 121
Hollings, Sen. Ernest, 223
Holtzman, Cong. Elizabeth, 270
Honam Oil, 92
Honolulu, Hawaii, 83, 94
Hoover, J. Edgar, 192, 193
Howard, Anne, 134
Howard, Frances, 134
Howe, Jimmy, 142
Howe, Nancy, 142
Hsu, Kevin, 125
Hummel, Arthur, 233
Humphrey, Hubert, 68, 84, 134, 135, 140
Hundley, William, 267–269, 271, 276, 282

Ichord, Cong. Richard, 157
Ikeda, Fumiko, 316
Immigration and Naturalization Service
foreign Moonies and, 323
Intelligence Select Committee (Senate)
Koreagate investigation, 251

Internal Security Committee (Senate), 156
International Conference for the Unity of the Sciences, 338–339
International Federation for the Extermination of Communism, 54
International Oceanic Enterprises, 172
International Organizations Subcommittee (House) (Fraser subcommittee)
hearings on KCIA activities in U.S., 238–240
human rights hearings, 7–8, 139–141, 142, 277
Korean lobbyists' concern about, 229–240
investigation of Moon and Unification Church, 307–324
Koreagate investigation, 250, 258–266, 285–288
Pak testimony, 313–318
Tongsun Park hearings, 230–231, 238–240
Moon subpoena, 320–321
International Relations Committee (House)
Fraser subcommittee, *see* International Organizations Subcommittee
Ishii, Mitsuharu, 171, 175

Jaffee, Jay, 249
Japan
kickbacks to Korea, 24–25
relations with R.O.K. after Kim Dae Jung kidnapping, 225–229
Japan Lines, 72
Jaworski, Leon, 255–257, 279–283
Kim Dong Jo case, 295–302
Joan of Arc Company, 128, 130
Johnson, Cong. Albert, 140
Johnson, Lyndon, 59, 62, 66, 79, 80, 81, 82
Joint Maritime Congress, 336

Jones, W. Farley, 178
Judiciary Committee (House), 111
Jung Nae Hiuk, 94
Justice Dept.
    Koreagate investigation, 247–248, 268–270
    Moon and, 347–348, 349

Kamiyama, Takeru, 154, 164–167, 174
Kang Young Hoon, 205
    Korean influence campaign and, 97–98
KCFF, see Korean Cultural and Freedom Foundation
KCIA, see Korean Central Intelligence Agency
Kelley, Ed, 233
Kennedy, John F., 22, 54, 86, 201
Kennedy, Dr. Joseph, 154–155
Kim (Moon's John the Baptist), 35–36
Kim, Alexander Juongwon, 205
Kim Chang Yong, Gen. ("Snake" Kim), 15
Kim, Charles, 169
Kim Chi Ha, 204
Kim Dae Jung, 207, 331
    harassment and kidnapping of, 224–226
    release from jail, 328
Kim, David S. C., 179
    Moon and, 154
Kim Dong Jo, Amb., 1–2, 4, 93, 97, 108, 110, 115, 207
    Korean influence campaign and, 279–283, 291–303
    opposition to Tongsun Park, 115–120, 131, 133, 137–138
Kim Dong Jo, Mme., 246, 294–295
Kim Dong Sung
    Radio of Free Asia and, 51–52
Kim, Hancho, 290, 291
    grand jury indictment of, 276–278
    conviction, 335
Kim Hyun Chul, Amb., 44, 48, 49, 59
Kim Hyung Wook, 49, 51, 60, 72, 73, 74, 86, 120, 122

KCIA head, 26, 46, 338
    Koreagate testimony, 258–260, 268
    Korean rice deal, 66–68
    named co-conspirator in Tongsun Park indictment, 272
    on Tongsun Park as KCIA agent, 76–77
Kim Il Sung, 2, 91–92
Kim Jae Kyu, 259
    shoots Park Chung Hee, 331
Kim Jong Pil, 15, 52, 159, 207, 233, 237, 292–293
    assassination of Park Chung Hee and, 331–332
    exile of, 25
    as fund raiser, 26
    KCFF and, 44
    KCIA head, 23–25
    Moon and, 39–40, 53
    plot to install Park Chung Hee in presidency, 17–23
    presidential ambitions of, 86
Kim Ki Wan, 298
Kim Kwan Suk, Rev., 237, 328
Kim Kwang, 100–101, 105, 106, 119, 193, 194, 218–220
Kim Kye Won, 330
    Minshall and, 103
Kim Kyong Eup
    Radio of Free Asia operations director, 51
Kim, S. K., 26, 86
Kim Sang In, see Kim, Steve
Kim Sang Keun, 163, 246, 252, 253
    Koreagate testimony, 268, 276–277
Kim, Cardinal Stephen, 209, 328
Kim, Steve (Kim Sang In), 38, 130, 132
Kim Sung Eun, 80
Kim Won Hee, 67, 69
Kim Won Pil, 175
Kim Woon Ha, 206, 207
Kim Yong Shik, Amb., 296, 298
Kim Young Oon, 39
Kim Young Sam, 328, 330–331
Kim Yung Hwan, 163
King College (Tenn.), 57

Kishi (Prime Minister, Japan), 112
Kissinger, Henry, 85, 88, 106, 110, 111, 138, 192–193, 207, 219, 243
    human rights and, 229
    Korean influence case, 192–197, 235–236, 238, 326, 349
Kleindienst, Richard, 198
Kodama, Yoshio, 54
Korea
    China and, 12–13
    mission of, in Moon theology, 34
    North/South division, 14
    "16 Colonels Incident," 19
    Tonghak Rebellion, 13
    under Japan, 11–14
Korea, North
    attempt on Pres. Park's life, 78–79
    establishment of, 14
    rejection of talks with Carter and Park Chung Hee, 329
    relationship to South Korea, 78–85, 332–333
    USS *Pueblo* incident, 79–80
Korea, Republic of (R.O.K.; South Korea)
    Colt rifle plant for, 83
    corruption of Park regime, 23–30
    economic success story, 27–29
    establishment, 14–15, 16
    Fraser subcommittee hearings on KCIA activities in U.S., 238–240
    human rights questions and, 7–8, 139–141, 142, 229–238, 328–329
    Johnson administration (U.S.) and, 78–84
    Korean/Japanese crisis over Kim Dae Jung kidnapping and Mme. Park assassination, 225–229
    North Korean infiltration of, 78–85
    U.S.–Korean rice sales, 61–72, 74–75, 102, 106–115, 116–131, 198–201
    U.S. military aid, 74–76

    withdrawal of U.S. troops, 87–95, 326–330
    Vietnam War support, 81
    see also Koreagate; Korean influence campaign; Park Chung Hee; Park, Tongsun
Koreagate, 241–266, 268
    first testimony on, 8
    Fraser subcommittee investigation, 230–231, 238–240, 250, 258–266, 285–286, 287–288, 313–318
    House Ethics Committee investigation, 248–250, 251–258, 291–306
    indictments and aftermath
        Hanna, 278–279, 333–335, 349
        Kim, Hancho, 276–278
        Passman, 286–287, 334–335, 336
        Tongsun Park, and efforts to return him to U.S., 271–276, 333, 335
    Justice Dept. investigation, 247–248, 268–270
    Kim Dong Jo case, 295–303
    Senate Select Committee on Ethics investigation, 250–251
    Senate Select Committee on Intelligence investigation, 251
    Tongsun Park interrogation, 281–289
    see also Korean influence campaign
Korean Central Intelligence Agency (KCIA), 60, 61, 66, 67, 68, 72, 86, 97, 98, 101, 102, 307, 310, 311
    assassination of Park Chung Hee and, 331
    Congress and, 194–197 (*see also* names of Congressmen and Senators)
    corruption of, 29–30
    East Berlin spy case, 27
    Gallagher and, 193–196
    harassment of Koreans at home and abroad, 224–227, 237, 238, 325
    House of Representatives listening post, 106

Korean Central Intelligence Agency
    (*cont'd*)
  kickbacks to, 24
  Kim Hyung Wook testimony
    about, 258–260
  Korean influence campaign in U.S.,
    1–8, 189–212, 325, 335–337
  origin and mandate, 23–24
  Radio of Free Asia and, 51–53
  relationship with Moon, 162–163
  rice deals and, 200
  Sohn Ho Young defection, 261–264
  Suzi Thomson agent for, 244–247
  Tongsun Park relationship to,
    76–77, 102
    Tongsun Report, 132–133
  Unification Church and, 39
Korean Cultural and Freedom Foun-
    dation (KCFF), 97, 156–157,
    191, 337, 338
  Children's Relief Fund, 321–322
  funding sources, 46–47
  origins, 43–44
  Radio of Free Asia and, 47–53
Korean influence campaign
  assessment of, 325–350
  Moon's role in summarized, 337–
    350
  official U.S. reaction to, 189–212, 349
  "Operation White Snow," 277–278
  Park Chung Hee cover-up,
    290–291, 305
  Ranard and, 213–220, 229
  see also Fraser, Cong. Donald; Kim
    Dong Jo; Koreagate; Park,
    Tongsun; names of Congress-
    men and Koreans involved
Korean stock market, 24, 25
Korean War, 16, 348
Korff, Rabbi, 160, 161
Kramer, Victor, 282
Krause, Alan, 210
Kuboki, Osami, 174
Kumi, South Korea, 11, 28

Lacovara, Philip, 249–250, 251–255,
    270

Lagomarsino, Cong. Robert, 278
Laird, Melvin, 75, 103, 104, 113, 131,
    132, 216, 222
Landauer, Jerry, 263
Lee Bum Jun (Mme. Park Chung
    Soo), 59, 212
Lee Chung Op, 15
Lee Hu Rak, 24, 26, 86, 117, 120, 199
  named co-conspirator in Tongsun
    indictment, 272
Lee Jai Hyon, 131, 250, 265
  defection of, 207
  with Korean Embassy, Washing-
    ton, 1–7
  testimony before Fraser subcom-
    mittee on human rights, 7–8,
    237–238, 295
Lee Sang Ho, *see* Yang Doo Won
Lee Tong Won, 19
Lee Young Woon, 206
Leggett, Cong. Robert
  Korean influence campaign and,
    245, 246, 335–336
Leigh, Monroe, 238
Lejeune, Judith, 174
Levi, Edward, 237
Lewin, Marty, 318–320
Liberace, 46
Lilly, Frank, 308
Lim Kyuil, Col., 104, 246, 305
Limb Man Sung, 206
Lindsay, John, 151
Little Angels, 160
  Moon front group, 42–47, 338
Lon Nol, 156
Los Angeles *Times*, 249
Lying, tenet of Unification Church,
    343–344

McCone, John, 39
McCormack, John, 62, 66, 72, 100
McFall, John, 242
  House reprimand of, 303
  and U.S. military aid to South
    Korea, 74–76
MacGregor, Clark, 133
McNamara, Robert, 39

McNelis, Charles, 279
Magruder, Gen. Carter, 20–21
Manchukuo, *see* Manchuria
Manchuria (Manchukuo), 14
Mardian, Robert, 196
Martin, David, 156
Martin, Graham, 221
Matsuda, Mitsuko, 157
Maw, Carlyle, 234
Maxwell Air Force Base, Alabama, 333
Mays, Larry
  on KCFF Board of Directors, 48
  Radio of Free Asia and, 47–52
Meany, George, 44
Meeds, Cong. Lloyd, 142
Meet the Press, 243, 283, 296, 297
Mesta, Perle, 44
Michaelis, Gen. John, 104
Michel, Paul, 239–240, 247, 262
  Koreagate, 268–269, 270, 271, 272,
    273, 284, 285, 286, 336
Miller, Donald, 158, 322
Mills, Wilbur, 88, 132
Min Byung Kwon, 259–260
Minshall, Cong. William, 102, 131,
  133, 140, 285
  Tongsun Park and, 103–104, 335
Miryung Sangsa oil tanker firm,
  Seoul, 59
Mitchell, John, 196, 197, 219, 245,
  267, 334
Moffett, Father, 232
Montgomery, Cong. Sonny, 140
Montoya, Sen. Joseph, 102, 132
Montoya, Joseph, Jr., 58–59
Moon In Ku, 284
Moon, Julie, 228
Moon, Sun Myung; Moon organiza-
  tion, 4–5, 15, 97, 99, 208, 290,
  291
  anti-Communist indoctrination
    program, 159
  avoidance of Fraser subcommittee
    subpoena, 320–321
  brainwashing, 347–348
  business enterprises, 168–177,
    339–341

Congressional contacts, 156–158
cult victims, 178–186
East Garden estate, Tarrytown,
  N.Y., 150
First Amendment protection, 344–
  346, 348–349
fishing industry and, 171–172
Fraser subcommittee investigation
  of KCIA activities in U.S.,
    238–239
  of Moon and Unification
    Church, 307–324, 342–347
immigration problems, 165
Justice Dept. and, 248, 347–348,
  349
KCIA connections, 162–163
Koreagate and, 243–244, 307–324
  effect of, on Moon, 339, 342
Korean Embassy in U.S. and, 291
Korean influence campaign
  role in, summarized, 337–339
  usefulness of, to Moon, 339–350
lawbreaking, 345–348
life of, 34–37
Little Angels choir, 42–47
manipulation of KCIA, 239
media exposure of Moon cult,
  176–177
newspaper and film connections,
  170–171
personnel of Moon enterprises,
  174–175
Radio of Free Asia, 197, 198
"save Nixon" campaign (Project
  Watergate), 151–161
strategy for recruiting converts,
  144–146
theology/politics of, 31–38, 54,
  343–345
"totalist" system, 173–175
UN demonstrations by Moonies,
  291
weapons manufacturing and,
  172–173
work in Korea, 159–160
see also Unification Church
Moon Sung Kyun, 173

Moonies, *see* Moon, Sun Myung; Uni-
    fication Church
Mun Se Kwang, 227
Murphy, Sen. George, 102
Murphy, Cong. John, 304
Myers, Carol, 295
Myers, Cong. John, 295

National Prayer and Fast Committee,
    152
National Security Agency, U.S.A.
    (NSA), 41, 243
National Security Council (NSC), 89,
    193
New Democratic party (R.O.K.), 328,
    330
New York State Board of Regents,
    323
    Unification Church lawsuit, 320
New York Times, 242, 243, 259, 260,
    309, 314, 347
    Unification Church lawsuit, 320
Newark Airport, 343
News World, 170, 171, 312, 319
Newsweek, 298, 303, 325
Nidecker, John, 207–211
Nields, John, 252, 255
Nixon, Richard, 3, 44, 53, 95, 96, 104,
    113, 133, 138, 326, 327
    "Asia after Vietnam" (*Foreign Af-
        fairs* article), 84, 85, 87
    Moon campaign for, 151–161
    Passman on, 108
    relations with Park administration,
        84–89, 201–207
    withdrawal of U.S. troops from
        South Korea, 87–95
Nixon Doctrine, 86–87
North Korea, *see* Korea, North
NSA, *see* National Security Agency,
    U.S.A.
NSC, *see* National Security Council

Ogata, Kiyomi, 150
Okamoto, Lieut. (Park Chung Hee), 14
One World Crusade, 146

O'Neill, Cong. Thomas P. ("Tip")
    Koreagate, 242, 255–257, 296, 298,
        299, 300, 302, 304
    Tongsun Park and, 138–142
Osami Kuboki
    Moon and, 154
Ottinger, Richard, 163

Pacific Development, Inc., 71
Packard, David, 83, 94
Paik Too Chin, 329
Pak, Bo Hi, 4–5, 158, 159, 172, 174,
    176, 178, 239, 248, 307, 308,
    310, 311, 312, 320
    anti-Fraser documentary film, 318
    and Korean influence campaign,
        97–98
    lawsuit against Fraser, 319–320
    Little Angels choir and, 42–43
    Moon's advance man in Washing-
        ton, 38–53, 154, 155, 337, 338,
        340
    Radio of Free Asia and, 47–53,
        197–198
    SEC complaint against, 322
    testimony before Fraser subcom-
        mittee, 313–318
Pak Keun, 228
    and House human rights hearings,
        230
Panmunjon armistice agreement, 16
Parents, Unification Church tenet re-
    garding, 344
Park Chong Kyu, 19, 98, 208, 209,
    210, 211
    Tongsun Park and, 97, 103
Park Chung Hee, 4, 7, 8, 48, 52, 55,
    59, 106, 139, 140, 141, 277
    birth and early years, 11–13
    marriage, 13
    in Japanese Army, 13–14
    takes Japanese name of Okamoto,
        14
    World War II service, 14
    at South Korean military academy,
        15

court martial, 15–16
Korean War service, 16
military intelligence work, 16
divorce and remarriage, 16–17
becomes president, R.O.K., through
    coup (1960), 17–23
anticorruption crusade and strong-
    arm tactics, 23–30
elected president of R.O.K., 25
reelection (1967), 26–27
as absolute dictator, 30
assassination attempt by North Ko-
    reans (1968), 78–80
relations with U.S. during Johnson
    administration, 78–84
relations with Nixon administra-
    tion, 84–89
deal with KCIA founder, 86
withdrawal of U.S. troops from
    South Korea, 87–95, 274,
    326–330
Korean influence campaign, 277
    benefits to Park, 326–330
    cover-up, 290–291, 305
    origins, 96–98
    summary and assessment, 325–
    339, 349–350
Yushin Constitution, 2–3, 88–89,
    201–207, 233, 235, 326, 330
meeting with Agnew (1970), 94–
    95
financing of 1971 election of, 92
rice/military aid deals (1971),
    113–115
defense of Tongsun Park, 131
Moon and, 158, 173, 177–178
Nixon and, 201–207
Kim Dae Jung kidnapping and,
    225–227
assassination attempt (1974), 227
human rights questions and,
    231–235, 328–329
Kim Hyung Wook and, 258–260
and Tongsun indictment, 274–275
meeting with Carter, 328–329
assassination of (1979), 330–331

Park Chung Hee, Mme., 17
    assassination of, 227, 228
Park Chung Soo, 59, 212
Park Hyon Kyu, Rev., 237
Park, Ken, 77, 122
Park Mu Hee, 15
Park Tong Jin, 274
Park, Tongsun, 4, 44, 304
    and American rice sales to Korea,
    61–72, 74–75, 102, 106–115,
    116–131, 198–201
    and Conference for the Develop-
    ment of Free Institutions, 98,
    99–101
    consulting services of, 72
    "cousin" of Park Chung Hee im-
    personation, 59–60
    customs inspection, Anchorage,
    Alaska (1973), 136–137
    education in United States, 57–58
    in England and Korea, following
    Koreagate exposure, 240,
    267–268, 269, 270–272
    family background and early years,
    56–57
    and Fraser subcommittee hearings
    on human rights, 230–231,
    238–240
    on KCIA activities in U.S.,
    238–240
    George Town Club business ven-
    ture, 61–63
    indictment of, 271–273, 333
    Justice Dept. investigation, 248
    KCIA and, 76–77, 102, 132–133,
    239
    Kim Dong Jo opposition to,
    115–120, 131, 133, 137–138
    and Korean influence campaign,
    59–77, 96–98, 101–143,
    189–212, 216, 241–248,
    258–260, 281–289, 336, 349
    benefits of, to Tongsun, 333–336
    Broomfield and, 108
    Chung Il Kwon and, 190–192,
    216

Park, Tongsun (*cont'd*)
  Edwards and, 110
  Gallagher and, 105–106, 335, 349
  Habib and, 221–224
  Hanna and, 61–63, 77, 100, 333–335, 349
  Minshall and, 103–104, 335
  "Tip" O'Neill and, 138–142
  Passman and, 106–115, 123–131, 134–136, 334–335
  Ranard and, 222–223
  oil and shipping interests, 142, 143
  personal characteristics, 57
  presidency of Miryung Sangsa firm, Seoul, 59
  U.S. military aid to South Korea, 74–76
  Watergate, 138
  yams deal, 128–130
Passman, Cong. Otto, 102, 222, 284, 285, 334–336
  indictment of, 286–287
  Korean rice deal, 109–115
  Nixon and, 108
  Tongsun Park and, 106–115, 123–131, 134–136
  trial and acquittal, 334–335
  and U.S. military aid to South Korea, 74–76
Patrick, Ted, 182
Patten, Cong. Edward, 140
Peace Corps, 107, 299
People's Temple, Guyana, 341, 342, 349–350
Phoenix, Ariz., 147
Porter, William, Amb., 220, 227
  Tongsun Park and, 64, 69–70, 78, 81, 87, 88, 89–91, 93, 96, 115, 189–192, 212, 216
Powell, Scott, 342
Price, Cong. Melvin, 140, 304
Prouty, Sen. Winston, 218
Pryor, Cong. David, 109
Pueblo incident, 79–80
Puget Sound, University of, 58
Pyongyang, No. Korea, 79

Radio of Free Asia (ROFA), 47–53, 158, 248, 307, 338
  investigated by Justice Dept., 197–198
Ranard, Donald, 21
  Korean influence peddlers and, 213–220, 222–229, 233, 235
  testimony before Fraser subcommittee, 239
Rarick, John, 304
Rayano, Fred, 313
Reischauer, Edwin, 205, 232
Religious freedom (U.S.)
  Moon and, 344–349
Research Institute of Korean Affairs, 97
Rhee, Jhoon, 40, 50
Rhee Min Hi, 225
Rhee, Syngman, 292, 330
  becomes president of South Korea, 14
  reelection, 16
  resignation from office, 17
Rhodes, Cong. John, 257
Rice sales (America to Korea), 61–72, 74–75, 102, 106–115, 116–131, 198–201
Richardson, John ("Jocko"), 134
Ridgway, Gen. Matthew, 44
Riley, Walter (Clyde Wallace), 311–313, 317
Rocca, Kurt, 74, 75
Rockefeller, Nelson, 45
ROFA, *see* Radio of Free Asia
Rogers, William P., 85, 219, 220
R.O.K., *see* Korea, Republic of
Roland, Robert, 45
  Unification Church and, 40–42
Row Chin Hwan, 208, 209, 210
Roybal, Cong. Edward
  House censure of, 303–304
Runyon, Michael, 175, 184, 311
Ryu, Jai Shin, 129

Safire, William, 243
Salonen, Neil, 151, 153, 154, 160, 161, 164, 174, 186, 309–312, 348

San Francisco, Calif., 86, 87, 88
Sasakawa, Ryoichi, 54
Saxbe, William B., 138
Scharff, Gary, 179, 181, 182
Scott, Sen. Hugh, 44
Securities and Exchange Commission
    complaint against Pak, 322
Sheftick, Dr. Joseph, 146
Shin Dong Shik, 61
Shokyo Rengo (Japanese Moon
    group), 54
Sikes, Cong. Bob, 249
Simcus, Laura, 192
Smith, Harry, 142
Smith, Michael, 323
Sneider, Richard, 211, 285
Soh Sung, 232
Sohn Ho Young
    defection of, 260–263, 305
Song Sun Keun, 206, 224
South Korea, *see* Korea, Republic of
Soyars, W. B., 195, 196
Spence, Cong. Floyd, 252, 300
Staggs, Allen, 149–150
Stephens, Charlie, 163
Stillman, Charles, 308, 320
Stone, H.P., 173
Stratton, Cong. Samuel, 218
Suicide, tenet of Unification Church,
    342
Sullivan, William, 195, 196
Sunchon rebellion (1948), 15
Supreme Council for National Recon-
    struction (Park govt.), 23
Suter's Tavern Corporation, 61
Swanner, John, 249, 252
Swope, George, 349
Symington, Sen. Stuart, 102

Talley, Martha, 279
Tanaka, Kakuei, 163
    visit to U.S. (1974), 228
Tarrytown, N.Y., 148, 323
Tet Offensive, *see* Vietnam War
Thompson, Cong. Frank, 304
Thomson, Suzi Park, 194, 196, 219,
    290, 291, 349

Korean influence campaign, 244–
    247, 336, 349
Three Star Navigation, 71
Thurmond, Sen. Strom, 55, 157
Time magazine, 325
Times (London)
    Unification Church lawsuit, 320
Tji Hak Soon, Bishop, 203
Tonghak Rebellion (1894), 13
Truman, Harry S., 44, 53
Tucson, Ariz., 343
Tully, Joe, 164–165
Turner, Shelley, 343

Udall, Cong. Morris, 132, 142, 247,
    304
Unification Church, 15
    business enterprises of Moonies,
        339–340
    converts
        indoctrination program, 146–150
        recruitment strategy, 144–146
    as cult, 342
    deprogramming and, 341
    First Amendment protection, 344–
        346, 348
    Fraser subcommittee investigation,
        307–324, 342–347
    fund-raising tactics, 148, 151, 167–
        168
    KCIA and, 39
    lawsuits against Fraser and investi-
        gators, *New York Times*, Lon-
        don *Times*, New York State
        Regents Board, 319–320
    Little Angels choir and, 46–47
    Radio of Free Asia and, 52–53
    status in Korea (1963), 43
    tax status, 176, 323
    theology/politics of, 31–38, 54,
        163–166, 343–344
United Nations, 79, 80, 107
United States
    Korean influence campaign and,
        326–330
    origins of, 96–98
    Park coup and, 19–23

United States (*cont'd*)
support for Park Chung Hee,
326–330, 332–333
USS *Pueblo* incident, 79–80
withdrawal of troops from South
Korea, 87–95, 326–330
see also Congress (U.S.); Korea,
North; Korea, Republic of;
Koreagate; Korean influence
campaign; Vietnam War;
names of persons involved in
Koreagate
United States Agency for International Development (AID), 107,
108, 114

Vance, Cyrus, 81–82, 282, 297, 298,
329
Vander Jagt, Cong. Guy, 278
Vietnam War, 76–77, 79
South Korean support for, 81
Tet Offensive, 80–81, 82
Viguerie [Richard] Company, 322

Waldheim, Kurt, 45
Walker Hill resort scandal, 24
Wall Street Journal, 263
Wallace, Clyde, *see* Riley, Walter
Warder, Michael Young, 174
Washington, Walter, 151
Washington Post
Koreagate scandal, 241, 242, 245,
248, 257, 266
Washington Star, 263
Watergate, 138, 152, 157
Western Illinois University, 7
White, Peter, 256, 257
Wiggins, Cong. Gerald, 247
Wilson, Cong. Charles
House reprimand of, 303
Winn, Cong. Larry, 278, 295

Wolff, Cong. Lester, 230, 231, 232,
244
Wonneberger, Elsie, 230
Wonsan, North Korea, 79
Wood, Allen Tate, 163
Moonies and, 54–55
Wood, James E., 342
Woodward and Dickerson, Philadelphia, 69
Woods, Rose Mary, 210
World Anti-Communist League, 54
World Mission Center (New Yorker
hotel), 149
Wright, Cong. Jim, 256, 257, 300
Wurster, William, 69–70
Wyman, Louis, 163–164

Yang Doo Won (alias Lee Sang Ho),
132, 206, 207
KCIA connections
in America, 1–2, 6
in Korea, 2
at United Nations, 76
ordered out of U.S., 227
Yang You Chan, 45, 48, 51, 59
KCFF and, 44
Yi Dynasty, 12, 13
Yoo Young Soo, 259
Yook Young Soo, *see* Park Chung
Hee, Mme.
Yosu rebellion (1948), 15
Yun Chan, 224
Yun Po Sun, 18, 26
Yushin Constitution, 2–3, 88–89,
233, 235
power to Park Chung Hee under,
201–207, 326

Zablocki, Clement, 44, 281, 299
Zion, Cong. Roger, 218
"Zombie" eyes, 344